PENGUIN BOOKS

Viking Age Iceland

Jesse — navian of the numer *Medie Saga* a *Saga* Byock in Icel — Viking studies, his work has been — the National Endowment for the Humanities, the Fulbright Foundation, the National Science Foundation and the John Simon Guggenheim Foundation.

JESSE L. BYOCK

Viking Age Iceland

PENGUIN BOOKS

PENGUIN BOOKS

Published by the Penguin Group
Penguin Books Ltd, 27 Wrights Lane, London w8 5tz, England
Penguin Putnam Inc., 375 Hudson Street, New York, New York 10014, USA
Penguin Books Australia Ltd, Ringwood, Victoria, Australia
Penguin Books Canada Ltd, 10 Alcorn Avenue, Toronto, Ontario, Canada m4v 3b2
Penguin Books India (P) Ltd, 11 Community Centre, Panchsheel Park, New Delhi – 110 017, India
Penguin Books (NZ) Ltd, Private Bag 102902, NSMC, Auckland, New Zealand
Penguin Books (South Africa) (Pty) Ltd, 5 Watkins Street, Denver Ext 4, Johannesburg 2094, South Africa

Penguin Books Ltd, Registered Offices: Harmondsworth, Middlesex, England

First published 2001
1

Copyright © Jesse L. Byock, 2001

Set in Linotype Sabon and Monotype Janson
Typeset by Rowland Phototypesetting Ltd, Bury St Edmunds, Suffolk
Printed in England by Clays Ltd, St Ives plc

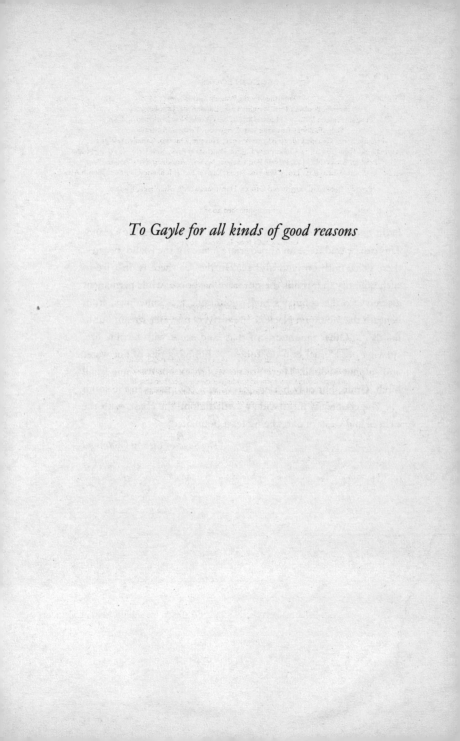

To Gayle for all kinds of good reasons

Latin books name that land Thule, but northmen call it Iceland. This can be said to be an appropriate name for the island, because there is ice both on land and sea. In the sea there is drift ice in such quantity that it fills the northern harbours, while permanent glaciers cap the country's high mountains ... Sometimes, from beneath the mountain glaciers, great rivers of water stream out in floods ... Other mountains of that land erupt with terrible fire, spewing out a cruel rain of stones ... Bubbling pits of hot water and sulphur abound. There are no woods except for some small birch. Grain, but only barley, grows in a few places in the south ... The country is most widely settled along the coast, with the eastern and western parts being least populated.

The Saga of Bishop Gudmund

Contents

List of Illustrations

List of Maps

Acknowledgements

I am indebted to my many Icelandic friends, especially Professors Helgi Thorláksson and Gunnar Karlsson for their reading of chapters. I consider it my great good fortune to have had their counsel and the benefit of their deep understanding of Iceland's development. I have adored maps since I was a child, when my father taught me the wonders of the atlas. An inordinate amount of time went into researching and designing the many maps and illustrations used in this book. Here I was aided by four especially skilful cartographers and artists: Robert Guillemette, Jean-Pierre Biard, Guðmundur Ól. Ingvarsson and Lori Gudmundson. Working with people of such knowledge was for me a great experience. Thanks also to Andrew Dugmore for his generous permission to use his illustrations.

My thanks to Guðmundur Ólafsson from Iceland's National Museum for sharing with me the archaeological floor plans to Grelutótt. Guðmundur has been a valuable colleague in the Mosfell Archaeological Project. I also want to extend my warmest thanks to Hörður Ágústsson, who gave me the use of his architectural drawings. With wit and humour, Hörður has over the years shared with me his wide knowledge of medieval Icelandic and Norwegian buildings. My thanks also to the architects Grétar Markússon, Stefán Örn Stefánsson and Hjörleifur Stefánsson, who so graciously and enthusiastically shared their expertise in turf construction. Kristján Jóhann Jónsson provided insightful comments on the manuscript. I want to thank my father, Lester Byock and my uncle, Harold Williams. Both are gone now, but I know they would smile at the turf

section. It would not have been written but for them. Growing up
with these wonderful men, and with my mother Cele Williams Byock
and her great interest in design, meant that before I could read
or write I knew something of construction and architecture. They
instilled a lifetime lesson in craftsmanship.

Scholars often groan at the amount of work, angst and pain put
into writing a book. Despite all that, I thoroughly enjoyed writing
this book. In part this is because the time of research and writing
corresponded to a period of grants which allowed me to spend almost
three wonderful years in Iceland. Thus I would like to thank these
generous benefactors: the Fulbright Foundation; the University of
California President's Fellowship; the National Endowment for the
Humanities; the John Simon Guggenheim Memorial Fund; the Icelandic Ministry of Culture and Education; the UCLA Academic
Senate, and Provost Brian Copenhaver and Dean Pauline Yu of the
UCLA College of Letters and Science.

Further, I offer my thanks to the Willard Fiske Center at the USIS
office in Reykjavík, and especially to the head of that office, Walter
Douglas, and his wife, Nancy. At the darkest moments of winter, the
Douglases rediscovered the art of mixing a Manhattan, and the light
almost returned. I also owe thanks to the American Ambassador,
Day Mount, who together with Walter Douglas arranged for me to
use an office, which was of much help. So, too, my deep gratitude to
my daughter Ashley and my wife Gayle, who read many drafts and,
as always, were filled with insightful comments. Grace Stimson, as
remarkable as ever, had much to say about making English flow.
Clare M. Gillis, an excellent student and dedicated assistant, worked
for me in Reykjavík. Clare held a Fulbright scholarship to Iceland
and acquired a great knowledge of Iceland and the sagas. Finally I
want to thank my friends at Sólon Íslandus and the old Kaffi List.
There was no end to the amusement and inspiration found at these
places.

Preface

I wanted to write a book that would explore the workings of Iceland's medieval society and would serve as a companion to reading the sagas. The result, I hope, deepens our understanding of the social forces and environmental factors which shaped the lives of medieval Icelanders in the period from the tenth to the end of the thirteenth century. These centuries, which saw Iceland's discovery and its subsequent development, coincide to a great extent with Scandinavia's Viking Age, and Iceland's experience is a rich part of that age.

A good portion of my life has been spent in Iceland. As a young man, I worked herding sheep on farms on the northern fjords, especially in the county of Húnavatnssýla. The experience has stayed with me, leaving an intimate awareness of the skills of survival so necessary in that far northern environment. In this book I have tried to bring this awareness to the fore. It is not only the cold and the hardship of keeping animals alive through the winter that I remember, but also the beauty of the landscape, the bright warmth of the summers, the wild horses in the highlands, and the friendship of the farmers. In particular I want to thank Karl, Margrét and Tryggvi from the farm of Stóraborg, and Vilhjálmur and Margrét at Gauksmýri.

At the time I was on the farms, the major form of mechanization was a strange mixture of Russian, American and British jeeps, small tractors, and clumsy milking machines for the cows. As a mechanic, I helped repair all of them. This skill gave me a certain value among the farmers and opened the door to the type of participatory fieldwork that has motivated my research. We ate traditional foods

– horse meat pickled in barrels of sour whey, for instance – herded sheep on horseback, and during the winter fished with nets in the freezing water for freshwater trout. During the day, while working, the men often told stories and recited long rhymed poems called *rímur*. Those who were said to have the gift composed endless small verses. A memory that never leaves me comes from early one morning in the late spring. Sitting on my horse on a mountain slope, I remember looking down into a broad river valley where thousands of wild geese and swans flew in and out of the low-lying morning mist, calling to each other. It was a sight and sound that could make a poet out of a mechanic, and one that I hope will be there for future generations.

Writing *Viking Age Iceland* has been a satisfying undertaking. The book elaborates on areas of new research since *Medieval Iceland* (University of California Press, 1988) was published. Some of the new research was incorporated into the expanded Danish edition, *Island i sagatiden* (C. A. Reitzel, 1998). Comprehensive studies are rare these days, and I am appreciative to Penguin Books for offering me the opportunity to write this book. It gave me the chance to fashion a broad reconsideration of the material, blending my interests in history, anthropology and archaeology as well as in sagas and the operation of law and feud.

Note on Names, Spelling and Pronunciation

In order to make the pronunciation of Icelandic names easier for the English-speaking reader, I have anglicized them. Thus Mörðr gígja becomes Mord the Fiddle. I have, however, left most of the place names and terms in the original Old Icelandic, apart from changing Icelandic *fjörðr* to English 'fjord'. Place names in the original are especially useful to the reader who wishes to find them on a map. An English translation is always provided at the first mention of a term. For example the contractual agreement called *handsal* is explained as follows: ' "handsale", referring to a witnessed slap or shake of hands at the conclusion of an agreement'. When many pages have passed between a first mention of a term and the next, I repeat the English name or translation. I do the same with place names when it is helpful. My goal was to provide a book easily read in English.

Icelanders in the Viking Age (and most of their descendants down to the present) derived their last name from their father, adding 'son' or 'daughter' to it. Thus a man named Eirik, who was the son of Thorvald, was named Eirik Thorvaldsson. Eirik's son Leif was Leif Eiriksson and his daughter Freydis, Freydis Eiriksdottir. (I have anglicized *dóttir* to 'dottir'.) With many different Eiriks and Olafs having sons and daughters, confusion was relieved by nicknames. One Eirik Thorvaldsson was known as Eirik the Red and his son was called Leif the Lucky. In rare but notable instances, sons and daughters took the name of their mother. Where the sources offer a nickname, I have included it. The medieval Icelanders apparently took pleasure in such names.

A *note for non-readers of Old Icelandic*: The letter þ ('thorn', upper case, Þ) is pronounced like the *th* in 'thought'; ð ('eth', upper case, Ð) is pronounced like the *th* in 'breathe'. For the convenience of readers unfamiliar with these characters, the publisher has replaced þ by *th* and followed English conventions for alphabetical order. For similar reasons I have conformed to modern Icelandic practice in using the vowel 'æ' for both Old Icelandic 'æ' and 'œ', and 'ö' for Old Icelandic 'ǫ' and 'ø'. In the names of medieval people, 'æ' is anglicized to 'ae', but it and accents are used when spelling the names of modern Icelanders.

Commonly Used Geographical Terms

á (pl. *ár*)	= river
dalr	= valley or dale
ey (possessive pl. *eyja*)	= island
eyrr (pl. *eyrar*)	= gravelly riverbank or small tongue of land running into the sea
fell	= hill
fjörðr (pl. *firðir*)	= fjord
holt	= a wood or a rough stony hill or ridge
hóll (pl. *hólar*)	= a hill or stone heap
jökull	= glacier
nes	= headland
tunga	= tongue of land at the confluence of two rivers
vatn	= lake
völlr (pl. *vellir*)	= plain

Introduction

This book focuses on the formative first centuries of the Old Icelandic Free State, and extends over the period from the tenth to the middle of the thirteenth century. Iceland's settlers came either from mainland Scandinavia or from the Viking settlements in the British Isles. The newcomers were forced to adapt to sometimes harsh environmental factors, as well as to a land of limited resources. From social-historical and anthropological viewpoints, early Iceland is a fascinating social laboratory. The society that evolved on this large island during the Viking Age avoided the establishment of most official hierarchies without going so far as to create egalitarianism. Consensus played a prominent role in decision-making, and Iceland's medieval governmental features find their roots in issues that specifically concerned the political and legal rights of free farmers.

The environment found by the first settlers was significantly different from that of mainland Scandinavia. The effects of active volcanic systems and of the subarctic ecology, as well as the climate, the distance from Europe, and the shortage of good building wood, helped to define the culture and its survival strategies. Working with the skills and practices of their homelands, the settlers adapted to their new surroundings, utilizing available resources and building materials. Directly or indirectly, the new culture group took advantage of a northern location made liveable by the warmth of the Gulf Stream. The settlers were prepared, and able, to live on often isolated farmsteads, and from the start they could let their livestock roam the highlands. The worst danger may have come not from nature, but from other men.

Law in medieval Iceland touched virtually all aspects of social intercourse, yet it was not implemented by the force of an executive arm of government. The operation of law was connected to advocacy, a core dynamic in the society which, together with 'friendships' (called *vinfengi*) and kinship ties, did much to shape social behaviour. The society's cultural focus on law, the crucial role played by advocacy and arbitrations, the course of legal and political decision-making, and the choices that individuals faced between violence and compromise in a feuding society are among the issues explored in the book.

As part of the colonization process, the settlers experienced a de-evolutionary change: the immigrant society moved down a few rungs on the ladder of complexity. This diminished level of stratification, which emerged from the first phase of social and economic development, lent an appearance of egalitarianism – social stratification was restrained and political hierarchy limited. The economy was from the start mixed, the settlers taking advantage of the resources of both the coastal and inland regions. The economic system that emerged in the earliest period was simple. It operated through the techniques and requirements of settled pastoralism and coastal hunter-gathering. With time, the system of livestock farming that the settlers imported proved disastrous to the ecology.

Up to the end of the medieval period (and beyond) Iceland remained entirely rural. There were no towns, not even villages, and early Iceland participated only marginally in the active trade of Viking Age Scandinavia. The devolution of the settlement period left its mark on the new island community, distinguishing Iceland from mainland Scandinavia, where extensive political and social hierarchies reached up to jarls and kings with well-defined military functions.

Out in the North Atlantic, Iceland became a headless polity. From early on, there was a rudimentary state apparatus, a central legislature and uniform, country-wide judicial and legal systems. Following the conversion to Christianity in the year 1000, the Church was quickly integrated into the chieftaincy system. Until the thirteenth century the Church in Iceland was less an independent power to be reckoned with than it was in contemporaneous Western societies. As leaders of their peers, Iceland's chieftains operated by gaining consensus among their followers. Having little coercive power, they were more like local 'big men' than regional military leaders. In a decentralized society with limited stratification, reciprocity among farmers and chieftains was essential. Especially important were the ties of mutual obligation between the chieftains and their acknowledged followers. Although the Icelanders were in touch with Europe, their society remained distant from most exterior forces of change.

The second of the three phases of the Free State's development was characterized by social and economic stability. Beginning in the tenth century with the end of the settlement period and the creation of the Althing (c. 930), this long phase continued well into the twelfth century. During this time Iceland functioned as a single island-wide community, or 'great village'. Inward-looking, highly litigious, and hardly military, the new society operated through consensual order. The sagas depict rivalry and competition among chieftains and farmers. We see the lives and ambitions of small farmers, something offered by few other medieval European narratives. In probing the sources of social power and the strategies employed by those with authority, I examine how leaders acquired wealth, primarily land, from the more vulnerable free farmers. Here as elsewhere in the book, women are considered as part of the social fabric. Rather than segregating the discussion along gender lines, I see women as players in a social life that includes feud and calls for moderation, bloodshed, vengeance, honour, shame and restraint.

The third phase of the Free State's history, the period beginning in the mid- to late-twelfth century, is characterized by the appearance of a new elite, the big chieftains who are called *stórgoðar*. First seeking regional control in the twelfth century, the *stórgoðar* struggled from the 1220s to the 1260s to win what had earlier been unobtainable for Icelandic leaders, the prize of overlordship or centralized executive authority. Numerous conflicting forces came into play. *Stórgoðar* faced rivals of their own rank but they also had to contend with opposition from another emerging group, the *stórbændr* or big farmers. In the last phase of the Free State, the older two-tiered system of chieftains and farmers gave way to a more complex three-tiered political structure of big chieftains, big farmers and farmers. The change took place in different parts of the country at different times.

A central feature of this study is that it provides a methodology for employing sagas as sources for socio-historical and anthropological study. I have tried to select episodes that earlier scholars have avoided, and so the reader should find much fresh material here. In particular I have taken long sections from two splendid sagas, *Vápnfirðinga saga* (*The Saga of the People of Weapon's Fjord*) and *Eyrbyggja saga* (*The Saga of the People of Eyri*). Insights drawn from these texts have in many instances changed the way I look at the better known sagas. Iceland has a rich treasure in its medieval writings, but scholars have had difficulty in utilizing these narratives for social and historical analysis. Not factual history, the sagas are stories by a medieval people about themselves. In many ways, they are rich ethnographic documentation, and this book treats them as such while also recognizing their creative aspects. The sagas are one of the world's great literatures and a knowledge of their social context increases our appreciation of their achievement.

I

An Immigrant Society

There was a man named Mord; he was called the Fiddle. He
was the son of Sighvat the Red, and he lived at Voll in the
Rang River Plains. He was a powerful chieftain and a great
lawyer – so great a lawman [*lögmaðr*] that no case was
thought to be legally judged unless he took part.

Njal's Saga, Chapter 1

Njal's Saga begins with a famous vignette that highlights issues
explored in this book. Set in tenth-century Iceland in the middle of
the Viking Age (AD *c.* 800–1100), the opening lines quoted above
describe a great leader. First we are told the name of Mord's impressive father and then the site of his family's landholding at Voll, located
on the broad plains that border the East Rang River in southern
Iceland. Next comes the reason for Mord's greatness. Those familiar
with chieftaincies and tribes, and the epics that such groups engender,
would have expected to hear of Mord's deeds of valour: enemies
slain, territories taken, and booty and slaves acquired. Instead the
saga relates a quite different story. Mord, an important leader, made
his mark not as a warrior but as a lawyer, an advocate with a deep
knowledge of law and legal procedures. This simple description of a
chieftain goes to the heart of early Icelandic society and its sagas.

Mord's fame is well known to readers of the sagas,[1] but neither
the nature of his power nor the source of his authority has received
much comment. In fact the society that developed on this large and

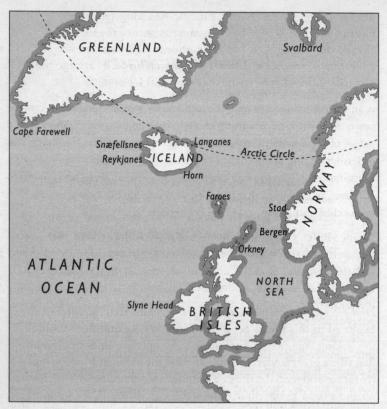

1. **The North Atlantic World of the Medieval Icelanders.** 'Wise men report that from Stad in Norway it is a voyage of seven days west to Horn in eastern Iceland, and from Snæfellsnes [in western Iceland] it is four days' sail west to Greenland at the point where the sea is narrowest. It is said that if one sails due west from Bergen to Cape Farewell in Greenland, one passes a half day's sail to the south of Iceland. From Reykjanes in southern Iceland it is five days south to Slyne Head in Ireland, and from Langanes in northern Iceland it is four days northward to Svalbard in the Arctic Sea.' (*The Book of Settlements*)

distant island in the North Atlantic has long perplexed scholars. Iceland was first settled by Norsemen as part of the seaborne expansion of the Viking Age, but the authority of its leaders was not that of warlords, warrior chieftains or regional lords. Years ago the legal historian James Bryce wrote that medieval Iceland

is an almost unique instance of a community whose culture and creative power flourished independently of any favouring material conditions, and indeed under conditions in the highest degree unfavourable. Nor ought it to be less interesting to the student of politics and laws as having produced a Constitution unlike any other whereof records remain, and a body of law so elaborate and complex that it is hard to believe that it existed among men whose chief occupation was to kill one another.[2]

Since Bryce's day, the study of Iceland has flourished, and numerous writers have explored different facets of the island's medieval culture. But the essential contradictions that Bryce noted remain unresolved. This book addresses these contradictions by examining the underlying structures and cultural codes that bound the different parts of Icelandic society into a cohesive polity. It is a social-historical study that employs the tools of history and anthropology and takes into consideration the ethnographic, literary and legal attributes of the sagas. It brings together the natural and human forces that shaped the new society, exploring the way Iceland's Viking Age social order came into being and how it functioned. The answers tell a great deal about society, saga and life in the medieval north.

The Norsemen who first settled Iceland in the late ninth century did not come as part of a planned migration, a political movement, or an organized conquest. Unlike many later European explorers and colonists, Norse explorers and settlers were not acquiring territory for sovereigns or for established religious hierarchies. Viking Age voyages into the far North Atlantic were independent undertakings, part of a 300-year epoch of seaborne expansion that saw Scandinavian peoples settle in Shetland, Orkney, the Hebrides, parts of Scotland and Ireland, the Faroe Islands, Iceland, Greenland and Vínland.

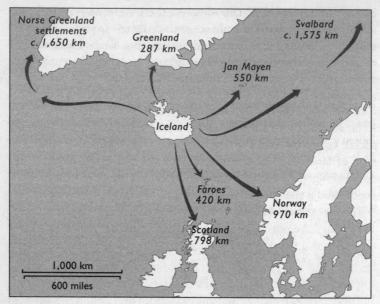

Norse Greenland
settlements
c. 1,650 km

Greenland
287 km

Svalbard
c. 1,575 km

Jan Mayen
550 km

Iceland

Fároes
420 km

Norway
970 km

Scotland
798 km

1,000 km

600 miles

2. Distance Between Iceland and Other Lands.

Iceland's settlement and subsequent development is a large chapter
in this story of migration. The island was discovered in about 850,
or perhaps somewhat earlier, by Scandinavian seamen who had
probably been driven off course. Shortly thereafter reports of large
tracts of free land on the island circulated throughout the Norse/
Viking cultural area, which stretched from Norway to Ireland. The
majority of immigrants to Iceland were free farmers. Among them
were a few small-scale chieftains who did not lead the migration but
came as independent settlers.

Iceland's medieval social order reflected the conditions of its settlement. As a culture group, the immigrants came from societies with
mixed maritime and agricultural economies and brought with them
the knowledge and expectations of European Iron Age economics.
The absence of an indigenous population on so large an island was
an unusual feature that permitted colonists the luxury of settling

in any location of their choosing. As there were no hostile native inhabitants, the settlers enjoyed extraordinary freedom to adapt selectively to their new surroundings. In this frontier setting they established scattered settlements in accordance with the availability of resources. The settlers and their immediate tenth-century descendants adapted quickly to life in the sometimes hostile environment. Called *landnámsmenn* (land-takers) by later generations, these early Icelanders had an extremely large 'founders' effect' on subsequent social, economic and political systems. They also set in motion a type of land and resource use that by the thirteenth century was diminishing the island's fertility. Iceland's history is that of both people and a changing ecosystem.

The first settlers were men and women asserting their self-interest. They seized the opportunity to bring their families, their wealth and their livestock nearly 1,000 kilometres (600 miles) across the North Atlantic in search of land. What they found was a mid-Atlantic island of striking beauty. The landscape varied from fertile inland valleys and richly grassed and forested lowlands to massive glaciers and forbidding volcanic mountain ranges. The higher mountains remained snow-capped throughout the summer. Today, glaciers and lava beds each cover approximately a tenth of the island, and the situation was roughly similar in the settlement period. In the autumn and early winter the far northern sky is often alive with the northern lights.

Most *landnámsmenn* (a term that includes women) came directly from Scandinavia, especially from Norway. Many also came from Viking encampments and Norse colonies in the Celtic lands. The Norse settlers from Ireland, Scotland and the Hebrides brought with them Gaelic wives, followers and slaves.[3] A few colonists were part or all Celt. In the sagas we find many Celtic names, such as Njáll and Kormákr (Old Irish *Níall* [Neil] and *Cormac*).

In the sixty or so years of the *landnám* (literally the land-taking, c. 870–930) at least ten thousand people, and perhaps as many as twenty thousand, emigrated to Iceland. Initially it was a boom period with free land for the taking. The settlers came in merchant ships

1. The *knörr*, the major ocean-going merchant ship of Viking Age Scandinavia. An exceptionally seaworthy craft, the *knörr* was the type of ship used in the exploration and settlement of Iceland, Greenland and Vínland (Wineland) on the North American continent.

(*knörr*, pl. *knerrir*) loaded with goods, implements and domestic animals. These sturdy single-masted, square-sailed ships were made to be sailed, but for short distances they could be rowed. They were used throughout the Viking Age, and at the time of the *landnám* they carried as much as 30 tons of cargo. Later in the twelfth century, when Norwegians used the *knörr* in the Iceland trade, the cargo capacity increased to about 50 tons. Many of the prominent settlers arrived in their own ships, as noted in the sources. It is also possible, although the later written records say little, that other ships went back and forth across the Atlantic, ferrying for hire land-hungry people out to the island.

The land which Icelandic immigrants took was uncultivated and, except for a few Irish monks, uninhabited. These monks, who had arrived earlier in their native *curachs* (boats constructed of hides sewn together and stretched over a wooden frame), had come seeking solitude. They were called *papar* (sing. *papi*) by the later Icelanders.[4] They left of their own accord or were driven out by the new settlers. Although it cannot be verified, it is possible that their presence is witnessed in a number of place names, such as the island of Papey off Iceland's south-eastern coast.

The task facing Icelandic immigrants was to prosper on an empty island with a limited habitable area. In the process they established a society with a rich blend of attributes. Beginning in the tenth century with the close (*c.* 930) of the *landnám*, they established a general assembly, the Althing, and Iceland functioned as a single island-wide community. In many ways, Iceland was a decentralized, stratified society, operating with a mixture of pre-state features and state institutions. This combination gave rise to the sagas, one of the world's great literatures. With its laws, sagas, archaeology and medieval historical writings about the settlement, early Iceland is an ideal laboratory for exploring the forces that cause and prevent social stratification. The settlement took place in a pristine ecosystem, and the *landnám* was one of the last colonizations of a large uninhabited land.

Language and the Term 'Viking'

The language of the settlers was called the Danish tongue, *dönsk tunga*. This was the common Old Norse language spoken by Viking Age Scandinavians at the time of Iceland's ninth-century settlement, but no one is quite sure why Scandinavians referred to their language as the Danish tongue.⁵ Throughout the Viking Age and into the following centuries, Old Norse speakers could easily understand each other despite the increased growth of dialects after the eleventh century. Old Norse was related to but different from the language spoken in Anglo-Saxon England. With some practice, however, Old Norse and Old English speakers could understand each other, a factor that significantly broadened the cultural contacts of Viking Age Scandinavians, including Icelanders.

Almost all written sources for the study of early Iceland, including the sagas and the majority of church writings, are in what is termed Old Icelandic. This was a branch of Old West Norse, the vernacular tongue shared by Iceland and Norway from the eleventh to the mid-fourteenth century. With relatively few changes, the original Old Norse of the ninth-century colonists remains the basis of modern Icelandic. Old Norse is also the root language of modern Swedish, Norwegian and Danish, but the connection is far more distant than with modern Icelandic.

The word 'Viking' is used frequently in this book. The early Icelanders themselves used the term, although they did not, as is popularly done today, employ it in an ethnic sense. Almost surely, they would have understood the concept of a Viking Age, but to them the idea that Scandinavian society was a 'Viking society' would have been a misnomer. Throughout medieval Scandinavia, a *víkingr* (pl. *víkingar*) meant a pirate or freebooter, and *víkingar* were men who grouped together in bands to raid from boats. The term applied both to those who honourably (in Norse eyes) sailed across the sea to steal and to those who robbed neighbours closer to home.

Although the meaning of the term *víkingr* is clear, its origin is uncertain. Probably it has something to do with the word *vík*, meaning an 'inlet' or a 'bay' – places where *víkingar* lived and lay in wait. The Icelanders did not, except in rare instances, raid each other from the coast. When they went abroad, however, especially to Norway, Icelandic men are frequently referred to in the written sources as having become Vikings for a time or having fought against Vikings. The description *hann var víkingr*, meaning 'he was a Viking', is not unusual. Sea-raiding voyages had their own term. They were called *víking*, and it was said that many Icelanders, while abroad or before settling down in Iceland, 'went raiding' (*fór í víking*).

Leadership

Icelandic chieftains, called *goðar* (sing. *goði*),* were more like political leaders than the warrior chiefs of many contemporary cultures. They possessed only slight formal authority to police, and until well into the thirteenth century had almost no military means to forcefully repress the surrounding population. As leaders they were unable to limit the access of other farmers to natural resources, and they had no privileged control over a region's surplus production. Like other prominent farmers, they were able to weather bad times, but there were no community works such as extensive irrigation systems, waterways or fortifications whose upkeep and defence offered the *goðar* a leadership niche. *Goðar*, both as individuals and as a group, had only limited ability to compel the free landholding farmers (*bændr*, sing. *bóndi*) to do their bidding. The situation did not change for those farmers who were a chieftain's *thingmenn* (sing. *thingmaðr*),† meaning legally recognized followers.

Although not a commanding nobility, the *goðar* functioned as leaders of interest groups composed of *thingmenn* drawn from among the *bændr*. These groups, established through personal alliances, were based on shared self-interest between leaders and their *thingmenn*. A *bóndi* who had become a thingman of a *goði* was referred to as being 'in thing' with the chieftain. The political office of a *goði* was called a *goðorð*, a term that means the 'word' (*orð*) of a *goði*.

---

* Hereafter the English term 'chieftain' and the Icelandic term *goði* (pl. *goðar*) are used interchangeably. Referring to *goðar* as chieftains is an old scholarly tradition, though the correspondence is not exact.

† *Maðr*, plural *menn*, is a word that appears frequently in Old Norse. Similarly to the English words 'man' and 'men', it can be gender specific, but often means 'people'.

To all appearances the *goðar* assumed leadership peacefully, with the consent of the free farmers, early in the tenth century. A chieftaincy or *goðorð* was treated as a private possession that normally passed to a family member, though not necessarily a first son. In addition to being inherited, a *goðorð* could be purchased, shared or received as a gift. There were perhaps more than twice as many chieftains as chieftaincies, because each of the several men who shared a *goðorð* could call himself a *goði*.

Scholars sometimes translate the term *goði* as priest-chieftain because it is derived from the Old Norse word *goð*, meaning 'god'. Probably the term stems from the responsibilities that early Icelandic chieftains had as priests of the old religion. The written sources originate in the later Christian period and are not reliable concerning pre-conversion religious practices.[6] Although we cannot be precise about numbers, there is no doubt that many *goðar* exchanged their previous religious function for that of Christian priests when Iceland converted to Christianity in the year 1000.[7] Having survived and in part engineered so dramatic a religious change, the *goðar* retained their traditional authority. Embracing the new beliefs, they held on to their occupational monopoly, solidifying their political control in the eleventh and twelfth centuries. Whether in heathen or Christian times, the *goðar* were a small-scale elite able to exert both ideological and political power.

Mord the Fiddle: A Leader and the Law

As noted earlier, acumen in the area of law was especially valuable for a leader. Returning to Mord the Fiddle, whose story comes from a saga and is not strictly factual, we find an account that shows a leader's use and abuse of the law. Mord's story involves questions of honour, and, like so many features of Icelandic culture, honour is repeatedly tied to competition. The common human concerns for the honour and ethics of the individual and his family play a significant role in the Icelandic texts, as they do in almost all medieval literatures.

Honour in the sagas, however, tends to exhibit a highly personal orientation. It is often more closely tied to maintaining life, property and status or to exacting revenge than it is to the more epic ideal of an individual's sacrificing himself for obligations to liege lord, religion or the defence of a people. In Iceland, loss of honour signalled that the individual was incapable of defending either himself or his property.

From the impressive introduction of Mord at the opening of *Njal's Saga*, we might guess that he is a man with a problem. Unn, his daughter, is unhappy in her marriage to a well-born and successful farmer named Hrut, half-brother to the chieftain Hoskuld Dala-Kollsson. For Mord, the young woman's complaint is important. He has only one child, and Unn is his heir. The matter she raises jeopardizes the future of his line and the integrity of his property. Mord quickly assesses that if Unn follows the proper procedure from the start, he will later, when he argues the matter at the assembly, have an airtight legal case against her husband. The passage below takes up the story shortly after Unn arrives at the annual Althing. She has ridden south to the general assembly from her new home in Laxárdalr (the Salmon River Valley) without her husband (Ch. 7):

Her father, Mord the Fiddle, was there. He welcomed her warmly, and invited her to stay with him in his booth during the Althing. She accepted.

'What have you to tell me of your companion Hrut?'

'I have nothing but good to say of him,' replied Unn, 'insofar as he is responsible for his own actions.'

Mord was silent for a while. Then he said, 'What is troubling you, daughter? For I can see that you want no one but me to know of it. You can rely on me better than on anyone else to solve your problems.'

They moved away so that their conversation could not be overheard. Then Mord said to his daughter, 'Now tell me everything about your relationship, and let nothing deter you.'

'Very well,' said Unn. 'I want to divorce Hrut, and I can tell you the exact grounds I have against him. He is unable to consummate our marriage and give me satisfaction, although in every other way he is as virile as the best of men.'

'What do you mean?' asked Mord. 'Be more explicit.'

Unn replied, 'Whenever he touches me, he is so enlarged that he cannot have enjoyment of me, although we both passionately desire to reach consummation. But we have never succeeded. And yet, before we draw apart, he proves that he is by nature as normal as other men.'

Having heard his daughter's plight, Mord devises a plan to get her safely out of both the marriage and the house, while laying the groundwork for a future legal claim against Hrut for a sizeable part of the couple's property. Mord sees that the crucial element is to have the husband away from home when the wife names witnesses at the couple's bedside. The threat of possible violence from Hrut is clear in the precision of the directions that Mord gives to Unn in order to throw off pursuit by Hrut:

'You have done well to tell me this,' said Mord. 'I can give you a plan which will meet the case so long as you carry it out in every detail.

'First, you must ride home now from the Althing. Your husband will have returned [Hrut was in the West Fjords collecting rents on his livestock], and he will welcome you warmly. You must be affectionate towards him and compliant, and he will think the situation much improved. On no account must you show him any indifference.

'But when spring comes you must feign illness and take to your bed. Hrut will not try to guess the nature of your illness, and he will not reproach you; indeed, he will tell everyone to take the greatest care of you. Then he will set off with Sigmund west to the fjords. He will be busy fetching all his livestock and rents from the west, and he will be away from home far into the summer.

'Later, when it is time for people to ride to the Althing, and when all those who intend to be there have left the Dales, you must get up from your bed and summon men to accompany you on a journey. When you are quite ready to leave, you must walk to your bedside with those who are going to travel with you. There at your husband's bedstead you must name witnesses and declare yourself lawfully divorced from him; do it as correctly as possible in accordance with the procedural rules of the Althing and the common law of the land. You must then name witnesses once again at the main door.

'With that done you must ride away. Take the path over Lax River Valley Heath and across to Holtavord Heath, for no one will search for you as far as Hrútafjord, and then carry straight on until you come to me here. I shall then take care of the case for you, and you will never fall into his hands again.'

Unn now rode home from the Althing. Hrut had already returned, and he welcomed her warmly. Unn responded well and was affectionate toward him. They got on well together that year. But when spring came, Unn fell ill and took to her bed. Hrut rode off west to the fjords, leaving orders that she was to be well looked after.

When the Althing was due, Unn made her preparations for the journey. She followed her father's instructions in every detail and then rode off to the Althing. The men of the district searched for her but could not find her. Mord welcomed his daughter and asked her how she had carried out his plan.

'I have not deviated from it at all,' she replied.

Mord went to the Law Rock, and there gave notice of Unn's lawful divorce from Hrut. People thought this was news indeed. Unn went home with her father, and she never set foot in the west again.[8]

Elements of law, honour, family, property and money are intertwined in this story, and in the course of this book we will unravel the different threads in stories like this one. But what of power and leadership? At least a part of the answer lies in what follows in the saga. Mord knows his law, and so far he has got his way. Now he makes an all-too-human mistake. He gets greedy. According to *Grágás*, Iceland's 'Grey Goose' Law (discussed in Chapter 17 along with issues of marriage and divorce), women involved in divorce had rights. If Unn's divorce had been initiated or caused by the husband (which had to be proved, at least to the satisfaction of the court), the wife's side could claim all the property that both families had committed in the marriage agreement.[9]

Unn's divorce is done; now comes the case over the couple's property. In order to win, Mord has to show that Hrut's failure to consummate the marriage initially caused the divorce. This is a messy business. It involves the public humiliation of Hrut, an otherwise

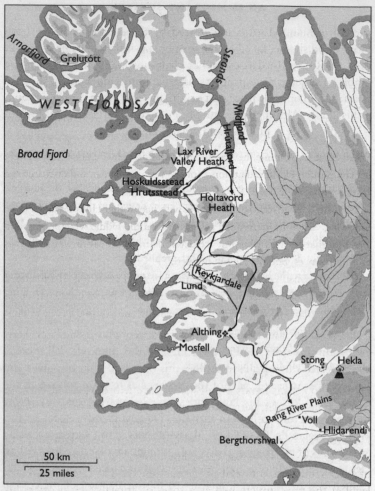

3. The Travels of Unn and Hrut. Mord, who lives in the south at Voll, advises his daughter Unn, who lives with her husband Hrut at Hrutsstead in the Western Quarter, on how to return home safely to Voll after she announces herself divorced from Hrut. In order to throw off pursuit, Mord tells Unn to first go east across the Lax River Valley Heath and then over the Holtavord Heath as far as Hrútafjord. Only then should she head south, because 'No one will look for you there'. The black arrows show Unn's route home to Voll. The grey arrows show the route of her former husband Hrut as he rides home to Hrutsstead from the Althing where, in the summer after the divorce, he and Mord dispute Unn's dowry.

successful man. Mord is undeterred by the consequences, in both money and shame, faced by his former son-in-law. The next year at the Law Rock, Mord assesses that Hrut must pay a sum equal to the whole of the marriage property, that is, both Unn's dowry and the contribution or bride price that originally came from the bridegroom or his family. Although presumably legal – the charge is still unproven – Mord's stance is punitive and grasping.

When Hrut came home, he was shocked to find his wife gone. But he kept his composure. He stayed at home for the rest of the year and discussed the matter with no one.

Next summer he rode to the Althing with his brother Hoskuld and a large following. When he arrived, he asked if Mord the Fiddle were present and was told that he was. Everyone expected that he and Mord would discuss their differences, but this did not happen.

One day, when people were assembled at the Law Rock, Mord named witnesses and gave notice of a money claim [fésök] against Hrut concerning the money affairs [fémál] of his daughter, which he assessed at ninety hundreds.* He demanded immediate payment of this sum, on penalty of a fine of three marks. He referred this action to the proper Quarter Court, and gave notice of it, in public, at the Law Rock.

Desiring to get his hands on all the wealth, Mord leaves little room for the type of quiet, personal negotiations called for by the delicacy of the matter. He drives his case forward in the public eye, pushing Hrut too far. Incensed by Mord's actions, Hrut challenges Mord to a duel (hólmganga).† Hrut's response moves the dispute from a test of legal acumen to a test of physical strength. The duel, which was legal at the time, functioned as a form of appeal.[10] Hrut offers his former father-in-law sporting terms: double or nothing.

---

* A considerable sum. Counted in ells of woven wool or vaðmál, it is approximately the value of ninety cows or several average farms.
† Hólmganga, literally 'island going', was a duel fought on a small island. At the Althing, this was a sandy islet in the Öxár River below the Law Rock. Duels were outlawed at the beginning of the eleventh century.

When Mord had made this announcement, Hrut replied: 'You are pressing this claim concerning your daughter with greed and aggression rather than decency and fairness, and for that reason I intend to resist it. You have not got your hands on the money yet; it is still in my possession. I declare, and let all those present at the Law Rock be witnesses, that I challenge you, Mord the Fiddle, to single combat for the bride price and dowry. I myself shall stake an equal sum, the winner to take all. But if you refuse to fight with me, you shall forfeit all claim to the dowry.'

Here the saga raises the question faced by each generation of Icelanders beginning shortly after the *landnám*: were disputes to be resolved by means of negotiation and compromise, that is through consensus, or by recourse to violence? Both courses of action were legal in this feuding society. The operation of power and authority in Iceland ultimately depended upon which course individuals and groups chose. A man like Mord had to mitigate his own greed so as not to give fighters like Hrut public approval to fall back on physical prowess. Moderation, or the lack of it, was articulated in terms of honour and shame.

The older man has overstepped the bounds of discretion. Mord finds no consensus of support for his position, and no one assists him against Hrut. Faced with the choice of life or death, Mord chooses life and loses both property and honour. The saga continues (Ch. 8):

Mord was silent, and conferred with his friends about the challenge. Jorund the *goði* told him, 'There is no need for you to ask our opinions; you know well enough that if you fight Hrut you will lose your life as well as the money. Hrut is a successful man; he is great by achievement, and he is a very good fighter.'

So Mord announced that he would not fight with Hrut. There was a great shout of derision at the Law Rock, and Mord earned nothing but ignominy from this.

The shamed husband's call for single combat is a rejoinder that focuses on honour, leaving no room for negotiation. Whereas Hrut, a young man, might otherwise have been too shamed to challenge an older man to single combat, in this instance Mord has given Hrut the opportunity.

It will never be known whether these events concerning Mord and his daughter actually happened. Certainly what we have just read was embellished by the saga author. For the original Icelandic audience the important point was that the story was plausible. It could have happened, and this very old story offers us considerable insight into the public and private worlds of medieval Iceland. Was there perhaps an element of social dialogue between the medieval storyteller and the saga audience? Surely the story points to the fact that duels and recourse to violence, although legal, rarely settled underlying economic and family issues. Such actions merely postponed the reckoning. Issues often churned in memory until later, setting off a feud. That happens in *Njal's Saga*. Hrut, triumphant in his manoeuvring at the Althing, keeps all the property, including Unn's dowry. No one in Mord's family forgets it. Long after Mord is dead, the issue of Unn's dowry brings an additional humiliation to Hrut and becomes the seed of a dangerous conflict. Eventually the matter leads to a feud, involving people who had nothing to do with the original dispute.

The Sagas: An Ethnography of Medieval Iceland

Jón Jóhannesson published a work on Iceland's early history in which he ... mentioned almost none of the events recounted in the *Íslendinga sögur* [family sagas], just as if they had never taken place. Yet Jón Jóhannesson was far from being extreme in his views. Shortly after his *History* appeared, I asked him whether he believed that the sagas were pure fiction. 'No, not at all,' he answered, 'I just don't know what to do with them.' – And this is still the situation today.

Jónas Kristjánsson, 'The Roots of the Sagas'

Mord's story is a good example of the nature of the family sagas. The most comprehensive extant portrayal of a Western medieval society, the sagas had both a social and a literary function, but their dual nature is often ignored. Historians and anthropologists, even those interested in social history, have tended to avoid using the sagas as source material. These vernacular prose narratives are relatively late sources, most of them dating from the thirteenth century. At times the storytellers invented characters and occurrences. When Icelanders are portrayed travelling abroad, the stories sometimes have an air of fantasy, but when the action is set in Iceland, even the supernatural episodes are usually framed in a formal social setting. In this latter context the stories reveal cultural patterns and normative codes, indicating to the reader basic guidelines for social and political conduct.

One small story like Mord's only hints at values. A whole collection of such stories is a different matter. In some, though certainly not all ways, the sagas approach the type of ethnographic material collected by anthropologists in the field. In one way the sagas may even have an advantage over most ethnographic observations, which have a weak point. Because they cannot cover an adequate span of time, anthropological observations rarely capture the full range of variability affecting the community under study. The sagas do not have this problem. They capture a wide range of variability, offering deep insight into the mentality of the culture group as well as the changing environment.

Whereas other European peoples often understood their historical roots in highly mythic terms, involving gods and semi-divine heroes, the Icelanders developed their sagas, a quasi-historical, linear reckoning of the past. They recognized that the origins of their community were not timeless or even very distant, but encapsulated in the relatively recent, memorable events of the Viking Age settlement of Iceland and the century following it. Collectively the family sagas are the Icelandic foundation myth. They can be described as a series of stories about a migration of farmers that are decidedly more history and legend than stories of mythic origin. These stories evolved over a period of centuries, providing later generations with an adaptable vehicle of social memory.[11] The sagas helped an immigrant people form a coherent sense of who they were, explaining how the traditional freeman values, so important to the Icelanders' self-image, came to the island. Tradition in medieval Iceland was not a block of historical fact. Nor was it a fixed text. Tradition was a living and growing heritage of quasi-factual social recollection that served as the thematic core of each saga story, uniting saga-teller and audience with life in the Icelandic environment, past and present.

The family and the Sturlunga sagas are invaluable sources for exploring the establishment and functioning of social order in early Iceland.[12] Together with the medieval laws and modern studies of the environment and archaeology, these written sources depict the workings of an island society that from the tenth to the thirteenth century was marked by strong continuity as well as by change. The sagas are a window into otherwise lost worlds of private life, social values and material culture. No other European society has such a detailed literature recounting its origin and development. The word *saga* is connected with the verb 'to say' (*segja*), and means both history and story. Not folk tales, epics, romances or chronicles, the sagas are mostly realistic stories about everyday issues confronting Icelandic farmers and their chieftains. They centre on disputes and feuds over insults, land, chieftaincies, seductions, inheritance, love, bodily injuries and missing livestock. There are passages of ecological description as well as claims to chattels, accusations of witchcraft, hauntings, fights over beached whales, scurrilous or erotic verses, cheating and stealing, harbouring of outlaws, and struggles for local status.

Focusing on conflicts and crisis situations, the sagas tell of virtue and deceit as well as the banality and humour of everyday life. We see a chilling picture of the hardships experienced by small farmers living with limited resources. The literature describes in detail the machinations of those aspiring to power and the responses of their weaker prey, who were often unable to undertake lawsuits in their own defence or to protect their lands from encroachment. The issue of the sagas as sources is treated in detail in Chapter 8. Here it is sufficient to point out that continued adherence to the older view, stressing only the literary value of the family sagas, is self-defeating. Because the sagas have literary value does not mean that they are devoid of sociological information. Medieval Icelanders wrote the sagas about themselves and for themselves. By exploring saga literature in conjunction with the other sources, we come a step closer to unearthing the essence of Iceland's functioning medieval society.

2

Resources and Subsistence:
Life on a Northern Island

Kjartan often went to the hot springs at Sælingsdal, and it
always seemed to happen that Gudrun was also at the baths.
Kjartan enjoyed talking with Gudrun, because she was intelligent and spoke so engagingly. It was common talk that
Kjartan and Gudrun were the best matched of the young
people growing up at that time.

Laxdæla saga, Chapter 39

Thorleif again invited Ketil and his men to stay there, warning them that the weather was not reliable. Ketil insisted
that he had to leave, but Thorleif urged him to turn back if
the weather began to worsen. Ketil set out, but it was only
a short time before the bad weather came, and they had
to turn back. They reached Thorleif's very late and were
completely exhausted. Thorleif welcomed them warmly, and
they spent two nights weatherbound there. The longer the
stay was, the better the hospitality.

The Saga of the People of Weapon's Fjord
(*Vápnfirðinga saga*), Chapter 5

At the same time that the Viking Age settlers of Iceland were setting
up an autonomous land with self-directed political and social
systems, they were adapting to an unusual combination of environ-

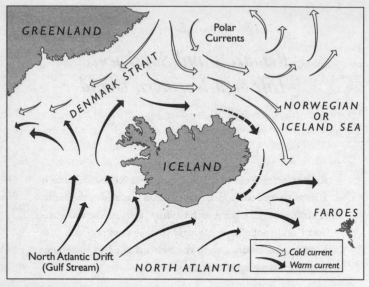

4. Ocean Currents Surrounding Iceland.

mental conditions. Although Iceland, at 103,000 square kilometres (39,769 square miles), is a fifth larger than Ireland, it cannot support a large population. Most of the interior is uninhabitable because of its distance from the warmth of the surrounding ocean, a northern branch of the Gulf Stream that flows around Iceland's coast. The glaciers, often at relatively low altitudes, are a reminder of the nearness of the Arctic Circle, which lies a few degrees above the northern tip of the West Fjords. The great Vatna Glacier (Vatna Jökull) in the south-east covers 5,800 square kilometres (2,240 square miles), and at its thickest point this snowcapped mass of ice is approximately 1,000 metres (3,000 feet) deep.

Iceland is situated between two different air masses – the cold, dry polar front and the warm, damp southern front – and between two different oceanic currents, the warm North Atlantic Drift and the East Greenland polar current. Because of this mix, the island's temperature and weather are frequently unstable. Cold northern winds which, having passed over the polar cap, are clear and dry alternate with moisture-laden maritime winds, which deposit heavy rains and snow. The run-off feeds the numerous rivers and lakes of the glaciated landscape, maintaining the extensive bogs and moorlands that support the island's abundant bird life.

Iceland sits on top of the Mid-Atlantic Ridge, and was almost entirely formed by volcanic activity. It remains today one of the most active volcanic regions in the world. The combination of glaciers and volcanic activity affected the early Icelanders in many ways. To a large degree, the valleys were shaped by the effects of glacial and water erosion on brittle volcanic rock. Young by geological standards, Iceland has more than 200 volcanoes, some of whose differing types reach deep into the Earth's unstable interior. Sheets of basalt, a dark rock of igneous origin, underlie almost all of Iceland's soil and surface cover. The landscape in parts of the island consists of dried lava flows and disintegrating pumice. Many of these areas are covered by a dense growth of multicoloured mosses and lichens. Volcanic activity under the huge ice mass of the Vatna Glacier has, over the centuries, caused harm to the surrounding population, including the medieval descendants of the *landnámsmenn* who settled on the coast directly south of the glacier.

Not all the effects of a volcanic environment were negative. The settlers found a landscape with more than 250 sites of natural hot springs, probably more readily accessible hot water than in any comparably sized area in the world. The medieval population never harnessed the hot springs or the volcanic vents for energy, but they did utilize this resource in other ways. These included washing clothes, boiling and steaming foods, attending to personal hygiene and comfort, and socializing in the natural hot pools. The quotation from *Laxdæla saga* at the start of this chapter mentions the baths at Sælingsdal in the Broad Fjord region, where the young Kjartan and Gudrun met. The mention indicates the role of hot springs in the social life of the rural community.

Almost all successful settlements were near the coast or in a few sheltered inland valley systems. There were no dangerous predatory animals. When the settlers arrived, the arctic fox and the field mouse were the only land mammals on the island, although periodically solitary polar bears travelling on ice floes from Greenland arrived in Northern Iceland. By the time the bears reached Iceland they were desperately hungry and, then as now, had to be hunted quickly. The settlers brought dogs, cats, pigs, goats, sheep, cattle and horses with them.[1] They also brought lice, fleas, dung beetles and a variety of other animal parasites. The lack of predators meant that from the start they could let their livestock roam the highlands. At first cattle raising, on the Norwegian model, was the most important activity, but within a century sheep farming became more prominent. Pigs and goats proved especially destructive to the grasslands, and by the year 1000 raising them was to a large extent discontinued.[2] The other imported animals adjusted well. The Icelanders were fortunate in their horses. The original settlers imported small Scandinavian horses with thick coats. While continental Europeans bred their horses with Arabian stock in the thirteenth century to produce larger animals, the Icelanders continued with their small, tough horses, which over the centuries proved well adapted to North Atlantic conditions and Iceland's uneven terrain.

The first settlers were prepared, and able, to live on often isolated farmsteads, surrounded by the hayfields and meadows necessary to maintain their herds, a settlement pattern that continued into the early twentieth century. They became a pastoral people based on fixed, dispersed farmsteads. Application of the concepts of freemen's rights turned on the ability of a farmer, called a *húsbóndi* (master of the house, related to English 'husband'), to feed his dependants. Households needed to control sufficient pasturage and hay meadows to provide the fodder necessary to keep a minimum of livestock alive through the winter. From the start, Icelandic society operated with well-developed concepts of private property and law, but, in an unusual combination, it lacked most of the formal institutions of government which normally protect ownership and enforce judicial decisions.

As the country participated only marginally in the active trade of Viking Age Scandinavia, subsistence was dependent on the strategies of settled pastoralism and hunter-gathering. The latter included hunting seals and birds, gathering eggs, fishing, and finding beached whales. Individual sagas tend to have different focuses. *Egil's Saga*, for example, reveals much about economic matters and subsistence strategies. It tells how the settler, the *landnámsmaðr* Skallagrim (Bald Grim), provisioned his main farm at Borg, which lay just above the coastal wetlands in Borgarfjord. The saga description, written several centuries after the land-taking by someone who knew the area and was aware that changes had occurred in the region since the settlement, in Chapter 29 assesses Skallagrim's wealth in terms of natural resources.[3]

Skallagrim was an industrious man. He always had many men to gather all provisions that might be useful for the household. This was because in the early stages of the settlement, people had little livestock, considering the number of them who were there. The livestock they did have were left to fend for themselves in the woods during the winter.

Skallagrim was also an active shipbuilder. Because there was no lack of driftwood to be found west of Mýrar [the Wetlands], he built and ran another farm at Alftanes [Swans' Headland]. From there he sent his men out fishing and seal-hunting. They collected wildfowl eggs and everything was plentiful; they also fetched in his driftwood.

Whales were often stranded, and anything one wanted could be shot. The wildlife was unfamiliar with man, and the animals waited peacefully when hunted. Skallagrim built his third farm by the sea in the west part of Mýrar where it was even easier to wait for the driftwood. He started sowing there, calling the place Akrar [Fields]. Because whales washed up on some offshore islands, they were called the Hvals Isles [Whale's Isles].

Skallagrim also sent his men up the rivers looking for salmon. He settled Odd the Lone-Dweller on the Gljufur River, where he attended to the salmon fishing. Odd lived at Einbuabrekkur [Lone-Dweller's Slope], and Einbuanes [Lone-Dweller's Headland] takes its name from him. Then Skallagrim gave

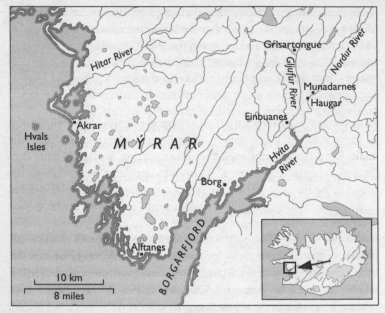

5. Skallagrim's Land-take in Borgarfjord. In the late ninth century, Skallagrim, the son of a Norwegian Viking and father to the Icelandic warrior-poet Egil Skallagrimsson, settled at Borg in south-western Iceland. In the Mýrar area (named after its moors and swampland), he established a series of outer farms in order to harvest the natural resources. His descendants, known as the Mýramenn, remained a prominent family in the region. Skallagrim's initial claim was large and he soon gave lands to other settlers. Within a generation several, sometimes contentious, families lived within the limits of Skallagrim's initial land-take.

a place on the Nordur River [North River] to a man called Sigmund. He lived at Sigmundarstead, or Haugar as it's called nowadays, and Sigmundarnes takes its name from him. Later on Sigmund moved his household to Mundarnes, a better place for salmon fishing.

As Skallagrim's livestock increased the animals started going up to the mountains in the summer. He found a big difference in the livestock, which were much better and fatter when grazing up on the moorland. Above all this was so with the sheep that wintered in the mountain valleys instead of being driven down. As a result, Skallagrim built a farm near the mountains and used it to raise sheep. A man called Gris was in charge of the farm, and Grisartongue was named for him. Thus the wealth of Skallagrim rested on many footings.

This picture of Skallagrim's land-taking corresponds well with what is known of the early society. Prominent settlers established their main farmsteads with smaller, self-supporting outlying farms that provisioned the main house. As is discussed later in this book, the attempt by the first settlers to install a system of territorial control would soon break down, with many of the outlying farms becoming independent households.

On the local level people harvested natural resources in the most suitable ways, with some specialization and division of labour. Among the regions of the island there was little significant variation in the production of goods or foodstuffs. Single-household farms became the rule, and since no towns or even small villages developed in Viking Age Iceland, the society was completely rural. In all regions of Iceland individual farmsteads were largely self-sufficient economic (though not political) units. Coastal fishing from small boats, manned sometimes by only two men, was practised widely. The richest catches were taken at the cod-spawning grounds off the south-western and western coasts in late winter and early spring, but abundant fish stocks were available in many places off Iceland's long coastline. With iron readily available in the form of low-grade bog ore, and with wood for charcoal to create the steady heat necessary to work it increasingly scarce everywhere, no individual or region cornered the market on iron-making.

The settlement of Iceland was financed to a large extent by wealth accumulated through Viking trade and depredations in Europe. The raids, beginning in the late eighth century, brought plunder to Scandinavia, stimulated shipbuilding, and invigorated commerce. These factors made possible the convergence of the wealth, experience and technology necessary to colonize so large and distant a place as Iceland. In the years after the settlement, whatever the initial wealth of the colonists, the descendants of the *landnámsmenn* saw their imported capital diminish. They found themselves in a remote place with a fragile subarctic ecology. The settlers soon learned that their new land allowed only limited agriculture and produced little on which the outside world placed a premium.

The settlers developed few new technologies to increase the productivity of their coastal and inland valley farmsteads. For archaeology this feature is especially significant, because it connects, in many ways, the far past with the near present. From the tenth to the nineteenth century, there was much continuity in Iceland's rural life. This continuity, seen more in the material culture and less in social arrangements, was reinforced by the durability of individual settlements. Many early-twentieth-century farm sites were the product of continuous habitation, beginning in the Viking Age and extending over a thousand years.[4] Numerous farms mentioned in the sagas are still occupied today, with many of them retaining their original names.

Similarities, however, can be deceptive. It is dangerous to view the tenth century through the perspective of the well-documented eighteenth and nineteenth centuries. It is important to remember that the erosion caused by the immigrants' herds had by the nineteenth century drastically diminished the island's biomass. This factor, in conjunction with a climate that after the thirteenth century became increasingly colder, meant that by the eighteenth century people lived somewhat differently than in the first centuries following the settlement. Even in the later years of the Free State there were already alterations in subsistence strategies, social arrangements and living conditions.

The variability of the weather and the short, often cool, growing season at Iceland's northern latitude influenced the way Icelanders farmed and lived. Native vegetation was limited mostly to birch and willow (with some alder and evergreens), shrubs, grasses, mosses, lichens and sedges. The settlers immediately saw that the grasses and shrubs were suitable for the type of cattle and sheep farming that they knew in their homelands. The original birch forests, which stretched in many places from the shoreline to the base of the mountains, did not hinder these herdsmen. The land was easy to clear of the relatively slender trees, and probably, as evidenced by excavations such as those in the Mosfell Valley at the farm of Hrísbrú, the technique for land clearing was to burn the trees and brush.[5] As the ownership of livestock was from the start the measure of status and wealth, the initial ease of adapting the new land to livestock farming fed from the beginning the temptation to overstock.

The native birch offered the *landnámsmenn* a supply of hardwood suitable for hearths and charcoal-making. The land clearings of the settlers, the ravenous fuel requirements for making iron from bog ore, and the uncontrolled grazing of livestock soon reduced the original forests to relatively small stands of trees. These remaining woodlands frequently appear in the sagas as valuable, contested property. Such a contest is at the core of a dispute in *The Saga of the People of Weapon's Fjord* (*Vápnfirðinga saga*, discussed in Chapter 13). After the first relatively few big trees had been cut down, the birch available was of only limited use in shipbuilding and house construction. From early on good timber had to be imported. This expense raised the cost of maintaining ships, a factor that over time severely limited the Icelanders' ability to compete with Norwegian merchants.

Lack of wood meant that the transplanted European farmers could not fence in large areas, a factor that limited the amount of land that could be devoted to hay production. Matters were not helped by the nature of Iceland's brittle volcanic rock, which with its many air bubbles chips easily and is hard to shape. Despite the difficulty of constructing high turf and stone walls, many had to be built to enclose grazing pastures.[6] Walls were also used to enclose the manured home fields, called *tún*. These productive hayfields were usually situated in front of the farmsteads, although sometimes, especially in the earliest period, the wall of the *tún* formed a ring around the farmhouse and the animal sheds. Both the home-field walls and the farm buildings were constructed of turf, the readily available natural material.

Turf Housing

With limited quantities of building wood, and with volcanic rock suitable mainly for foundation stones and rough walls, the Icelanders depended on turf for constructing their houses. Around frames of timber they constructed sod homes with thick, heat-retaining walls. The timbers were fashioned from imported wood or driftwood. Most of the latter was carried by currents from Siberia, collecting in many places along Iceland's coast. With the damaged portions cut away, driftwood timbers were often short and imperfect. By the end of the settlement period, the supply of stout timbers was not sufficient to satisfy the needs of the population.

The turf farmhouse was a focal point of everyday life, and its development was a crucial chapter in the settlers' adaptation to their northern environment. In the few centuries of the Viking Age, the Icelandic and the related Greenlandic turf house grew in complexity. With some sleuthing, the construction and the history of these buildings can be determined from archaeology, written sources, and comparison with architectural developments in mainland Scandinavia, especially Norway.[7]

At the time of Iceland's settlement, the turf longhouse (*langhús*) already had a long history in Scandinavia, reaching far back into prehistory. In the North Atlantic region of the ninth-century Viking world, most houses were built of turf. The *landnámsmenn* brought to Iceland the turf-building techniques used in their homelands. The traditional turf longhouse, called both a *skáli* (hall) and an *eldskáli* (fire-hall) in the sources, was a narrow, oblong structure, slightly wider in the middle than at the ends. The entrance was through the front wall, under a small gable near one of the ends.

Turf houses were built in stages, and required a significant degree of expertise. The outside walls were built first and then left to settle. Next came the wooden frame, and then finally the roof. From later centuries it is known that rock and driftwood timbers for building were gathered in summer and autumn. During the winter these materials were transported by sled to the construction site. Turf (grass with the underlying sod attached) was usually cut near the site in early summer. The walls of some Icelandic buildings were made of rock; they resembled turf construction because soil and turf were wedged between the uncut rocks to seal and keep them steady. Depending on the location, turf walls were often easier to construct than stone ones.

Well-built turf walls lasted from thirty years to a century, whereas whole buildings were often much older. The difference was maintenance, especially when there was water damage. Sections of the walls and roofs had to be replaced at intervals, and turf buildings required a substantial amount of upkeep. At times stray sheep and even cows might climb on to a turf roof, where the grass was usually particularly rich. With the passage of years, grass often grew over the lower outside walls, and turf buildings tended to melt into the surrounding ground, looking like small hillocks from a distance.

In Norway as the Viking Age advanced, the turf house gradually gave way to the timber house.[8] This change did not occur in Iceland or in the Norse/Icelandic settlement in Greenland, where the scarcity of large building timbers and the presence of suitable sod favoured turf construction. In keeping with the building techniques of Greenland and Iceland, the Norse settlement in about the year 1000 at L'Anse aux Meadows in Newfoundland relied on turf houses.[9]

In Iceland, the ruin of a settlement-period farmhouse, called Grelutótt, in Arnarfjord (Arnarfjörðr) in the West Fjords is a good example of a traditional Scandinavian longhouse (*skáli*).[10] Many similar settlement-period longhouses, such as Granastaðir in Eyjafjord and the larger Hofstaðir in the Mývatn district, have been found.[11] Grelutótt was a small house with room for little more than a family and a few workers. Animals were housed in separate buildings. The site showed

2. Grelutótt in Iceland's West Fjords. The reconstruction shows a small, typical longhouse from the settlement period.

evidence of considerable iron-working, and two smithies were found near the longhouse. There were also a number of everyday Viking Age artifacts radiocarbon dated to AD 800–900.[12] The finds included fragments of soapstone bowls and containers, common Norwegian exports during Viking times. No evidence exists of an earlier house on this *landnám*-period site.

Archaeologically, Grelutótt fits well into the picture of a small Icelandic Viking Age house. The interior of the Grelutótt building was 13.4 metres long and 5.4 metres wide. It was equipped along the inside walls with wide benches, called *set*, a word related to the English 'sit'. Here people sat, worked, ate and slept. In the centre of the floor was the long-fire (*langeld*), where wood and peat were burned. The smoke exited through a hole in the roof, and the interior was probably smoky, especially during rains.

In Iceland's wet maritime climate people were forced to spend considerable time indoors, and traditional longhouses such as Grelutótt were not very comfortable. In order to improve their housing, the settlers combined the most useful aspects of two types of structure. One was the outside turf shell of the traditional Scandinavian turf longhouse; the other was the internal timber framework used in the construction of contemporary Scandinavian wooden buildings. Other Norse communities may have also devised or incorporated these changes to turf buildings during the Viking Age, but the major evidence for such a development comes from archaeological work in Iceland and Greenland, where the innovations were spurred by environmental conditions.

In houses where an internal wooden frame relieved the relatively weak turf walls of the weight of the heavy sod roof (see Appendix 3), passageways could be cut through the walls, allowing rooms to be added. One room frequently added was a communal latrine. In the older longhouses, such as Grelutótt, the latrine had been built as a separate outhouse, but by the eleventh century the *kamarr* (chamber), as it is frequently called in the sagas, was often placed indoors.[13] This alteration, which improved living conditions and

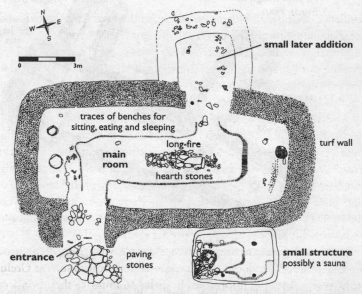

3. **Archaeological Floor Plan of Grelutótt.** The small back room was added later and is an early example of Icelanders expanding the basic longhouse design. The sunken rectangular structure in front of the house had stones for an oven-like hearth and what appears to be earthen support for benches. This 'pit house' may have been a sauna or a smokehouse, perhaps both.

dairy and food storage room

latrine

living hall

entrance room

entrance

main hall

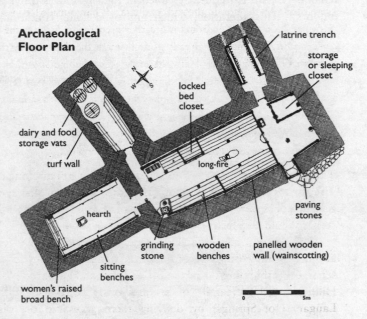

Archaeological Floor Plan

latrine trench

storage or sleeping closet

locked bed closet

dairy and food storage vats

turf wall

long-fire

paving stones

hearth

grinding stone

wooden benches

panelled wooden wall (wainscotting)

sitting benches

women's raised broad bench

0   5m

4. The Stöng Longhouse Ruin. Located in the Thjórs River Valley (Thjórsárdalur) in southern Iceland, this is an example of the multi-roomed buildings that Icelanders were constructing by the late Viking Age. The farmhouse sat on a rise in a hilly inland valley that was fully settled by the end of the tenth century. Stöng, which was average-sized for the farm of a well-to-do farmer or chieftain, was abandoned when nearby Mt Hekla erupted, destroying as many as twenty farms. The floor plan shows the layout of the interior woodwork.

increased safety in the feuding culture, is corroborated by both archaeology and saga. For example, *Eyrbyggja saga* (Chapter 26) recounts the following short episode about an unfortunate fellow named Svart, who was sent to the farm of Helgafell to kill the chieftain Snorri goði. The plan was to attack Snorri in the evening when it was assumed that he and his men would head for the latrine:

Svart went over to Helgafell and broke through the roof over the outside door, climbing into the loft. This action took place while Snorri and his men were sitting by the fire. In those days the farms had outside latrines. When Snorri and his men got up from the fire, they prepared to go out to the latrine. Snorri went first and had already gone through the doorway by the time Svart made his thrust. Mar Hallvardsson was just behind Snorri, and Svart struck him with his halberd [a combination of spear and axe]. The thrust landed on Mar's shoulder, slicing across the arm. It was not a serious wound. Svart scrambled out on to the roof and jumped down from the wall. But the paving stones were slippery and he took a bad fall when he landed. Snorri had his men grab hold of Svart before he could stand up.

This story also hinges on a couple of other features of turf longhouses. The saga author assumes that his audience knows that over the outside doors were gables into which a man could fit; and that paving stones would have been placed in front of the door.

Laxdæla saga, in relating the story of Kjartan's vengeance, gives another example (in Chapter 47) of the danger of having latrines as separate outbuildings. Kjartan, who lived at Hjarðarholt (Herd's Hill), shamed the family of his previously betrothed Gudrun at Laugar (Hot Springs) by denying them access to the outdoor latrine:

Kjartan assembled a group, getting sixty men together . . . He took with him tents and provisions and rode until he came to Laugar . . . In those days it was the custom to have the latrine outside, some way away from the farm-house, and this was the layout at Laugar. Kjartan, seizing all the house doors,

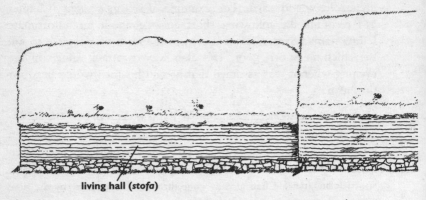

living hall (*stofa*)

5. Front View of the Longhouse at Stöng. The reconstruction postulates a row of small holes for letting in light at the base of the roof. These holes, together with oil lamps, the two fires and the smoke holes in the roof, provided interior light for the building's two large longhouses, the *skáli* (main

refused to let anyone go outside. For three days he forced them all to stay indoors without access to the latrine. After that incident Kjartan rode back to Hjarðarholt and his followers went home.

By the eleventh century, Icelanders were building large farmhouses. The farmstead excavated at Stöng in southern Iceland is an example of the home of a prosperous farmer or chieftain, with room for twenty or more people. Its exceptionally well-preserved foundations and turf walls were buried under pumice and ash in 1104, when the Mount Hekla volcano erupted for the first time since the area had been settled.[14] Spacious and liveable, Stöng included several different rooms, including an indoor latrine. The floor plan shows the front door opening into a large entrance room, a kind of 'mud room' for wet clothes, dirty footwear and equipment. This entrance room also contained a wooden closet used for storing smoked and dried fish and meat, or possibly for sleeping, and was separated from the central

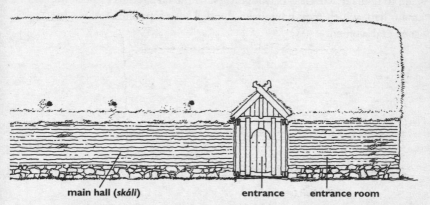

main hall (*skáli*)   **entrance**   **entrance room**

hall) and the *stofa* (living hall), which were connected end to end. The length of the two longhouses, in which about twenty people could live with some comfort, was about 30 metres (95 feet).

part of the main hall by a wooden partition. People entering from the outside went through the entrance room before opening the door to the main hall. This arrangement kept those inside the main hall from being exposed to cold drafts from the outside.

Most of the cooking at Stöng was done on the long-fire in the centre of the main hall. The hearth was lined with stones and partly covered with slabs. As in earlier longhouses, smoke found its way out through a hole in the roof. The steep pitch of the roof gave room for the smoke to rise, decreasing the amount of smoke in the living spaces. There may also have been a row of small holes at the base of the roof for letting light into the hall. Along the walls on both sides of the main hall were the usual low wooden longhouse benches, 1.5 metres (almost 5 feet) wide. The household members probably used foldaway tables for meals. The sagas often mention a locked bed closet for the master of the house. The floor plan shows such a private, protected sleeping place for the *húsbóndi* and the mistress of the house on the bench against the back wall, but other inhabitants had to manage with less privacy. Most of the farmhands slept in the main hall, which may have been divided into separate sections for men and women.

3

Curdled Milk and Calamities:
An Inward-looking Farming Society

Volcanic eruption at Hekla Mountain with great fall of ash and pumice and such large breaks in the earth that cliffs collided in the fires in such a way that it was heard almost throughout the whole land. It was so dark while the ash fall was at its greatest that there was not enough light to read books in those churches that stood closest to the source of the fire. Great hunger. Great death of livestock, both of sheep and of cattle, so that between the Travelling Days [at the end of May] and Peter's Mass [1 August] alone eighty head of cattle from Skálholt's possessions died.

Entry in the *Annals of Skálholt* for the year 1341

On the edge of the habitable world and separated from their home-lands by a dangerous ocean, the ninth- and tenth-century immigrants to Iceland established a social order that lacked many characteristics of a state structure and operated without regional or local military arrangements. Even at the height of Viking times, the country was never invaded, nor was it a base for attacks against other lands. Nevertheless, Iceland remained in contact with events in the Viking world, and some individuals went abroad to join Viking or mercenary bands.

Beyond the consensus that it was wise to be on friendly terms with the Norwegian king, Iceland for centuries had no foreign policy and no defensive land or sea force. The kings of Norway, Iceland's major potential enemy, were for centuries too weak or too absorbed in their own wars and their own domestic problems to play more than a sporadic role in Icelandic affairs. Although many Norwegian kings, including Olaf Tryggvason, St Olaf and Harald Hardradi, showed interest in Iceland, until Norwegian royal power became formidable in the mid thirteenth century foreign monarchs and churchmen rarely had direct influence on events in Iceland. Politically, the island became an inward-looking country that was in contact with, but was largely independent of, the rest of Europe.

Limited agricultural production, coupled with a lack of organized commercial fisheries, restricted Iceland's trade with the outside world. This situation, and the self-sufficiency in staple subsistence which it imposed, did not change until the early fourteenth century. In that period, which is well beyond the scope of this book, dried cod or *skreið*, called stockfish in English, began to be exported and fishing changed from a subsistence to a commercial activity.[1] Once started, the trade in stockfish grew rapidly. Foreign ships from Norway, northern Germany and England began coming regularly to Iceland to purchase stockfish, and by the mid fourteenth century stockfish export and the industry that grew up around it became firmly entrenched. The arrival of these new foreigners was a significant change. From the end of the eleventh century, few Icelanders owned ocean-going ships, and trade with the outside world had become dependent on Norwegian merchants and their boats. After the late eleventh century, Norwegian importance increased still further with the growth of merchant towns in Norway. At this time, because of its export value, the production and export of standardized homespun or woollen cloth, called *vaðmál*, became increasingly important in Iceland.[2] At home and abroad *vaðmál* was used not only for clothing but also, waterproofed with animal fat, for sailcloth.

From the settlement period on, *vaðmál* was woven on upright warp-weighted looms. Much of this indoors work was done by women. The looms were usually a little more than a metre wide, and this width determined the size of the bolts of cloth. Viking Age

Scandinavians had not yet learned to knit, and buttons were still an invention many centuries off. Clothes, including gloves, were cut from woollen cloth and sewn together. Sleeves to some garments, as is mentioned in sagas, were fastened by sewing them shut at the wrists. Some Icelanders wore linen undergarments, but these were expensive and often imported.

Both men and women tended to follow the styles of mainland Scandinavia. Men wore a long shirt and dressed in trousers. Wearing coloured clothes beyond the natural brown, black, grey and white of the sheep signified wealth, and both men and women dressed in their finery for meetings of the Althing. Styles and details of dress changed with time, but Icelandic women during the Viking Age generally wore a long shift, sometimes pleated. This dress was overlaid front and back by a long apron held in place by brooches attached to the front of the dress just below the shoulders. A number of these distinctive brooches have been found in Icelandic excavations and they date their surroundings to the Viking Age.

Icelanders never had a sufficiently large or stable source of silver to replenish the precious metals brought in by the first settlers. Over the years, travelling Icelanders and successful traders brought new supplies of silver to the island, but by the eleventh century the reserve seems to have become sharply depleted. From the earliest period Icelanders substituted commodities for silver, and several mediums of exchange – ranging from silver to livestock, woollen cloth and dairy products – coexisted in medieval Iceland. In particular, homespun replaced silver as a more common unit of exchange. Each grade of *vaðmál* was equivalent to a weight of silver, though the ratios fluctuated over the years.*

* The principal monetary unit was the law ounce (*lögeyrir*), which equalled six ells of homespun cloth two ells wide (an Icelandic ell seems to have been a little more than 49 cm or approximately 19.5 in). The ratio of the law ounce to an ounce of silver varied from 8:1 in the eleventh century to 6:1 in the latter half of the thirteenth century, with a ratio of 7.5:1 recorded in the twelfth century. Prices of goods were calculated in standardized ounces (*thinglagsaurar*), whose values were set at the local springtime assemblies and thus varied from district to district. Usually the standardized ounce was

Until stockfish became important in the fourteenth century, imported goods not paid for in silver were purchased with bulk wool, homespun, skins and, to a lesser extent, agricultural products, in particular dairy goods. Without a renewable supply of money, Icelanders going abroad took with them woollen cloth or other goods to sell. It was a basic fact that Iceland had only limited supplies of foodstuffs to export. Sulphur and such luxury items as white falcons (mostly later) and walrus ivory were exported. One can only guess at the relative importance of such trade, which probably was small. The written sources suggest that the country had an active cottage industry producing woollen goods and dairy products. These products served as an internal barter currency and were the means by which most debts were settled and landlords received payment.

Provisions, Subsistence Strategies, and Population

Although descended from Norse peoples with rich seagoing traditions, the Icelanders soon lacked a ready, cost-effective supply of ocean-going ships. This factor restricted their fishing and limited their subsistence strategies. With their herds, they became a largely landlocked livestock farming society in the midst of a fertile ocean which teemed with whales and other sea mammals. Even for a journey down the coast, characters in the sagas most frequently resort to long overland horseback rides. An extensive system of horse paths connected the whole island. These led to almost every part of the country, and formed a highly serviceable communications web. There were, however, no roads for wheeled carts to cross the highlands, and few if any such roads in the valleys.

In the relatively small boats that the Icelanders could build inexpen-

---

equal to three or four ells of homespun cloth. Livestock was also frequently used as currency. The value of a cow was set at each district assembly, a practice that again made prices variable. Taxes and tithes were paid mostly in *vaðmál*, butter, cheese, livestock and other farm products, including bulk wool and skins.

sively from driftwood, their close coastal fishing often yielded large quantities of fish. They wind-dried for the winter, as will shortly be discussed, several types of fish, especially cod. Given the limitations of their boats, the Icelanders, like most other Scandinavians of the period, avoided or were unable to hunt whales on the open sea. It is unlikely that Icelanders routinely herded whales into bays, forcing them aground. Instead they remained on the lookout for dead whales washed ashore.

Inevitably the new society's development was dictated by competition among succeeding generations for the land's limited resources. Because the population was not nomadic but lived at settled farmsteads, livestock farming required that each farmer have at his disposal sufficiently large expanses of grazing land. During the summer common lands and pastures in the highlands, often called *almenning*, were used by a region's farmers for grazing. The majority of lambs and wethers (gelded rams) were driven up to the highest mountain pastures. During the summer ewes and cows were kept in the lower uplands at dairies called *sel*, many of which were owned by specific farms. There the cows and some of the ewes were milked, and butter and cheeses were produced.

Ewes that are not milked produce more and better quality wool, the cash product of Iceland's sheep-farming society. Because of the trade value of wool, dairy activity centred on the products of cows' milk. Most important was *skyr*, a form of coagulated milk high in protein, which would keep over the winter. *Skyr* was curdled by introducing rennet, found in the membrane of calves' stomachs. *Skyr*, which is still eaten today, had in the Middle Ages the consistency of a thick yoghurt. It was stored at the main farm in large, cool wooden vats of sour whey which were partly buried in the ground. People drank *skyr* when it was mixed with additional whey. Because there was no fresh milk for much of the year, *skyr* was the major dairy food. Cows, which were smaller than today's, were kept alive through the winter on the limited amount of hay each farm could produce, and their milk dried up until the spring.[3]

Dairy farming is extremely labour-intensive. Much time was spent during the summer milking the cows, preparing the *skyr*, and transporting it down from the *sel*. The production of wool and homespun, which paid for imports, was supported by the labour invested in *skyr* and in caring for the cattle. Much of the milking and *skyr* production was done by women. Men were more concerned with the care and herding of animals, the maintaining of turf buildings, fishing, the gathering of natural foods and driftage, and the transportation of the *skyr* down from the summer dairies.

With its many entries about food, *Grettir's Saga* gives a good idea of how the lowland farms were provisioned. For example, in Chapter 28 the description of a prank played by Grettir the Strong on Audun, a fellow farmer, gives one a feeling for the dimness within the turf houses, and shows how *skyr* was transported – by pack horses rather than carts:

Audun was bringing back dairy products [from his *sel*] loaded on two horses. One of the horses carried *skyr* placed in skin bags, which were tied shut at the top and were called *skyr* bags. Audun unloaded the horse and carried the *skyr* into the house. As he came inside, he couldn't see in the dark. Grettir stuck his foot out from the bench so that Audun fell on his face. He landed on top of a *skyr* bag, forcing the top open. Audun jumped up and asked what idiot was there. Grettir named himself.

Audun said, 'That was foolishly done. What is it that you want here?'

'I want to fight you,' said Grettir.

'Let me take care of the food first,' said Audun.

'As it should be,' said Grettir, 'if there's no one else to do it for you.'

Audun bent down and picked up the *skyr* bag. He flung it straight into Grettir's arms, telling him first to deal with what had been given to him. Grettir was covered all over with *skyr* and was more insulted than if Audun had given him a serious wound.

Common lands were called *almenning*.[4] Especially along the coast these public lands offered opportunities for enterprising individuals to increase their store of provisions and to find saleable merchandise. Leaving the protection of one's farmstead and neighbourhood to hunt and gather foodstuffs in often desolate *almenning* could be dangerous. Competition might be fierce and disputes arose. Seal-hunting was highly important, but bloated whales, which had washed ashore with their huge quantity of meat and blubber, were the real prizes among the driftage. *Grettir's Saga* recounts the dangers encountered by Thorgils Maksson, a farmer from Midfjord (Miðfjörðr) in the northern quarter, when he ran afoul of two landless troublemakers, the foster-brothers Thorgeir and Thormod. These famous foster-brothers, who are the lead characters in *Fóstbrœðra saga* (*The Saga of the Foster-Brothers*), had acquired a boat and were causing trouble on the Strands, a section of the eastern shoreline of the West Fjords. The story is told because Asmund, the man who leads the prosecution against the foster-brothers, is Grettir's father. According to the saga, Asmund's successful handling of the case resulted in a legal precedent advantaging prosecutions against land-less individuals who killed men of property on the common lands.

Thorgils worked hard at acquiring provisions, and every year he went out to the Strands. There he collected wild foods and found whale as well as other driftage.[5] Thorgils was a brave man and searched all through the common lands.

At this time the foster-brothers Thorgeir Havarsson and Thormod Kol-brun's-Skald were making their reputations. In their coastal trading ship they sailed over a wide area, landing in many places. They were thought to be unjust men.

One summer Thorgils Maksson found a beached whale on the common land, and he and his companions immediately started to cut it up. When the foster-brothers learned about it, they went there as well, and at first the discussion seemed reasonable enough. Thorgils offered them half of the whale meat from the part that was still uncut. But the newcomers claimed for themselves all of the part that was still uncut or wanted to divide in two the parts already cut as well as those that were uncut. Thorgils flatly refused to give up the part that was already cut.

Tempers flared. Both sides armed themselves, and they began to fight.

Thorgeir and Thorgils fought each other for a long time with no one interfering. Neither gave way and each fought furiously. Their long and hard
exchange ended when Thorgils fell dead, killed by Thorgeir. Meanwhile
Thormod fought in another place with Thorgils' followers. Thormod won
the victory in this exchange, killing three of Thorgils' companions.

After Thorgils' killing, his men returned to Midfjord, taking Thorgils'
body with them. People felt his death was a great loss. The foster-brothers
took the whole whale for themselves. Thormod tells of this encounter in the
memorial *drápa*[6] which he composed in honour of Thorgeir.

Asmund Grey-Streak learned about the killing of his kinsman Thorgils.
Asmund was the person principally responsible for prosecuting the legal case
for Thorgils' death, so he set out to name witnesses and to verify the type of
wounds. He and his supporters interpreted the law such that they referred
the case straight to the Althing because the event had taken place outside
their quarter. Time passed for a while.

When a dead whale was found like this, how were the pieces
of meat and blubber stored? *The Saga of Gudmund the Worthy*
(*Guðmundar saga dýra*) provides some information. It mentions that
after a long stand-off, a chieftain rewarded the men who had stood
by him by opening his brother's whale storage pits [*hvalgrafir*]. He
gave each man three loads of whale meat, which they carried home
with them. In such pits the meat and blubber fermented, a form of
preservation. In a similar manner, Icelanders down to modern times
preserve and eat rotten shark and skate fermented in their own juices,
the process benefiting from the ammonia found in the urine.

In the first years of the settlement, farmers depended heavily on
birds, seals, fish and other forms of wild food while they were building
up their herds. After the herds reached full size, probably by the mid
to late tenth century, livestock farming, including the management
of semi-wild horses used for meat, became the major form of subsistence.[7] Animals, however, were valuable and fresh meat was mostly
only eaten in the autumn. If we are to judge from later times, little
from the slaughtered animals was left unused as households prepared

for winter. Sheep heads, rams' testicles, udders and jelly from the feet were all prepared for storage. Some meats were smoked, but most were boiled and then placed in large wooden vats of sour whey. Called *súrr*, related to English 'sour', this liquid acted as a preservative, bacterial fermentation turning the milk sugar to lactic acid. Food stored in *súrr* takes on a sour taste, and in modern times the food was not considered fit to eat until properly sour. As the forests diminished, dried dung became a major fuel for heating, and was the preferred fuel for smoking both meat and fish. Foods conserved in *súrr* were ready for the table straight from the barrel, and the large percentage of pre-cooked or prepared foods resulted in a considerable saving in winter fuel.

Most early Icelandic farms had little if any salt for preserving, but meat and suet were made into different kinds of sausages and boiled, as were liver and blood-pudding preparations. These and other fatty foods were stuffed into skin bags made from animal stomachs. The butter made at the summer dairies was easily stored in wooden boxes and small barrels and during the winter was an important complement to most foods. Without salt, the stored butter fermented during storage, turning sour. In this state, it would keep for a very long time.

Again from later times, we know that edible lichens such as Iceland moss (*fjallagrös*) were widely used in place of ground meal. Northern grouse or ptarmigan was an important game bird. Ptarmigan, which have feathered feet and plumage that is brownish in the summer but changes to white in the winter, are found widely in the northern Arctic and subarctic regions. Iceland also offered a wide abundance of water fowl and migratory birds, including many varieties of ducks, geese and swans. There are several fjords along the coast that are named Álptafjord, meaning swans' fjord, where large numbers of wild swans still congregate today.

Diet in early Iceland often depended on location. For people on farms along the coast, fresh fish, seals, seabird eggs and seabirds themselves, such as puffins, were important foods. Place names, such as Rosmhvalanes (Walrus' Headland), and a few bones found at excavations indicate that in the earliest years there were walruses (*rosmhvalar*). These were soon hunted to extinction for their meat, fat and ivory. In the inland valleys and even on farms not especially far from the coast, people probably ate relatively little fresh fish from the sea, but seal products and fresh eggs were transported inland. There are many seals around the coast of Iceland. In cold winters, seals ride the ice flows from the north, arriving off the Icelandic coast. Seal blubber became an especially important product. Along with fat from other sea mammals, it was used for frying foods and eaten in the place of butter. Seal fat was also used to grease leather clothes, making them water repellent. Iceland lacked pine forests for tar to caulk ships, but for small boats seal blubber was a successful substitute. Boats were caulked by placing strips of homespun wool or *vaðmál* between the planks and then coating them with hot seal oil. *The Saga of Eirik the Red* reports that when treated with 'seal tar' (*seltjara*) boats resisted wood-boring sea worms.

Seal and shark oil were considered the best fuel for indoor oil lamps. Such lamps were simple affairs, fashioned by chipping out the centre of a stone to form a crude bowl. Wicks were woven from a grass called *fífa* (cotton grass), which grows wild in swampy ground. In late summer, the flowering portion becomes cotton-like and has often reminded people of a woman's long white-blonde hair. The burning wick extended out over the lip of the bowl and oil that dripped from the wick was caught beneath in a second, larger stone bowl. When the lower bowl filled, the unused oil was poured back into the lamp.

Trout and char, a species related to trout, are abundant throughout Iceland. These fish were a year-round resource for many farms, especially because during the winter they can be fished with nets through the ice. Sea trout and brown trout often grow very large. In modern times, brown trout weighing over 14.5 kg (32 lb) have been caught. Like salmon, which was an important food for many farms, trout can be smoked.[8] Stockfish, that is wind-dried cod or *skreið*, also reached the inland valleys. The cod, which is rich in oils necessary for preservation, was dried on outdoor racks. The fish was split open and hung on a length of wood called a *stokkr*, hence the name stockfish. Needing no salt, the process required little investment and fishermen could do it themselves. Iceland and northern Norway around the Lofoten Islands are among the few regions in the world where cod, despite its oil content, can be successfully wind-dried. The crucial factor is the cold, dry polar winds. These alternate with the relatively mild northern maritime climate, with temperatures moving above and below freezing. These dry, cold winds are not routinely found further south in Norway, for example.

There is only scant information about the internal trade in dried fish during the earliest centuries of the Free State. We know that stockfish was an important staple food by the twelfth century, especially during the periods of religious fasting. Archaeology helps fill in the gap. Archaeozoology (the study of vertebrate animal remains) from the inland site of Granastaðir, occupied in the mid tenth century, shows that some fish was brought up from the coast and eaten along with livestock, including pigs and horses.[9] Again *Grettir's Saga* offers insight into this lost world, when it tells (in Chapter 42) of a trip to purchase provisions undertaken by Grettir's brother, Atli. In this instance, the specific coastal settlement that Atli rides to with his packhorses may reflect the situation more in the thirteenth century than in the earlier period:

Atli now became a successful farmer, and he had many men. He was a good provider. Toward the end of the summer he travelled out to Snæfellsnes to purchase dried fish. He took with him many packhorses ... They rode west through Haukadalsskard, following the route which leads out on to Snæfellsnes. There they bought a lot of dried fish and loaded it on to seven horses. Once they had done this, they set off on the route home.

Seven packhorse loads of cod is a considerable amount of fish. It would have been interesting to know with what Atli is supposed to have paid for this food.

Hay harvesting on lowland meadows was vital in order to feed as many cattle and sheep as possible during the long winter. Farmers kept a few rams for breeding, but wethers were the staple of the sheep herds. These castrated rams grew fat. They produced ample quantities of wool and could stay outside for much of the winter, foraging for themselves. In later times such rams were thought to be especially clever. In severe winter periods they were known to survive by digging themselves into the protection of the insulating snow, leaving only their nostrils above the surface. The ability of animals to graze outside throughout the winter was crucial to subsistence. Ólafur Steffensen, governor of Iceland from 1793 to 1803, remarked after one of Iceland's most severe famines that the grazing of domestic animals in the winter was 'the main pillar of our farming'.[10]

The consistent central importance of livestock farming and land-ownership indicates the continuity that characterized the experience of Icelanders from the tenth to the mid thirteenth century. Through-out these centuries, land sufficiently productive to satisfy the type of agriculture practised was scarce. Iceland's northern location meant that it had short, cool and often damp summers, which made the growing of cereal crops unpredictable. Grain and flour became mostly imported luxury items, even though some farmers, especially in the south, cultivated cereal crops such as barley on a small scale. With the vast interior of the country uninhabitable because of the severity of the long winters, the population remained concentrated along the coast and in a few sheltered inland areas. In these areas population pressure increased and claims to ownership of valuable land became a primary source of contention, not least because such property produced the food resources on which the population depended.

All population estimates for Free State Iceland (c. 930–1264) are guesses, even though some remarkable data are available. According to the early-twelfth-century Icelandic historian Ari the Learned (inn fróði), writing in his Book of the Icelanders (Íslendingabók), Iceland's second bishop, Gizur Isleifsson, carried out a census at the end of the eleventh century. At this period, at the close of the Viking Age, Bishop Gizur determined that there were thirty-eight 'hundred' farmers liable to the thing tax, that is, heads of households who possessed enough property to enjoy all rights in courts and at assemblies. The term 'hundred' probably stood for 120, as was customary (the medieval 'long hundred' was based on the number twelve), so the number of self-sufficient farmers at this time was approximately 4,560.

So large a number of property-owning free farmers is an indication of the social levelling that had transpired in Iceland in the centuries following the settlement. The figure also suggests the political import-ance of the landowning farmer class, individuals who, from all accounts, looked after their own rights and interests. Most estimates of the total population in the early Free State are based on Ari's information about Gizur's census. Reckoning an average of ten to twenty people on a householder's lands – figures that included tenant farmers – gives a rough estimate of somewhere between 45,000 and 90,000 people, but the larger figure seems high. In the late seventeenth century, when the size of the population was better known, there were approximately 55,000 people in Iceland.[11] The population during the early Free State period, when the land was more fertile and the grasslands were less eroded, was probably somewhat larger. Hence an estimate of 60,000 to 70,000.

Bad Year Economics: Difficulties of Life in the North Atlantic

When all went well, the country was relatively prosperous in the early centuries, but bad times hit hard. The sagas often speak of these periods, giving a glimpse of the ways in which things might go wrong. With the possibilities for calamity strong, most Icelanders who sur-vived to old age experienced several rough periods. The natural limitations of Iceland's productivity did much to shape its social development. Indications are that by the late tenth century the popu-lation began to strain the natural resources. By the thirteenth century the pressure on resources is clearer, and there were significant increases in tenant farming and the rise of fisheries as an alternative form of subsistence.

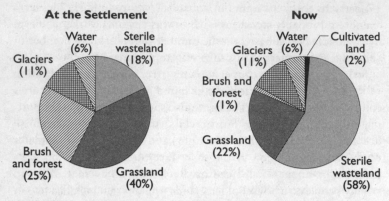

6. The Effects of Erosion. Erosion drastically changed Iceland's landscape from the ninth century to modern times. Almost all the forest and brush as well as more than half the grasslands were lost. (Source: Landmælingar Íslands)

The effect of human habitation on the island was rapid. Beginning as early as the tenth century, erosion and overgrazing diminished the productivity of the grasslands, a factor that increased the value of good lowland properties. Iceland is a large island and, in the early years, it is likely that it had a biomass sufficient to feed the herds.[12] Problems stemming from overgrazing were caused less by the lack of grasslands, which were extensive, than by the way they were used. Because animals were often sent to the fragile highlands early in the short summer, the grasslands were grazed just at the time when the grass, which needed time to recover from the winter, was most vulnerable. Because the upland soils were shallow, the effects of early grazing were severe, and in many areas the herds quickly diminished the available grasslands. This upland and then lowland erosion of its grazing lands, coupled with a more or less finite number of lowland hay meadows, meant that Iceland differed from many contemporaneous European lands. In many areas of the Continent the environment was less fragile and large tracts of forest, marshlands capable of being drained and uninhabited wilderness provided the medieval population with room to expand.

Although reliable data for the Icelandic climate in the Middle Ages are scarce, the evidence suggests that from c. 870 to 1170 the climate in the western North Atlantic was unusually mild.[13] During this Little Climatic Optimum, temperatures appear to have been about 1°C higher than the more recent average of 4°C. The timing of the settlement was thus especially good for a seaborne migration and drift ice, which endangered shipping, was at a minimum. In the mid to later twelfth century, the warm spell that marked the initial phase of settlement ended. A long-term cooling trend began which, among other things, resulted in the more frequent appearance of drift ice along the north-western and north-eastern coasts. The climate did not, however, consistently worsen, and there were intermittent periods of relative warmth. One of these warm spikes occurred at the end of the Free State, lasting from approximately 1200 to 1260, that is during most of what is often referred to as the Age of the Sturlungs.

The onset of centuries-long cooling affected the subsistence economy by limiting the land's productivity, especially at higher elevations. Predicting fodder yields in a gradually worsening or fluctuating climate must have become more difficult. These changes almost surely increased the sense of competition in an already competitive society oriented to private property. The transformation to a changing climate, sometimes colder and sometimes warmer, may also have contributed to the political turmoil at the end of the Free State in the thirteenth century.

From the tenth century on, Iceland suffered periodically from famine and sickness. This island country is a classic example of 'bad year economics', where matters went well only if nothing went wrong.[14] The short-term variability of the climate played a significant role. In some years, after weeks of especially good weather in the summer and autumn, the rich green valleys and grasslands produced bumper hay crops. Being so close to the Arctic Circle, bad weather had the opposite effect. A series of cold, rainy summers was especially troublesome. Matters worsened when drift ice appeared along the north-western to north-eastern coasts, lowering the air temperature. Such times of small-scale climate fluctuations might cut down the

Highland Sequence

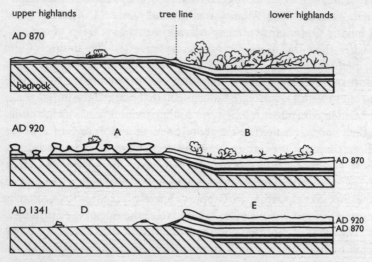

7 and 8. Highland and Lowland Erosion Sequences from the 870s to the mid 1300s. The diagrams trace changes in the Eyjafjöll region of southern Iceland. The soil cross-sections are dated by tephra (ash) layers formed by volcanic outbreaks (marked on the soil profiles as thick black lines). The first cross-section is dated by the *landnám* tephra layer from 871 ± 2, below which there is no evidence of human habitation. At the beginning of the settlement the upper highlands above the tree line had shallow, often fertile, grass-covered soil. The lower highlands supported an often dense covering of brush and dwarf forest. The lowlands were heavily forested, mostly with birch.

Livestock grazing rapidly affected the fragile subarctic ecology, and by 920 the soil of the upper highlands was eroding fast. Following natural patterns, the erosion was irregular. Some surfaces were increased by aeolian soil (soil carried by the wind) and particles carried by water, which were deposited on surrounding areas in the upper highlands (A), across the lower highlands where the brush was disappearing (B) and in the lowlands where the original forests were being reduced by grazing and cleared by the settlers to make way for pastures (C).

By the mid 1300s the upper highlands (D) were almost completely denuded,

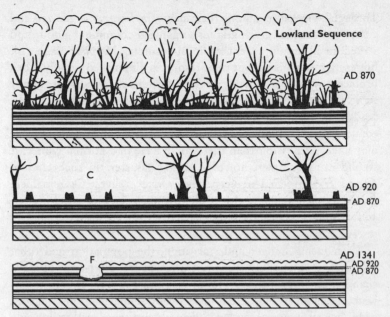

and the soil level of the lower highlands (E) had been significantly raised. Almost all of the original lowland birch forest was gone by the 1300s. At the same time, the raised soil in the lowlands was beginning to erode toward the bedrock (F), a process continuing into modern times. The wavy upper line that appears in the illustration for the year 1341 denotes the uneven surface of Iceland's grasslands. Frost heaves due to water collected in the soil mean that the treeless grasslands are characteristically covered by small bumps. (Diagrams courtesy of A. Dugmore and I. Simpson.)

population somewhat, but a buffer period separated the initial bad times from a subsequent population drop.

In a summer too cold and damp for either harvesting or drying hay, there was not enough fodder to keep many of the livestock alive over the winter. Farmers might initially turn for assistance to the local communal unit called the *hreppr* (discussed in detail in Chapter 7).

Through cooperation among their members, *hreppar* organized and controlled summer grazing lands, organized communal labour and served to a certain extent as local insurers. *Hreppar* were risk buffering mechanisms, but their resources diminished rapidly when problems were region-wide. In such instances, farmers, especially those on smaller farms, had little choice but to severely cull their herds. The resulting slaughter translated into meat, sausages and edible suet, all of which put fat on the household inhabitants. People may have eaten better than they would have in a normal winter. A second rainy summer, however, meant disaster. In such circumstances farmers tried to keep alive whatever livestock remained. Problems such as the health of the livestock, lack of good fodder, and a hungry household complicated efforts to keep supplies in reserve.

When facing hunger and starvation, the population had other resources that possibly were not affected by short-term climatic changes. Emergency foods – foods that under normal circumstances were not eaten or only eaten in relatively small quantities, such as edible lichens – came into play. Expanded gathering and exploitation of natural resources included increased fishing (a dangerous start-up enterprise) and seal-hunting, the collection of seaweed (*söl*) for human consumption and for livestock fodder, and searches for wild foods and driftage in the common lands (*almenning*). In most instances the population seems to have rebounded quickly. Because enough young childbearing women survived, famines were often followed by high birthrates.

However resilient the general population was, hard times severely affected individuals. The sagas show farmers becoming quarrelsome. Passages such as the following from *The Saga of the Sons of Droplaug* (*Droplaugarsona saga*) are frequent: 'Later that year it was a very bad season, and many sheep died. Thorgeir, the farmer at Hrafnkelsstead, lost many of his animals.' As Thorgeir was soon to learn, not all of his sheep disappeared because of the weather. Another farmer had them in his pens.[15] So, too, the following passage from *The Saga of Hen-Thorir* (*Hænsa-Þóris saga*) precedes a quarrel over the remaining hay resources: 'That summer the grass grew sparsely and was poor. For this reason little grass was dried, and as a result people's hay stores were very small.' Such stories reflect the reality that in a series of bad years only the wealthiest farmers could count on having sufficient supplies.

Less frequent than weather calamities, periodic volcanic activity on the geologically new island brought its own problems. From 1500 onwards, Icelandic eruptions are estimated to have accounted for a third of Earth's total outpouring of lava. Activity from the *landnám* to 1500 was roughly similar, and the ash layers embedded in the soil of wide regions attest to repeated eruptions from the start of the settlement. Every decade or so saw an outbreak in some part of the island, but in most localities of volcanic activity, one or several generations often passed between outbreaks. This time factor, small by geological standards but large by human ones, made preparations for outbreaks almost useless.

Though no good description of a volcanic outbreak from the earliest period exists, *The Annals of the Bishopric of Skálholt* give the following report of a major eruption in 1362 in south-eastern Iceland. The outbreak, under the great Vatna Glacier, destroyed a long stretch of settlements on the coast immediately below or south of the glacier and caused death and damage over a wide area, especially in southern Iceland.

Fire came up in three places in the south. It continued from the Travelling Days [in late May] until the autumn with such extraordinary happenings that it destroyed all of Litla District [now Öræfi] and much of Hornafjord and the Lon Region. In that area *c.* 100 miles [160 kilometres] were laid waste. Along with this, the Knappafell Glacier gave way and flowed down into the sea. Where previously there had been 30 fathoms of deep water, the stone, soil and waste made it into flat sands. Two whole parishes were wiped out, at Hof and at Rauðalæk. The ash settled on the plains up to the middle of a man's leg, blowing together into large drifts so that the houses could barely be seen. The ash fall was carried north over the land and was so thick that tracks could be seen in it. And this also happened: great heaps of pumice were drifting outside the West Fjords so that ships could scarcely make their way through.[16]

Depending on wind direction, eruptions covered the grass, sometimes at long distances from the point of the outbreak, with grit and ash. These substances were so damaging to teeth and mouths that animals could no longer graze. As in other instances of bad times, the resulting hunger and starvation first affected indigents, tenants, landless workers and the more marginal small landowners.

4

A Devolving and Evolving Social Order

> Further general processes were 'Devolutions' – movement
> back toward rank and egalitarian societies – and a cyclical
> process of movement around these structures, failing to
> reach permanent stratification and state structures. In fact,
> human beings devoted a considerable part of their cultural
> and organizational capacities to ensure that further evolu-
> tion did not occur.
>
> Michael Mann, *The Sources of Social Power*

> Many 'autonomous' chieftains and tribes may simply be
> devolved societies temporarily cut off from the larger system
> of which they had historically been a part.
>
> Timothy Earle, *Chiefdoms: Power, Economy and Ideology*

Defining early Iceland is no easy task. Historians tend to describe the
island as either a free state or a commonwealth, two general and
useful terms. Anthropological concepts, which have not been widely
applied in Icelandic studies, help to sharpen the definition by charac-
terizing the similarities and differences between early Iceland and
recognized types of societies.[1] From the start, however, it should be
recognized that this Viking Age immigrant group does not easily fall
into any of the standard categorizations of evolutionary development. For this reason I employ throughout the book the suitably

loose term 'Free State', while often looking at the Icelandic experience with an anthropological eye.

The term 'Free State' has much to recommend it. *Fristat* is the word currently used to describe early Iceland in modern Swedish, Danish and Norwegian. (Icelanders use the term *Þjóðveldi*, meaning 'Republic'.) In English, 'free state' means an independent, loosely organized polity, often at a pre-state level but already containing elements and the knowledge of statehood. This depiction fits Iceland well, and is more accurate than the old romantic notion of a commonwealth. In a straightforward manner, 'Free State' reflects the reality that medieval Iceland was independent and that the Icelanders were conscious of belonging to a single, island-wide polity.

The immigrants who founded Iceland became participants in what in some ways was a headless or stateless society. Early Iceland can loosely be so described because its leaders, the *goðar*, wielded little executive power and did not rule over territorial units. The concept of statelessness, however, should not be carried too far. Iceland did have specific elements of statehood: a formal national legislature (the *lögrétta*) and a well-defined judicial system that embraced the entire country. Social stratification, although it existed, was restrained by the absence of kings or even regional princes or warlords. Among the landed there were differences in wealth and prominence. Distinct cleavages existed between landowners and landless people and between free men and slaves. Although early Iceland was essentially headless, it did have distinct aspects of an embryonic state. How can this mingling of attributes be explained? The answer is that early Iceland experienced a complicated evolution. This dynamic has been largely overlooked, yet it holds the key to understanding Iceland's medieval society and culture.

The mixture of state and stateless existed because Free State Iceland was the product of two different cultural forces. On the one hand, it inherited the tradition and the vocabulary of statehood from its European origins. On the other, Iceland was headless because of the class values of the immigrants. On this very large island, a late Iron Age European culture group took advantage of the safety afforded by the North Atlantic to eliminate the hierarchy of command and the taxation necessary for defence. As a result the society simplified, moving down a few rungs on the ladder of social complexity.

What has not been recognized about the settlement of Iceland is that the evolutionary machinery was in many ways running in reverse. Rather than a simple society that had reached a modest level of complexity as part of an evolutionary progression, Iceland at the start went the other way. Initially it 'devolved', shedding most of the aristocratic strata of Viking Age society. In their own eyes the tenth-century settlers and lawgivers almost certainly had limited goals. By emphasizing the rights of free farmers, they adjusted social arrangements, making them less complex than in Norway with its king, aristocrats, regional warlords and legally defined levels of free and unfree. Reflecting the desires of landowning farmers, Icelandic institutions eliminated a significant number of the roles played by elites and overlords. By avoiding the formation of self-perpetuating executive structures, the farmers collectively retained control over coercive power. In doing so they denied would-be elites the crucial state function of monopolizing force. Leadership was limited to local chieftains who often operated like 'big men', individuals whose authority often was temporary.

The social order that emerged in Iceland displays a mixture of features affected by its initial devolution. It was marked by aspects of statelessness and egalitarianism as well as by elements of social hierarchy. Characteristics of both ranked and stratified societies were present, as the immigrant society evolved in new ways. Although Iceland was not a democratic system, proto-democratic tendencies existed. The rich variety of features makes Viking Age Iceland a fertile ground for examining theories of cultural and social change. Early Icelanders repeatedly opted for legally based governmental solutions that for centuries hindered the development of executive authority. In this respect social and governmental developments in Iceland were at variance with those in mainland Scandinavia.

On the mainland, kings were enlarging their authority at the expense of the traditional rights of free farmers. The emigrants to

Iceland were well aware of this process. Although it would be going too far to assume that the settlers and their descendants knew exactly what they wanted, available evidence does suggest that the early Icelanders knew quite well what they did not want. In particular, they were collectively opposed to the centralizing aspects of a state. This vital factor led to a significant amount of experimentation in social and governmental arrangements, which can be seen in the sagas and the laws. From the viewpoints of both anthropology and sociology, Iceland is an example of a self-limiting pattern of state formation.

Ranking, Hierarchy and Wealth

Icelandic society shares many characteristics of 'ranked' societies, which often include significant numbers of small-scale farmers who exhibit formalized, if limited, social differences. 'Big men' tend to assume leadership roles in ranked societies. Icelandic leaders in many ways resembled such individuals, but again the comparison is not exact. In particular, Icelandic social arrangements provided for more continuity of power than did arrangements usually found in big-man societies. Although the goðar often acted like big men, they can better be described as small-scale Scandinavian chiefs. As in ranked societies, some chieftains and farmers in Iceland were richer or more powerful than others; their dependants included tenant farmers (who worked for their landlord in return for their smallholdings), landless free labourers and slaves. Slavery mostly died out in the eleventh century.

In ranked societies, those in politically superior positions often compete for followers while openly seeking prestige, honour and sometimes wealth. In early Iceland, goðar competed for status and for followers (thingmenn) from among the bændr. Goðar and other prosperous landowners were often recruited to participate in disputes and feuds among farmers or between other chieftains, and such participation offered wealth. At times advocating the position of others and arbitrating resolutions could be dangerous; the person intervening might even be killed. The *goðar*, in return for risking their wealth, honour and lives, sought to reap economic profit from owning all or part of a chieftaincy. (The related question of the use of coercive force is discussed later in this book.)

One of the roles of the *goðar* was to facilitate the redistribution of wealth. Through their participation in the settlement of disputes, chieftains were actively engaged in the transfer of property, including land. Leaders extended hospitality to farmers and to other chieftains and made loans to tenants and farmers in need. *Goðar* and other prominent farmers also took an active part in a prestige economy based on gift-giving, which served to cement political and kinship alliances. Norwegian merchants came to Iceland, but Icelanders also continued to sail to Norway in their own ships until some time in the eleventh century. There they sold their native woollen cloth and other goods in exchange for high-status items such as weapons, tapestries, imported clothing, linen and coloured cloth, tools, flour, wax, soap-stone bowls, jewellery, barley and hops for brewing ale, and quality timber.

Icelandic leaders regularly held feasts. In displays of luxury con-sumption, they exhibited their foreign items and offered their guests feast goods, including the imported ingredients for making ale. Such feastings, including wedding and funeral banquets, were often care-fully planned to take place in times of plenty, especially the autumn, so as not to overly reduce a household's wealth. *Laxdæla saga* gives a sense of the planning and the honour involved in conspicuous feasting, when describing (in Chapter 7) the intended arrangements made by the great matriarch and *landnámsmaðr* Unn the Deep-Minded for the marriage of Olaf Feilan, her favourite grandson:

Unn held him [Olaf Feilan] in higher regard than all other men, and made it known publicly that Olaf was to inherit everything at Hvammr after her death.

Now Unn was growing weary with old age. She summoned Olaf Feilan and said to him, 'I have been thinking, kinsman, that you ought to establish yourself and take a wife.'

Olaf agreed readily, and said he would rely on her guidance.

'I have had it in mind,' said Unn, 'that your wedding feast should be held towards the end of this summer, for that is the best time for getting all the necessary provisions; I am sure that our friends will be coming in large numbers, because I intend this feast to be the last one I shall hold.'

'That is a generous offer,' said Olaf. 'But I shall marry only a woman who will deprive you of neither wealth nor authority.'

That autumn Olaf Feilan married Alfdis, and the wedding feast was held at Hvammr. Unn went to great expense over it, for she invited many eminent people far and wide from other districts.

Despite the obvious connection between wealth and power, there is little indication that Iceland's Viking Age chieftains enjoyed a significant income through either taxes or tributes from the farmers. The labour of slaves, landless workers and tenant farmers, and the rental of property and livestock, were significant sources of wealth for all prominent farmers. Many free farmers, like the *goðar*, were prosperous landowners who were frequently called upon to act as advocates or arbitrators. Over time, however, chieftains proved to be the best qualified people for this public endeavour. They found a significant and, to some degree, a proprietary source of revenue by actively participating in dispute management and conflict settlement.

From the tenth into the twelfth century, social differentiation was relatively fluid, with few rigid class barriers. Aggressive farmers could become chieftains, and the degree of ranking throughout the society was limited by convention, law and economics. The outward trappings of rank in Viking Age Iceland were so few that it is frequently difficult to determine whether a prominent individual was a chieftain or just a farmer. In the late twelfth and early thirteenth centuries (that is, after the Viking period) the situation began to change, and a movement toward rigid stratification and incipient statehood can be perceived. The Church became a factor, and small groups of more powerful thirteenth-century chieftains, called in modern studies 'big *goðar*' (*stórgoðar*) or 'big leaders' (*stórhöfðingjar*), emerged from among the most wealthy and powerful chieftain families. Yet even in this late period, stratification in Iceland did not limit access to strategic resources or approach the degree of differential ranking in other more hierarchical Norse societies, where kings, jarls and regional military leaders had assumed the right to wield executive authority much earlier.

That a chieftain might gain widespread territorial control, thus centralizing political and governmental power in a region, was always a threat. This development was avoided, however, until the late twelfth century and, in some regions, the early thirteenth century by a system of checks and balances aimed at limiting the power of individual chieftains. Farmers, as in the example of conflict between the two chieftains Arnkel goði and Snorri goði from *Eyrbyggja saga* (see Chapter 6), openly granted authority to their *goðar*, and during much of Iceland's early history dissatisfied farmers could take authority from one leader and give it to another.

Complex Culture and Simple Economy

The immigrant Viking Age community was a cultural mix. It brought a cultural legacy from the complex Scandinavian culture, but at the same time a simple economy was dictated by the ecology and limited resources of Iceland. This unusual combination has caused confusion. Early Icelandic society is occasionally described as primitive, and it did have some features in common with such societies (though 'simple' is a far better term than 'primitive'). Among these features were the oral stage of the culture in the early centuries; the widespread presence of relatively self-sufficient family-based economic units; the role of feud as a means of settling disputes; and the absence of towns or concentrated communities. Nevertheless, primitive is an unsatisfactory way to describe early Iceland, which was not really a simple community.

The connotations of 'primitive' are not easily reconciled with Iceland's situation as the major northern offshoot of Viking Age Scandinavia, a culture whose technology was sufficiently sophisticated to

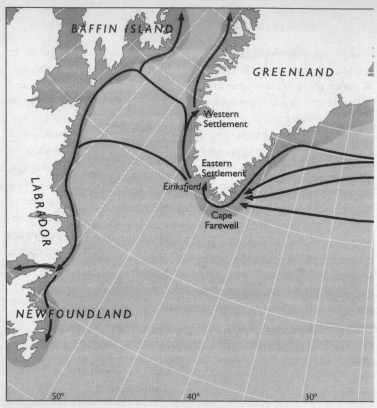

6. Viking Age Sailing Routes to Iceland and Beyond. Navigation across the North Atlantic was based upon land sightings and simple astronomical observations. Weather permitting, an east–west course (i.e., one running along a line of latitude) could be fixed by noting the height of the sun at its midday zenith. It is possible that Norse mariners used a simple sun compass. During the night, sailors navigated by the stars. The shaded areas on the map show distances out to sea from which land could regularly be seen in good weather.

Leaving Norway, seamen sailed due west to the Shetlands and then on to the Faroes. At this stage of the journey the distances between land sightings were relatively short. Farther out into the Atlantic, the stretches on the open sea were larger. Birds, marine life, cloud formations, changes in currents, the colour of the water, and light reflected off the great icecaps all aided sailors in locating Iceland and Greenland when these large landmasses lay over the horizon. The *Hauksbók* version of *The Book of Settlements* gives the fol-

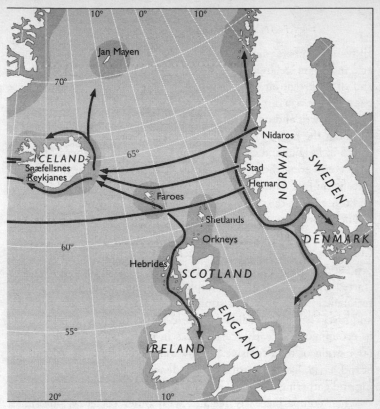

lowing sailing directions: 'Setting off from Hernar in Norway [near Stad] for Hvarf [? Cape Farewell] in Greenland, one sails due west. The course lies to the north of the Shetlands, so that they may be clearly seen from the sea, and then to the south of the Faroes, so that the sea on the horizon stands halfway up the face of the cliffs, then close enough to the south of Iceland so that the sailors can recognize birds and whales from there.' Once in Greenland, North America was well within the reach of a competent ship's crew.

Sailing an east–west course was routine, but Atlantic crossings could be hazardous. Clouds and fogs made holding a course difficult, and storms, high seas and drift ice could be deadly. The twelfth-century *Book of the Icelanders* reports that of twenty-five ships that left Iceland in the year 988 to colonize Greenland only fourteen reached their destination. Close to land the dangers of shipwreck increased. *Kristni saga* says that in 1118 a large merchant ship was driven ashore below the mountains of Eyjafjöll in southern Iceland: the ship 'spun in the air and landed bottom-up'.

allow its members routinely to cross the North Atlantic. Scandinavians, including Icelanders, possessed a wide knowledge of the world and of its geography and political systems. Administratively these people were equal to the task of setting up and maintaining major trading towns and powerful small states in various parts of Europe. At about the time of Iceland's settlement, Norsemen set up trading towns in Ireland and established the Danelaw in northern England, later conquering the whole country. Vikings founded the Norman state within the Frankish empire, rose to prominence in old Russia, and traded with the caliphate of Baghdad and the Byzantine empire.

The knowledge of Scandinavia's expansive mother culture was embedded in early Iceland's underlying social codes and values. Culturally, the early Icelanders inherited centuries of northern European social development. As part of this heritage their community started out with, and soon expanded upon, complicated constitutional concepts as well as sophisticated laws of contract, property and tort. They also produced a world-class literature. It is in regard to economics that early Iceland was in many ways simple. On the far margin of the extensive international commerce of Viking Age Scandinavia, Iceland, with its dependence on pastoralism and hunting and gathering, became largely self-sufficient.

When comparing early Iceland with other societies, one might keep in mind additional factors. Unlike early Ireland with its history of chieftains and warlords dating from at least the Bronze Age, medieval Iceland was not a tribal society, and the authority of its leaders did not depend on ownership of or rule over defined territorial units. What, then, was Iceland? Briefly, it was a society whose development was determined by the dynamics of its Scandinavian past and immigrant experiences. Having shed a good part of the military and political structures of Viking Age culture, the settlers and their descendants built a society on a combination of choices rarely, if ever, possible over so long a period of time on the European mainland. Beginning in the tenth century, the Icelanders established a rudimentary state structure that declared to the outside world the island's independent status. Internally, with most executive institutions in private hands, the country operated with only the bare bones of public institutions of statehood. Internal cohesion was maintained by stressing lateral social arrangements. These were invigorated by the general acceptance of the principle, pleasing to farmers, that government was to be dominated by the requirements of consensus rather than by the authority of overlords.

Cultural focus, a long-established anthropological concept, is the tendency of every culture to exhibit more complexity and a wider scope in some of its aspects and institutions than in others.[2] When a society focuses on a particular dimension of culture, that dimension is more likely to develop new ways and to generate innovation because more activity and closer scrutiny are directed to it than to other aspects. In Iceland the cultural focus was on law, and disorder was avoided through dependence on legalistic solutions arrived at through arbitration and court cases.

Icelandic law was based on custom, and it proved to be highly adaptable to change over time. To an unusual degree, law became the catalyst in the conceptualizing of life outside the family. Law set the parameters of successful arbitration, and served as an element of continuity throughout Iceland's medieval history. This reliance was more pronounced in times of crisis and dispute, when judicial process was used as a model even in private arbitrations, thus supplying the means to reconcile the most divisive forces within the society. An example (discussed in Chapter 16) is the conversion to Christianity in the year 1000. This potentially explosive situation was channelled into the normal procedures of legalistic dispute processing, where it was treated as a feud between two groups and settled at the Althing through negotiation and compromise.

Privatization of Power in the Tenth Century

Leadership functioned in a kind of market economy, with the forces of supply and demand playing a significant role. Candidates competed for the supporters necessary to claim a chieftaincy (goðorð), which offered prestige and an opportunity to amass wealth and power through privileged access to processes of law. Depending on the acumen of the individual, the results could be significant. Alliance with a chieftain gave a farmer the promise of present or future services. In many ways, it was a pay-as-you-go system. Services, or the expectation of them, were negotiable and exchangeable, and had monetary value.

With coercive power privatized, Icelanders did not need to pay taxes for the upkeep of state institutions of enforcement. The solution was economically efficient.[3] It avoided a governmental hierarchy and lowered the cost of government to almost nothing, yet it provided a minimum of state-like, executive branch services. Once private enforcement was established, the rights to vengeance-taking were often sold by family members to advocates, who sometimes were aspiring farmers but for the most part were chieftains. Through the office of chieftaincy, a seat in the national legislature, the lögrétta, was marketable personal property. Nevertheless, acquisition was only the entry price: a leader needed personal abilities to succeed as the head of a following of thingmen. Farmers in conflict who were unable to enforce their claims turned to advocates, especially goðar, who had the support of a group and enjoyed superior opportunities to manipulate the legal system. For their support of farmers and other chieftains in lawsuits and feuds, goðar expected to be paid, even though transferable wealth was in limited supply in Iceland.

The marketable nature of the goðorð had a profound effect. The availability of this relatively low-level yet paramount position of authority contributed significantly to the stability of the Free State in the early centuries. As class distinctions did not constitute formal barriers to acquiring the office of chieftaincy, an ambitious, successful farmer could set his sights on becoming a goði. Reward could be sought within Iceland's social and political systems rather than in changing them. Until the appearance of overlords in the thirteenth century (discussed in Chapter 19), there is no evidence that Iceland's peasantry was disgruntled.

A Proto-democratic Community?

In the absence of national or regional leaders who might foster dissension with other countries over trade, wealth, dynastic claims, conquest or territorial dominance, Iceland developed in response to its own circumscribed needs. The society that emerged was based on a system of decentralized self-government that functioned largely through personal relationships between leaders and followers. This system fostered a political stability that lasted from the end of the settlement period (*c.* 930) until the thirteenth century.

The Viking Age settlers began by establishing local things, or assemblies, which had been the major forum for meetings of freemen and aristocrats in the old Scandinavian and Germanic social order. The tenth-century Icelanders altered the equation. They excluded overlords with coercive power and expanded the mandate of the assembly to fill the full spectrum of the interests of the landed free farmers. The changes transformed a Scandinavian decision-making body that mediated between freemen and overlords into an Icelandic self-contained governmental system without overlords. At the core of Icelandic government was the Althing, a national assembly of freemen[4] which operated through a socio-political system in which the governmental elite, the *goðar*, were not linked by a formal hierarchy. Theoretically, and often in fact, the *goðar* acted as equals.

To some extent the value of possessing a *goðorð* was enhanced because so few chieftaincies existed. Around 965, as part of a series of constitutional reforms, the number of *goðorð* was limited to thirty-nine by agreement at the Althing. As part of the arrangement (see Chapter 9), an additional nine men were given the title of *goði*. The duties of these new chieftains, however, were limited mostly to participation in the legislative and political functions of the Althing. It is important to keep in mind that the actual number of chieftains (individuals calling themselves *goðar*) at any particular time in early Iceland was more than the number of chieftaincies, because each of the men who shared a *goðorð* could call himself a *goði*.

The sources mention many chieftains in the early centuries. Just how they acquired the capital necessary to function as leaders during the early period has not been well explained. Yet the answer to this question opens the path to an understanding of how the different elements in Iceland's medieval society were able to function as a cohesive political body. To succeed, a *goði* had to have charisma as well as skill in managing relationships with thingmen, in supervising disputes and feuds, especially in the final court and arbitration stages, and in winning legal cases. Despite the deference accorded to success-ful *goðar*, the society's egalitarian ethos was so strong that the *goðar* participated in governmental processes that were often proto-democratic.

For the chieftains, permanent coercive power remained unobtain-able until the very end of the Free State. Even then, in the thirteenth century, they were unable to translate their power into operable state structures. Repeatedly during the history of the Free State the rights of free farmers tempered the demands of the *goðar*. Throughout this study I explain the prerogatives enjoyed by the *bændr* and the strategies by which they defended their rights. Here too there are hints of early democratic development as well as signs of a self-limiting pattern of state formation.

The tenth-century settlers developed economic and legal processes that institutionalized barter, the public brokerage of power, and the conduct of feud, all of which hindered the emergence of overlordship. Farmers chose their personal *goði* from among the available chief-tains of the quarter. Thus an individual free farmer or *bóndi* enjoyed more self-determination than he would have in a society dominated by lords. For several centuries the island enjoyed stability free of the internal dynastic dissension that existed in petty states in the Viking Age homelands or in areas controlled by kings or regional rulers. During this time, however, low-intensity feuding continued through-out the country.

Icelandic Feud: Conflict Management

As an effective way to diminish the damages of feuding, a revised form of conflict management evolved. Feud in Iceland was more a public than a private matter. As such it was discussed at the assemblies and directed to the law courts. This public trajectory assisted peacemaking regardless of whether arbitrations and settlements were made in or out of court. Iceland's overseas Norse community was culturally split between the military values of the mother country and the more peaceful realities of the new land. When involved in disputes, Icelanders postured in the manner of Viking Age warriors, yet the threatening and the posturing described in the sagas led only to mild battles. 'Warfare', to use the anthropological term for small-scale feuding and socially structured violence, occurred mostly at the individual or the family level. Even when several hundred farmers assembled, there were very few deaths. As seen from the sometimes exaggerated crisis situations in the sagas, small groups might be sufficiently motivated to kill a few of their opponents, but larger groups found solutions, avoiding large-scale fighting. As a society Icelanders consistently acted with restraint. They learned to ritualize and even to limit the use of force. Only at the very end of the Free State did the endemic feuding reach the level of open warfare, and even then random violence was sporadic.

The Saga of Thorgils and Haflidi (*Thorgils saga ok Hafliða*) recounts an episode of feud, restraint and compromise. Two powerful chieftains were at loggerheads, and a mediator, a man with clerical ambitions, intervened. Set in the early twelfth century, the saga, which is found in the Sturlunga compilation, tells the story of two powerful chieftains, Thorgils Oddason and Haflidi Masson. Other men frequently tried to arbitrate the dispute between these *goðar*. Both leaders went to the Althing of 1121, Haflidi with 1,440 men and Thorgils with 940. Earlier, when the two men had discussed a settlement at the Althing, Thorgils, defying attempts to reach a settlement, had viciously attacked and maimed Haflidi.

The situation was unusually dangerous because Haflidi, having been betrayed, was intransigent. Seeking vengeance, he steadfastly refused to engage in reasonable negotiations. Normally third parties would have intervened to arbitrate a compromise solution, but the two weeks of the Althing slipped by without intervention by 'men of good will' (*góðviljamenn*), and a major clash became more likely. At this juncture (Chapter 28) Ketil Thorsteinsson, who was not involved in the feud, comes forward. He tells Haflidi about an experience of his own which concerned issues of honour, prestige and the call for blood-taking:

'It seems a great pity to your friends if a settlement is not reached and this case is not brought to a good end. Yet many think it is hopeless now, or nearly so. I know of no advice to give you, but I have a parable to tell you.

'We grew up in Eyjafjord, and it was said that we were promising. I made what was thought to be the best possible match – with Groa, the daughter of Bishop Gizur. But it was said that she was unfaithful to me.

'I thought it hard that there was such talk. Trials were held and they went well. But nevertheless the persistent tales were offensive to me, and for this reason I grew very hostile toward the other man [his wife's seducer]. One time when we met each other in passing, I attacked him. But he ducked under the blow and I found myself under him. Then he drew his knife and stabbed me in the eye so that I lost my sight in that eye. Then he, Gudmund Grimsson, let me get up, and it seemed to me there was something wrong about this. I had twice his strength, and so I thought we would compare similarly in other things.

'I fiercely wanted to avenge his wounding me with the strength of my kinsmen and to have him outlawed. We prepared our case. But some powerful men offered to support him, and therefore my suit came to nothing. It may now also happen that men come forward to support Thorgils, even though your case is more just.

'When my case had reached this point, they [Gudmund's party] offered to pay a fine in settlement. I thought about what I had had to endure and how heavily it had all weighed on me, and I refused the offer ... And I found, when thinking about my honour, that no offers could have been paid which would have sated my honour.'

Ketil, helped by his religious nature (with Haflidi's backing, he later became a bishop), came to realize that his demand for absolute justice was not reasonable and settled the dispute. The point of Ketil's tale is well made, for shortly thereafter Haflidi submits his case to reasonable arbitration, and a settlement is arranged which both men then honour. This adherence to rules, which made it honourable to address order more than justice, was inherited from Scandinavian legal tradition and underlies Njal's famous statement in his saga, when feuding parties would no longer play by the rules: 'Our land must be built with law or laid waste with lawlessness.'

Rather than a socially destructive force to be controlled by sheriffs, bailiffs and royal agents, as in many contemporaneous European societies, feud in Iceland became a formalized and culturally stabilizing element. Respected men served as negotiators, and feuding became the major vehicle for channelling violence into the moderating arenas of the courts and into the hands of informal arbitrators, where public pressure was applied. In Iceland's single 'great village' environment *goðar* found honour in containing disruptive behaviour. Leaders gained prestige and standing by publicly playing the role of men of moderation (*hófsmenn*) and goodwill (*góðviljamenn*). Churchmen acted as advocates, and small farmers and even free labourers participated in the settlement process, acquiring status and prestige by serving as jurors (*kviðir*). The law courts had no judges in the modern sense directing the jury. Instead some farmers, usually twelve, would be called to say what they thought were the facts, and in that way give evidence. Another panel of jurors would act as judges, deciding the outcome of a case by agreement among themselves.

The feuding process and the complex social and legal mechanisms that evolved to contain it were characteristic features of Iceland's medieval culture. In the absence of institutionalized chains of command, feuding took over the burden of adjusting status, wealth and power. Although this system, with its intricate court procedures and its emphasis on resolution by compromise, did not always work smoothly, it did provide manageable solutions in disruptive situations.

5

The Founding of a New Society
and the Historical Sources

Many men say that writing about the settlement is unneces-
sary. But it seems to me that we would be better able to
answer foreigners who censure us for our descent from
scoundrels or slaves if we knew our true origins for certain.
Similarly, for those men who want to know old lore or to
reckon genealogies, it is better to begin at the beginning
rather than to jump right into the middle. And of course all
wise people want to know about the beginnings of their
settlement and of their own families.

The Book of Settlements

Iceland is the first 'new nation' to have come into being in
the full light of history, and it is the only European society
whose origins are known.

Richard F. Tomasson, *Iceland: The First New Society*

Icelanders emerged as a separate people because they chose to migrate
overseas. A fundamental ingredient in the development of this immigrant society of freemen was its formation at a time when Scandinavian kings were enlarging their authority at the expense of the
traditional rights of freemen.

The Effect of Emigrating from Europe

The sociologist Richard Tomasson argues that Icelandic society shares some of the characteristics of 'new societies' formed in later periods by overseas migrations of Europeans. In these offshoot societies, which sociologists call 'fragments' of larger and older groupings, the influence of kin and traditional community lessened, and law took precedence over kinship as the source of authority.[1] By detaching itself from a 'whole' or parent society, a fragment may lack the stimulus to take part in the developing social issues of the mother culture. European fragment societies experienced internal transformations; philosophical concepts current in the mother country at the time of separation were played out in a manner not possible in the homeland within the confines of the European continuum.[2] Inward-looking and freed from those confines, the fragment society often developed in a form 'unrecognizable in European terms'.[3]

Iceland in the late ninth century looked especially attractive to Norse colonists, in part because of the growing resistance to Viking expansion in some parts of Europe. In England and Ireland, native populations under leaders such as Alfred the Great were counter-attacking and defeating the invaders. In Scandinavia, the expansion of royal authority continued throughout the Viking Age. In particular, Norway, the original homeland of most of the Icelandic settlers, was in the late ninth century experiencing major political and social adjustments. The long-standing tradition of local independence was challenged by Harald Fairhair, a petty king from south-eastern Norway who became the first ruler to seek control over the greater part of the country. Allied with the jarls (earls) of Lade (*Hlaðar jarlar*) from the northern Trondheim region, Harald subjugated regional petty kings, local leaders and free farmers. Although he then claimed to be Norway's overlord, in actuality he seems to have controlled mainly the south-western coastal region. In other parts of the country his sovereignty appears to have been nominal, with real power being held by jarls, petty kings, and local military leaders called *hersar* (sing. *hersir*).

According to Snorri Sturluson, the thirteenth-century Icelandic author of *Heimskringla* (*A History of the Kings of Norway*), King Harald levied property taxes on men who had traditionally not paid any land taxes because they owned their lands directly (rather than being granted them by the king), as inalienable family possessions. In imposing the concept that state ownership took precedence over private ownership, King Harald disturbed age-old customs of allodial, or family-based, landholding, called *óðal* in Old Norse. The character of Harald's overlordship, especially his policy concerning *óðal* rights, is one of the issues most disputed by students of Norway in the Middle Ages.[4] Historians today generally believe that Snorri and other saga authors overstated Harald's tyranny. Nevertheless, it is instructive to consider the financial policies and hierarchical governmental arrangements which thirteenth-century Icelanders believed Harald introduced into the mother country at the time of Iceland's settlement and the establishment of its Althing system of government:

King Harald claimed possession of all *óðal* land wherever he gained power and had each farmer, powerful or not, pay him a tax for the land. He appointed a jarl in each province [*fylki*] who would give judgements at law and collect the fines and the land tax; the jarl would keep a third of the tax for his food and living expenses. Each jarl would have four or more *hersar* under him, and each of the latter would have a revenue of twenty marks. Each jarl would provide the King's army with sixty soldiers and each *hersir* would provide twenty men.[5]

Harald's long reign (*c.* 885–930) roughly coincided with the period of Iceland's settlement. According to Icelandic narratives, many landowners reluctant to accept Harald's demands left Norway. Some went to Iceland and some to Norse settlements in the Shetlands, the Orkneys, the Hebrides, England, Scotland and Ireland. From the Viking Age settlements in the British Isles a few of the displaced

Norwegians returned to raid the coast of Norway, a challenge that Harald answered by mounting an expedition (*c.* 890) against the Shetlands, Orkneys and Hebrides. This countermove, if it indeed occurred, seems to have stimulated a new wave of emigration from these islands to more distant Iceland. Later medieval Icelandic writers who stress Harald's greed for power may have exaggerated his influence on the Icelandic *landnámsmenn*. Yet clearly it was the growth of royal authority in Norway to which Icelandic writers attributed the decisions of many of their forefathers to leave that country. And Harald's autocratic actions may indeed have impelled some men to seek a fresh start in a newly discovered land.

Land-taking and Establishing Order

When first discovered in the mid ninth century, Iceland was attractive to land-hungry people accustomed to the rugged North Atlantic climate. There had been no prior exploitation of resources and, in the beginning, valuable land was free for the taking. The fjords and coastal waters teemed with the food resources of the North Atlantic seaboard, and in the early period the island was fertile. After a few generations of rapid deforestation and extensive livestock farming, the productivity of the land began to decline.[6] On the European continent grazing often created permanent grasslands, but in Iceland it was mostly devastating to the environment.[7]

The earliest *landnámsmenn*, often shipowners who arrived as the heads of families with dependants and slaves, took huge portions of land, sometimes even entire fjords; Helgi the Lean, for example, claimed all of Eyjafjord in the north. Within a few years, however, disputes arose between the initial settlers and those who arrived a little later, including settlers who may have purchased transport on others' ships. According to the *Hauksbók* version of *Landnámabók* (*The Book of Settlements*), the latecomers accused the early arrivals of taking too much land and asked King Harald to mediate. Whether or not the King did intervene is not known for certain, but *Landnáma-*

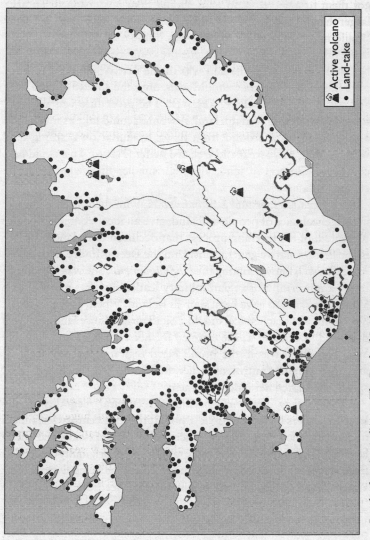

7. Land-takes According to *The Book of Settlements*.

that an agreement was reached: 'King Harald Fairhair
agree that no man should take possession of an area
he and his crew could carry fire over in a single day. They
should make a fire while the sun was in the east. Then they should
make other smoky fires so that one fire could be seen from the next,
but those made when the sun was in the east would have to burn
until nightfall. Then they should walk until the sun was in the west
and make other fires there.' (H294)* The procedure was different
for women wishing to claim land. A woman could take as much land
as she could walk around from dawn to sunset on a spring day,
while leading a two-year-old well-fed heifer (H276). This could be a
considerable parcel of land, although smaller than what could be
claimed by a man.

Both *Laxdæla saga* and *Landnámabók*, with their intense interest
in the genealogies of people and land, give an idea, even if fictionally
presented, of the levelling process that occurred in Icelandic society
in the first formative generations. Unn the Deep-Minded, also called
Aud, was well known among the *landnámsmenn*. She was the daughter of a powerful Norwegian military leader and was married to a
Viking king said to have been slain in Ireland. When, as the leader of
her family, she reached Iceland, like Skallagrim whose land-take was
discussed in Chapter 2, she claimed for herself a huge and valuable
area. Her claim was in the Broad Fjord region in western Iceland,
and to maintain control over her followers, who included freed
slaves, she shared her land with them.

Laxdæla saga offers insight into the cultural mentality of the
later Icelanders by letting us view how thirteenth-century Icelanders
understood the tenth-century processes of manumission and social
levelling. That important Icelandic families were originally descended
from slaves is addressed by showing freedmen as being worthy individuals, even nobles in their original lands. According to *Laxdæla*

---

* The letters 'H' (*Hauksbók*) and 'S' (*Sturlubók*) refer to different manuscripts of
Landnámabók. These manuscripts are discussed later in this chapter.

saga (Chapter 6), Unn, after bequeathing lands to her family and loyal freemen, said to her men:

'There is no shortage now of the means with which to repay you for your service and goodwill. As you all know, I have given freedom to the man called Erp, the son of Earl Meldun; it has never been my wish that a man of such high birth should be called a slave.'

Thereupon she granted him Saudafellslands, between Tungu River and Mid River. Erp's children were Orm, Asgeir, Gunnbjorn and Halldis, who was the wife of Alf of the Dales.

To Sokkolf she granted Sokkolfsdale, and he lived there till old age.

Another of her freed slaves was called Hundi, a Scotsman by birth; to him she gave Hundadale.

The fourth of her slaves was called Vifil; and to him she granted Vifilsdale.

Whether or not Erp was a man of such 'high birth' we will never know. We do know, however, that many prominent families were descended from the union of his daughter Halldis and Alf of the Dales, and that Vifil, the fourth freed slave given lands by Unn, was the grandfather of Gudrid Thorbjarnardottir. This young woman is spoken of in *The Saga of the Greenlanders* (*Grænlendinga saga*) and in *The Saga of Eirik the Red* (*Eiríks saga rauða*).[8] Together with her husband Thorfinn Karlsefni, Gudrid set out from Greenland to colonize North America shortly after the year 1000. From Gudrid, whose voyaging is discussed in Appendix 4, came a line of important twelfth- and thirteenth-century Icelanders, including several bishops.

Unn's death occurred around 900 and within a few decades the initial stratification among the immigrants changed. Although Unn's family, like Skallagrim's, retained a certain prominence, they were not a dominant elite. The new generations descended from followers of these important first settlers no longer honoured claims of 'first' families – if they made such claims – to regional authority. There was no reason to do so. The way land was apportioned in early Iceland established social and economic differentiations, but it did not encourage a system of vassalage or extensive dependence. In the succeeding generations, the original vast land claims throughout the island were divided up into many farms. Some of the larger land claims appear to have been sold off as plots almost in a modern land-development sense.[9]

To whom were lands sold? Mostly to newcomers and freed slaves. The productivity of the type of labour available to landowners probably influenced both the freeing of slaves and the rapid settlement of the country. Beyond a minimum number of free labourers and slaves necessary to work a farmstead, neither the additional hay harvested nor the wild provisions gathered seem to have offset the extra food necessary to feed these dependants throughout the whole year.[10] Landowners faced the reality that adding more slaves or long-term labourers did not increase their farmstead's productivity. At the same time, holding excess land could be dangerous, since excess property had to be defended against encroachment. In this situation, slaves were often more burden than use, and the slave population was controlled by exposing infants and by grants of freedom. Later, labourers and freed slaves became tenant farmers. In the earliest period, however, when land was plentiful, the sources are filled with references to freedmen becoming landowners, a factor which hastened the full colonization.

As part of the levelling process, land became, through a patrimonial type of ownership, the possession of the family that held it. As the tenth century evolved a pattern emerged: the ties of interdependence that had formed when the first settlers transferred parcels of property to latecomers and freedmen weakened. The rights of thingmen to choose their own political ties took precedence. In the absence of an external military threat, farmers were unwilling to take orders from would-be local warlords. The *goðar* had to cast about for other ways to institutionalize their power.

Dating the Settlement: Volcanic Ash Layers

Iceland's settlement is traditionally dated to around 870. This dating originally relied solely on the written sources, especially the twelfth-century *Book of the Icelanders*. Today it is reinforced by archaeological finds whose dates are often successfully established by stratigraphic comparisons with volcanic tephra (ash) layers.[11] Tephra, a generic term for solid particles thrown out from a volcanic eruption, includes ash, rock fragments, pumice and large stones. Because tephra layers are widely dispersed by winds, similar layers can be compared in different areas. Often they can be referenced to historical records and serve as a reliable means of establishing chronology. The layers striate the soil, and tephra is often easily seen in soil profiles on the sides of simple trenches dug during archaeological or geological work. Because the various tephras are composed of different elements, coming from different volcanic systems, including Hekla, Katla, and the Vatnaöldur fissure, they have identifiable trace-element signatures. Icelandic geologists have correlated the most widely distributed layers found in soil profiles throughout Iceland into a comprehensive system useful for dating over a wide area of the North Atlantic, wherever Icelandic volcanic ash was carried by the wind.

A tephra layer which is especially important for Viking Age excavations is that known as the *landnám* tephra. Through comparisons of trace elements found in ice-core samples drilled from the Greenlandic ice pack, the *landnám* tephra layer is dated to 871 ± 2 and effectively marks the start of Iceland's settlement.[12] There is no evidence of human impact on the landscape in the soil below the *landnám* tephra. When trenches are dug in boggy ground it's often easy to see the difference between the rich, undisturbed organic landscapes immediately below the *landnám* tephra layer and the far more sterile soils (often the result of erosion and the effects of human habitation) immediately above,[13] as in the marshy valley bottom at Mosfell. Two other tephra layers, the Katla R tephra of *c.* 920 and

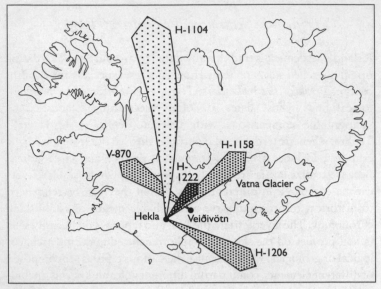

8. The Main Axis of Ash Fallout from Volcanic Eruptions, 870–1222. The ash deposits, which form datable tephra layers in the soil, spread over much wider areas than indicated by the main axis. They are useful to archaeologists, biologists and geologists for dating. The *Landnám* tephra of 871 ± 2 is marked with a V, signifying its origin in the Veiðivötn system in southern Iceland. The other eruptions are from the Mt Hekla system. (Source: A. Dugmore)

the Eldgjá tephra of about 935, mark the end of the settlement period in about 930. Remains from the later Free State period are also frequently datable by what is known as the medieval tephra layer of about 1226, which is thought to have resulted from an eruption off Iceland's south-western coast.

Although the geological evidence agrees with archaeological finds about the dating of the major migration, it is also reasonable to assume that at least a few people, aside from the previously men-

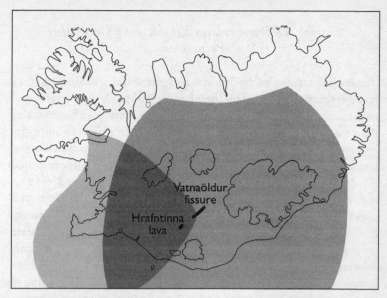

9. The *Landnám* Tephra Layer, Showing the Extent of the Deposit. The eruption occurred in 871 ± 2 at two related parts of the Veiðivötn system in southern Iceland. Today the ash layer is often readily identifiable in the soil. Deposits from Hrafntinna lava are lighter in colour and were carried by the winds mostly to the west. The darker ash from the Vatnaöldur fissure is distributed more widely over the island. Over a significant area, especially in western Iceland, there are deposits from both sources (indicated by a darker tone on the map), making the layer multicoloured. (Source: *Íslenskur söguatlas*)

tioned Irish monks seeking solitude, would have washed up on the shores of such a big island before the 870s. In any event, our understanding of the basic process of colonization beginning in the ninth-century Viking Age does not depend on an exact date.

Closing the Frontier and Establishing Governing Principles

The leading families of the original settlement soon realized that they had a leadership problem on their hands. Although their wealth and perhaps the number of tenants on their lands may have been greater than many of the surrounding free farmers, their claims to authority and regional control had little viability in a dispersed rural society of landholders enjoying the rights of freemen. The situation accelerated the development of a system of political relationships based more on the offering of service obligations than on a flow of payments and goods between thingmen and *goðar*.[14] Economic hierarchy among the early settlers is hard to quantify but there were large estate owners, from among whose ranks most of the *goðar* were probably selected, middle-sized significant landowners, and what appears to have been a majority of economically viable householders, some of whom may have been dependent.[15] Archaeologically there is generally little distinction in artifacts between the different categories of farms, although grave goods from the larger estates tend to be of greater value.

According to *The Book of the Icelanders* the *landnám* period ends about the year 930, when all the usable land was taken. With the closing of the frontier at this time, the second- and third-generation Icelanders recognized the need for some form of governmental structure. Turning to the king of Norway to settle disputes was a dubious practice if Iceland was to be independent. Further, the settlers came from various Scandinavian and Norse-Celtic areas, and had brought with them the different legal customs under which they had lived. With the steady increase in population the colonists came into contact with one another more frequently, and the lack of a common law must have created serious problems.

In particular, legal differences disrupted the solidarity of the extended families that had migrated to Iceland but whose members had settled in different parts of the country.[16] The problems could probably have been tolerated had not the idea of some form of unified country-wide structure appealed to the self-interest of the colonists. The initiative for establishing the Althing, the national assembly, seems to have come from a large and powerful kin group which traced its ancestry to an early ninth-century Norwegian *hersir* (war-lord) named Bjorn buna. Years ago, the Icelandic scholar Sigurður Nordal developed the idea that kinship with Bjorn buna was the basis for selecting those who were first chosen to be chieftains, and the concept is still intriguing.[17] The children of all Bjorn's sons, among them the matriarch Unn the Deep-Minded, came to Iceland. One problem is that the sources about Bjorn and his descendants may be somewhat skewed. For instance, Ari the Learned, the chieftain, Christian priest and historian who wrote *The Book of the Icelanders* may have been one of Bjorn's many descendants.

The actual events that lay behind the founding of the Icelandic government are not recorded and can only be surmised. According to Ari in *The Book of the Icelanders*, a man named Ulfljot was sent to Norway, probably in the 920s, to adapt the West Norwegian law of the Gula Assembly (Gulathing) to Icelandic exigencies. With good reason some scholars, especially the legal historian Sigurður Líndal, doubt the authenticity of Ari's story and question the existence of Thorleif the Wise (an important figure in Ari's account) and the age of the Gulathing.[18] They suggest that the Gulathing and its law, rather than being ancient tradition, came into existence after the establishment of the Althing in Iceland.

Even Ari's intent in telling the story raises questions. Because of his own political and family ties, Ari may well have exaggerated in his writings the importance of Norwegian influence, masking the influence of other Scandinavians and Celtic immigrants. Concerning the latter there are place names, especially in the western quarter, such as Brjánslækr (Brian's Stream) and Patreksfjord (Patrick's Fjord). If Ulfljot did, as Ari says, undertake his trip back to Norway, his task was probably to seek clarification on certain matters about which the Icelanders, in fashioning their own laws, were unsure, rather than to bring back an entire legal code. Most importantly, the laws of the

Gulathing and the Free State's *Grágás* show few consistent similarities. Jakob Benediktsson sums up the dissimilarity between them:
'Norwegian legal traditions applied only to a limited extent to the
society that was being created in Iceland. In many areas establishing
new constitutional arrangements and new legal procedures was
unavoidable. The innovations were then little by little hallowed by
custom.'[19]

Whatever the truth in Ari's story, a decentralized government
specifically designed to satisfy Iceland's needs was established about
930. Initially there appear to have been approximately thirty-six
chieftaincies (*goðorð*), and a higher number of *goðar*, since each
goðorð could be shared by two or more individuals. The number of
goðar in the early centuries was perhaps double or more the number
of *goðorð*. Selection was made on the basis of kinship alliances
(some among the descendants of Bjorn buna) and local prominence.
Although scholars generally agree that no other governmental or
societal structure could have served as a direct model for the Icelandic
chieftaincy, the word *goði* was not new. It may have been written in
runes in Norway around the year 400, and it is found on several
Danish rune stones from the island of Fyn dated to the ninth and
perhaps to the early tenth century.[20]

As noted earlier, the word *goði* is derived from the word *goð* (god),
reflecting a religious connection, and *Landnámabók* (S297, H258)
refers to one Thorhadd from Mæri(n) as a temple priest (*hofgoði*) in
Norway. In Iceland, Thorhadd settled in the East Fjords. In the
absence of a recognized priesthood, the chieftains seem to have been
responsible for hallowing the local assemblies and performing official
sacrifices. Since religious life centred on ceremonial cult acts, these
duties may have been substantial, at least in the earlier period. The
religious functions of the *goðar* lent an aura of importance to the
individual, distinguishing him from neighbouring rich and influential
farmers. Attendance by a farmer at a chieftain's ceremonial feast
served as a public announcement of a *goði*–thingman relationship,
and *goðar* competed with each other in holding such feasts.

Written Sources: The Book of Settlements *and* The Book of the Icelanders

The student of early Iceland is fortunate in having a collection of extensive written sources. The laws and sagas are discussed in later chapters. Here we consider the Icelanders' major historical writings. The chief historical sources are *Landnámabók* (*The Book of Settlements*) and *Íslendingabók* (*The Book of the Icelanders*).[21] Both texts include genealogies as well as historical sections and together offer considerable information about the island's settlement.

Íslendingabók is the smaller of the two, and is a concise overview (thirteen or so pages in a printed edition) of Iceland's history from 870 to 1120. It was probably written between 1122 and 1132 by Ari Thorgilsson, called the Learned (*inn fróði*), who was mentioned earlier. Two versions – the 'older' and the 'younger' – were extant in the medieval period, but only the younger has survived, in two seventeenth-century copies.

Íslendingabók is an invaluable source. It touches on a wide variety of subjects, albeit on many of them only briefly. Among the ninth- and tenth-century events it records are Iceland's settlement, the adoption of Iceland's first oral laws, the founding of the Althing, the subsequent reform of the constitution in the mid 960s, and the adjustment of the calendar. *Íslendingabók* is also a primary source for information concerning the settlement of Greenland and the discovery of Vínland (in Chapter 6):

The country that is called Greenland was discovered and settled from Iceland. A man called Eirik the Red from Breiðafjord [Broad Fjord] went there from here and claimed the land later called Eiríksfjord. He called the country Greenland, saying men would be encouraged to go there if it had a good name. They found human settlements, fragments of boats, and stone artifacts. From these remains it could be concluded that the same type of people had lived there as had settled in Vínland – the ones whom the Greenlanders called Skrælings. Eirik began the settlement fourteen or fifteen winters before

Christianity came here to Iceland, according to what a man, who himself
followed Eirik the Red on the voyage, told Thorkel Gellisson in Greenland.

This entry is characteristic of Ari's work. The statement is based on
verified information, which includes dating the Greenland settlement
to about 985. Here, as elsewhere, he is careful to tell us his sources.
For instance at the beginning of *Íslendingabók* Ari states that Thorkel
Gellisson was his paternal uncle and a man 'who remembered far
back', and that another of his sources, Thurid, the daughter of the
chieftain Snorri goði, was both very learned and 'unlying', that is,
accurate. On the other hand, Ari offers little information about the
social, economic or political factors which caused Icelanders to make
certain decisions. For instance, some people chose in 985 – only
fifty-five years after the establishment of the Althing – to emigrate to
Greenland, a place that to people already accustomed to Iceland
must have seemed to be close to the very end of the world.

Almost three-quarters of *Íslendingabók* is devoted to selected
events occurring between 996 and 1120. This period included the
lifespan of the author and of the older men and women who served
as his oral informants. Ari covers Iceland's conversion to Christianity,
the presence of foreign missionary bishops, the establishment of
Iceland's two bishoprics, the introduction of the Fifth Court (for
appeals), the first tithe law, the census of farmers eligible to pay the
thing tax before the introduction of the tithe, and the first writing
down of the laws.

There is no doubt that Ari was a careful historian. At times,
however, his objectivity and his choice of subject matter were influenced by his interest in strengthening the Church, his predilection for
stressing the Norwegian ancestry of the settlers, and his desire to
record events of special significance from his local region of Breiðafjord in western Iceland.[22] Most of the people Ari mentions are
individuals with whom he has some link of kinship. In genealogies he
traces his own ancestry through the kings of Norway and Sweden back
to the gods Njord and Frey – a respectable lineage for an Icelander.

Landnámabók is much larger than *Íslendingabók*, the extant versions filling several hundred pages in a modern printed volume. It was an important and popular book in the medieval period and several different versions are extant. *Landnámabók* was written as a record of the settlement and a genealogy of the Icelanders. Through a welter of predominantly terse entries, it accounts for approximately 400 of the most prominent *landnámsmenn*. Sometimes it tells where these colonists came from and who their forefathers were in Scandinavia. We learn where the *landnámsmenn* settled and some details about their land claims. At times the kinship lines of *landnámsmenn* are traced through succeeding generations of Icelanders.

The first *Landnámabók*, now lost, was written in the early decades of the twelfth century. Ari the Learned may have been one of the authors, or at least he may have had a hand in the work. The major extant versions of *Landnámabók* – *Sturlubók*, *Hauksbók* and *Melabók* (the last a fragment of only two vellum leaves) – date from the thirteenth to the fifteenth century.[23] These mention 1,500 farm and place names as well as more than 3,500 people. The material, arranged geographically, gives a seemingly complete picture of the whole country.

Although *Íslendingabók* and *Landnámabók* report specific information, the entries are often so concise that they merely hint at a picture of the functioning society. For example, the following passage from *Landnámabók* (S86, H74) names major characters but leaves us in the dark as to the nature of what appears to have been, in the late tenth century, a serious dispute in a small fjord in western Iceland called Álptafjord (Swans' Fjord):

Thorolf Lamefoot was the father of Arnkel goði and of Geirrid who married Thorolf from Mávahlíð. The sons of Thorbrand from Álptafjord were named Thorleif kimbi, Thorodd, Snorri, Thorfinn, Illugi and Thormod. They quarrelled with Arnkel over the inheritance of their freedmen and they, together with Snorri goði, killed him at Örlygsstaðir.

This passage encapsulates a feud narrated in *Eyrbyggja saga*, which is discussed in Chapter 6.

The reliability of many entries, particularly in *Landnámabók*, is questionable.[24] The thirteenth- and fourteenth-century editors of the *Sturlubók* and *Hauksbók* versions extensively altered the older texts. For example, there is little doubt that Sturla Thordarson, the thirteenth-century editor of the *Sturlubók* (S) version of *The Book of Settlements*, was familiar with, and drew on, several family sagas in expanding his edition. Not only did these medieval historians use the family sagas to augment or to replace what appeared in earlier, now lost, versions of *Landnámabók*, but at times genealogies are traced to what seems to be the editors' own families.

In summary it can be said that the Icelanders' earliest historical sources show a distinct interest in the founding of their society. This interest sparked the inquiries of people such as Ari the Learned, writing 250 years after the settlement. From its foundation, this farming society with its cultural focus on law and its strong leaning toward consensual decision-making faced the threat that the rights of farmers would be diminished if the power of the chieftains grew too large. In the next chapter we turn to an example of how social codes and political mechanisms worked to prevent this transfer of power.

6

Limitations on a Chieftain's Ambitions, and Strategies of Feud and Law: Eyrbyggja saga

'Don't think that I will hesitate to swing this axe at Arnkel once you are ready.'

Eyrbyggja Saga, Chapter 37

Revenge is a dish best served cold.

Old Sicilian adage

In exacting payment for his services, a *goði* was subject to restraints. Such limitations are particularly evident in a feud related in *Eyrbyggja saga* (*The Saga of the People of Eyri*) between two strong chieftains whose contest over power and land polarized the local community. The prospect of arousing the vengefulness of local farmers often frustrated the ambitions of a chieftain. In *Eyrbyggja saga*, Arnkel goði chooses to ignore this risk. In return for his services he acquires through a contractual agreement called *handsal* ('handsale', referring to a witnessed slap or shake of hands at the conclusion of an agreement) the rights to properties to which he had no prior claim. By this action, involving *arfskot* (cheating of heirs, or transferring land without the heirs' consent), Arnkel arouses the animosity of neighbouring farmers who are willing to fight to maintain their claims to the lands. The story of Arnkel marks the limits that a chieftain, greedy for wealth, exceeded at peril of his life. Set within the context of a long-standing rivalry between Snorri goði and Arnkel goði, the

10. The Location of *Eyrbyggja saga* on Snæfellsnes. The feud between Arnkel goði and Snorri goði takes place in the blackened area.

events that develop from the machinations of a *bóndi* named Thorolf Lamefoot form a narrative unit (Chapters 30–34) with ramifications immediately following (Chapters 35–8).[1] The story frequently turns on actions that stem from greed, fear, ambition or downright meanness, as it describes coldhearted bargaining between farmers and chieftains.[2] Timing, that is the knowledge of when to take vengeance, is crucial.

All the events take place in one small region of Snæfellsnes, shifting between Álptafjord, which cuts into the northern shore of the peninsula, and Helgafell, the farmstead on Thórsnes where Snorri goði lives. Álptafjord (Swans' Fjord) is named for the large number of swans that to this day congregate there. Helgafell means holy mountain: the god Thor was thought to reside there. The legal case arising from Thorolf's actions is settled at the local Thórsnes Thing. The action is limited to disputes that embroil the two chieftains and the owners of four farms that lie near Bólstaðr, Arnkel's farm at the inland end of the fjord. The main characters are known from *Landnámabók*, where the events are sketchily outlined (S86, H74).

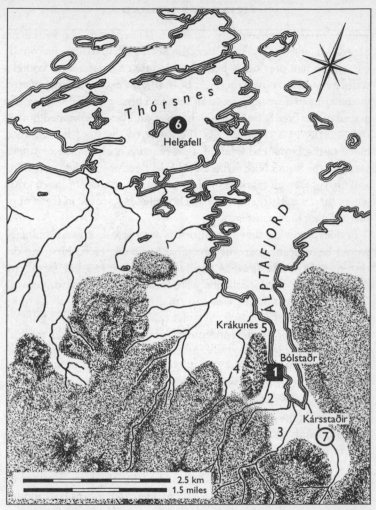

11. Landownership in Álptafjord (Swans' Fjord). At the start of the incidents described in this chapter, the pattern of ownership was: **1** Bólstaðr (Arnkel goði); 2. Úlfarsfell (Ulfar the Freedman); 3. Örlygsstaðir (Orlyg the Freedman); 4. Hvammr (Thorolf Lamefoot); 5. Krákunes (the woodland); **6** Helgafell (Snorri goði); **7** Kársstaðir (the six sons of Thorbrand). The circled numbers designate land owned by the chieftain Snorri or by his thingmen, the sons of Thorbrand. The square designates the property of chieftain Arnkel. Kársstaðir, at the innermost point of the fjord, was a major prize in the feud. Its broad, low-lying hay meadows were the most extensive in the area, and through the middle of the farm ran one of the best salmon and trout rivers in the region.

In 1931 the archaeologist Matthías Thórðarson conducted an excavation at Arnkel's farm.[3] Because Bólstaðr had so little surrounding land, it had previously been doubted that a chieftain of Arnkel's stature would have lived there. At Bólstaðr, the excavation uncovered the remains of a small habitation that had been replaced in the early period of the Free State by a much larger and better equipped house, well worthy of a chieftain. As the water of the fjord has claimed much of the farmstead land, all that remains is an outline of stones marking the house. The farms of the two freedmen in the saga, Ulfar and Orlyg, are still marked by distinct square patches of green grass where their manured and enclosed homefields once lay in front of or surrounding the farmsteads.

Besides knowing that Álptafjord is very small, a local audience would have been aware of several other basic facts. First, as the eastern side of the fjord is too steep to provide good farmland, no habitations of consequence were located there. Second, because Bólstaðr, Arnkel's farm, was too small to support the needs of so ambitious a chieftain, one would expect him to be land-hungry. Third, Kársstaðir, at the innermost point of the fjord, was the real prize. Its broad, low-lying hay meadows were the most extensive in the area, and through the middle of the farm ran one of the best salmon and trout rivers in the region. The surrounding mountains, by keeping out the harshest winter winds and in the summer retaining the heat from the sun, contributed to the productivity of Kársstaðir's rich grasslands. As testimony to its inherent value, Kársstaðir is the only farm in Álptafjord which is still inhabited today.*

---

* My thanks to Gísli Gíslason, the *bóndi* at Kársstaðir, for discussing with me the relative merits of the lands and streams in Álptafjord.

Arnkel's Quest for Wealth and Power

The danger inherent in Arnkel's territorial ambitions is sensed by the sons of Thorbrand, who live at Kársstaðir in the inner fjord. With impassable mountains at their backs, these farmers need a safe route to Helgafell, where their chieftain Snorri goði lives, as well as free access to the Thórsnes Thing. As the story progresses, their adversary Arnkel is claiming the properties on the western side and at the mouth of the fjord, thus cutting off their lifeline. Arnkel is also interfering with their expected inheritance of some of these properties.

The sons of Thorbrand are determined to retain their freedom of movement, property rights and local status. Their frustrations illustrate the limitations of Iceland's system of consensual order. Thorolf, Arnkel goði's father, had been a Viking in his youth before emigrating to Iceland, and this experience seems to have added to his unjust and overbearing nature (*mjök ójafnaðarfullr*). Arriving in Iceland late in the settlement period, he used his warrior training to acquire a sizeable piece of land by challenging an elderly *landnámsmaðr* to a duel and killing him. Wounded in the duel, Thorolf became known as Lamefoot. Later he sold part of his land to Ulfar and to Ulfar's brother Orlyg, two slaves freed by Thorbrand of Kársstaðir.

Ulfar the Freedman (*leysingi*) has prospered on his farm, called Úlfarsfell, and Thorolf, who lives at Hvammr, resents the freedman's skill at farming and weather forecasting. Now an old man himself, Thorolf is increasingly difficult to deal with, and he wants to hurt Ulfar. On the ridge that separates the farms, the two men jointly own a mountain meadow. One summer day Thorolf goes with a few slaves and gathers in all the hay, even though part of it clearly belongs to Ulfar. The latter, who is younger than Thorolf, confronts the old man in the act of stealing the hay, but Thorolf refuses to listen to reason. Rather than come to blows, Ulfar chooses to take the matter to his neighbour and *goði*, Arnkel, son of Thorolf. (Thorolf has no share in Arnkel's chieftaincy.)

Though reluctant to take part in the dispute, Arnkel does ask his father to pay Ulfar for the hay, but Thorolf refuses. His refusal strains the relationship between father and son and puts Arnkel in a difficult position. When his friend and follower Ulfar chides him for not acting more decisively on his behalf, Arnkel himself pays Ulfar for the hay and seeks reimbursement by slaughtering some of his father's oxen. Thorolf, who does not approve of Arnkel's solution, swears that he will make Ulfar pay for the loss of his livestock.[4]

Ulfar's Land Shifts to Arnkel

The conflict, which hitherto has been a neighbourly squabble over hay, becomes more serious. Thorolf, though taking no immediate action, continues to brood over the wrong done to him. At his Yule feast he serves his slaves strong drink and incites them to burn Ulfar in his house, but the plot fails when Arnkel sees the fire and puts it out. The next day Arnkel has Thorolf's slaves led to a promontory and hanged.

Frightened by the attempt on his life, Ulfar places himself under the protection of his chieftain Arnkel (Chapter 31): 'After that [the attempted murder and the hanging of the slaves], Ulfar transferred to Arnkel by *handsal* agreement all his property, and Arnkel became his guardian [*varnaðarmaðr*].' Arnkel's acceptance of the burden of guardianship is not gratuitous. In return for Arnkel's protection, Ulfar assigns all his wealth (*fé sitt allt*)[5] to the chieftain in a formal agreement (*handsal*), which we later learn was duly witnessed. With one variation, the transaction between Ulfar and Arnkel is, according to the law books, an example of *arfsal*, cession of the right of inheritance. *Arfsal*, a binding agreement, differs from *arfskot*, fraud or cheating in matters of inheritance.[6] In *arfsal*, one of the two parties agrees to take the other into his household and care for him in return for an assignment of inheritance rights. The variation in this instance is that Ulfar continues to live on the property he is relinquishing instead of moving to Arnkel's farm.

The *handsal* between Ulfar and Arnkel especially affects a group of neighbouring farmers, the six sons of Thorbrand, who are the foster-brothers of Arnkel's rival, Snorri goði. Ulfar had been freed by Thorbrand, who is now an old man and whose sons have taken over his property and rights. Thorbrand's sons feel they have been cheated by Arnkel's transaction with Ulfar: 'The Thorbrandssons did not like this *handsal* because they had thought themselves owners of Ulfar's wealth, as he was their freedman.' In accordance with the laws on *arfsal*, those who originally stood to inherit may nullify a transaction if they are not in agreement with the assignment. In the instance of a freedman without children, *Grágás*, the record of Iceland's early laws, is very precise: the manumitter (*frjálsgjafi*) is the heir.[7] If a freedman such as Ulfar signs away the rights of his manumitter, he can be accused of *arfskot*, according to *Grágás*.[8]

Icelandic law assumed that a freedman (*leysingi*) might have difficulty earning his living. *Grágás* specifies that if a freedman could not maintain himself and did not have a son or daughter to look after him, then his manumitter was required to support him.[9] The manumitter was compensated by becoming the legal heir if his freedman died childless. Freedmen (*leysingjar*) were in this respect a single generation of former slaves who were not completely free from their manumitters. They remained united to manumitters by bonds of quasi-kinship, remaining dependent on them as minor children were on their fathers.[10]

Ulfar has done well for himself; far from having difficulty earning his living, he has accumulated enough wealth to arouse the greed of those around him. Because he has presumably never looked for support to his manumitters, the Thorbrandssons, he may well think that he owes them nothing, that his self-earned property is his to dispose of as he pleases, without recognizing their claims. The Thorbrandssons, on the other hand, are within the letter of the law in considering themselves heirs of the childless Ulfar, even if they never maintained him in his lifetime.

By promising protection to a farmer in need of support, Arnkel has, through the legality of *handsal*, taken possession of a valuable piece of property. In establishing a claim to the land by means of Ulfar's *arfsal*, Arnkel has ignored the inheritance rights held by the well-born sons of Thorbrand. Nevertheless, he is still manoeuvring within legal limits. Ulfar, for his part, is considered to have committed *arfskot* and is stirring up animosity in the district by selecting Arnkel as his protector. Yet few other viable options are available to him. Consider Ulfar's position. His most direct procedure would be to attack and kill Thorolf, but he wisely refrains from choosing a solution that would be foolhardy for a simple farmer (a freedman) whose opponent is kin to a chieftain. By killing Thorolf, Ulfar would force Arnkel to seek redress, perhaps even blood vengeance. Possibly Ulfar fears that he would be injured in a confrontation with the tough old Viking. Another choice open to Ulfar is to seek protection from the sons of Thorbrand, who are his legal heirs. As powerful warriors they would be dangerous enemies to any opponent. Because they do not possess a *goðorð*, however, they cannot exercise the full power of the law in Ulfar's favour. Further, their chieftain lives much farther away from Ulfar than does Arnkel, whose land is no more than a long arrow-shot away.

The Thorbrandssons also have options. They can attack Arnkel with the intention of killing him. Although in the end the Thorbrandssons do just that, at this stage they are not willing to go that far. As Arnkel is a skilful opponent and a powerful chieftain, these farmers choose to handle the dispute through the proper legal channels. Their next move is to seek the advocacy of their *goði*. Ulfar's, and initially the Thorbrandssons', rejection of a violent solution is similar to farmers' restraint in similar situations in other family and Sturlunga sagas; under duress, farmers consciously avoid initiating action against their chieftains. As the *goðar* guard the privilege of their official position, so, too, the *bændr* keep their conduct within the limits imposed by that position.

The sons of Thorbrand choose not to act alone, even legally. Theoretically they could have summoned Arnkel either to the local thing or to the Althing. The reality of Icelandic legal procedures, however, did not support freemen challenging a chieftain alone, i.e., without the support of other chieftains. Court cases often depended on bold posturing and displays of manpower. Without a following of thingmen, these *bændr* would stand little chance against Arnkel goði and his thingmen. The saga does not suggest that Thorbrand's sons even consider taking independent court action. Instead, they turn to Snorri goði.

Snorri, apparently seeing little opportunity for self-aggrandizement in taking on a case against Arnkel, refuses to support the Thorbrandssons. Snorri was an astute power-broker who was revered as an ancestor by many of the prominent people of the thirteenth century, including the Sturlungs. As the present example reveals, Snorri's reputation was based on shrewdness rather than on physical prowess. In view of Arnkel's clear intention to push his claim, a confrontation at the courts on behalf of Thorbrand's sons would be dangerous for Snorri. On the other hand, what has Snorri to gain by supporting his foster-brothers? If Arnkel wins the case, he keeps the rights to the land. But if Snorri wins, he would be expected to turn the rights over to the Thorbrandssons. If Snorri exacts from them a price commensurate with the risks involved, such as Ulfar's property, he would himself arouse the hostility of these potentially dangerous men. Snorri, who is not a rash man, chooses not to put himself in a precarious position. Snorri's refusal to support his thingmen makes them legally impotent. Even though they are powerful and well-born farmers with clearly established rights, they are helpless without an advocate.

Theoretically, Ulfar might have turned to Snorri goði for assistance, but that option is not realistic. Snorri, who lives at a distance out on Thórsnes, could not effectively aid Ulfar if Arnkel or Thorolf should harass him. Furthermore, an agreement with Ulfar would probably be counter-productive for Snorri. By accepting what Ulfar has to offer (assignment of his land) in return for protection, Snorri would probably anger the sons of Thorbrand. Such action might even force them to unite with Arnkel against Ulfar. Given the choices, Arnkel is really the only suitable advocate for Ulfar, though it is questionable what advantage Arnkel would have in seeing Ulfar enjoy a long life.

Thorolf's Land Shifts to Snorri goði

Financial considerations again enter into the continuing legal process when a bargain is struck between Thorolf Lamefoot and Snorri goði. Once more, a farmer requests the support of a chieftain in return for a specific payment. As the details are different from Ulfar's transfer of his land to Arnkel, however, the situations of Ulfar and Thorolf present a notable contrast. Ulfar is a freedman who desperately needs protection; Thorolf is a well-born man under no physical duress. Thorolf's intention is to exercise his rights in order to obtain personal revenge against Arnkel. He is prepared to go to Snorri and to contract for the support of his son's chief enemy, a man with whom he has no ties of friendship or kinship. Presented in unusually sharp detail, the scenes are tightly narrated examples of how a clever leader bargains with a determined *bóndi* and gains land in return for his advocacy.

Thorolf is especially irked by Arnkel's refusal to pay compensation for the hanging of his slaves after the failed attempt to burn Ulfar to death. According to two complicated entries in *Grágás*,[11] Thorolf's claim for compensation is probably justified. A master whose slaves have been killed has the right to demand that the issue be settled in court. Here is another example of a *bóndi* who knows his legal rights but lacks the strength to uphold them. Thorolf needs an advocate.

Determined to seek vengeance, Thorolf swallows his pride and solicits support from the other local broker, Snorri goði. As the meeting begins, the *goði* offers food to his unexpected guest, but Thorolf refuses it, saying that he 'has no need to eat his host's food'. Thorolf informs Snorri that, as a major leader in the district (*héraðshöfðingi*), the chieftain is obligated to support those who have suffered injury. The appeal to Snorri's sense of justice or duty is a waste of time. When he hears that Thorolf wants to prosecute his own son, Arnkel, Snorri viciously humbles the old man. Reminding Thorolf of his family ties, Snorri declares that Arnkel is a better man than his father.

The positions of the two men are clear. Neither likes the other, and Snorri, who is in complete control of the situation, sees no reason even to be civil to the father of his rival. If Thorolf wants Snorri to use his power, he will have to appeal to an interest other than the chieftain's sense of duty. Thorolf, aware that something more is required, offers to give Snorri some of the compensation for the slaves if Snorri will take the case. Snorri flatly refuses his support, saying that he will not interject himself into the dispute between father and son.

Thorolf then realizes that if he wants to uphold his rights he will have to offer Snorri something of real value. And Thorolf does indeed possess a worthwhile bargaining unit, a property in Álptafjord called Krákunes, on which stands a valuable forest. He offers to transfer this property, 'the greatest treasure in the region', to Snorri by a formal *handsal* agreement if Snorri will prosecute Arnkel. With all the power of understatement the saga author lets us know that Snorri feels a 'great need' to possess the forest. So in return for taking on the case of Thorolf's loss of his slaves, Snorri accepts a *handsal* of the land.

At the local spring assembly, the Thórsnes Thing, Snorri brings the case against Arnkel for the killing of the two slaves. When the two chieftains arrive at the thing, each has a large following. After the accusation has been made before the court, Arnkel calls witnesses to prove that he caught the slaves in the act of burning a farmstead. Snorri replies that Arnkel could have killed the slaves with impunity if he had done so at the scene of the burning. *Grágás* supports Snorri's contention, specifying that men may be struck down as being outside the law when caught in the act of setting a fire ('*með ellde tecnom til breno*').[12] According to Snorri, Arnkel forfeited his right to kill the slaves when he did not act immediately but later had them taken to a promontory to be executed. Therefore, Snorri claims, Arnkel has failed to observe the law and thus is unable to use it in his own defence.

After a discussion of legal points, the arbitration process begins. Men come forward offering to help in the resolution of the dispute. Two brothers, who have connections with the opposing parties, are chosen to arbitrate, and they arrange a settlement. Arnkel pays a modest sum to Snorri, who in turn passes the pouch to Thorolf; Snorri has already been paid in land. But Thorolf, who expended so much energy in bringing about this confrontation between Arnkel and Snorri, feels cheated: 'I did not expect, when I gave you my land, that you would pursue this case in so petty a manner, and I know that Arnkel would not have denied me such compensation for my slaves if I had left it up to him.' Apparently it does not occur to him that Snorri is less concerned with discrediting Arnkel and getting a large sum for the slaves than in winning his legal point in order to keep Krákunes.

The forest acquired by Snorri carries a price beyond the aid promised to Thorolf. As the saga makes clear, Arnkel believes that Snorri has unlawfully acquired title to the Krákunes woods. Arnkel's view is that his father Thorolf 'committed *arfskot* when he transferred the forest to Snorri goði'. Here Arnkel seems to be in the right: Thorolf's transfer of the forest to Snorri is an instance of *arfskot* in that the title was conveyed without the prior agreement of Arnkel, Thorolf's rightful heir. According to *Grágás*,[13] Arnkel, as the heir, has the right to bring an action to remove the testator, in this case Thorolf, from control of the property. Arnkel, however, has little to gain from such an action, as Thorolf is no longer in control of the forest and as he himself will inherit his father's other property. Arnkel therefore waits until he thinks the time is ripe; then he rides over to Krákunes and kills a man named Hauk, one of Snorri's freeborn followers, who is transporting wood from the forest to Helgafell. By killing Hauk, Arnkel is openly claiming that Snorri has no right to take wood from Krákunes. At the same time he is asserting his own control over the forest.

Ulfar Claims Orlyg's Land

By becoming Ulfar's guardian, Arnkel had acquired control of a property at the expense of the sons of Thorbrand. The transaction brings still other advantages to Arnkel. Not only is Ulfar a childless landowner, but his brother Orlyg also has no children. When Orlyg dies, Ulfar, backed up by Arnkel, claims that he is his brother's heir and takes possession of all of Orlyg's property, including his farm Örlygsstaðir. In doing so he is once again openly thwarting Thorbrand's sons, who had expected to inherit because Orlyg, like Ulfar, was their father's freed slave.

Although Ulfar's and Orlyg's farms are both small, together they make up a substantial portion of the usable land within the fjord. Furthermore, Örlygsstaðir borders on Kársstaðir, the farm of the Thorbrandssons. By acquiring control first of Úlfarsfell and then of Örlygsstaðir, Arnkel has extended his property to the borders of Kársstaðir. The question of what he intends to do next makes the situation dangerous for the sons of Thorbrand. Their confrontation with Arnkel over Orlyg's property (Chapter 32) clearly shows that the owners of Kársstaðir feel cheated:

And when Orlyg died, Ulfar sent immediately for Arnkel, who came quickly to Örlygsstaðir. Together Ulfar and Arnkel took into their possession all of Orlyg's property. When the Thorbrandssons learned of the death of Orlyg they went to Örlygsstaðir and laid claim to all the property there. They declared that whatever their freedman had owned was their property. Ulfar, however, said that he held the right to his brother's inheritance. The sons of Thorbrand asked Arnkel what he intended to do. Arnkel replied that if he had a say in the matter Ulfar would not be robbed by any man as long as they were partners. Then the sons of Thorbrand left and went immediately out to Helgafell [Snorri goði's farmstead].

As noted earlier, *Grágás* clearly stipulates that the manumitter is the rightful heir of a childless freedman. (Again the sons of the manumitter, Thorbrand, are concerned with protecting their inheritance.) As the law, to our knowledge, does not allow a brother's claim in such a situation, Arnkel is acting illegally in asserting his right to Orlyg's property. Although the law explicitly upholds the sons of Thorbrand as Orlyg's heirs, Arnkel through his previous experience knows that they will not act without the backing of their chieftain Snorri.

By taking the property Arnkel is humiliating Snorri; he seems convinced that Snorri will back down in the face of an open challenge, and that is exactly what happens. When the sons of Thorbrand go to Helgafell to seek Snorri's aid, the chieftain again refuses to support his thingmen and foster-brothers. He even manages to blame them for the dispute, stating that he 'would not quarrel over this issue with Arnkel because they [the Thorbrandssons] had been so careless as to let Arnkel and Ulfar arrive at the property first and take it into their possession'. Without the support of their *goði*, Thorbrand's sons again find themselves outmanoeuvred. As in the earlier exchange with Arnkel over Ulfar's property, they back down and do not openly contest their neighbour's seizure of their inheritance. Snorri, however, cannot fail to understand the threat made by his foster-brothers when they remark, as they leave Helgafell, that their chieftain 'would not long retain his authority if he did not concern himself with a matter such as this'.

Ulfar's Demise

Ulfar does not enjoy for long the use of Orlyg's property, for old Thorolf Lamefoot is still plotting. While riding home alone from Arnkel's customary autumn feast, Ulfar is ambushed and killed by a man sent by Thorolf. By chance Arnkel is standing outside his house and sees the killer running across a field. Now, though his protection has proved ineffectual in keeping Ulfar alive, he acts quickly in his own interest. Sending some of his followers to kill the runner,* he immediately rides to Ulfar's farmstead where he claims that, as Ulfar's protector, he should inherit the property.

Meanwhile, Thorbrand's sons, having learned of Ulfar's death, set

---

* To kill so quickly a man whom he only suspects to be an assassin is curious. Few details would need to be changed in the story to implicate Arnkel in the killing of Ulfar. Certainly Ulfar's death was to Arnkel's advantage. The few sentences towards the end of Chapter 37 eulogizing Arnkel may be a later interpolation.

out to claim the property of their freedman for themselves. When they reach the farmstead they find Arnkel, supported by a following, already there. Arnkel, denying the precedence of their claim (*tilkall*), supports his own by bringing forward witnesses who were present when Ulfar assigned his property to Arnkel by *handsal*. Displaying an intense interest in legal manoeuvrings, the saga-teller has Arnkel declare that 'he would hold firm to his right to the property since the original agreement had not been challenged at law. Arnkel warned them [Thorbrand's sons] not to encumber the property with a legal claim because he intended to hold on to it as though it were his patrimony.' Again Arnkel is master of the situation, both legally and physically.[14]

Outmanoeuvred and overpowered, the sons of Thorbrand leave the farmstead and once again seek the help of their chieftain, Snorri. As before, Snorri refuses to support his thingmen. He does, however, point out to the Thorbrandssons that, although Arnkel has established a legal claim to the lands and has taken possession of the chattels, the property lies equidistant between them and in the end 'will fall to the stronger'. Snorri reminds his foster-brothers that they 'will have to put up with the situation as others do, since Arnkel now stands above all men's rights here in the district. And that will continue as long as he lives, whether it is longer or shorter' (Chapter 32). In this way Snorri incites his followers to violence.

Snorri's prediction that the lands will fall to the stronger party is an accurate assessment, for in the end Arnkel does not realize his ambitions. Yet before he meets a violent death at the hands of Snorri and the Thorbrandssons (Chapter 37), he gains control of almost all of Álptafjord. After Thorolf Lamefoot dies (Chapter 33), Arnkel acquires his father's farm at Hvammr (4 on Maps 11 and 12). This acquisition further reduces the Thorbrandssons' freedom of movement. Both sides of the ridge between Úlfarsfell and Hvammr, site of the meadow where Ulfar and Thorolf first came into conflict, are now controlled by Arnkel, hemming in the sons of Thorbrand whose property is the only one in the fjord still outside Arnkel's control (see Map 12).

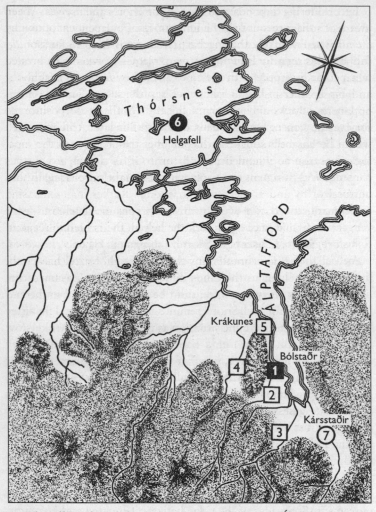

12. The Effect of Arnkel's Actions on Land Claims in Álptafjord (Swans' Fjord) Immediately Before His Death. The squares indicate land that Arnkel had acquired or claimed. A circle designates land owned by Snorri goði or by his thingmen, the sons of Thorbrand.

In considering their position the sons of Thorbrand may have been aware of stories recounting the limitations of independent action by *bændr* when asserting their rights. The tragedy of Gisli Sursson, as told in *Gísla saga Súrssonar*, is an example. Gisli becomes embroiled in a personal dispute with his chieftain, who is also his neighbour and his brother-in-law. Gisli, who is physically a match for his opponent, attacks and kills him. Legally Gisli is in no position to survive the consequences of his act. By killing the chieftain with whom he has been allied, he has at one stroke removed the most logical person to whom he could turn. Gisli's action has further consequences. It signals to people with political clout that he is both untrustworthy and unsuccessful at feuding. Rather than exercising self-control, and coolly waiting for the proper moment to take his vengeance, Gisli's passions become enflamed. In his need to respond to his exaggerated concept of honour, he acts too quickly.

As Gisli finds out, no matter how honourably motivated his action, there is little willingness by others to defend him or to seek a settlement for him in the courts. The disaffected include the members of Gisli's close family, who give him very little support. His sister becomes a determined enemy and his brother is angered because of Gisli's violent act. In killing a chieftain to whom he is related by marriage, Gisli has lowered his relatives' status and undermined their political strength. The brother of the chieftain whom Gisli has killed, after assuming the vacant *goðorð*, quietly and determinedly seeks vengeance against Gisli. Gisli is virtually powerless in the court system against the force of a chieftain supported by his followers at the thing, and he is declared a full outlaw.

The End of Arnkel's Ambitions

The story of the conflicting claims in Álptafjord reveals the profits accruing to an ambitious leader, such as Arnkel, as well as the dangers and the choices he faces. Arnkel repeatedly manipulates the law to gain possession of new and valuable properties while abusing the rights of freeborn farmers. However, he miscalculates. The sons of Thorbrand can be cheated, but they cannot be ignored. Snorri, no rash opponent, is well aware of the dangers that he faces. He has been biding his time, waiting for the proper moment for revenge. What Snorri needs is determined allies to face Arnkel, and he knows it. Perhaps not by chance, the moment to secure these allies comes at his own autumn feast, when he allows himself to be shamed into supporting his thingmen. It is a negotiation, a freely entered into contract between *goði* and *bændr*. Both sides get what they want, with Snorri agreeing finally to take part in an attack on Arnkel. In response to their taunts, Snorri gives one of them an axe, remarking that it would be a suitable weapon with which to kill Arnkel. The farmer Thorleif kimbi, who is equally hard-nosed, replies: 'Don't think that I will hesitate to swing this axe at Arnkel once you are ready.'

Once they are assured of a chieftain's backing, the sons of Thorbrand become a serious threat to Arnkel. Events move quickly. Snorri and Thorbrand's sons await the right opportunity. One night they learn that Arnkel has gone alone with only a few slaves to tend to the hay on his newly acquired lands. At a distance from his men at Bólstaðr, Arnkel is an easy target. Although he defends himself courageously, the sons of Thorbrand, with Snorri in command, kill him.

Details of the ensuing court case are sketchy, but the outcome is clearly a success for Snorri. The only sentence of outlawry – banishment for three winters – for the killing of Arnkel falls on Thorleif kimbi, one of Thorbrand's sons who had publicly taken responsibility for administering the death blow. As to the lands, the saga later tells that Bólstaðr, Arnkel's farm, is deserted while Örlygstaðir and Úlfarsfell return to the possession of Thorbrand's sons.

For all his local wealth and power, Arnkel seems not to have made many friends among his fellow chieftains. Nor had he created a successful system of family or political alliances, and no competent advocate steps forward to prosecute his killers. Perhaps what is not said but understood is that Snorri, a master politician in other tales such as *Njal's Saga* and *Laxdæla saga*, was not sitting idle during the time that he was suffering abuse from Arnkel. Instead, he was quietly gathering assurances from other *goðar* that when the moment came, he and his followers would not be attacked in the courts for the killing.

Left on their own, Arnkel's female heirs take over the responsibility of bringing a court case, but they lack the power to pursue the suit successfully. According to the laconic description in *Eyrbyggja saga*, the result of the suit is 'not as honourable as one might have expected for so important a leader as Arnkel. The leading men of the country then made it law that never afterwards should a woman or a youth less than sixteen winters be the chief prosecutor in a case of manslaughter; and this law has held ever since.'[15]

In its story of Arnkel, *Eyrbyggja saga* shows a system of order in which the ambitions of a chieftain could be frustrated by *bændr* who know how to assert their rights. In order to maintain these rights, freemen needed to know the law and their rights and had to be prepared to choose between options, including compromise and violence. Farmers kept chieftains from gaining the upper hand through extralegal mechanisms. These mechanisms, which protected the freemen's rights, operated only when freemen could establish consensus among themselves to oppose the unreasonable demands of a chieftain. *Eyrbyggja saga* shows *bændr* entrusting their *goðar* with power and threatening to withdraw that support when the agreement was no longer beneficial to them.

7

Chieftain–Thingmen Relationships and Advocacy

All societies have authority structures and values concerning the allocation of authority. In stateless societies, the proper unit for the analysis of such phenomena is not the total society, where we are likely to mistake lack of a central political hierarchy for egalitarianism, but the maximal decision-making unit (or some cohesive subgrouping within it).

Robert A. LeVine, 'The Internalization of Political Values in
Stateless Societies'

In Iceland, where no such need of defence existed, where there was no foreign enemy, and men lived scattered in tiny groups round the edges of a vast interior desert, no executive powers were given to anybody, and elaborate precautions were taken to secure the rights of the smaller communities which composed the Republic and of the priest-chieftains who represented them.

James Bryce, *Studies in History and Jurisprudence*

The medieval Icelanders possessed a well-developed vocabulary for describing social and political stratification. They employed the words and attendant concepts when writing the kings' sagas about the rulers of Norway and Denmark or when composing saga histories about other Norse lands, such as *Orkneyinga saga*, an account of the Norse earls of Orkney. But when Icelanders wrote about their own society, whether in sagas, laws or stories, the roles and the vocabulary of statehood seldom appear. This striking contrast is the result of a central development in early Iceland: leadership evolved in such a way that a chieftain's power and the resources available to him were not derived from an exploitable realm. Territorial lordship, an element of authority which permeated the Western concept of landownership and legal and economic jurisdiction, was largely absent in early Iceland; the lord–peasant relationship, so prevalent elsewhere in the medieval West, barely existed.

In more stratified European societies, religious and military hierarchies provided models for structuring social, legal and political relationships. Iceland developed differently. In place of overlordship, the early Icelanders, with their focus on law, developed their own set of mechanisms for maintaining order. As they modified traditions and customs they had known in their homelands, a new system of law and political behaviour emerged. It compensated for the absence of the executive institutions that accompanied territorial leadership in other Norse lands. This chapter concentrates on the basic relationships that underlay the operation of Iceland's system of consensual governance. One, the *goði*–thingman bond, was defined by law. Another, which can best be described by the term 'advocacy', was not legally defined. It found its authority in private contractual agreements whereby one person, not necessarily a chieftain, gave support to another by speaking or acting for him, and so became involved as a third party to a dispute. The usefulness of advocacy was reinforced by the presence of additional extralegal arrangements, such as political friendships and frequent recourse to arbitration.

The Nature of the Goðorð

In principle, the legal *goði*–thingman bond was created by a voluntary public contract which did not depend upon a geographical base. A key factor that has received scant attention in previous studies is that this relationship provided little sense of either permanency or protection to either leader or follower. For an ambitious individual, at least in the early centuries, becoming a *goði* was not entry into a formally defined class. To become a *goði*, a farmer – that is a *bóndi* – did not undergo formal investiture; there was no oath of office, no swearing before a deity. The *goði* was answerable only to minimal guidelines set by law and to the pressure of public opinion.

Possession of all or part of a *goðorð* (the political office of chieftaincy) granted a leader little formal authority over his followers. Although it would be naive to assume that all social systems function according to their laws, in the instance of early Iceland, it appears that a chieftain, in accordance with *Grágás*, had little power to command a thingman to act against his will. Instead, a chieftain's power rested, to a large degree, on the consent of his followers. Thingmen, for their part, could formally demand very little of their *goði* beyond requiring that he carry out the few duties prescribed in the laws. These responsibilities included holding thing meetings and setting prices on imported goods. Such duties assured the availability of arenas for settlement of disputes and helped to prevent friction among the farmers. In fulfilling these obligations the *goðar* had little latitude, for in most instances they were accountable to their followers and to other chieftains.

Advocacy

Advocacy arrangements existed alongside, and sometimes in place of, *goði*–thingman and kinship ties. These agreements established between any two individuals a set of third-party contractual obligations, which could be freely entered into by advocates and clients living in any part of the quarter or, for that matter, in any part of the country. Unlike the *goði*–thingman bond, which was defined in the laws, advocacy was an informal, extralegal association that came into being in response to specific needs. Functioning as a form of third-party intervention, it assumed unusual prominence in early

Iceland because both farmers and chieftains frequently required more assistance than public institutions offered.

The fact that government was often permitted to operate by means of private intervention, particularly at the assemblies, provided many opportunities for advocates. Some of these, especially chieftains, increased their influence to the point where they became power-brokers. Such individuals, who were often also called on to act as arbitrators, did not constitute a separate class or a semi-official body, for theirs was a temporary role. They were farmers and chieftains who enjoyed credibility and inspired the trust of others. Examples mentioned in the sagas of especially powerful advocates who frequently acted as power-brokers are Snorri goði, Jon Loftsson, Gudmund the Worthy, Gudmund the Powerful, and the prominent farmer Njal Thorgeirsson.

Sometimes advocates, even as brokers, acted out of high-mindedness (*drengskapr*), charging no fee for their efforts to solve the problems of others. The motivation for such acts of goodwill might be the desire to enhance one's prestige or to reaffirm kinship, political alliances or goði–thingman ties. But at other times an advocate might set a fee which was often substantial, perhaps even requiring the transfer of property or inheritance rights in return for his services. The fee, which made it worth the while of a third party to intervene in the affairs of others, is frequently referred to in the sagas by the term *sæmð*, meaning honourable recompense. *Hallfred's Saga* (*Hallfreðar saga*) offers an example of how an advocate, in this instance a kinsman and a goði, was engaged. Hallfred, a cantankerous poet, has slept with another man's wife. In a confrontation the next day he kills one of the husband's kinsmen, named Einar. The husband initiates a lawsuit against Hallfred; when Hallfred is summoned to the local Húnavatns Thing (Chapter 8), his brother Galti asks him:

'What do you intend to do about this case?'

Hallfred replied, 'I intend to seek the aid of my kinsman Thorkel [Thorgrimsson, a goði].'

In the spring thirty of them rode north to Hof [Thorkel's farm in Vatnsdalr] and spent the night. Hallfred asked Thorkel what support he could expect from him. Thorkel responded that he would take on the case if he were offered some honourable compensation (*sæmð*). [The kind of payment is not disclosed.]

Seeking an advocate was a basic step in building the partisan support required for success at the assemblies. People often turned first to kinsmen, as Hallfred did, since kinship was a basic field of relationship that provided a claim to potential supporters. Shared blood, however, beyond providing an entry to ask for assistance was no guarantee that support would be forthcoming. If only partly reliable during feud, kinship relationships did have more dependable features throughout the Free State: cognatic kinship ties (placing nearly equal value on both the mother's and the father's families) remained important in determining inheritance rights and deciding who should take the responsibility for seeking vengeance. Like the *goði*–thingman relationship, kinship ties were often augmented by extralegal arrangements, for once a right or a duty had been ascertained, a farmer or a chieftain might need help in validating his claim or carrying out his responsibility. In the absence of court-appointed officials to warrant that justice be done, who was to supply the assistance? Private advocates filled the void by undertaking specific aggressive or defensive action. These voluntary relationships, whether entered into with an individual's regular chieftain or with another leader, supplied the support required to achieve a sense of security. A large part of saga narrative is devoted to descriptions of people seeking advocates. Individuals are routinely shown protecting their rights through specific advocacy agreements, rather than simply relying on the *goði*–thingman bond or on kinship.

Third-party advocacy relationships complemented rather than supplanted *goði*–thingman alliances and kinship ties. Informal, voluntary and sometimes covert, the different advocacy roles provided a framework within which individuals could manipulate political forces at different stages of a dispute. Icelandic feuds tended to survive many attempts at resolution. Settlements, both those that were final and those that were temporary, were frequently arrived at through arbitration.[1]

Arbitration and Legalistic Feuding

The Old Icelandic legal and narrative texts about the Free State contain many terms for arbitrators and arbitration. Sometimes arbitration is referred to as *jafnaðardómr*, a case judged by one or more umpires. More often the term *görð*, meaning simply arbitration, is used. A settlement or reconciliation brought about through arbitration was called *sætt* or *sátt* (the forms are used interchangeably; the plural for both terms is *sættir*), and arbitrators or peacemakers were frequently called *sáttarmenn* or *görðarmenn*. Arbitrators were often influential advocates who possessed the wide-ranging family and political alliances required to arrange compromises. So it is in the example above from *Hallfred's Saga*; Thorkel, after having taken on Hallfred's case, chooses to seek an arbitrated settlement rather than to defend his client in court: 'Now men came to the thing. When Hallfred and Galti arrived they went to Thorkel's booth and inquired what was to happen. Thorkel replied, "I will offer to set up an arbitration [*görð*], if both sides will accept this. Then I will try to arrange a settlement [*sætt*]."'

In many instances when arbitration had a chance of success, supporters of both sides united to aid the arbitrator. A famous example is from *Eyrbyggja saga* (Chapter 10) where Thord Gellir arbitrates between two local groups, the people of Thórsnes (*Thórsnesingar*) and the descendants of Kjallakr (*Kjalleklingar*). Usually the farmers and chieftains who backed the arbitrator were concerned with achieving a compromise that adjusted for the new status quo but did not seriously disturb the existing balance of power. Here again consensus came into play, since compromise resolutions often involved many people. These and other *sættir* had a chance of success because they were based on a common standard of compensation or blood money recognized throughout the island as suitable recompense for torts and physical injury. Like advocacy, which in many instances served to promote the common good, arbitration was intended to accomplish specific goals.

Advocacy and arbitration tended to cool hotheadedness by taking the conduct of a quarrel out of the hands of the original, perhaps more emotionally engaged, rivals and entrusting decisions to third parties. That is what eventually happens in Hallfred's case. Hallfred's brother is attacked at the thing and killed by the brother of the woman Hallfred seduced. When the killer is allowed to get away, Hallfred doubts the commitment of his advocate Thorkel and instead challenges the husband to a duel (*hólmganga*). Reason prevails, and in the end Hallfred withdraws his challenge to the duel, and the husband agrees to let Thorkel resume arbitration. Thorkel pronounces that the killings of Einar, the husband's kinsman, and Galti, Hallfred's brother, cancel each other out, with the provision that Hallfred's visit with the wife made up for any difference that might have existed between the two fallen men. For the scurrilous verses he had composed about the husband, Hallfred has to pay one article of value. When Hallfred shows reluctance to do so, Thorkel chides him; Hallfred then gives the husband an arm-ring of great value.

Perhaps because of its efficacy, advocacy became the accepted procedure for guiding conflict and violence into legal channels – into the courts or private arbitration. This development, which influenced the alignments of the political networks between leaders and the social networks between leaders and followers, was determined largely by the status of the free farmers. As the ones who would suffer most if a case came to violence, Icelandic *bændr* could demand that their chieftains show restraint, even during feuds. Thingmen were not beholden to their leaders by oaths of unswerving loyalty. Thingmen were mostly landowners and householders whose interests were better served by compromise solutions than by pitched battles. Advocacy, brokerage and arbitration facilitated problem-solving by compromise rather than by military victory.

The absence of pitched battles does not mean that the island inhabitants eschewed all forms of militant show, only that they ritualized the actual use of force. Parties to a dispute that was moving toward resolution frequently assembled large numbers of armed *bændr*. Sometimes these groups confronted each other for days at assemblies and at other gatherings, such as when a successful party was trying to enforce a judgement at the home of the defendant (*féránsdómr*). Although opposing sides often clashed briefly, and a few men might be killed, protracted battles were consistently avoided. It was not by chance that the parties showed restraint. Leaders really had few options if they hoped to retain the allegiance of a large following, since the *bændr* were not dependable supporters in a long or perilous confrontation. They had no tradition of obeying orders, maintaining discipline, or being absent from their farms for extended periods. The *goðar*, for their part, were seldom able to bear the burdens of campaigning. They lacked the resources necessary to feed, house, equip and pay followers for more than a brief period.

Rather than signalling the outbreak of warfare, a public display of armed support revealed that significant numbers of men had chosen sides and were prepared to participate in working toward an honourable resolution. With chieftains and farmers publicly committed, a compromise resting on a collective agreement could be reached. Conforming to the expected practice, third parties, termed men of goodwill (*góðviljamenn*) or well-wishing men (*góðgjarnir menn*), intervened between the armed groups, publicly displaying *góðgirnð* or *góðgirni* (the words normally mean goodness, kindness, or benevolence). Consider the description from Chapter 20 of *The Saga of Thorgils and Haflidi* (*Thorgils saga ok Hafliða*) of the gathering of men for a court of confiscation after Haflidi Masson succeeded in obtaining a judgement of outlawry against Thorgils Oddason in the year 1120:

And as the time approached for holding the *féránsdómr* [the court of confiscation, i.e., carrying out the sentence at Thorgils' home], Thorgils gathered men around him, assembling almost 400 in all. Haflidi had from the north a picked band of 100 men, each chosen for his manliness and equipment. And in a third place the men of the district gathered together for the purpose of intervening with *góðgirnð* [benevolence]. The leaders of this group were Thord Gilsson and Hunbogi Thorgilsson from Skarð. With them were also other *góðgjarnir menn* [men of good wishes] – Gudmund Brandsson and Ornolf Thorgilsson from Kvennabrekkr, with 200 men for the peacemaking.

Góðgjarnir menn might simply be concerned neighbours. Frequently, as in the above example, they were chieftains and ambitious *bændr* who by stopping a violent clash often enhanced their own reputations. One of the *góðgjarnir menn* in the above example, Thord Gilsson, was a *bóndi* who became a chieftain. His son was the famous chieftain Hvamm-Sturla. In some instances, after separating the opposing sides, *góðgjarnir menn* served as arbitrators, thus improving their own status by arranging suitable resolutions. For approximately three centuries, or until the last decades of the Free State, there were in Iceland no pitched battles with casualties comparable to those that routinely took place elsewhere in medieval Europe. Avoiding warfare, the Icelanders esteemed political flexibility and legal acumen, a cultural focus that is seen in their literature.

The Flexibility of the Goði–Thingman Relationship

From the ninth century to the twelfth the concerns of free farmers dominated the spectrum of governmental activity. Legal and administrative decisions were fashioned within the context of a widespread belief in the inviolability of the rights of freemen. These rights were contained in a system of law which served less to protect privileges than to allow the individual to exercise specific rights. The *goðar*, in their capacity as advocates, enjoyed no legal authority to act in defence of their supporters; conversely, they were under no obligation to do so. This situation left a *goði* open to prosecution by other freemen, a factor that apparently discouraged rashness on the part of leaders.

Being a *goði* was a professional vocation with entrepreneurial overtones. In an island society with limited economic opportunity, *goðar* were individuals poised to intervene, upon request and when remuneration was likely, in the disputes of others. They, along with influential farmers who chose to play the role of advocates, were experts in conducting feuds, whether arbitrated, adjudicated or fought. A *goði* was willing to help others for reasons of self-interest, kinship, political obligations or payment. Although the law in Iceland held out the promise of equal rights, the political reality was that only consensus among leaders, representing their followers, could make the complex legal system work satisfactorily. As a result of the advocacy process, violence was reduced to an acceptable level; rash acts and overbearing conduct became marginal.

From early on a major threat to Iceland's internal cohesion was the possibility of regional fragmentation. The lie of the land, with its uninhabitable interior, isolated fjords and remote valleys, made communications difficult and might easily have fostered the growth of regionalism. The Althing system of government, however, successfully countered this danger. When situations started to get out of hand, regional antagonisms or serious feuds triggered the safety mechanisms of the island-wide legal community. In particular, brokerage and arbitration came into play. In extreme instances, as in the major feud between Thord gellir and Tungu-Odd in the mid 960s, legislated constitutional change was deemed necessary: the quarter courts were instituted to lessen the likelihood of future escalations of regional confrontations.

Over the years there has been confusion as to how best to describe the authority of the *goðar* and their participation in the consensual order. The uncertainty stems to a large degree from the very nature of the *goðorð*. As the basic cohesive subgroupings within the social order delineated by the reach of the Althing, *goðorð* were not geographically defined. In the past scholars, attempting to interpret conditions in Iceland in terms appropriate to northern Europe, have tended not to concentrate on this distinguishing characteristic or on processes such as advocacy. Likening the authority of a *goði* to the power of an overlord, they have compared the *goðorð* with the small political entities or petty kingdoms that flourished in early Viking Norway or early Ireland. In keeping with this comparison, early Iceland has often been characterized as a union of petty states.[2]

The concept of *goðar* as leaders of small states reflects the outward aspects of the politics of confrontation among chieftains while failing to take into account the complex relationship between chieftains and farmers. Unlike petty kingdoms in Norway or Ireland, which often fought to defend or extend their borders, a *goðorð* had no defined boundaries. Icelandic chieftaincies were units of power not based on the resources of an exploitable realm. Differing from the Norwegian and Irish leaders, who lived surrounded by followers sharing a common loyalty, the chieftains lived interspersed among farmers who might be thingmen of other, sometimes rival, *goðar*. Thingmen of competing *goðar* might also be advocacy clients of chieftains other than their own, as well as clients of prominent *bændr* who themselves might be thingmen of still other *goðar*. In order to understand Iceland we must remember that farmers and chieftains had many choices. One possibility is exemplified in Thorolf Lamefoot's advocacy arrangement with Snorri goði, described in *Eyrbyggja saga*. Thorolf, who is under no duress, enters into an agreement with Snorri whereby Snorri, as Thorolf's advocate, prosecutes Thorolf's own son, Arnkel goði, who happens to be Snorri's major rival.

The Saga of Gudmund the Worthy, written shortly after the death of Gudmund the Worthy (*dýri*) in 1212, gives a detailed and basically reliable picture of *goði*–thingman alliances in the region of Eyjafjord in the Northern Quarter at the end of the twelfth century. The two accompanying maps portray the network of criss-crossing ties, with chieftains relying for support on farmers, some of whom lived far away from their *goðar*. In this Sturlunga saga at least five chieftains are claiming the allegiance of farmers while at the same time feuding over land and power. The leaders (marked by boxes) did not control territorial entities but, in keeping with centuries-old Icelandic traditions, lived scattered among thingmen loyal to other chieftains. The network of public *goði*–thingman associations pictured on Maps 13 and 14 does not reflect advocate–client agreements, which were often covert.

The following list of *goðar* and their thingmen mentioned in *The Saga of Gudmund the Worthy* includes only those whose areas of residence and affiliation can be verified from the saga. The numbers and letters refer to designations on Map 13.

A. *Gudmund the Worthy at Bakki*

2A. Soxolf Fornason at Myrkárdalr
3A. Thorvald at Bægisá
4A. Kalf Guttormsson at Auðbrekka
5A. Hakon Thordarson at Arnarnes
6A. Sons of Arnthrud at Sakka (later sent to Ogmund Thorvardsson)
7A. Sumarlidi Asmundarson at Tjörn
8A. Thorstein Halldorsson at Brekka
9A. Nikulas Bjarnarson at Grindill

B. *Onund Thorkelsson at Laugaland* (he later moves to Langahlíð [5B], and Thorfinn, his son and follower, moves to Laugaland)

2B. Erlend Thorgeirsson at Myrká
3B. Bjorn Steinmodarson at Öxnahóll
4B. Tjorvi at Rauðalækr
5B. Langahlíð (Onundr Thorkelsson)
6B. Halldor or Bjorn Eyjolfsson (farms in Reykjadalr not specified)
7B. Einar Hallsson at Möðruvellir (shares *goðorð* with Onund)
8B. Helgi Halldorsson at Árskógr
9B. Bjorn Gestsson at Sandr (location approximated)
10B. Eyvind and Sighvat Bjarnarson at Brekka
11B. Runolf Nikulasson at Mjóvafell (residence of father)

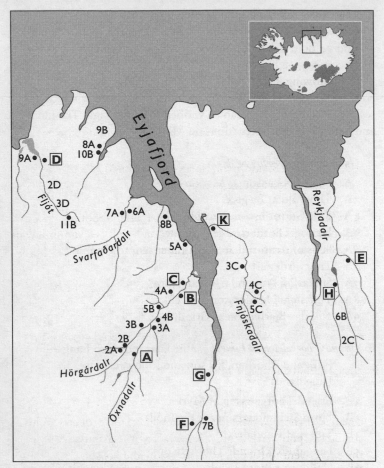

13. **Eyjafjord (*c.* 1190): Locations of Chieftains and Their Thingmen as Mentioned in *The Saga of Gudmund the Worthy*.** A chieftain (marked by a box) and his thingmen are designated by a letter and numbers: **A** stands for a chieftain; 2A, 3A, and so on stand for that chieftain's thingmen.

C. *Thorvard Thorgeirsson at Möðruvellir*

  2C. Halldor or Bjorn Eyjolfsson (farms not specified)

  3C. Brand Knakansson at Draflastaðir

  4C. Hall Asbjarnarson at Fornastaðir

  5C. Ogmund Thorvardsson sneis at Háls (later becomes *goði*)

D. *Jon Ketilsson at Holt* (*goðorð* later given to Gudmund the Worthy)

  2D. Thorvard Sunnolfsson (farm not specified)

  3D. Mar Runolfsson (farm not specified)

E. *Eyjolf Hallsson at Grenjaðarstaðir* (a priest, later abbot of Saurbær); acts as though he were a *goði*. Eyjolf is a son-in-law of Olaf Thorsteinsson at Saurbær [F].

F. *Olaf Thorsteinsson at Saurbær* (probably a chieftain; may have shared a *goðorð* with Kleppjarn Klaengsson)

G. *Kleppjarn Klaengsson at Hrafnagil* (may have shared a *goðorð*)

Farmsteads that changed ownership:

H. *Helgastaðir*

The first owner, Gudmund Eyjolfsson, gave the property to his son Teit. Upon Teit's death, the property was disputed, but in the end it went to Kleppjarn Klaengsson and his son Klaeng. A marriage was arranged between Klaeng and the daughter of Thorvard Thorgeirsson. Kleppjarn and Klaeng sold the property to Asbjorn Hallsson, the brother of Eyjolf Hallsson.

Farmsteads whose owners changed allegiance from one *goði* to another:

K. Laufáss

Thord Thorarinsson was a follower of Thorvard Thorgeirsson; his sons were followers of Gudmund the Worthy.

The Social Effects of Concubinage

At least in the early centuries, a chieftain was both a *bóndi* and a *goði*. More precisely, he was a farmer (*bóndi*) who controlled all or part of a chieftaincy (*goðorð*), and the sagas and other sources refer to a chieftain as *goði*, *bóndi*, *goðorðsmaðr* (literally, *goðorð*-man) or *höfðingi* (leader, pl. *höfðingjar*). For most of the Free State's history the *goðar* lived as prosperous farmers among farmers without the distinction of being a legally defined class. The closeness between *goðar* and *bændr* was maintained by routine intermarriage. The ties were further strengthened through chieftains taking concubines from *bændr* families. Through such arrangements, illegitimate children were often provided with substantial property. In this environment the *goðar* were not under pressure to establish lineages along the exclusionary lines of many European aristocracies.[3]

Wives in Old Icelandic society were usually of the same economic and social rank as their husbands, but they were often not the only women in their husbands' lives. At the same time, to judge from numerous saga examples, husbands were not always the only men in their wives' lives either. Given the living conditions, on separated farms, extra-marital relationships were seldom secret. In the earliest period after the settlement, many married men, whether farmers or chieftains, kept slave women as concubines. These women were called *frillur* (sing. *frilla*). As slavery died out in the eleventh century, men continued to maintain *frillur*. No longer slaves, these women came at times from families of equal status as well as, more commonly, from families of lower station than those of the men with whom they lived. Becoming a concubine of a prominent man often increased a woman's status and influence among her siblings and

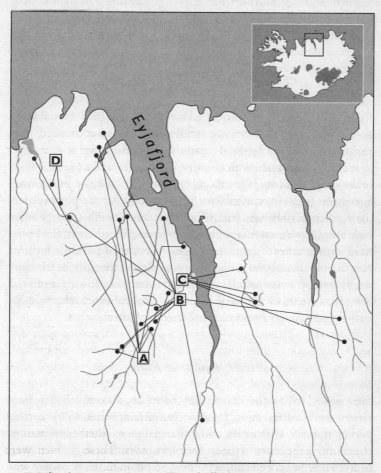

14. Eyjafjord (c. 1190): Showing Ties of Allegiance Between Four Chieftains and Their Thingmen as Mentioned in *The Saga of Gudmund the Worthy*. The farms of the chieftains are indicated by boxes.

kinsmen, and chieftains often treated male kinsmen of their concubines as trusted brothers-in-law. In some instances concubines had
wider latitude to act in their own interests than they might have had
in poor marriages. An Icelandic folk saying of uncertain age goes,
'Better a good man's *frilla* than married badly.'[4]

Grágás says almost nothing about concubinage, but the sagas
relating events of the twelfth and thirteenth centuries speak so frequently of them that one scholar has written, 'It is scarcely possible for
anyone who reads the Sturlung and Bishops' sagas not to notice that
concubinage was the national custom in Iceland during the Free State
period.'[5] In these thirteenth-century sources, as well as probably in
earlier usage, concubinage among landowning groups was a formal
agreement. In taking concubines, prominent *goðar* are portrayed as
casting their kinship nets farther out than was possible through marriage arrangements. *Frilla* agreements strengthened chieftains' positions with families of important farmers. For their part, the farmers
were allying themselves with the power elite. Especially in the thirteenth century, when judicial courts and assemblies no longer offered
farmers adequate tools of self-protection, concubinage relationships
became increasingly important to farmers of lower status.

Distinctions of Rank

Norwegian law, in contrast to Icelandic law, distinguished among
various ranks of freemen. These included freeborn labourers, free-
holding farmers, aristocrats, and low and high government functionaries. Among the ranks of the freeborn, an individual might be classed
as: a *reksthegn* or freeman, who depending upon the province was
often not an independent householder; an *árborinn maðr* or head of
an independent farm, though one not on inherited ancestral land; a
hauldr or *óðalsbóndi*, who was a free farmer in possession of inalienable ancestral land, which was called *óðal* (related to the Latin term
allodium, meaning family ownership of the land); a *hirðmaðr* or paid,
royal household retainer; a *lendr maðr* or aristocratic landowner and

liegeman of the king (a *lendr maðr* often held local authority in the tradition of a *hersir,* an older title of military and political authority which died out in the eleventh century); a *stallari* or marshal; or a *jarl* or earl. Different monetary values, according to rank and class, were assessed to redress personal injury to members of each of these groups.[6] In *Grágás* the right to lawful redress for injury and the legal amount prescribed, 6 marks (48 legal ounces), was the same for all freemen, whether farmers or chieftains.[7] The sagas, however, show awards being adjusted for the relative respect accorded to different individuals.

The absence of rigid class distinctions between chieftains and farmers in early Iceland is corroborated by the terms of the treaty between the Icelanders and the Norwegian king, Olaf Haraldsson (1015–30). The treaty, which was originally oral, was first sworn sometime during Olaf's reign. Later in the century it was committed to writing when representatives from Iceland came to Norway and swore to it for a third time.[8] A copy of this written version, preserved in *Grágás,*[9] is the oldest extant Old Norse document about Iceland. Remaining in force until the end of the Free State (1262–4), the treaty does not differentiate between *goðar* and *bændr* but states that 'in Norway Icelanders are to have the right [*réttr*] of a *hauldr'. Réttr* refers to lawful claim for redress possessed by an individual subjected to personal injury. *Hauldr* (Old Icelandic *höldr*) is a Norwegian legal term for a type of higher yeoman, an owner of inherited land.[10]

Apparently the category of *hauldr* (pl. *hauldar*) was acceptable to all leading Icelanders. The older version of the Norwegian Gulathing Law established a time period before an Icelander's social station could be re-evaluated: 'The Icelanders shall have the rights of *hauldar* while they are here on trading voyages. If they have stayed here through three winters, then an individual shall be accorded such rights as men bear witness to.'[11] The treaty with Olaf also granted rights to subjects of the Norwegian king when they were in Iceland. Without distinction of Norwegian rank, the Icelanders gave the Norwegians the same rights enjoyed by Icelandic freemen: '*slikan sem landz menn'.*[12]

Adding to the lack of significant distinction between chieftains and farmers in early Iceland was the tradition whereby *goðar* dealt directly with their followers. *Grágás* clearly defines a freeman's right to choose his *goði*,[13] a right characteristic of a non-territorial concept of authority:*

A man shall declare himself in thing [part of the chieftain's assembly group] with whatever *goði* he wishes. Both he and the chieftain shall name for themselves witnesses in order to attest that he [the farmer] declares himself there, along with his family and household and livestock, in thing [with the chieftain]. And that the other accepts him.[14]

Once a farmer had chosen a *goði* he was not bound to him but had the right to change:

If a man wants to declare himself out of the thing [relationship with his *goði*], it is the law that he declare himself so at the springtime thing [local assembly], if he enters into a thing relationship with another *goði* who is a *goði* of the same springtime thing. So also if he enters into a thing relationship with another *goði* who has an assembly group within the same thing district. It is the law that at the Althing he declare himself out of the chieftain's assembly third [a chieftain's following, called a third as there were three chieftains] at the high court at the *lögberg* [the Law Rock], if the *goði* hears [or listens]. If the *goði* does not hear, then he must say it to him directly, and in that instance it is the law that he declare himself out of the thing in the presence of witnesses for himself. And on the same day he must declare himself to be in a thing relationship with another *goði*.[15]

By the same token, a chieftain could break off a relationship with a thingman:

---

* The major territorial restriction was that a farmer could not choose a chieftain outside his quarter of the island. There were, however, a few exceptions: *bændr* who lived on Hrútafjord in the north-west were allowed to cross the fjord, and a chieftain could accept a thingman from outside his quarter if permitted to do so at the *lögberg* at the Althing (*Grágás* 1852a: 140–41 (Ch. 83)).

If a *goði* wishes to declare himself out of thing with a thingman [thus ending their thing relationship], then he shall notify him [the thingman] a fortnight before the springtime thing or with more notice. And then it is the law that he should tell the man at the springtime thing.[16]

In practice, the free exercise of the right to change leaders – an essential element in chieftain–farmer reciprocity – was tempered by traditions of personal and family loyalties, as well as by practical considerations, such as proximity to a chieftain. Probably freemen did not change chieftains frequently, yet the option was available. *The Saga of Hvamm-Sturla* offers a concise example from the early 1170s of a farmer, Alf Ornolfsson, switching his allegiance from Einar Thorgilsson to Hvamm-Sturla. The two *goðar* are involved in a series of contests in the latter half of the twelfth century. Farmers, particularly rich and prominent ones, could, if dissatisfied, shift their allegiance. In extreme instances, disaffected farmers moved to other areas.[17] Although the laws give the impression that all freemen were required to be in thing with a chieftain, it is probable, especially in the absence of a policing authority, that some freemen chose not to enter into such arrangements.

Hreppar: *Communal Units*

The status of farmers as free agents was reinforced by the presence of communal units called *hreppar* (sing. *hreppr*). Composed of a minimum of twenty thing-tax-paying farmers (*thingfararkaupsbændr*), these geographically defined associations of landowners were independent of the *goðar* and later of parish arrangements.[18] We do know that the *hreppar* were self-governing, but precisely how they functioned is unclear. It appears that each *hreppr* was guided by a five-member steering committee. The age and origin of the *hreppar* are also obscure. They are not known elsewhere and may have been an Icelandic development. As early as the 900s, the whole country seems to have been divided into *hreppar*, but they are only mentioned much later in the narrative sources. *Hreppar* provided a blanket of local security, allowing the landowning farmers a measure of independence to participate in the choices of political life. In 1703 there were 162 of these units.[19] Given the territorial nature of the *hreppar* and the conservatism of Icelandic rural arrangements, the number may have been somewhat the same in the Free State period, though we have no evidence of this.

Through cooperation among their members, *hreppar* organized and controlled summer grazing lands, organized communal labour, and provided an immediate local forum for settling disputes. Crucially, they provided fire and livestock insurance for local farmers. Probably they also arranged tithe collection, distributed the tithe portion that returned to the locality, saw to the feeding and housing of local orphans, and administered poor relief to people who were recognized as inhabitants of their area. People who could not provide for themselves were assigned to member farms, which took turns in providing for them. New people could not move into a locality without recommendations and then formal acceptance, restrictions that seem to have been aimed at stopping the swelling of relief rolls. *Hreppar* continued in operation long after the end of the Free State, contributing to social continuity in the rural society.

The local thing structures and the *hreppar* appear to have developed at roughly the same time in the tenth century. Together these two institutions form cooperative clusters that overlap in membership.[20] The springtime assembly (*várthing*) was not territorial, while the *hreppr* was. Once attached to the local *hreppr*, a farm's affiliation could not be changed. At the same time, a farmer could switch attendance among the *várthing* of the quarter by switching alliance to a new *goði*. The *hreppr* was essentially non-political and addressed subsistence and economic security needs. Its presence freed farmers from depending on an overclass to provide comparable services or corresponding security measures. In the *hreppar* we can see the self-limiting nature of what otherwise might have been state structures controlled from above.

The Orkneys: A Comparison

The uncertain hold of *goðar* on their thingmen and the competition among leaders for the allegiance of *bændr* made it difficult if not impossible for individual chieftains to impose burdensome taxes on their followers. Leaders in other, more stratified Norse settlements were not so constrained. For example, in Orkney leaders had the right to impose taxes and to demand extensive services from the farmers. Like Iceland, the Orkney Islands were settled by Norwegians during the Viking Age. The Orkneys, however, were nearer Norway and the British Isles, and were threatened by both.

Orkney was ruled by jarls, and *Orkneyinga saga*, written in thirteenth-century Iceland, presents Orkney from early on as a state with a central political hierarchy and a military structure. Along with the accounts of other jarls, the saga tells the story (in Chapter 13) of Einar Sigurdarson, who in 1014 seized control of two-thirds of Orkney after his father was killed near Dublin while aiding Viking allies against the Irish in the battle of Clontarf:

Einar became a strong ruler and assembled a large band of followers. During the summers he was often out raiding and called out large levies of ships and men from throughout the land. The resulting plunder, however, was not consistently rewarding. The farmers became tired of serving, but the jarl held them harshly to their duties and taxes and made sure that no one spoke publicly against him. Einar was a thoroughly tyrannical man, and all the payments and services that he imposed on the farmers caused a serious famine in his part of the earldom [*jarldómr*].

It does not seem likely that leaders in the Orkneys spent much time advocating the claims of farmers as happened in Iceland, where leaders were solicitous of the demands of *bændr*. Because the *goðar* could not claim obedience, they competed among themselves for supporters and advocacy clients. A chieftain's authority depended upon bonds of blood and alliance with members of the society's politically important population, the thing-tax-paying farmers, *thingfararkaupsbændr*. At the same time, the collective wealth of the *bændr* posed a challenge for the chieftains. The private lands and possessions of these farmers were a major source for the wealth required for the *goðar* to function as leaders. How to acquire resources from the independent-minded farmers and still retain their support was a dilemma faced by those seeking power, since checks and balances in the system, discussed in examples in later chapters of this book, worked to protect property owners against overly aggressive chieftains.

Freedmen

The Icelandic respect for freemen's rights was also extended to freedmen (freed slaves) and their heirs. The slaves, many of them were probably of Celtic stock, were brought by the early settlers and were rapidly integrated into the society.[21] The number or proportion of slaves to freemen is unknown. Slavery in Iceland may have been primarily a household phenomenon, with female slaves serving as nurses and foster-mothers as well as concubines. Most slaves were freed in the tenth century, although a few instances of slavery may have continued into the early twelfth century.[22] Some freedmen became landowners, though the majority probably became tenant farmers. It is difficult to define the latter, called *búðsetumenn* (tenant farmers who owed work services to their landlords) and *leiglendingar* (land renters not obligated to provide labour), because Icelandic tenant farmers enjoyed most freeman's rights, including the taking of vengeance and the collecting of blood money.[23] According to *Grágás*, only hired hands and impoverished fishermen were denied the right to choose their own *goðar*:

A man who begins householding in the spring shall declare himself in thing wherever he wishes; it is a household where a man has milking stock. If, however, a man is a landowner he shall declare himself in thing even if he has no milking stock. If he is not a landowner and has no milking stock, he follows the thing choice of the householder in whose care he places himself. If he is living in a fishing hut, then he follows the thing choice of the man who owns the land on which he is living. A man shall declare himself in thing with the *goði* he prefers at the Althing or, if he wishes, at a local springtime assembly [*várthing*].[24]

8

The Family and Sturlunga Sagas: Medieval Narratives and Modern Nationalism

Each society's social drama could be expected to have its own 'style', too, its aesthetic of conflict and redress, and one might also expect that the principal actors would give verbal or behavioural expression to the values composing or embellishing that style.

Victor W. Turner, 'An Anthropological Approach to the Icelandic Saga'

The Sagas differ from all other 'heroic' literatures in the larger proportion that they give to the meanness of reality.

W. P. Ker, *The Dark Ages*

The family sagas, dealing with the tenth and early eleventh centuries, and the Sturlunga sagas, covering the years from approximately 1120 to 1264, are the most important, as well as the most extensive, source for a study of social and economic forces in medieval Iceland. These two related groups of vernacular prose narratives are rich mines of information about the normative codes in Iceland's medieval community.*

---

* The family and Sturlunga sagas are discussed in relation to social groups in the section 'Big Farmers and the Family Sagas' in Chapter 19.

The Family Sagas

The family sagas are called in modern Icelandic *Íslendingasögur*, 'the sagas of the Icelanders'. They have no close parallels in other medieval European narratives, which are mostly in verse and are often of a more epic character than the sagas. Some family sagas tell us about the settlement of Iceland, but most of them concentrate on the period from the mid tenth to the early eleventh century. In a crisp and usually straightforward manner they describe the dealings between farmers and chieftains from all parts of the country and among families from diverse elements of the society. They explore the potential for an individual's success or failure in the insular world of the Old Icelandic Free State.

Whereas the Sturlunga sagas are mostly about individuals engaging in the power struggles of an emerging overclass and give almost no information about the personal lives of ordinary farmers and local leaders, the family sagas tend to concentrate on precisely these concerns. With regularity the stories focus on private matters and offer insights into personal problems of families and the health, good or ill, of marriages. The family sagas often exaggerate situations of crisis. They deal less with extended kin groups, as the name 'family sagas' might imply, than with regional disputes in Iceland. Similar actions involving different characters are repeated in different locales. With constantly changing detail, the literature presents potential issues and the responses that individuals in the society needed to make to them if they were to succeed. Among the matters stressed were methods of reacting to overly ambitious or otherwise dangerous characters, precedents for various legal positions and modes of action, successful interventions by advocates, different means of settlement, and the principles underlying the establishment and maintenance of ties of reciprocity.

In the oral saga, as elsewhere in oral tales, one may assume that adherence to strict fact was never an issue. Nor was the saga-teller required to memorize a fixed text; a general outline of a story that was perhaps of historical origin was sufficient. The medieval audience expected the narrator of a family saga to observe certain strictures. Most importantly, the saga had to be credible; that is, the story had to be portrayed as possible, plausible, and therefore useful within the context of Iceland's particular rules of social order and feud. The sagas served as a literature of social instruction.

In an earlier book, *Feud in the Icelandic Saga*, I suggest that feud served as a cohesive and stabilizing force in Old Icelandic society.[1] Because the rules of feuding, as they developed in Iceland, regulated conflict and limited breakdowns of order, violence was kept within acceptable bounds throughout most of the history of the Free State. The ways in which feud operated provided a structure for the sagas. In examining the question of the oral saga, I found probable the existence of a pre-literate stage of well-developed saga-telling employing a compositional technique that became the foundation for the written saga. This simple, easily adaptable technique was based on the use of active narrative particles that occur in no particular order and fall into three categories: conflict, advocacy or broker-age, and resolution. Guided by the parameters of socially recognized conduct, the storyteller or storywriter arranges these action particles in various orders and with different details.[2] By using the particles he (or she) translates social forms into narrative forms. In anthropo-logical terms the particles reflect the phases of Icelandic feud. These discrete units of action, the hallmark of saga style, were a convenient means for an oral or a literate teller to advance the narration of a complex tale.

Working within a tradition of known characters, events and geo-graphy, the saga-teller chose his own emphasis. He (or she) was free to decide what details and known events to include and what new actions to introduce. These choices not only made for variety in the small clusters of actions that linked together to form chains of saga events, but also served to distinguish one saga from another. Although the medieval audience probably knew in advance the out-come of a particular dispute, the essence of a tale could be put forward differently each time. This economical and effective technique of

forming narrative prose applied to both oral and written saga composition. Freedom from reliance on a fixed, memorized text allowed
individual authors to incorporate new elements, such as Christian
themes and changing ethical judgements.

Thirty or more major family sagas are extant.* These texts vary
markedly in length: some, like *Hrafnkels saga*, are approximately
twenty pages in modern volumes; others, such as *Njáls saga* and
Laxdœla saga, fill 300 or more pages. The family sagas are preserved
in a wide variety of manuscripts, none of which is an original text
definitely attributed to a specific author, despite the educated guesses
of scholars. The oldest surviving examples of saga writing are fragments; the earliest are usually dated to the mid thirteenth century,
although it is possible that some fragments pre-date 1200. Among
the presumed oldest fragments are sections from *Eyrbyggja saga*,
Heiðarvíga saga, *Laxdœla saga* and *Egils saga*. These, like later
copies of entire sagas, give no information as to when the earliest
versions of the texts were composed; thus dating the sagas has always
been a difficult task, and scholarly conclusions are open to question.
Decisions on the age of the family sagas have been influenced by
different theories of saga origins, a point underscored by Hallvard
Magerøy: 'A chief argument for placing the production of the family
sagas in the thirteenth century is that only by this means can saga
literature be seen as a natural branch of European literature in the
High Middle Ages.'[3]

---

* The major family sagas are *Egils saga Skalla-Grímssonar*, *Hænsa-Thóris saga*,
Gunnlaugs saga ormstungu, *Bjarnar saga Hítdœlakappa*, *Heiðarvíga saga*, *Eyrbyggja
saga*, *Eiríks saga rauða*, *Grænlendinga saga*, *Laxdœla saga*, *Gísla saga Súrssonar*,
Fóstbrœðra saga, *Hávarðar saga Ísfirðings*, *Grettis saga Ásmundarsonar*, *Bandamanna
saga*, *Vatnsdœla saga*, *Hallfreðar saga*, *Kormáks saga*, *Víga-Glúms saga*, *Svarfdœla
saga*, *Valla-Ljóts saga*, *Ljósvetninga saga*, *Reykdœla saga ok Víga-Skútu*, *Thorsteins
saga hvíta*, *Vápnfirðinga saga*, *Hrafnkels saga Freysgoða*, *Droplaugarsona saga*, *Fljóts-
dœla saga*, *Thorsteins saga Síðu-Hallssonar*, *Brennu-Njáls saga*, *Kjalnesinga saga*,
Thórðar saga hreðu, *Finnboga saga ramma*, *Harðar saga ok Hólmverja*, and *Flóamanna
saga*. There are also a number of smaller sagas, fragments, and short stories called
thættir (sing. *tháttr*).

Copies of complete family sagas are preserved in vellum books dating from the fourteenth and fifteen centuries. For example, the fourteenth-century compilation *Möðruvallabók* is the chief source for many of the eleven sagas it contains. Many other sagas are preserved in paper manuscripts from the sixteenth century and later. In the medieval period there were many more family sagas than have survived. *Landnámabók*, for example, names several that are now lost. Except for *Droplaugarsona saga*, which notes at the end that a certain Thorvald, descended from one of the main characters, 'told this saga', all the family sagas are anonymous.

The Sturlunga Compilation

Sturlunga saga is a large compilation of sagas named after the Sturlungs, an influential family in the last century of the Free State.[4] The name *Sturlunga saga* first appears in a surviving seventeenth-century source, although the collection may have borne this title earlier. Along with the bishops' sagas, the sagas in the Sturlunga compilation are often called contemporary sagas (*samtíðarsögur*) because the twelfth- and thirteenth-century events they describe transpired about the same time as the sagas were written. *Sturlunga saga* provides a wealth of information about this later period. The individual sagas included in the compilation were written by many authors, all but one of whom remain unknown. The one identified author, Sturla Thordarson (d. 1284), nephew of the Icelandic chieftain and writer Snorri Sturluson, was an active chieftain at the end of the Free State.

The different texts contained in *Sturlunga saga* were first gathered into a single large book around 1300, a time when many such compilations were being assembled. These costly vellum books, often impressively illustrated, preserved many texts that otherwise would have been lost. Compilations might be mainly a gathering of sagas of one kind, such as the surviving *Flateyjarbók* (c. 1390), consisting of 225 large-format leaves of sagas and shorter narratives pertaining for the most part to Norway's kings, or the surviving *Möðruvallabók* (*c.* 1350), an assortment of family sagas filling 200 leaves. The modern names of these manuscripts derive from the localities where the books were found in the sixteenth and seventeenth centuries. Flatey is a flat island in Breiðafjord (Broad Fjord) in western Iceland and Möðruvellir is a farm in Eyjafjord in the north. Compilers might also assemble writings with little or no common thread as, for example, in the partly extant *Hauksbók*, put together in the first decades of the fourteenth century. *Hauksbók* is named for its compiler, the lawman Hauk Erlendsson, and contains among its texts one of the major versions of *Landnámabók* (H) spoken of earlier.

The initial Sturlunga compilation had been copied several times before it was lost. Two of these transcriptions, vellum manuscripts from the second half of the fourteenth century, fortunately survived intact as late as the seventeenth century, when many of the sagas were copied into books made from relatively inexpensive imported paper. Once their contents had been transferred to a more easily read format, the vellum books lost almost all value to the contemporary population. In fact, they were viewed as so unimportant that the stiff pages of one of them were cut up into patterns for making clothes.[5] Many medieval manuscripts were similarly damaged, or disappeared altogether, after manufactured paper became available in the sixteenth century. From the seventeenth until the early twentieth century the transcribing of sagas and laws from older documents, including earlier paper manuscripts, became a popular pastime in Iceland. To this custom we owe the survival of many medieval Icelandic texts.

Like the family sagas, the Sturlunga sagas often concentrate on conflict and feud. Yet the two groups differ from each other in social emphasis. Whereas the more numerous family sagas narrate disputes and concerns of all kinds, including petty issues involving obscure local people, the Sturlunga sagas focus on quarrels among the most powerful chieftains. This feature is especially evident in *The Saga of Thord Kakali* (*Thórðar saga kakala*), *The Saga of Thorgils Skarði* (*Thorgils saga skarða*) and *The Saga of the Icelanders* (*Íslendinga saga*). Detailing events of the last decades of the Free State, these narratives frequently touch on issues that affect the political future of the country.

The literary quality of the sagas in the Sturlunga collection varies widely. Some of them, including parts of the longer ones, are gripping tales of people and events. On the other hand, many are collections of loosely connected material. Frequently the accounts are filled, even cluttered, with names and places, as though the authors were determined to record every scrap of information they had accumulated on a subject. If the Sturlunga sagas are burgeoning with factual information, the reader must nevertheless be wary. The authors are certainly not disinterested parties. On occasion they are partial to particular personages and families; at times, it seems that the purpose behind a story is to redeem the author's reputation or that of a friend, a kinsman, or an ancestor. Still, one is often struck by the seeming objectivity of the sagas, which were written for a contemporary audience with a knowledge of the families, farms, events and characters. The absence or distortion of essential details in a particular account would have been noticeable.

Sturlunga saga, it seems, was compiled in western Iceland at Skarð, a prosperous farm owned by a family famed for its interest in the law. Whoever the compiler was, he was decidedly concerned about the history of his country during the preceding two centuries. With the goal of creating a chronological history, he integrated various accounts from different sagas and thereby mixed the texts. As customary in Icelandic compilations of the period, he tended to respect the original wording of the sagas and left whole pieces of the older narratives intact. In general his emendations were restrained. This medieval historian shortened some of the originals, spliced together overlapping texts, added a number of transitions, and wrote a few of the shorter narratives. Modern scholars have spent years unravelling his chronological arrangement in order to re-establish the integrity of the separate sagas.[6] Because the sagas in the compilation were contemporaneous, *Sturlunga saga* is usually considered to contain reliable, if at times subjectively reported, information, and it remains a primary source for numerous innovative historical studies on the twelfth and thirteenth centuries.[7] Literary scholars, on the other hand, have often judged the texts in this compilation to be less sophisticated than the family sagas.

The Sagas as Sources

The family sagas are a register of the basic values of medieval Iceland's conservative rural society, yet since the mid twentieth century historians and social scientists have shied away from using them as sources. This curious development is largely attributable to a series of theoretical obstacles against historical analysis raised by a group of Icelandic scholars who have come to be known as the Icelandic school. The ideas that animated the Icelandic school may be traced, first, to the nineteenth-century German scholar Konrad Maurer and then, in the early decades of the twentieth century, to Björn M. Ólsen, the University of Iceland's first professor of Icelandic language and literature. Under the commanding leadership of Ólsen's successor, Sigurður Nordal, and strongly reinforced by the writings of other Icelandic scholars such as Einar Ól. Sveinsson and Jón Jóhannesson, the movement itself reached its full international momentum after the 1960s.[8]

The Icelandic school championed 'bookprose', a term derived from German *Buchprosa* and first employed by the Swiss scholar Andreas Heusler to denote belief in the written rather than the oral origin of the sagas. The theoretical positions of the bookprosists formed the foundation of saga studies in the second half of the twentieth century.[9] In particular, the forceful position of Sigurður Nordal has dominated the issue of the sagas' historical value. While serving from 1951 to 1957 as ambassador from his newly independent country to Denmark, he prepared a detailed position paper, aptly entitled 'The Historical Element in the Icelandic Family Sagas'.[10] Nordal's view leaves the historian (or any other social scientist) with little option but to ignore the sagas; it has successfully discouraged analysis of the social substance in the sagas and of indigenously derived creative elements in Icelandic society. In the past, scholars have disputed specifics in Nordal's arguments,[11] but the basic bookprosist position against historical use of the sagas remains intact, inhibiting the innovative kinds of socio-literary and socio-historical analysis which could deepen the study of saga and society.

It is informative to review some of Nordal's statements in order to understand the division among saga critics concerning the historical value of the sagas. According to Nordal, a historian's interest should be confined to the limited facts of a chronicle; as literature the sagas lie beyond the scope and competence of the historian:

A modern historian will for several reasons tend to brush these Sagas aside as historical records. He is generally suspicious of a long oral tradition, and the narrative will rather give him the impression of the art of a novelist than of the scrupulous dullness of a chronicler. Into the bargain, these Sagas deal principally with private lives and affairs which do not belong to history in its proper sense, not even the history of Iceland. The historian cuts the knot, and the last point alone would be sufficient to exempt him from further trouble. It is none of his business to study these sagas as literature, their origin, material and making.[12]

The modern reader may find this attitude to history limited, and perhaps even naive, but it was not so regarded when Nordal was formulating his position in the first half of the twentieth century. Nordal wrote at the end of a period during which scholars were attempting to separate truth from fantasy in early Norse sources. Time and energy were spent determining the veracity and the chronology of reported events in Scandinavia's earliest historical period. In order to determine the chronology of events in medieval Scandinavia, historians of the early twentieth century began implementing a stricter criticism of sources than had been practised in earlier studies. The Swedish historian Lauritz Weibull spearheaded this movement with a series of critical studies questioning a number of sources previously presumed reliable, among them the family sagas.[13]

Debates raged over small issues. Did the Icelander Kjartan Olafsson (in *Laxdæla saga*) have an affair with Princess Ingibjorg of Norway, sister of King Olaf Tryggvason, while she was being courted by a foreign prince? Was the description of the fight at Vínheiðr (in *Egils saga*) an accurate portrayal of the tenth-century battle between the English and the Scots at Brunanburh?[14] Nordal judges such red herrings, rather than the private lives and affairs of medieval people, to be the principal concern of historians.

Modern Nationalism and the Medieval Sagas

Determining the origin of the sagas was more than just an obscure academic question, yet hardly any attention has been directed to the relationship between the bookprose theory and Icelandic nationalism. An attempt to analyse the viewpoint of the Icelandic bookprosists is well served by taking into consideration the political climate at the time their theory was being formulated and propounded. The late nineteenth and the first half of the twentieth century in Iceland were marked by intense agitation for independence from Denmark. The island had not been independent since the end of the Free State in 1262–4; it was ruled first by the Norwegians and then, after 1380, by the Danes. At first foreign control was not particularly onerous.[15] Especially during the period of Norwegian suzerainty, Iceland functioned under its own code of laws and the Althing maintained a good measure of legislative power. There were some relatively prosperous periods in Iceland in the late Middle Ages when Scandinavian control over the island weakened and German and English merchants came for fish and sulphur. Later the country went through some dark periods, especially after the Protestant Reformation when the power of the Danish monarchy increased. By the end of the sixteenth century royal authority had taken on many characteristics of absolute rule, which in effect deprived the Althing of much of its legislative power. With the formal introduction of absolutism in 1662, all legislative power was officially vested in the Danish king, and the yearly Althing became a court of appeals until it was replaced in 1800 by a court in Reykjavík.

The eighteenth century was a low point in Icelandic history. The country was ravaged by an epidemic of smallpox and by famine brought on by volcanic eruptions. In 1801 the second largest island in Europe had only 47,000 inhabitants.[16] At the same time foreign dominance blocked Iceland's economic growth. The Danish trade monopoly, established in 1602, became by the middle of the eighteenth century oppressive and unresponsive to Iceland's needs. In the period 1783–5 famine claimed the lives of approximately one-fifth of the population, yet during the famine year of 1784 the island was required to export food. Trade policies instituted in Copenhagen continued to stunt economic development until well into the nineteenth century. Only in 1854 did the Icelanders begin to enjoy the same foreign trade rights as the Danes.[17]

Despite such problems the Icelanders managed over the centuries to hold on to their language, culture and literacy, and in the mid nineteenth century the situation began to change. In 1845 the Althing was re-established in Reykjavík as an advisory body. Although the king renounced absolutism in Denmark in 1848, for a time there was no similar diminution of royal authority in Iceland. The ensuing struggle, led for decades by Jón Sigurðsson (d. 1879), is narrated concisely by Thorkell Jóhannesson, professor of history at the University of Iceland in the first half of the twentieth century:

The Danes refused to recognize the justice of Iceland's claim for self-government while united with Denmark under the person of the king, a claim based on the ancient rights of the country first stipulated in the *Gamli sáttmáli* [the covenant of union with the king of Norway] in 1262. Drafts for an Icelandic constitution were frequently submitted by the Danish authorities, but the Althing, led by Jón Sigurðsson, remained firm in its demands. In 1871 the king at last issued an act defining the status of Iceland within the Danish realm, but the Icelanders refused to recognize its validity because they had not been consulted. In 1874 ... Iceland was granted a new and better constitution, although the Icelanders were by no means wholly satisfied. The

Althing was given legislative power conjointly with the Crown, domestic autonomy and control of the national finances. The executive authority in Iceland, however, was vested in the governor [*landshöfðingi*], but he was responsible to the Minister for Icelandic Affairs, who lived in Copenhagen and was answerable not to the Althing but to the Danish Rigsdag. Despite Icelandic dissatisfaction, the existence of a conservative government in Denmark until the end of the century prevented any further changes. In 1901 a liberal ministry took office in Denmark, with the result that in 1903 a Minister for Icelandic Affairs was appointed to reside in Reykjavík and to answer to the Althing. This was a great step forward, but the independence movement was now stronger than ever and dissension still continued.[18]

Towards the end of the nineteenth century towns began to grow in Iceland. In 1880 the country had only three townships, whose inhabitants together numbered 3,630 and accounted for only 5 per cent of the entire population.[19] With all its attendant problems and benefits, urbanization had progressed rapidly by 1920, when seven townships with 29,000 inhabitants between them accounted for 31 per cent of the total population.[20] Yet, despite the growth of towns, the island was largely a rural land of fishermen and farmers. The capital Reykjavík, with a population soon growing past 30,000, was the country's administrative and commercial centre, proud of its new university founded in 1911.

By 1918 Iceland had gained complete internal autonomy. The island's foreign affairs, however, continued to be conducted by Copenhagen, and the Danish king remained head of state. The country did not become completely independent until 1944, when it declared a final separation from Denmark just before the end of the Second World War. The movement for independence engendered a nationalistic phase which influenced many aspects of Icelandic cultural life in the twentieth century, including the socialist movement. One of the most renowned novels by Halldór Kiljan Laxness, *Sjálf-stætt fólk* (*Independent People*),[21] published in two volumes in 1934–5, was characteristic of many social and intellectual currents in Iceland between the wars. It both extolled the virtues of the nation and treated Icelandic nationalism with irony.[22] Nationalism spilled over into analyses of the national treasure, the family sagas.[23] A problem that stirred Icelandic intellectuals was how to remove the sagas from the realm of traditions of unlettered storytelling farmers and place them in the front rank of world literature while still contending that they were Icelandic in origin.

To provide the sagas with so rich a lustre was an uphill battle. Since the late Renaissance, educated Icelanders had been of two minds about the sagas. Some, probably the majority, including Icelandic scholars in Copenhagen such as Arngrímur Jónsson the Learned (lærði) and Árni Magnússon, the manuscript collector and scholar, venerated the stories. Others tended to look down on the native sagas as crude quasi-historical tales, hardly on a par with the great literary traditions of Europe. One scholarly eighteenth-century Icelander characterized the sagas as stories about 'farmers at fisticuffs [bændur flugust á]'.[24] Almost everyone considered them the product of an old oral tradition. By the twentieth century, however, perception of the sagas began to change among educated Icelanders. In particular, the bookprosists' view that the sagas are a written creation gained ascendancy.

At this time many Icelandic intellectuals lived in Reykjavík or Copenhagen. They frequently moved back and forth between the two cities, and many of them were strong nationalists. From this cultured urban milieu the bookprosists drew their leaders, who at times found themselves at odds with older scholars such as Finnur Jónsson and with the more conservative Icelandic farmers. The tone of the disagreement is discernible in Finnur Jónsson's statement, 'I will uphold and defend the historical reliability of the sagas, however "grand" this may sound, until I am forced to lay down my pen.'[25] The modern-day farmers, many of whom lived on the farmsteads mentioned by name in the sagas, also believed in the accuracy of the sagas, which they were in the habit of reading. Laxness, who won the Nobel Prize for Literature in 1955, playfully touches on this element of division among Icelanders in Atómstöðin (The Atom Station), a novel published in 1948, dealing with the tensions in

Icelandic society at this time. His main character, a young woman who was brought to Reykjavík from the countryside to be a maid in a wealthy household, says, 'I was taught never to believe a single word in the newspapers and nothing but what is found in the sagas.'[26]

The stakes were high. A defined literary origin for the sagas did more than furnish credibility for what Nordal describes as 'one of the most powerful literary movements in recorded history';[27] it equipped Iceland with a cultural heritage worthy of its status as an independent nation. Here the Icelandic intellectuals were following a well-established pattern: a similar development had occurred in several European countries in the nineteenth century. In Germany and Norway, for example, folk tales and fairy tales were embraced as a national heritage that could be appreciated by a literate culture. But the Icelanders were moving toward full independence in the twentieth century, and (particularly after the First World War) the nineteenth-century national romantic adoration of oral heritage was no longer flourishing. The bookprosists were influenced by the intellectual currents of their own day. They wrested the sagas from their base within oral culture and reinterpreted the origin and nature of the national texts in a manner compatible with contemporary literary criticism.

Nordal was, of course, aware that the sagas are not an ordinary medieval literature, yet he circumvented the issue of their historical content by concentrating on the far more limited issue of authorship. He justified the social content of the stories as satisfying the medieval audience's demand for the appearance of 'historical reality'. Within this limited context he believed that the artistic success of the writers lay in their ability to meet the audience's desire for realism. He never doubted that the thirteenth-century author was equipped for this undertaking, though he did not pursue the obvious implications of his statements:

Not only through their access to older written sources, but in certain other ways too, the writers of the Family Sagas were better off than might be expected when describing times so long past. The changes in the social and material conditions, in housing, clothes, weapons, seamanship, and so on, were not very remarkable from the tenth to the thirteenth century, and obvious anachronisms in such descriptions are rare. The writers were quite conscious of the distance in time, and they had a considerable historical sense.[28]

Nordal was quite right: medieval Icelandic society was marked by a strong element of cultural continuity. As it evolved from chiefdoms to a more stratified arrangement, Iceland – escaping as it did foreign invasion, religious wars, and rapid social or economic upheaval – was at most points in its history part of an unusually stable cultural continuum.[29] From the eleventh century the island gradually entered into less marginal membership in the distant and richer European medieval culture, losing its self-confident and secure position in the more parochial Norse world. Change came most quickly in the thirteenth century, with periods of political disequilibrium particularly from the 1230s to the 1260s.[30] Despite the turmoil caused by these changes, Iceland remained completely rural, with the majority of the population scattered in accordance with the centuries-old settlement pattern, based on family landholding. The country retained much of its traditional law, culture and social structure throughout the transition leading to Norwegian control, and even beyond the end of the Free State.

Conclusions

Past theories have not treated the sagas as representations of the social processes of medieval Iceland. The early Icelanders, during the two centuries when their culture was completely oral, were intelligent and capable enough to establish an efficient system of courts, laws and institutions widely variant from those they had known in their homelands. If we acknowledge these achievements, then we must also admit the likelihood that they could develop a form of narrative suitable for telling stories about themselves and about important events in their daily lives and in the life of their society. The sagas are not like contemporary European histories or chronicles written in Latin; they are stories that tell of feuds, horse fights and conflicts over shared hayfields, love, dowries, taunts, and the like. They are an indigenous development, the product of a long tradition of storytelling which responded in both pre-literate and literate times, to the particular needs of Iceland's insular population.[31]

The various small stories that together form a saga are linked by the logic of dispute, the pulls of obligation and the brokering of aid. They reveal the different ways in which disputes were started and resolved in medieval Iceland. Within this context saga-tellers were able to develop character and to explore new ideas brought in from Europe. They were free to consider all aspects of social intercourse in their culture, including the ramifications of love, the souring of friendship, and the development of new concepts. The context was sufficiently broad to include Christian concepts and beliefs. Beginning in the late twelfth century and ending in the early fourteenth, saga-writing became a national passion in Iceland. As new and often foreign elements became important to the society, they too were incorporated into this creative form of narration, thus enriching the oral saga as it was transformed into a written genre.

The arguments that the sagas could not be both oral and sophisticated are based on a form of long-discredited anthropological reductionism which maintains that without writing people lack the ability to produce complex oral narratives. Whereas in the past it was assumed that the introduction of reading and writing was in itself an overwhelming cultural change,[32] evidence from the post-colonial world has given us a wider perspective from which to assess the transition of cultural elements from an oral to a written state.[33] One does not have to look outside medieval Iceland for proof that adaptation to writing was rapid. Sometime between 1140 and 1180 an unknown Icelandic grammarian wrote an essay that has come to be called 'The First Grammatical Treatise'.[34] This vernacular book, which provided a modified Latin alphabet for Icelandic as well as an accurate, phonologically based system of orthography, was written 'in order to make easier writing and reading which have now become common in this land'.[35]

Throughout this book I examine certain sagas for information about social behaviour, social patterning, and economic and environmental issues. These same texts have long been analysed for their literary nature and structure. Instead of demanding that one field of inquiry overshadow the other, it is far more productive to acknowledge the complementary possibilities of different approaches. The sagas are indisputably a major literature. They are at the same time the indigenous social documentation of a medieval people, and as such they contribute a wealth of information about the functioning of a tradition-bound island culture.

15. The Locations of the Family Sagas. The following maps show the geographical locations of the family sagas (*Íslendingasögur*). Included are the major short stories (*þættir*, sing. *þáttr*) that take place in Iceland.

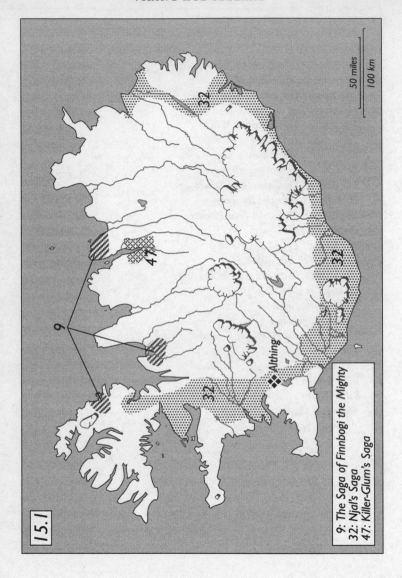

15.1

50 miles
100 km

Althing

9: The Saga of Finnbogi the Mighty
32: Njal's Saga
47: Killer-Glum's Saga

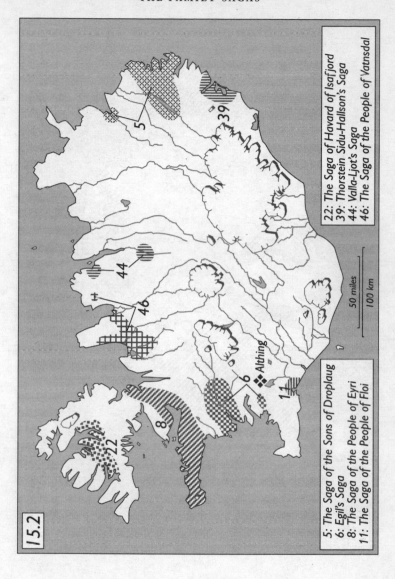

15.2

5: The Saga of the Sons of Droplaug
6: Egil's Saga
8: The Saga of the People of Eyri
11: The Saga of the People of Floi

22: The Saga of Havard of Isafjord
39: Thorstein Sidu-Hallson's Saga
44: Valla-Ljot's Saga
46: The Saga of the People of Vatnsdal

Althing

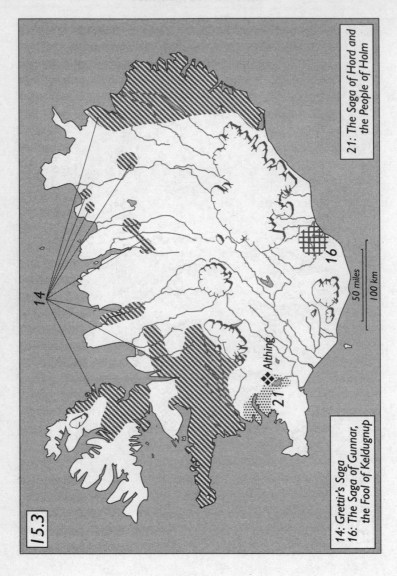

15.3

21: The Saga of Hord and
the People of Holm

14: Grettir's Saga
16: The Saga of Gunnar,
the Fool of Keldugnup

50 miles
100 km

Althing

14

16

21

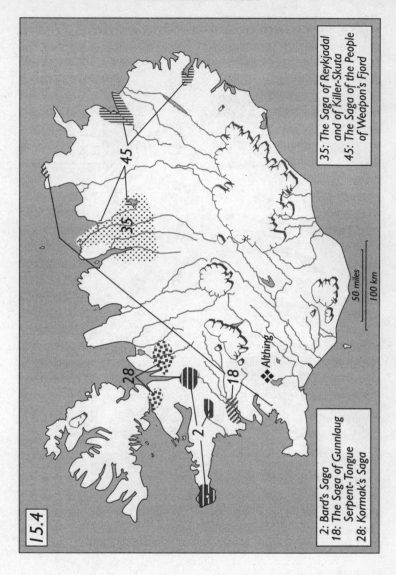

15.4

35: The Saga of Reykjadal
and of Killer-Skuta
45: The Saga of the People
of Weapon's Fjord

Althing

50 miles
100 km

2: Bard's Saga
18: The Saga of Gunnlaug
Serpent-Tongue
28: Kormak's Saga

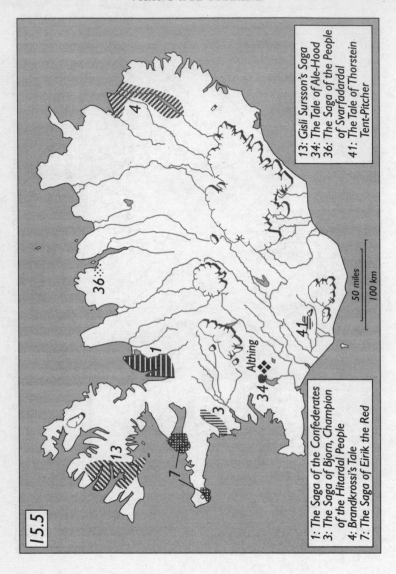

15.5

13: Gisli Sursson's Saga
34: The Tale of Ale-Hood
36: The Saga of the People
     of Svarfadardal
41: The Tale of Thorstein
     Tent-Pitcher

1: The Saga of the Confederates
3: The Saga of Bjorn, Champion
   of the Hitardal People
4: Brandkrossi's Tale
7: The Saga of Eirik the Red

Althing

50 miles
100 km

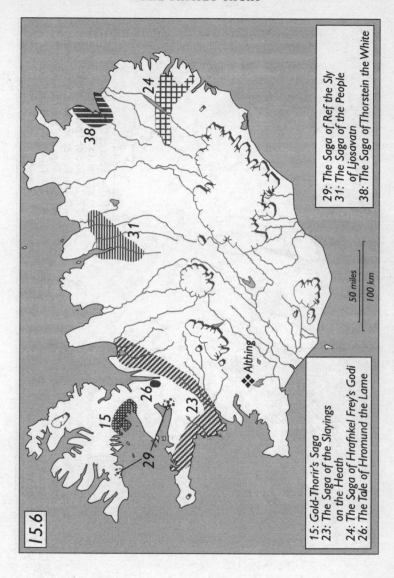

15.6

24
38
31
Althing
15
26
29
23

50 miles
100 km

29: The Saga of Ref the Sly
31: The Saga of the People
    of Ljosavatn
38: The Saga of Thorstein the White

15: Gold-Thorir's Saga
23: The Saga of the Slayings
    on the Heath
24: The Saga of Hrafnkel Frey's Godi
26: The Tale of Hromund the Lame

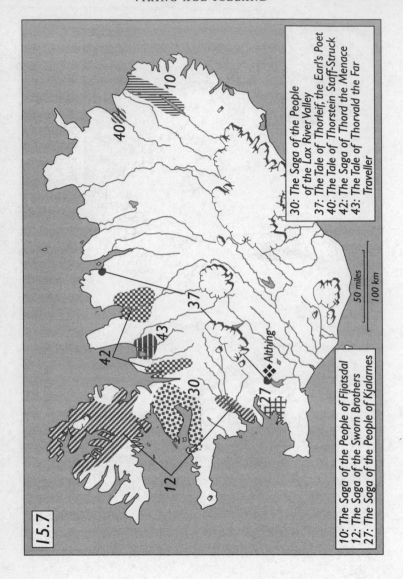

15.7

10: The Saga of the People of the Lax River Valley
37: The Tale of Thorleif, the Earl's Poet
40: The Tale of Thorstein Staff-Struck
42: The Saga of Thord the Menace
43: The Tale of Thorvald the Far Traveller

10: The Saga of the People of Fljotsdal
12: The Saga of the Sworn Brothers
27: The Saga of the People of Kjalarnes

Althing

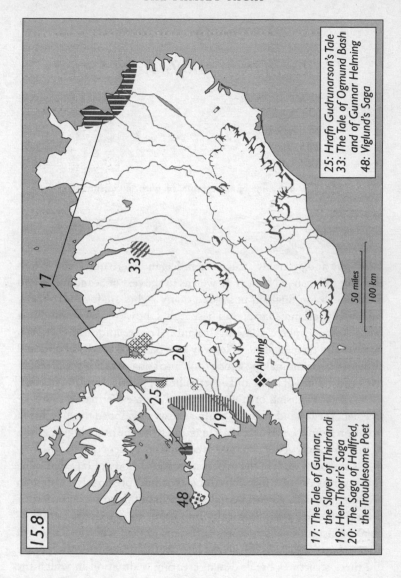

15.8

25: Hrafn Gudrunarson's Tale
33: The Tale of Ogmund Bash
      and of Gunnar Helming
48: Viglund's Saga

17

33

50 miles
100 km

20

25

Althing

19

48

17: The Tale of Gunnar,
      the Slayer of Thidrandi
19: Hen-Thorir's Saga
20: The Saga of Hallfred,
      the Troublesome Poet

9

The Legislative and Judicial System

> With law must our land be built, or with lawlessness laid
> waste.
>
> *Njal's Saga*, Chapter 70

The court and assembly structures in Iceland were unusually extensive, but freemen in Norway as well as in the rest of Scandinavia and in Anglo-Saxon England possessed many rights analogous to those enjoyed by Icelandic farmers. These rights, however, were valid in a more limited sphere than in Iceland. The relationship between farmers and their leaders in Norway was part of a local and national system of decision-making which took into consideration the prerogatives and designs of kings and other military, political and, later, clerical leaders. Focusing on the traditional Norse-Germanic rights of freemen, the Icelanders in the tenth century developed those rights in isolation from the privileges of kings and from the other higher strata of Viking society. They expanded the ancient concept of the local freemen's assembly and, in the process, created a body of law that in its entirety was distinct from anything that had previously existed in Scandinavia. This governmental system maintained social order for several hundred years. Critically important to it was the establishment of institutional structures sufficient to deal with the danger of inter-group conflicts.[1] Only in the late twelfth and thirteenth century did these structures break down, creating a situation in which the Norwegian Crown could successfully claim hegemony over Iceland.[2]

Thing: *Assemblies*

All Icelandic things (assemblies) were *skapthing*,[3] meaning that they were governed by established procedure and met at regular, legally designated intervals at predetermined meeting places. Except for the *leið* (discussed below), no special announcement was required for meetings of the different things. We do know that the *goðar* were officially responsible for seeing to the upkeep of the earliest local things, but we do not know the composition of the assemblies and their courts before the constitutional reforms of the 960s. After these reforms the design of the different meetings becomes much clearer, as both assemblies and courts are discussed in *Grágás*. From the beginning, however, the most important local assembly was the springtime thing (*várthing*) which met each year in May and might last a week. At these assemblies cases of local farmers and chieftains were tried, if they could not be settled out of court. Three local chieftains were responsible for each *várthing*, and by law all their thingmen were required to attend. By the mid tenth century there were perhaps twelve springtime assemblies, distributed rather evenly around the perimeter of the country. Only two of them, the Kjalarnes Thing and the Thórsnes Thing, are known to have preceded the establishment of the Althing. After the island was divided into quarters (*c.* 965), a thirteenth *várthing*, along with three additional *goðorð*, was added in the Northern Quarter.

The *várthing* were divided into two parts, courts of prosecution (*sóknarthing*) and courts of payment or panels for dealing with debts (*skuldathing*). Each assembly began with the court hearings and judgements of the *sóknarthing*. After four days the *skuldathing* opened with people settling debts and putting values on goods traded within the district. The *goði* named twelve *bændr* who served on the panels of judges, bodies that acted much like juries. As chieftains took no official part in the judicial process beyond naming the twelve judges, they were free to participate in litigation and out-of-court manoeuvrings. The *várthing* was empowered to set the local value

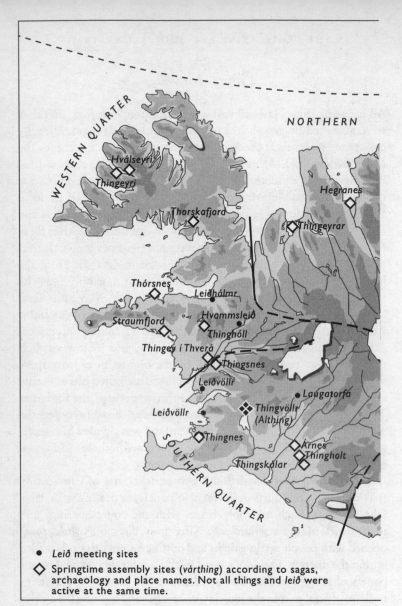

Leið meeting sites ●

Springtime assembly sites (*várthing*) according to sagas,
archaeology and place names. Not all things and *leið* were
active at the same time. ◇

16. **Quarter Boundaries and Assembly Sites During the Free State** (*c.* 930–1264). The broken lines mark the boundaries between the quarters. The names of the things are not identical with the names of the places they were held (see Illustration 9).

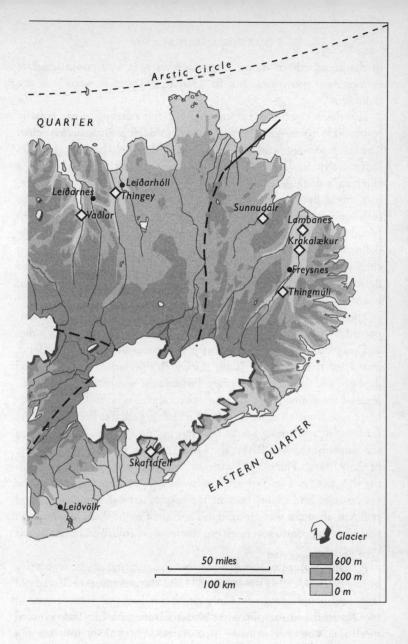

QUARTER

Arctic Circle

Leiðarnes

Leiðarhóll
Thingey

Vaðlar

Sunnudálr

Lambanes

Krakalækur

Freysnes

Thingmúli

EASTERN QUARTER

Skaftafell

Leiðvöllr

Glacier

50 miles

100 km

600 m
200 m
0 m

of the standardized ounce (*thinglagseyrir*). It also could legislate certain local provisions, but to what extent and in what way are unknown.[4]

The three chieftains responsible for the *várthing* were equally responsible for the *leið*, the autumn assembly, usually held in August. The *leið* had no judicial function and could be held by each chieftain individually, in which case the meeting was attended largely by a chieftain's thingmen. Its official purpose was to report to those who had stayed home what had taken place at the summer Althing and to announce any new laws. The *leið* meeting had an additional function within the context of the political economy. It publicly defined who a chieftain's thingmen were at the conclusion of that summer's dispute season. The group noted thingmen who had defected during the season when push had come to shove, and counted the current membership.

The Althing was the annual meeting of all *goðar*, each accompanied by some of his thingmen. This crucial gathering, which met at Thingvöllr (the Thing Plain) in the south-western part of the island, lasted for two weeks in June, during the period of uninterrupted daylight and the mildest weather. Its business was more than governance of the country. At the time when travel was easiest, hundreds of people from all over Iceland, including pedlars, brewers of ale, tradesmen, and young adults advertising for spouses, converged on the banks of the Axe River, the Öxará, which runs through the site of the Althing. Thingvöllr, with its large lake and the mountains in the distance, is a site of great natural beauty. For two weeks the ravines and lava plains became a national capital. Friendships and political alliances were initiated, continued or broken; information was passed; promises were given; stories were told; and business was transacted.

A major feature of the Althing was the meeting of the legislative or law council, called the *lögrétta*.[5] Here the chieftains reviewed old laws and made new ones. Only chieftains had the right to vote in the *lögrétta*, and each brought two advisers with him into council meetings. When two or more men shared a chieftaincy only one at a time attended the *lögrétta* and performed the chieftain's other official duties at the Althing. The *lögrétta* was also empowered to grant exemptions from the law. It acted for the country in foreign affairs by making treaties, such as the one with the Norwegian King Olaf Haraldsson (1015–30) delineating the status of Icelanders in Norway and of Norwegians in Iceland.

Formal government at the Althing was public. The *lögrétta* and the courts were held in the open air. At the *lögrétta* the participants sat on benches arranged in three concentric circles. The *goðar* occupied the benches of the middle circle while their advisers sat on the inner and outer benches. In this way each chieftain sat with one adviser in front of him and another behind him. The only fixed buildings at Thingvöllr were a small church, built after the conversion, and a farm. A second small church was added, probably in 1118. Most people pitched tents, but *goðar* and other important personages maintained turf booths from year to year; these they roofed with homespun for the duration of the meeting.

From the beginning of the Free State until its end the only significant national official was the law-speaker (*lögsögumaðr*), who was elected chairman of the *lögrétta* for a three-year term. Annually at the Law Rock (*lögberg*) the law-speaker recited a third of the laws from memory. Attendance at this ceremony was required of each *goði* or two stand-ins, selected from among the advisers at the *lögrétta*.[6] They and other interested people sat on the surrounding grassy slope, probably offering emendations or corrections and taking part in discussions of legal issues. Among other duties, the law-speaker had to announce publicly any laws passed by the *lögrétta*. When needed, the *lögrétta* could also call on the law-speaker to furnish any part of the law its members needed in considering legislation. If faced with a difficult point of law or a lapse of memory the law-speaker was required to consult five or more legal experts (*lögmenn*).[7]

Although the position of law-speaker was prestigious, it brought little or no official power to its holder, who was allowed to take sides and to participate in litigation and in feuds as a private citizen. We do not know to what extent the law-speaker decided what to recite, and the choice may have provided him with some leverage. Since the law-speaker functioned as an authority prepared to answer questions only when asked, it was the duty of the individual to learn the proper questions. To a large degree, knowledge of these came through the telling of stories about dispute, feud, legal cases and settlements arranged in and out of court. The names and duties of the law-speakers are preserved in the sources. Ari the Learned dates events by naming the current law-speaker. (A list of the law-speakers and their dates is given in Appendix 1.)

The position of 'supreme chieftain' (*allsherjargoði*) was largely ceremonial. It carried with it the duties of hallowing the Althing and setting boundaries for the different sections of the assembly area. The hallowing marked the official opening of the assembly. The position of *allsherjargoði* was held by the individual who owned the hereditary *goðorð* of Thorstein Ingolfsson, the son of Iceland's first settler, Ingolf Arnarson. It is possible that the honour was given to Thorstein and his descendants in recognition of services rendered at the time the Althing was established.

The constitutional reforms of the mid 960s were carried out in the wake of a serious clash between two powerful chiefs, Thord gellir (the Bellower) and Tungu-Odd (Odd from the Tongue Lands).[8] As a consequence of the court system's inability to contain the violence of this conflict, the Icelanders reorganized the judicial system so that the courts could more successfully regulate feud. The original law had specified that a case of manslaughter be tried at the local assembly nearest the scene of the killing. This arrangement seems to have worked in regulating disputes among individuals who lived within a thing district, but a defendant from outside the district could hardly expect to have his rights upheld in the home territory of his accuser. To remedy this potential for disorder, the law was altered. Such cases were now permitted to be brought to the Althing where four new courts, one for each quarter, were established. We catch a glimpse of this development in Ari's *Book of the Icelanders* (Chapter 2):

A great lawsuit occurred at the thing between Thord gellir, the son of Olaf Feilan from Breiðafjord, and Odd, the one who was called Tungu-Odd; he was from Borgarfjord . . . They first brought suits against each other at the local thing which was in Borgarfjord at that place which since is called Thingnes. At that time it was the law that suits for manslaughter were required to be brought before that thing which was nearest to the place where the manslaughter had been committed. But they fought there, and the assembly could not be carried on according to the law . . . Thereafter the case was brought before the Althing and there again they fought . . .

Then Thord gellir delivered a speech at the Law Rock concerning how badly it suited men to go to things outside their local regions in order to sue for manslaughter or for other injuries. He related what had happened to him before he was able to bring this case to law. He said that many in their turn would experience difficulties if this matter was not remedied. Then the country was divided into quarters, so that three things were established in each quarter where thingmen should bring their own lawsuits.

With the island divided into quarters, four new quarter courts (fjórð-ungsdómar; sing. fjórðungsdómr; dómr means court) were established at the Althing. These met yearly and were courts of first instance. This meant that individuals from any quarter could begin an action at the Althing rather than at a local várthing as long as the matter was of more than minimal consequence. The quarter courts also served as appellate courts: a case that was deadlocked at a vár-thing could be referred to that region's quarter court at the Althing.

Dividing the island into quarters was a change that required fixing the number of full chieftaincies at thirty-nine. The Western, Southern and Eastern quarters each held three fixed springtime assemblies under joint control of three chieftains, making a total of nine chieftains in each quarter. At the same time a fourth várthing was added to the Northern Quarter. The combination of geographical conditions and the needs of people in Iceland's most populous quarter required four assemblies, one more than in each of the other quarters. Ari the Learned also speaks about this development:

THE ALTHING

This systematic picture of the Althing's legislative and judicial functions and their relationship to other governmental structures is based on information found principally in the thirteenth-century lawbooks. In reality Iceland did not operate so systematically.

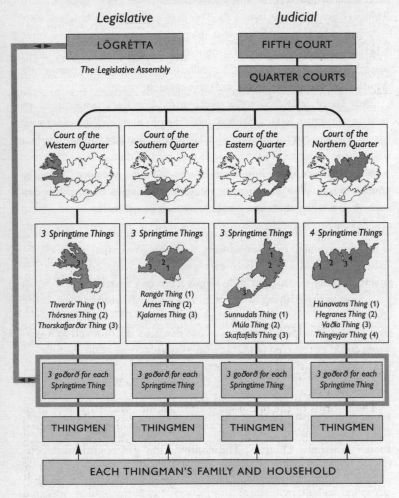

9. The Governmental Structure.

However, in the Northern Quarter, there were four things, because they could not reach any other agreement. Those living north of Eyjafjord were not willing to go there to attend the thing. Likewise, those who lived to the west of Skagafjord were unwilling to go there.

The Northern Quarter thus had twelve *goðar*, although its three new chieftains were not empowered to appoint judges to the quarter courts. To maintain a balance of power among the quarters at the Althing, the title of *goði* was conferred upon three new chieftains each from the Eastern, Western and Southern quarters, bringing the total number of *goðar* to forty-eight. These nine new *goðar* sat in the national legislative assembly but were not allowed to nominate judges to the quarter courts or even to take part in the local assemblies as chieftains.[9]

Through these measures the Icelanders, after a trial period of three decades, remedied the most serious inadequacies of the original system of government. The presence of such an extensive court system did not mean that all disputes were resolved in court. Many, perhaps even a majority, were not. The courts set a standard to which out-of-court arbitrations and other resolutions adhered, and a legalistic settlement could be reached even though a case was not formally adjudicated. If a private, negotiated solution could not be achieved, then one of the parties could turn to the public arena of the courts. That such action would involve third parties in what were otherwise personal affairs was a factor that encouraged private settlement. The sagas often present us with cases stemming from intractable dispute and escalating feud, but most dispute settlement was routine, not worthy of a saga.

The reforms of the mid 960s reaffirmed the essentially decentralized nature of the earlier governmental and judicial structures, based as they were on the relationship of mutual dependency between chieftain and farmer. The more centralized judicial system resulting from the reforms is the one we know from the laws and the sagas. It provided Iceland with legal and judicial structures which operated as a balanced system. Each *goði* had approximately an equal number

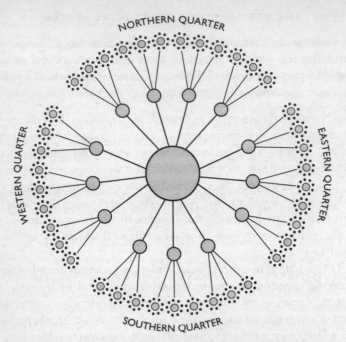

NORTHERN QUARTER

WESTERN QUARTER

EASTERN QUARTER

SOUTHERN QUARTER

10. An Alternative Concept of the Governmental Structure of Free State Iceland.
How did the medieval Icelanders conceive of their governmental institutions?
They surely understood regions and compass directions, but it is doubtful that
they had a firm geographical picture of the island as presented on modern maps
of Iceland. Likewise, the flow-chart model found in the preceding illustration is a
modern construction based on the probably too systematic information found in
the law books. The diagram above is more organic. Circles of differing size show
the central Althing, the local assemblies in each quarter, and the chieftains (who
were more numerous than the number shown) surrounded by their thingmen. Its
elements of symbolic design (Jon Høyer 1997) may come close to showing how
early Icelanders conceived of the interlocking nature of their government and
their society.

The image presents a restrained connection with geography. At the same time,
it provides a picture of the public channels of decision-making, whereby decisions
initiated at the Althing moved to the fringes. Actions from the local districts also
worked their way to the centre, passing through concentric rings of authority.
Without the need for literacy, the design visualizes Viking Age Iceland's political
economy, in which the *goðar* served as local 'big men' or leaders of interest
groups, offering services and gathering the consensus of their thingmen. As part
of the unitary island-wide system, the Althing was connected to the four quarters,
each with its own local springtime assemblies (thirteen in all).

of thingmen, and the widely dispersed springtime assemblies served approximately equal numbers of local inhabitants. Local groups from any part of the country had equal access to the central Althing, where proportion was also maintained in the balance of chieftains and judges from the different quarters.

The Althing system made Iceland into one legal community: it was a maximal group which had the obligation to end fighting by peaceful settlement and the machinery to arrange such resolutions. The *goðar* and their non-tribal cluster of followers formed the major sub-groupings within this political and legally defined world. (Chapters 11 and 12 discuss how this arrangement affected the type of feud practised.)

Yet another intermediary assembly existed. Called the quarter assembly (*fjórðungathing*), this thing was devoted entirely to the legal affairs of each quarter and was a further innovation instituted some time after the reforms of the mid 960s. The four *fjórðungathing*, about which there is little information, were overshadowed by the courts at the Althing. Although it is generally held that they were soon discontinued, some scholars such as Ólafur Lárusson have argued that they functioned for a longer period than has been assumed.[10] The quarter assemblies are not counted among the regularly convened assemblies. *Grágás* names them only once and does not mention them as having been regularly constituted.[11]

People quickly came to regard the quarter courts at the Althing as better suited than the local assemblies to solve serious problems. A case was normally heard in the court of the quarter in which the defendant was domiciled. Built into this system of annual Althing courts was the concept of impartiality, embracing an intense desire to avoid partisanship. The sources are unclear as to whether thirty-six judges sat in each of the four courts at the Althing or whether a total of thirty-six judges were chosen for all the *fjórðungsdómar*.[12] Since the courts at the *várthing* had thirty-six judges, most experts now believe that the quarter courts at the Althing had the same number.

The panel of judges functioned as a kind of jury, with the power to examine facts, weigh evidence and deliver a verdict. The national character of the Althing courts is apparent in the composition of the panel of judges. The holders of the 'old and full chieftaincies', as the thirty-six pre-reform *goðorð* came to be known, each nominated judges from their own assembly districts. These judges, required to be free males at least twelve years of age, to have a fixed domicile and to be responsible for their commitments and oaths, were then apparently assigned by lot to each of the quarter courts.[13] An individual who initiated an action at the Althing or a person who was summoned there thus entered one of four courts, whose panels of judges were drawn from all four geographical divisions of the country.

The Althing convened on a Thursday evening, and on the following day all judges were appointed. On Saturday the nominees could be challenged and disqualified for various reasons, such as kinship. The process, governed throughout by strict rules of procedure, was open to public scrutiny. The system of seating judges further discouraged regionalism: farmers became acquainted with issues and disputes in other quarters, and decisions were standardized throughout the country. In this way a large segment of the politically important population took part in the decision-making process. Verdicts had to be almost unanimous to avoid legal deadlocks: if six or more judges were in disagreement the case was legally deadlocked. In that event the panel entered two opposing judgements, each favouring one party to the dispute. No legal resolution was possible until a court of appeals was later established. Although every freeman had access to the courts, success in judicial cases often depended on a litigant's ability to muster political support. Settlements usually required negotiations among influential individuals, especially *goðar*.

Because a consensus at court was not always possible, after another forty years (*c.* 1005) the court system of the Althing was again altered by the establishment of a court of appeals, called the Fifth Court (*fimtardómr*). As in the other courts, the jury was composed of farmers.[14] The new addition proved to be effective as a court of last instance, in which verdicts were determined by a simple majority. Establishment of the Fifth Court was the penultimate reform of the governmental structure in the Old Icelandic Free State; the final alteration was to expand membership in the *lögrétta* to include the two Icelandic bishops, who, unlike the *goðar*, were not permitted to bring advisers with them.

The regularity and the dependability of the Icelandic courts reveal the society's desire that parties quickly find acceptable and publicly approved solutions to disputes. The courts had another function, of equal importance. Both local and Althing courts offered Icelandic leaders an outlet for their ambitions. To a large extent the events at these courts reflected the political climate of the country, and because their solutions were based on agreement, they brought workable solutions to problems that otherwise could have been disruptive. Farmers and chieftains met there to settle differences, to broker their power, and to advocate the positions of those individuals whose cases they were supporting. Legal assemblies became political arenas where leaders contested with one another for status.

Options

The presence of elaborate court and assembly structures gave the individual Icelander many alternatives in handling a grievance. Ideally, two individuals could resolve personal differences by compromise. One party to a dispute might offer self-judgement or *sjálfdæmi*, allowing the other party to fix the terms of the settlement. *Sjálfdæmi* was granted when the party offering it assumed that the opponent would act with moderation, or when the opponent was so strong that he could demand the right to set the terms. *Hólmganga*, formal duelling, and *einvígi*, unregulated single combat, were used less frequently as direct methods of resolving disputes.[15] The duel was outlawed at the beginning of the eleventh century, probably because it embodied outdated values incompatible with the system of negotiation and compromise which by then had become firmly entrenched.

An injured party frequently had other options. For instance, the aggrieved could engage in manslaughter or even a protracted blood feud. More so than in other types of action, resort to blood vengeance depended on the support of kinsmen. Hoping, perhaps, to avoid the consequences of blood feud or to end a feud, an individual could turn to the formal legal system with its prescribed rules for summoning, pleading, announcing, and so on. Then there was the less formal option of arbitration, which tended to introduce into a quarrel the influence of new, often more neutral parties. Each of these techniques of settling disputes could be interconnected. For example, arbitrated settlements were most effective when announced (published) at an assembly, and many court cases were, as Andreas Heusler has noted, a stylized form of feud.[16] At different times contending parties might be involved in all aspects of settlement including violence, legal redress and arbitration.

The close connection between political and legal success in Iceland was owing in part to the institutionalized concept that the government bore no responsibility for punishing an individual for breaking the law. Criminal acts were regarded as private concerns to be settled between the injured and the offending parties or their advocates. Penalties could be restitutions or fines paid in the form of damages to the successful party. The duty to exact vengeance in cases of manslaughter fell on the kin of the slain, who, if they wished to act, had to choose among the different available methods of processing a claim. Far less than a duty, violence was an option.

10

Systems of Power:
Advocates, Friendship, and
Family Networks

Immediately after receiving the legal summons, Thorir Akraskegg rode to meet with Thorir Helgason. He told the chieftain what had happened and asked for help – 'because I am
your thingman'.

Thorir Helgason answered, 'I am hesitant to get involved
with you, but I may give you some support.' He rebuked
Thorir Akraskegg for his quarrels and wrongdoing.

'I will,' said Thorir Akraskegg, 'give you gifts of friendship
[*vingjafar*] if you will throw your support behind me in this
matter.'

The Saga of the People of Ljosavatn (Ljósvetninga saga),

Chapter 14

Chieftains had an advantage over farmers in being closer to the inner
workings of the legal system, an advantage that was sustained by the
workings of justice in medieval Iceland. The courts were less likely
to base judgements on the evidence than to adjust decisions to satisfy
the honour and resources of powerful individuals. Icelandic society
acknowledged the legal rights of the free farmers but provided no
formal executive institutions to enforce those rights. Farmers
involved in conflict and unable to enforce their own claims turned to
advocates, especially *goðar*, who had power at their disposal and
superior opportunities to manipulate the legal system. An ordinary

bóndi had little chance of success in facing opponents of substance without the help of advocates such as *goðar*. With their stake in maintaining the status quo, the *goðar* dealt in power politics, influencing the course of conflict resolution. Participating as advocates, both aggressively and defensively, permitted them to influence the behaviour of others while enjoying the sanction of public opinion.[1]

As the *goðar* were not territorial lords, the question remains: what were they? The answer is that they were leaders of interest groups that were continually jockeying with one another for status. These negotiations, political manoeuvrings and compromises, strikingly portrayed in the family and Sturlunga sagas, followed a pattern of action in which leading individuals, whether prominent *bændr* or *goðar*, gained their own ends by intervening on behalf of others. As advocates they gave counsel, functioned as lawyers and, in extreme circumstances, were willing to fight.

Advocacy

Advocacy was third-party intervention. It took different forms and had both overt and covert functions. The overt function was to provide clients and their leaders with a mechanism for arriving at a consensus necessary to settle disputes in a way that satisfied law and honour. The covert function was to allow leaders to maintain or increase their own power. *Goðar* were especially well placed to participate in advocacy. They played Iceland's proto-democratic game of upholding rights through open disputing, but anyone who was asked could be an advocate. The trick was to be a successful one. Advocacy became the keystone of a system of reciprocal arrangements in which people carefully kept track of assistance rendered, and balanced the books of obligations. The social fabric depended upon the maintenance of this balance, a process that forms the basis of much of the action in the sagas.

Some advocates made better use of their advantage than others. Their fame rested on their ability to mediate and to use the law intelligently on behalf of themselves and of others. Through the mechanisms of advocacy, *goðar* and some *bændr* acquired lands and received gifts. Success bred success, and the better an individual's reputation for bringing about advantageous settlements, the more often questions of inheritance, prosecution and mediation were submitted to him. As Preben Meulengracht Sørensen has noted, 'It was to the farmers' own advantage to be thingmen of those *goðar* who could best look after their interests, and the more thingmen that a *goði* could turn up with, the stronger his position at the thing and in armed conflicts.'[2]

Arriving at an assembly with a large following was more than a display of status. It might be profitable. Consider the account from *Ljósvetninga saga* (Chapter 10) where two chieftains, Eyjolf Gudmundarson and Thorvard Hoskuldsson, are locked in a desperate struggle. One of Thorvard's followers has killed Eyjolf's brother, and Eyjolf prepares a case. Each of the rival chieftains offers to pay other *goðar* in return for support. Eyjolf, who is very wealthy, offers his 'friend' (see *vinfengi* or friendship, below), the chieftain Gellir Thorkelsson, one ounce of silver (*eyrir silfrs*, one-eighth of a mark) for each man plus half a mark for each chieftain whom Gellir can bring with him to the Hegranes Thing (Chapter 15 [25]).* Further, Eyjolf offers a gold ring to the chieftain Skegg-Broddi. Thorvard, who is less wealthy, also sends a gold ring to Skegg-Broddi. In this example, the 'friendship' of a chieftain and his thingmen was for sale.

---

* Events described later in the saga show that the two chieftains, although 'friends', did not really trust each other (Ch. 17 [27]). The different chapter numbers refer to the two major manuscripts of the saga.

The Role of Kinship

The advocacy system, together with the temporary interest groups that gathered around Icelandic leaders, diluted the strength of kinship bonds. Kinship arrangements were highly egocentric, and kinsmen in the same region might be attached to different and sometimes rival *goðar*. At times they might switch from one advocate to another. Shifting allegiances clouded loyalties during feuds and legal actions; the sagas frequently show kinsmen on opposing sides of feuds.

Families were basically nuclear with thing-tax-paying farmers and their wives living in their own households and forming independent units of production and consumption. Kinship centred on categories of kinsmen rather than on corporate groups, a feature, as is discussed later, which had a marked effect on the kind of feud practised. The sagas often distinguish between blood kinsmen (*frændr*) and the nearest male relatives by marriage, such as fathers-, brothers- and sons-in-law (*mágar*).* Fictive kinship bonds complemented these relationships. They were formed when individuals, after a ritual blending of blood, became, for example, foster-brothers (*fóstbróðir*),† sworn brothers (*svarabróðir*) or oath brothers (*eiðbróðir*). In the sagas such arrangements, usually including obligations to take vengeance, were frequently more reliable than blood ties.

In Iceland's individualistic society, blood and non-blood kinship served principally to form a network of pre-established relationships that could be mobilized according to the talents and resources of the individual. An Icelander could primarily expect support from his nearest relatives – parents, children, siblings, maternal and paternal uncles, and brothers-in-law. Except in matters of domestic conduct, such as incest, kinship in Iceland was a malleable concept. For

---

* *Mágar* (sing. *mágr*, fem. *mágkonur*) constituted a category of *sifjar*, a broader term designating general relationship by marriage. *Frændsemi* (blood relationship) is contrasted with *sifjar* (affinity).

† *Fóstbróðir* also referred to men who were brought up together.

example, there was no proscription, or rule, against close cooperation among those related only by marriage, with the result that in-laws often cooperated against consanguine relatives in legal matters and in feud. This situation would be very unusual in a society that used kinship as a principle for organizing political and legal relations (for example, in so-called patrilineal societies).

Reflecting a distinct patrilineal emphasis, the laws of wergild (compensation for manslaughter), known as *Baugatal*,[3] seem to be very old.* They presuppose a society, such as Norway's, which was to a greater extent than Iceland's organized around groups that traced their descent through the male line, and they are at variance with the information provided in the sagas about how Icelandic society operated. It is not surprising that older concepts of social, political and kinship organization, such as elements of *Baugatal*, were carried to Iceland. These concepts served as a point of departure for the new society, and to a certain extent remnants of all imported concepts remained operative throughout the history of the Free State and beyond. However, the new associations that emerged in Iceland could not be based on traditional Norse corporate groups because only a few individuals from these groups migrated. Furthermore, the settlers claimed land individually. In order to defend his patrimony from encroachment the landowner in the early period had to look to anyone capable of lending support – cognates (relatives through either parent), in-laws, or non-kin landowners who would find an advantage in lending assistance. In the situation of a developed social group in a frontier setting, support for maintaining landownership claims was the crucial issue in the early period. Political associations provided this support more readily than kinship groupings. Reciprocity was widespread and advocacy was systematized. Talent in

---

* *Baugatal* means 'a list' (*tal*) 'of arm-rings' (*bauga*, the genitive plural of the masculine strong noun *baugr*). *Baugr* also had the meaning of money, since precious metals were often rolled into spiral-formed rings, and pieces cut off these and weighed were used as a medium of payment. In Old Icelandic legal usage the payment of wergild was often simply called *baugr*, hence the naming of the section of *Grágás* listing the different sums to be paid to different relatives for killings.

acquiring allies rather than reliance on an external rule of law defined through kinship or through the *goði*–thingman relationship determined how well one would fare in a crisis. This is the social background to the system of wealth accumulation that rewarded politically able individuals.

A Balancing Act

Success in maintaining reciprocal agreements and playing the role of advocate required conformity to a standard of moderation, termed *hóf*. An individual who observed this standard was called a *hófsmaðr*, a person of justice and temperance. *The Saga of Gunnlaug Serpent-Tongue* tells of the successful and revered chieftain Thorstein Egilsson. The great-grandson of the Norwegian landowner Kveldulf and the son of the Viking warrior-poet Egil Skalla-Grimsson, he is described in the following way (Chapter 1):

There was a man named Thorstein. He was the son of Egil, the son of Skallagrim, the son of Kveldulf, a chieftain from Norway; and Thorstein's mother was named Asgerd and was the daughter of Bjorn. Thorstein lived at Borg in Borgarfjord; he was wealthy and a great leader [*höfðingi mikill*], a wise [*vitr*] man and gentle [*hógværr*], and a man of moderation [*hófsmaðr*] in all respects.

The opposite of *hóf* was *óhóf*, a failure to observe restraint denoting excess or intemperance. Displays of *óhóf* alarmed both friend and foe. They called forth the exercise of peer pressure against an overbearing individual with the result that rarely did one leader succeed in imposing his will on other leaders for very long. The practice of *óhóf* was known as *ójafnaðr*, meaning unevenness, unfairness or injustice in dealings with others. *Ójafnaðr*, which is often translated as 'being overbearing' or 'unjust', disturbed the consensual nature of decision-making and set in motion a series of coercive responses; for example, when an individual's greed or ambition threatened the balance of power, other leaders banded together in an effort to counter his immoderate behaviour. This was the dynamic that came to Snorri goði's assistance in his conflict with Arnkel goði. Action against an unruly man (ójafnaðarmaðr), instead of causing an upheaval in governmental authority, led to small adjustments in the balance of local power, as recounted in saga feuds. Without slipping into the realm of ójafnaðr, leaders sought to reap profit, status and perhaps social good from their activities as advocates.

When a leader overstepped the bounds of propriety many people, including members of his own family, could take offence. *The Saga of the People of Ljosavatn* (Chapters 2–3) tells a curious story about the problems that befall two leading goðar, Gudmund the Powerful and Thorgeir goði, when they grossly manipulate the law to their own advantage. A pair of troublesome brothers who live in the northern part of the country are outlawed for three years as punishment for their misdeeds. They go to Norway where they gain the esteem of Jarl Hakon, Norway's ruler. After only two years abroad, one of the brothers, Solmund, returns to Iceland in violation of his sentence. For the two chieftains, Gudmund and Thorgeir goði, he brings gifts that have been provided by the Norwegian jarl to buy protection for the outlaws. Gudmund is described as a retainer of the jarl, whereas Thorgeir's interest in the gifts seems only pecuniary.

The situation is difficult because other local men, including Thorgeir's sons, have strong feelings against Solmund. In order to protect him, the chieftains decide to use their legal powers to nullify the earlier court judgement. In preparing the case, the chieftains apparently intend to use to their advantage Thorgeir's position as lawspeaker, supposedly the final arbiter of law in unclear cases. Thorgeir tells Gudmund: 'And I will support you, but you are to defend the case.' Gudmund replies: 'I cannot speak against this since you have the law in your power.' Thorgeir's sons, however, are of a different mind. They kill Solmund and, before a settlement is reached, Thorgeir barely escapes impeachment.

In addition to demonstrating *hóf*, an advocate had to have knowledge of the law in order to be successful, especially when he played the role of power-broker. The *goðar* had no monopoly on legal knowledge; in the sagas prominent *bændr* such as Njal Thorgeirsson and Helgi Droplaugarson show exceptional skill at law. Although they did not possess *goðorð*, they moved in the circles of the *goðar* and benefited from being advocates and brokers. At times the influence of such *bændr* rivalled the authority wielded by *goðar*, although it is not clear how successful they were in the long run. A *bóndi* was at a disadvantage without the privileges normally enjoyed by a *goði*, especially the ready support afforded by a legally constituted following of thingmen. The story of Helgi Droplaugarson in *The Saga of the Sons of Droplaug* (*Droplaugarsona saga*) illustrates this disability. For several years Helgi competes at the law courts as an equal with a local chieftain, whose *goðorð* he apparently covets.[4] His opponent, however, shows a remarkable ability to absorb damage, a resiliency that Helgi as a *bóndi* finally is unable to equal.

As important advocates, power-brokers maintained social stability when feuds escalated and threatened serious disruption. Turning to a broker with wide-ranging alliances was a way for a disputant to involve others, both chieftains and farmers, in his case. A resolution arrived at through such third-party intervention was likely to gain broad social approval. Because the courts required unanimity, or a general consensus, before arriving at a decision, brokerage and arbitration became commonplace.

*Friendship (*Vinfengi *and* Vinátta*)*

In striving for consensus, advocates and arbitrators frequently relied on ties of contractual political friendship called *vinfengi* and *vinátta* – the two terms are often used interchangeably, although *vinátta* is employed more frequently than *vinfengi* to describe genuine affection.

Vinfengi agreements allowed leaders to achieve the collaboration necessary for social control, and *vinfengi* is mentioned repeatedly in the sagas. Yet this device for augmenting power has received little attention. Translations of the sagas tend to gloss over the contractual political nature of *vinfengi*. The specific Icelandic terms are almost always dropped and saga characters become 'friendly' with each other or are simply 'friends'. Once aware of their importance, we see for example that *vinfengi* relationships described in *The Saga of the People of Weapon's Fjord* are particularly illuminating, and these are discussed in Chapter 13. That saga portrays a feud between the chieftain Brodd-Helgi, who frequently establishes *vinfengi* based on deceit, and the chieftain Geitir Lytingsson, who bases his survival on more honourable conduct.

Vinfengi and *vinátta* relationships complemented kin or *goði*–thingman obligations and put individuals in a position to demand reciprocity. Here the formal exchange of gifts and the holding of feasts played an important role. The author of *Njal's Saga* underscores this when in describing the friendship between Hoskuld the *goði* at Hvítanes and Njal's family, he tells us, 'their *vinátta* was so great that they invited each other to a feast every autumn and gave each other handsome gifts'.

Vinfengi was yet another way to supplement blood kinship relationships and the non-blood kinship bonds formed by marriage, fosterage and sworn brotherhood. The number of alternatives available in building temporary relationships made protecting oneself in Icelandic society a complex procedure. In Chapter 6 we saw the choices faced by a freed slave, Ulfar the Freedman, who found himself threatened by a neighbouring farmer. Ulfar turned for support to a local chieftain who, among other signs of friendship, invited him to feasts and gave him handsome gifts. This same episode from *Eyrbyggja saga* also illustrates the choices confronting a family of farmers, the sons of Thorbrand, forced into the difficult, but ultimately successful, position of opposing an ambitious chieftain.

A *vinfengi* arrangement might be concluded between individuals of equal political status, as between chieftains or between thingmen of different chieftains. *Vinfengi* agreements might also be reached by people of different status. Such relationships might be kept secret, especially if, as often happened, chieftains and farmers who entered into them shared nothing but a mutual need for support. Should a friendship not prove rewarding – by not providing assistance during a feud, for example – the arrangement could be terminated. *The Saga of the People of Weapon's Fjord* describes how a farmer, Stout (Digr) Ketil, terminated a covert agreement of friendship between himself and a *goði*. In some ways the extralegal bonds of *vinfengi* corresponded to the lawfully defined 'thing relationship' between a *goði* and a *bóndi*, as both alliances could be ended when one of the parties was dissatisfied.

Chieftains who were careful to cultivate good reputations as advocates and were successful in their power-brokerage often defined the terms of a friendship before entering into it. *Njal's Saga* (Chapter 139) describes in detail how Snorri goði, one of the cleverest chieftains portrayed in the family sagas, is supposed to have weighed the options available to him as a third party well situated to intervene in a coming armed clash at the Althing. The scene begins when the major prosecutors of the killers of Njal and his sons come to Snorri's booth at the assembly to seek assistance in the upcoming court case. After an initial discussion in which Snorri predicts that the case will not be settled in court but will turn into an armed confrontation, one of the prosecutors, Asgrim Ellida-Grimsson, asks Snorri the crucial question:

'I want to know what help you intend to give us, if it goes as you predict.'

Snorri replied, 'I shall make this friendship [*vinátta*] agreement with you, Asgrim, since your honour is at stake. I will not go into court with you. If you should come to blows at the thing, then attack only if you see no danger whatsoever, because there are valiant champions on the other side. But if you give way you should retreat in this direction to join up with us, for I will have drawn up my men in preparation and will be ready to assist you. And if, on the other hand, they are the ones who give way, it is my guess that they will make for the vantage point of Almannagjá [a rift in the lava near the Law Rock]. If they make it to that place you will never be able to overcome them. I shall undertake to draw up my men in front and bar them from the vantage point, but we will not go after them if they retreat north or south along the river. And when you have killed as many of their men as it seems to me you can afford to pay compensation for and still keep your chieftaincies and your domiciles, I will come forward with all my men and separate you. If I do that for you, you should follow my instructions.'

This account shows how a leader as cunning as Snorri might aid his friend's side to carry out limited vengeance and then, at the right moment, might assume the role of a man of goodwill intent on intervening between the feuding parties in order to terminate the violence. It is obvious here that honour is a related issue.

Christian priests, including many who were not *goðar*, also participated in feuds and played the role of advocate. According to *The Saga of Gudmund Arason the Priest* (*Prestssaga Guðmundar góða*), Gudmund, later (1203) bishop of Hólar, took on a prosecution for a killing in the early 1180s. Like most advocates, Gudmund depended on the support of others. In this instance he was counting on the assistance of his prominent kinsman, the *goði* Sturla Thordarson (Hvamm-Sturla) of Hvammr (1116–83), the father of Snorri Sturluson. Unhappily for Gudmund, Sturla died soon after Gudmund won a legal sentence of outlawry against the killer, named Odd. Gudmund then faced the dishonour that accrued to one who had obtained a sentence in his favour but had no means of executing the penalty prescribed by law. A solution, in keeping with the nature of advocacy, was found when 'Almighty God supported him by putting ideas into his mind so that he decided to make a vow that he would give Almighty God all the wealth that came to him because of Odd's outlawry, as long as the case was brought to an end without peril to Gudmund's soul' (Chapter 8).

WOMEN AND CHOICES OF
VIOLENCE AND COMPROMISE

Freeborn Icelandic women had legal responsibilities which were often comparable to those of men. These women maintained a measure of control over their own lives, including their right to own property independently. When acting as heads of households, they were required to tithe 'in the same manner as men',[5] and like men they were subject to outlawry for a wounding or a killing.[6] Some women may have served as temple priestesses in the pre-Christian period.*

Despite their influence in some areas, Icelandic women played no substantial role in open political life and did not enjoy full legal equality with men. Women did not serve as advocates, because they were not entitled to lead prosecutions, either for revenge or for material compensation. From *Grágás*, which says nothing on the subject, it appears that women were not permitted to speak publicly at a thing. When present at assemblies, they probably attended as onlookers – the rules concerning judges mention only men[7] – and they were not allowed to serve as members of a *kviðr* (a verdict-giving panel) or probably to act as legal witnesses.[8] Although a woman could inherit a *goðorð*, she was ineligible to act as a *goði* and had to appoint a man to act in the chieftaincy on her behalf.[9]

Icelandic women did, however, frequently play an influential role in the extralegal workings of advocacy. They contributed to the private consensus underlying decisions that determined relations between families and the outcome of feuds. In depicting personal life and the constellation of factors which affected decisions about legal entanglements, the sagas reveal ways in which women of property-holding families set in motion actions that escalated or prolonged feuds. At times the sagas also show women resolving and preventing

---

* *Vápnfirðinga saga*, Ch. 5, calls a woman named Steinvor a *hofgyðja*, a temple priestess, although this information cannot be confirmed.

them.[10] The literature suggests that women frequently achieved their objectives by inciting, shaming or goading their kinsmen into action.

Vengeance and Feud: Goading in Laxdæla saga

> Bolli then rode home to Laugar and Gudrun [his wife] went out to meet him. She asked him how late in the day it was. Bolli said it was around noon of that day. Then Gudrun said, 'Morning tasks are often mixed: I have spun yarn for seven ells of cloth and you have killed Kjartan.'
>
> *Laxdæla saga*

Icelandic women, though not permitted to enter the law courts, often played influential roles in shaping the long-term interests of families. 'Cold are the councils of women' reads a famous line from *Njáls saga*, and in times of feud women are repeatedly portrayed in the sagas as demanding blood vengeance. Demanding and getting are not the same, and the self-willed women of *Njáls saga* at times found it difficult to goad their men into action. Despite laws granting rights to vengeance,[11] Icelandic men frequently chose not to seek blood vengeance for close kinsmen, seeking compensation instead. Here we can see a gender distinction. Within the realms of honour and vengeance, the sagas regularly portray Icelandic men and women as having separate goals. Women could not participate in the legal processes that brought violence to an end, but they could affect the hatred and animosity that drove feud. Occasionally women are seen as restraining their kinsmen, although the sagas, with their conflict-driven narrative, show more interest in women opposing compromise and demanding blood vengeance.

Laxdæla saga portrays differences between the sexes concerning the goals of feud in the disagreement between Thorgerd Egilsdottir and her husband Olaf the Peacock. The couple's son, Kjartan, was killed by Bolli, his cousin and foster-brother. Thorgerd is determined to take blood revenge, but her husband disagrees. Here there is a small but crucial distinction. The killer, Bolli, is Thorgerd's nephew by marriage rather than by blood. The difficulties encountered by Thorgerd in motivating the men of her immediate family (more closely related to Bolli than she is) to seek vengeance against her son's killer highlights the entanglement of ties and the contrasting spheres of authority separating the genders.

For Thorgerd the problem is not a lack of respect, love or status. The saga tells us this about their relationship, beginning with the early years of their marriage: 'Olaf and Thorgerd lived at Höskuldsstaðir and came to love one another dearly. It was obvious to everyone that Thorgerd was an exceptional woman. She was not an interfering person as a rule, but whenever she did take a hand, she insisted on having her own way.' Thorgerd's problem was that Olaf the Peacock is a man of moderation (*hóf*), a leader proud of his restraint. He is a local big man who feels the responsibility of his authority and deliberately chooses to ignore calls for him to take blood in return for Kjartan's death. Olaf's actions are not dominated by the *lex talionis* (law of retaliation), in biblical terms 'an eye for an eye'.

Olaf is ready to strike back, but only in a careful way. His choice of target for reprisal respects the complex family structure built on multiple connections between in-laws. Olaf puts the group solidarity of his *goðorð* above the need to engage in protracted homicidal exchanges. A logical and careful man, he is thinking of the economic and political source of his family's wellbeing. Specifically, he refuses to harm Bolli, the son of his half-brother. As part of the numerous fostering arrangements whereby families increased the number of kinship and non-kinship relationships, Olaf had raised Bolli in his home as his own son. In saga style, the text explores the dilemma of having several choices, none of which are particularly appealing or even clear-cut.

The author of *Laxdæla saga* works with a personal knowledge of the conflicting ties and obligations of Icelandic kinship. In doing so, the writer lays bare underlying emotions among families immersed

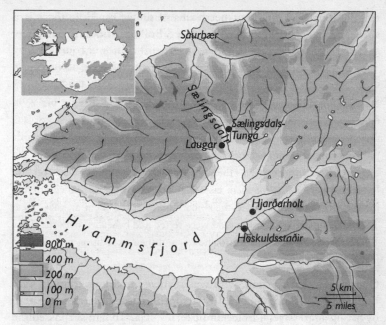

17. Thorgerd's Feud. Locations of households involved in the feud between the family of Olaf the Peacock from Hjarðarholt (Herd's Hill) and the people of Laugar (Hot Springs) in Sælingsdalr. Setting out from her home at Hjarðarholt, Thorgerd, accompanied by her sons, rode north to visit her woman friend at Saurbær. On the way up the Sælings Valley she passed Sælingsdals-Tunga, the farm of her enemy Gudrun Osvifrsdottir.

in a feuding environment confused by the pulls of restraint. Olaf, a grieving father, masters his emotions and carefully chooses the targets of his vengeance:

When Olaf Hoskuldsson heard the news, he was deeply affected by Kjartan's killing, although he bore it with fortitude. His sons wanted to attack Bolli at once and destroy him.

'Far from it,' said Olaf. 'Bolli's death would not bring back my son. I loved Kjartan above all others, but I could not bear to see any harm befall Bolli. I see a much more fitting task for you: go after the sons of Thorhalla [implicated in Kjartan's killing], who have been sent off to Helgafell to gather forces against us; any punishment you see fit to mete out to them will please me.'

The sons of Olaf set off at once and boarded a ferryboat belonging to Olaf. There were seven of them in all and they rowed away down Hvammsfjord, pulling as hard as they could. There was a slight breeze in their favour, and they rowed with the sail up until they reached the Skor Isle; they paused there briefly to ask about people's movements. Soon afterwards they saw a boat coming across the fjord from the west, and recognized the men on board at once; it was the sons of Thorhalla. Halldor Olafsson and his companions made for them instantly. There was no resistance offered, for the Olafssons leapt on to their boat and attacked them at once. Stein Thorholluson and his brother Odd were seized and beheaded over the side.

The Olafsssons then turned for home, and their expedition was thought highly enterprising.[12]

Olaf knows that Kjartan, who was involved in a love triangle with Bolli and Bolli's wife Gudrun Osvifrsdottir, caused his own downfall by acting aggressively. In Icelandic terms, Kjartan had surpassed the acceptable limits of immoderation.[13] Whereas Olaf wants to maintain the solidarity of the larger family, keeping workable relations with his siblings and their children, Thorgerd's concerns are different. She focuses more narrowly on the honour of her nuclear family. Concerning Olaf's intentions, the saga says that 'Olaf chose not to have Bolli prosecuted, but instead asked his nephew to pay compensation for his killing'. Thorgerd views material compensation as dishonourable. She and her female opponent, Gudrun Osvifrsdottir, demand a life for a life. In the score-keeping between the two women, Gudrun, who lives at the farm of Laugar, is ahead for the moment. She incited the men of her family to kill Kjartan, and Thorgerd is determined not to rest before achieving parity with her rival.

As a reflection of cultural mentality, Thorgerd's and Olaf's struggle with the issue of revenge is instructive. Kjartan is a well-born man, the son of a *goði*. Nevertheless, the men of his immediate family are prepared to compromise and accept payment. Thorgerd employs the persuasions of honour and shame, and places her husband and sons in a position where they will want to appease her. Psychologically the Icelandic situation was complex, more so perhaps than in societies where the imperative for taking vengeance is clearer. The sagas reflect the laws, in that both violence and compromise are legally acceptable options. In this instance, as in numerous others, the issue is not who is right, but which choice will prevail.

Although she does not get her way at first, Thorgerd continues to feel a duty to shed blood. She is patient. Unable to get her husband to strike at Bolli, she waits until after Olaf's death. Then she goads her sons into action. Her problem is that her sons, once eager to attack Bolli, are now unwilling to break their father's settlement of the feud. Faced with her sons' lack of motivation, Thorgerd, who lives at Hjarðarholt in the Salmon River Valley (*Laxárdalr*), commands the young men to accompany her on a visit to a friend living farther north, in the district of Saurbær. As a result, mother and sons ride past the farm at Sælingsdals-Tunga where Bolli and Gudrun now live. Again, Thorgerd relies on shame to bring on hatred, animosity being an essential ingredient in this kind of feuding. She invokes the courage of her own father, the warrior-poet Egil Skalla-Grimsson. She even asserts that her sons have dishonoured Olaf by their inaction, an accusation that highlights the element of ambiguity frequently surrounding calls to defend family honour:

Toward the end of the winter following Olaf Hoskuldsson's death, Thorgerd Egilsdottir sends word to her son Steinthor, requesting that he come see her. When mother and son meet, she tells him that she wants to go west [in fact, north] to Saurbær to see her friend Aud. She tells Halldor that he is also to come. He does so, and they make a party of five altogether. They continue until they come opposite the farm of Sælingsdals-Tunga. There Thorgerd turns her horse up toward the farm and asks: 'What farm is this?'

Halldor answers: 'You are not asking this, Mother, because you do not already know. This farm is called Tunga.'

'Who lives here?' she asks.

He answers: 'You know that too, Mother.'

Then Thorgerd snorts. 'I do indeed,' she says. 'Bolli, your brother's killer, lives there. You have certainly turned out very differently from your noble kinsmen if you don't want to avenge a brother like Kjartan. Egil, your mother's father, would never have acted this way. It's a sad thing to have shirkers for sons. Indeed, to my mind it would have suited you better had you been your father's daughters and married off. It just goes to prove the old saying: "There are black sheep in every family." The way I see it, this was clearly Olaf's worst misfortune, that he was cheated when it came to the kind of sons he got. I am telling this to you, Halldor, because you seem to be the foremost of your brothers. Now we shall turn back, for the sole purpose of my coming out here was just to remind you of this situation, in case you did not remember it before.'

Then Halldor answers: 'It certainly won't be any fault of yours, Mother, if we don't remember.'

Other than that Halldor had little to say about it, but all the same a fiery hate against Bolli welled up inside him.[14]

But even such goading was not quite enough. A while later, when the brothers finally set out to attack Bolli, Thorgerd is on hand (Chapter 54), demanding that she go with them. They try to dissuade her, saying that this is no journey for a woman. But she insists on going, saying 'For I know you well enough, my sons, to realize that you will need spurring on.' So they let her have her way.

Laxdæla saga shows many literary touches, and Thorgerd's story may be an authorial invention. Her plight, however, as a high-status woman forced to rely for assistance in feud on a reluctant family group, is no fiction. On the contrary it is a dramatic portrayal of a deeply rooted social conflict.[15] Because Icelandic men tended to put their faith in the political culture, preferring material compensation to blood vengeance, Icelandic women, if they were to get their way, had to pull out all the stops. In a type of incident found in many feuding societies, *Eyrbyggja saga* (Chapters 26–7) depicts a widow (also named Thorgerd) carrying her husband's severed head around the region in order to shame the dead man's kin to take vengeance.[16] Other women are shown waiting sometimes for years for the right moment to throw an old cloak caked with blood over their menfolk so that the dried blood would rain down on those to be shamed into action. Goadings were a distinctive feature of Icelandic feud for a number of reasons. Icelandic political groups were more important than kin-based structures or blood groups, and could not be counted on to have enough hatred against their enemies to engage in long-term feuding. In feuding, Icelandic women found their source of man-power limited to immediate kinsmen or to farm workers and slaves on their property. *Njal's Saga*'s famous feuding wives, Hallgerd and Bergthora, carried out a series of killings by mobilizing almost all gradations of rank on their respective farms. Starting with the lowest and least important in their households, they worked up the labour and honour scale, following the general rule that the lower the man's status, the easier it was for the woman to manipulate him. In the process of goading, Iceland again shares similarities with other feuding communities, including Corsica.

To be sure, Thorgerd Egilsdottir and other goading women in the sagas acted in the manner of feuding women elsewhere. In the language of feud, they seek to wash clean the stain of blood with the blood of their enemies. Armed with the long-term commitment to vengeance-taking which Icelandic men's groups lacked, Thorgerd succeeded in overcoming the confusions of identity that reached down into the smallest family units. Yet how did it all end? After a limited exchange of killings, the feud between Olaf's family and the people at Laugar was concluded with arbitration, compromise and compensation. Thorgerd's determination to take blood succeeded in prolonging the conflict by triggering a series of killings. Ultimately, however, the forces of compromise and compensation which she fought against defined the long-term settlement.

A Goading Woman from Sturlunga saga

Influential women such as Thorgerd Egilsdottir are not found only in the family sagas. *Sturlunga saga* also has examples of women participating in the decision-making of Iceland's contentious society. It portrays mothers and wives goading sons and husbands, and sisters inciting brothers to take blood even when they were Christian priests. *The Saga of Gudmund the Worthy* (*Guðmundar saga dýra*) recounts an example from Eyjafjord in the year 1197. Gudmund the Worthy, from the farm Bakki, burns to death the neighbouring *goði* Onund Thorkelsson at his home. At the time, Gudmund was attempting to uproot the still-functioning, centuries-old system of non-territorial *goðorð* (see the map of Eyjafjord in Chapter 7 showing *goðar* and thingmen alliances).

Initially Onund's killing was settled through an arbitrated agreement. Gudmund, however, was slow in paying the full compensation price. In 1198, almost two years after the burning, the dead man's three sons, two of whom were priests,[17] visited their sister Gudrun Onundardottir. Gudrun recognizes the dishonour in Gudmund's tardy payment. For her, the time for blood vengeance has come. When her husband and brothers sit down for breakfast, she serves them only *svið*, singed sheep heads, a clear reference to her father's death by burning. Asked by her husband whether this food is proper for guests, she replies that as far as she is concerned, 'singed sheep heads were what she easily had on hand' (Chapter 17). Her brother Vigfus, one of the two priests, then comments: 'There is no doubt of what you are reminding us of with *svið*.' That same day the men, including the priests, ride out to seek blood vengeance.

Restraint Within a Major Chieftain's Household in the Sturlung Age

Despite the famous statement in *Njáls saga* about women's counsel, the Icelandic texts sometimes show women acting with *hóf* (moderation) and working to limit the ravages of feud. One especially significant example of this is found in *The Saga of the People of Weapon's Fjord* and is discussed in greater detail later in this book. There a two-generation blood feud is resolved partially due to the wishes of the wife of one of the feuding chieftains. Sometimes such episodes ran deep in medieval family life, as is illustrated in the following account from *Thorgils saga skarða* (*The Saga of Thorgils Skardi*). The incident involves Groa Alfsdottir, the mistress of Gizur Thorvaldsson (d. 1268), a chieftain of the southern Haukdaelir family, who at the very end of the Free State became a jarl (earl).

The saga recounts that shortly after Gizur took part in the killing of Snorri Sturluson in 1241, a boy from the extended Sturlung family, Thorgils Bodvarsson skarði (later a powerful chieftain), comes to live as a hostage in Gizur's household at Tunga in Biskupstungur.[18] The fifteen-year-old Thorgils quarrels with another boy, Sam Magnusson, over a game of *tafl*.* The status of the 'young men' is very different. Sam is Gizur's kinsman, whereas Thorgils is there without choice. As it turns out, Gizur is fond of Thorgils, whose position in the household is much like that of a foster-son. The quarrel between the boys over the chess game escalates when Thorgils sweeps the game-pieces off the board and strikes Sam on his ear. Because Sam's wound bleeds, the action is a serious insult if left uncompensated. Upon entering the room, Gizur reprimands Thorgils, who answers him in a challenging manner.

The older man and the younger one are verging on a quarrel when Groa intervenes. Groa, whom the saga refers to as *húsfreyja*, the mistress of the house, perceives the danger in the situation. Thorgils has

---

* A kind of chess, where the pieces are initially set in the centre of the board and in the corners rather than lined up on opposite sides.

acted violently while in Gizur's home, and it is best that the matter simply be dropped. Everybody's honour is at stake and Groa knows that if Gizur were to quarrel with Thorgils, the way would be open for the type of smouldering dispute which could eventually claim lives. She takes Gizur's hand and leads him aside, asking (Chapter 1):

'Why are you so angry? To me it seems that it is you who will have to answer for it, even if he [Thorgils] does something that calls for compensation.'

Gizur replied, 'I do not want to listen to your opinion in this matter.'

She answered, 'Then I will, on my own, offer compensation, if that is what is necessary.'

The sharp-witted Groa is portrayed as having a cooler head than Gizur. A prolonged quarrel between the boys or between Gizur and Thorgils would have provided an entry point for third parties to intervene, harming her and Gizur's family. Because slights rankle, it was crucial to settle even the smallest dispute immediately. In this instance it is the woman who ignores the principle of retaliation and demonstrates her understanding of the politics of Icelandic feud. Opposing Gizur, Groa preserves the peace of the household when Gizur yields to her. The saga recounts that the matter was dropped, but 'Gizur was less friendly toward Thorgils than he had been earlier'. So matters continue until Groa again intervenes, this time at Christmas (1242) when she and Gizur reconcile the household with gifts: 'Before Christmas Groa had a green tunic made for Thorgils out of new green cloth, while Gizur gave Sam a blue tunic that he had previously owned. And they were good friends ever after.'

As portrayed here, Groa was a decision-making individual in this important household. *Sturlunga saga* leads readers to believe that Gizur loved Groa: together they had had several children and Gizur had wanted to marry her for years, but because of their close kinship the Church denied them permission. Finally, in 1252, some form of dispensation seems to have been arranged and the two apparently were married.

II

Aspects of Blood Feud

> It is the structure of society that demands and generates a
> specific standard of emotional control.
>
> Norbert Elias, *The Civilizing Process*

The hardest part of ending feud is overcoming hatred. The system of
dispute settlement that evolved in Iceland got around this central
obstacle by splitting vengeance-seeking from blood-taking. The two
were not the same. Blood vengeance in Iceland became an option
rather than a duty. Vengeance, that is action that satisfies the needs
of hatred and the debts of loss, could be routinely achieved through
compromise, material compensation or even limited manslaughter.
The combination of Iceland's northern climate, the tyranny of bad
year economics, the settlement pattern of fixed farmsteads, and the
systems of political and social life limited the number of options
available to groups. Blood feuding in Iceland was difficult to conduct
over long periods. The Icelandic methods of feud management were
not original to Iceland. In all feuding societies, peace is sometimes bought, and compromise exists. Icelanders, however, were
especially good at peacemaking. Early in Iceland's development,
different elements converged to the point where they systematically
promoted psychological and political motivations for compromise
and enemies routinely controlled their hatred. Even after exchanges
had reached the level of feud, arbitrators and third parties were
regularly allowed to intervene and to arrange compromises. This

penchant for settlements in which groups surrender demands, make concessions and adjust principles is no small matter, especially when we remember with whom feuding parties must compromise their differences. The difficulty in controlling animosity when making peace underlies the adage, 'It is not with one's friends that one must make peace.'

Feuding in Iceland was not always blood feud. At its simplest, feud involves prolonged animosity leading to exchanges of insults and/or violent acts against property or persons, including injury and even manslaughter. Feud can happen between individuals, but blood feud is a conflict that involves protracted violence between groups. This group aspect of the animosity is decisive, often involving repeated killings. We can define the type of blood feud that occurred in early Iceland in the following way: Icelandic blood feud was a form of vengeance-taking. It involved deep, smouldering animosities leading to repeated reprisals. Score was kept of injuries and killings inflicted on enemies. The taking of vengeance was understood as action that satisfied honour, and exchanges of violence could go on for a very long time, frequently over generations. Each vengeful act engendered a response. Although subterfuge often occurred, rarely was there true secrecy surrounding the general source of the action. The exchanges, which frequently escalated rapidly in the early stages, were rooted in competition, not always but often economic, involving access to resources. The spilling of blood and the attendant animosity resulting from such actions gave both identity and cohesion to the groups by openly distinguishing their enemies – 'them' as opposed to 'us'. With time the initial offence or offences that set the dispute in motion diminished in importance and may even have been forgotten, but the feud could take on a life of its own. Each new offence remained fresh in the minds of the victims even after considerable time and demanded a response, hence the 'duty' of vengeance and the 'sweetness' of revenge. The exchanges continued until the parties either wore themselves out, sought settlement, were forced by others to settle, or procreated new generations who were not committed to the animosities.

Social life in early Iceland displayed the dense and often complex personal ties that sometimes led to reprisal killings. But this aspect of 'warfare', to use the anthropological term for quasi-organized social violence, was held in check in Iceland by a combination of features that are explored in this and the next two chapters. These features included: non-territorial chieftaincics (goðorð); common judicial structures that extended across regions and chieftaincies; extensive processes of private and public dispute settlement; and marriage and kinship arrangements that moderated the cycle of vengeance. These combined in a society that saw itself as more unitary than multi-territorial and in which individuals, despite their dependence on livestock, saw themselves as farmers rather than herders.

Comparative material about feud offers considerable perspective on Icelandic conditions. Examples of societies at somewhat similar levels of economic and social integration give us the material to explore subtle differences among feuding societies. And we can avoid some problems. It is often forgotten that although feuding is a widespread human process, different peoples feud in different ways. Despite this basic fact, feud has mostly been studied in its more blatant forms, particularly in tribal and clan settings.[1] Attempts to explain Icelandic feud have tended to take the easy path, regarding Iceland as though it were tribal or divided into warring clans.[2] The problem is that early Iceland, with its mixture of pre-state and state institutions, was only marginally tribal and not very clan-like.

Willingness to find compromise solutions is one of early Iceland's distinguishing features. Comparative material is helpful in defining issues. For example, the situation among feuding tribes is often rather different from inter-group contests in Iceland. Tribes are frequently territorial, and compromise is not especially common. Iceland's mix of family and political alliances did not resemble the cohesive forces that usually bond members of tribes and feud-ready clans. Consider the Bedouin tribes of north-east Libya (formerly Cyrenaica). There, the anthropologist E. L. Peters points out, group discreteness is the basis for decisive action, making it possible to dispense with compromise: 'Feud is present in Cyrenaica because any one corporate group is sufficiently discrete in relation to a limited number of others that its members can decide not to compromise. The ability to make this decision is central to feud.'[3] In such environments, the obligation to take vengeance and the taking of blood go hand in hand. The anthropologist Christopher Boehm notes that a key to understanding blood feuds among tribes is awareness of 'effective tribal military and political organization and a code of values that placed merit upon maintaining the honour of a true warrior'.[4] The need for the warrior to prove himself through violence propagates feud and leads to more violence.

The local mentality of feud and feuding parties is often evident in the narratives of societies that have feud at their core. It is not surprising, therefore, that the treatment of warfare in the epics of the South Slavic region,[5] which has frequently been used by scholars as a well-documented example of feuding, is so different from that in the sagas. Although the warrior mentality existed in Iceland, its fierceness did not flourish as it did, for example, among the tribal groups of Montenegro, and the surrounding South Slavic areas.[6] The anthropologist Christopher Boehm's description of Montenegrins of two centuries ago reveals a mentality and a social order very different from those of the early Icelanders. Montenegrins were

warriors living in large territorial groups [who] regulated their own political affairs, and were organized to fight fiercely and effectively to defend their tribal lands. The tribesmen spent much of their energy in warfare, headhunting and raiding against external enemies; but they also carried on vicious blood feuds among themselves in which the males of one clan had free licence to kill any male in an enemy clan and vice versa. In short, the Montenegrins were warrior tribesmen of a type to be found all over the world.[7]

The above description highlights the crucial role that territorial arrangements can play in shaping the nature of feud. As far as Icelandic feud is concerned, the presence or absence of territoriality and the related issues of group cohesion and identity are central matters.

Territory

The lack of geographically defined chieftaincies in Iceland during the first centuries after the settlement had ramifications. Few if any blood, political or other groups had exclusive or long-time control over any one area. This feature made sustained feuding difficult because in Iceland there were so few territorial 'refuge areas', that is, a defined area where feuding parties lived protected, at least to a certain extent, by a cluster of kin and friends.

Without a territorial pattern under the control of groups, successful blood feuding in Iceland required participants to go to extremes in order to isolate themselves from attack. In Chapter 13, about blood feud in *The Saga of the People of Weapon's Fjord*, Geitir, one of two feuding *goðar*, retreats with all his household to Fagradalr, an isolated but defendable tiny valley (see Map 20). This withdrawal proves a successful strategy. Geitir bides his time, secure in the protection of the furthermost mountains that jut out into the sea at the mouth of the fjord. Action such as Geitir's is not unique in the sagas, but it is unusual. As the saga makes clear, Geitir was particularly clever and tenacious. He also seems to have had unusual access to ample resources. Fagradalr, his retreat, is located on the edge of the sea, close to rich fishing grounds.

For most Icelandic farmers and chieftains, sequestering themselves to engage in an extended feud carried too high a price. Such a withdrawal endangered their survival because they were not present on their farms to lay up stores for winter. Long-term feuding also ended participation in the normal aspects of social life – open meetings, games and assemblies. The psychological dread of exclusion from social life is not to be underestimated. Life during the long winter in this northern country was confined, isolated and lonely. Removing oneself and one's family from the excitement and bonding opportunities of annual gatherings and assemblies during the relatively short spring, summer and autumn was virtually unthinkable as a regular long-term strategy. Blood feud and other forms of private warfare periodically broke out in Iceland, but the costs, when weighed against the benefits, did not favour prolonged violence over peaceful settlement.

Evaluations of costs and benefits came into play in disputes between neighbours over control of basic resources. In such instances, private property was a central concept. Encroachment on a household's hay meadows signalled a contest. Boundary lines were public and trespass, which might mean the control of grassland, was reason for fighting. Because Icelanders tended to put issues concerning trespass into the perspective of law rather than emotion, the way was open to legal settlement, even after killings occurred. *Egil's Saga* (Chapter 81) recounts the conflict between Thorstein Egilsson at Borg and his neighbour, Steinar at Anabrekka, over a pasture owned by Thorstein, but lying between their two farms.

'I can see you must be very proud of yourself,' said Steinar, 'putting up such a mighty defence of your land by killing a couple of my slaves, but I don't think it all that much of a triumph. So now I'll offer you the chance of something much better, since you're so keen to defend your land: I'm not asking others to herd my cattle any more, and I want you to know that my herd will be grazing on your land day and night.'

'It's true that I killed your slave last summer,' said Thorstein, 'the one you'd told to graze your cattle on my land. Since then I've let you have all the grazing you wanted till winter came. And now I've killed another slave for you, for the same reason I killed the first. Now, if you want, you can use my pastures as much as you like for the rest of this summer; but when next summer comes, if you try to graze my land and send men to drive your cattle over to this side, I'll kill every single man herding them, you included, and I'll carry on doing that every summer as long as you make a habit of using my pasture.'[8]

There is a history to these lands. Steinar's grandfather was a trusted follower of Thorstein's grandfather Skallagrim, who granted Steinar's grandfather his farm at Anabrekka from the core of Skallagrim's original land-take. Now, later in the tenth century, relationships between the families have changed. This conflict among the grandchildren of the *landnámsmenn* is told as a saga example of Thorstein's attempt to hold on to what remains of his family's diminished authority and property.

A basic tenet of Icelandic law was that trespass forfeited a person's immunity to attack, and a trespasser while still on someone else's land could be killed with impunity. Thorstein is depicted as a man of moderation, and his dilemma is framed not in the light of the wrongs that have been done to him, but of his ownership rights. His forceful actions are legal and appear calculated to leave open a negotiated settlement. The choice of peace, like the choice of aggression, is in Steinar's hands. To end the conflict, Steinar simply has to end the encroachment. The problem facing Thorstein and his brand of self-help is that this path of action, however measured, could get him killed before his neighbour stops and a settlement is reached. In the sagas, tragedy befalls threatened individuals when they are neither as self-confident nor as lucky as Thorstein. Then they need advocates. Once Thorstein has called Steinar's bluff, Steinar is the one who needs supporters. After their meeting,

Steinar rode off back home to Anabrekka, and a little later he rode over to Stafaholt, where the Chieftain Einar was living. Steinar asked for his support and offered him money in return.

'My support won't make much difference to you,' said Einar, 'not unless you get other men of substance to back you up.'

Steinar succeeds in assembling a group of paid advocates, but in the end they fail him when it becomes clear that Thorstein can be pushed no further. Aided by his tough old father, Egil, he would rather fight than compromise. Having signed on for a legal case not a blood feud, Steinar's advocates drop out, and the contest between Steinar and Thorstein ends abruptly with all the main players still alive.

Marriage and Confused Loyalties

Marriage arrangements influenced the type of feud practised in Iceland. Within a household each individual, whether wife, husband or child, reckoned his or her kinship bilaterally, that is to both the mother's and the father's families. Thus a woman given away in marriage did not abandon her blood family; she continued to belong to her original kindred, as did her children, who also belonged to their father's family. Marriages outside the local group and often at considerable distances were frequent, extending alliance networks among members of different chieftain–thingmen groups. Such arrangements watered down the discreteness of the local group, adding to the already rich mix of potentially conflicting political and kinship alliances among individuals.

The extent of these cross-cutting ties helps to explain why the loyalty of Icelanders, whether male or female, was not to a single group. In-laws frequently cooperated against blood relatives in legal matters, but when the disagreement came to blood feud, people were reluctant to take part in killings. It was because this general rule was broken that the conflict between the uncompromisingly antagonistic kinsmen in *The Saga of the People of Weapon's Fjord* becomes a blood feud. Some of the most serious blood feuds in the written sources developed when the restraints against kinsmen harming one another were bypassed.

Usually, however, family members are portrayed as wanting to avoid harming even distant kinsmen. Because of this factor, hostility between families or among *goði*–thingmen constituencies was often a confusion of conflicting loyalties. The situation might be obvious, as when one's best ally was the worst enemy of one's first cousin. There were no set guidelines for choosing whom to support, and Icelanders routinely faced the dilemma of being called upon to uphold pre-existing kinship, fosterage or political obligations to individuals on opposing sides in a dispute. This tendency can be seen in *Laxdæla saga* (Chapter 61) in the quandary faced by Thorstein the Black. He was pressured to take part in a reprisal against his wife's brother, a seemingly well understood plight: 'Thorstein stated, "It is not proper for me to be party to a plot against Helgi, my own brother-in-law. I would much rather buy peace with as much money as is considered right and honourable."'

Linking the wife's and husband's families into wide, though fragile, support networks, the bilateral kinship system combined with other factors of Icelandic social life to help limit or at least control animosity between groups. The cultural acceptance of networks based on the numerous options available through a combination of family, shifting political alliances and covert friendship (*vinfengi*) arrangements diminished the potential in Iceland for the type of clan solidarity frequently important within feuding societies. In giving away a daughter in marriage, a father or the head of a household, sometimes a woman, was investing the family's limited marriage capital in a new kinship alliance that was frequently independent of what might have been a larger clan policy. If the union did not produce children it could be terminated. In such instances it was important to retrieve both the woman and the dowry (*heimanfylgja*) that had 'followed her from home [*fylgir henni að heiman*]'. So too, when there was no increase in status, wealth or security for the bride's family, ways could be found to end the marriage. Many Icelandic women married several times, and neither age nor lack of virginity was a hindrance. When a former husband did not return the dowry, the consequences could be especially serious. The parties had a tangible and easily recognizable issue of dispute which could develop into feud.

Contrary to Icelandic practice, rules of marriage among tribes where blood feud is endemic often stress the discreteness of the individual group and limit confusions of loyalty. Describing feuding among the Bedouin of Cyrenaica, Peters observes: 'Since external marriages are concentrated into a relatively small number of other corporate groups, Bedouin are able to satisfy their needs without compromising the discreteness of their groups.'[9] He also notes: 'Where groups are discrete, the possibility for feuding is also present; but where an entanglement of ties precludes decisive action, threat of feud may be used to arrive at compromise.'

Because of their structural make-up, Icelandic dispute groups could not easily dispense with compromise. Whether *goði*–thingmen constituencies (interest groups), family groupings or *vinfengi* (friendship) alliances, these relationships were neither discrete nor territorially defined. As a result, it was difficult for Icelandic groups to distinguish enemies collectively for long-term vengeance-taking. Even small landowning families normally had sufficient ties to other groups that they could rarely refuse calls to compromise. The difficulty of refusal was reinforced when, in keeping with established custom, third parties intervened. The contractual nature of the *goði*–thingman relationship also contributed to Iceland's loose concept of group solidarity. Self-interest was never far from the minds of medieval Icelanders. *Ljósvetninga saga* attributes the following words to the successful northern chieftain Gudmund the Powerful: 'I am looked on as your chieftain and judge it to be in the spirit of our relationship that each aids the other in just cases. You should support me against my opponents and I am your ally when your needs require it.'

Early on, Iceland's legalistic institutions adapted to a structural situation in which the focus of activity shifted more toward reducing the threat of feud than toward dealing with its continuance. Whereas often in blood feuding the threat of violence grows stronger as the feud progresses, because both animosities and expected responses become institutionalized, Icelandic blood feuds usually dissipated rapidly.

Again the nature of Iceland's feuding groups played a key role. Such groups were not sufficiently cohesive for the 'us against them' mentality to reign over the long term. Once a series of initial violent acts took place, possibly followed by escalation over a period of time, the threat of continuing, generations-long exchanges diminished. In their place came ritualized forms of menace and armed posturing. Finally, legalistic compromise took centre stage. The combination of these processes was in part a response to the geographical constraints of the island environment. The lack of spatial mobility did not allow people to escape easily from feuds.

The gatherings of hundreds of farmers on each side were public displays of force by groups which, until the thirteenth century, were not made for fighting. Such displays of manpower, as in the conflict between Thorgils and Haflidi discussed in Chapter 4, limited or replaced the need for repeated homicidal exchanges. They signalled consensus. It was time to get on with a settlement. Men of goodwill (*góðviljamenn*), such as Ketil, were ready, even competing, to come forward to convince men of honour, such as Haflidi, to settle the feud. As part of the process violent acts were translated into heavy financial burdens. The sagas repeat the adage that 'one should not kill more men than one can pay for'. In extreme cases, when no settlement could be reached, a leader might even face the added burden of compensating the relatives of his followers. As might be expected, such costs dampened the willingness of leaders to resort to violent confrontation.

Some Conclusions

At this point, we can draw some conclusions. Icelandic groups were not well equipped for extensive blood feuding. Lacking the concept and the leadership of military structures, they were not in a state of readiness to fight. The inherent confusions of loyalty among group members tended to rule out serious warfare, and the *goðar* were not warlords, warrior chieftains or aristocrats controlling regions. Within Iceland's 'great village' situation, discussed in the next chapter, thingmen of rival *goðar* maintained cross-chieftaincy networks based on blood, politics, marriage and 'friendship'. The general absence of group territoriality in Iceland's political system diminished the solidarity of a chieftaincy. It was difficult, though not impossible, to establish the consensus or cohesion necessary for long-term feuding exchanges. Even the most successful *goðar* found it hard to concentrate forces and resources, or even to protect followers from reprisals.

A century after the end of the Viking Age, or down into the thirteenth century, Iceland's 'warfare' was more on a family or individual level than is often found among ranked or stratified groups, whether big man collectivities, chieftaincies or incipient states. The *goðar* early became political entrepreneurs adept at forming ad hoc interest groups of often unrelated backers. They specialized in advocating clients' interests through arbitration both in and out of court, and found it honourable and profitable to engage in resolving moderately mature, that is 'court ready', conflicts.

For several hundred years following the initial settlement, feud operated as a form of limited, coercive violence. With its patterned actions and structured legalistic responses, it replaced (on both the local and countrywide levels) formal governmental institutions. The result was a cost-effective, mostly private means of resolving disputes, which also regulated wealth and power. In the horse-trading atmosphere of the Icelandic court system, *goðar* and *bændr*, even those who had once been firm allies, frequently changed sides. With old groups dissolving and new groups forming, the 'duty' of blood vengeance, so important in a tribal setting, was often observed more in lip service than in actuality.

12

Feud and Vendetta in a 'Great Village' Community

> Never kill in the same family more than once, and never
> break a settlement which good men make between you and
> others.
>
> *Njal's Saga*, Chapter 55

We come closer to understanding early Icelanders by focusing on their perception of themselves as people. Their cultural setting gave individuals an incentive to keep the peace. Peer pressure demanding moderation and consensus emerged as a potent force because Icelanders lived in what might be called a 'great village'. The island was a single but dispersed community. Socially it was a large, spread-out, village-like environment that shared common judicial and legislative institutions. In some ways it functioned like an incipient city-state.[1] The different quarters of Iceland were meshed together and united by strong ties of interdependence. Within regions the subsistence of independent households depended upon economic cooperation.

These common bonds can be seen in other cultural features. Despite the segmented geography, the Icelandic language became so standardized that no dialects developed. Years ago the Scottish medievalist Walter P. Ker noticed the island's distinctive unity, although the point has often been ignored by modern researchers:

Iceland, though the country is large, has always been like a city-state in many of its ways; the small population though widely scattered was not broken up, and the four quarters of Iceland took as much interest in one another's gossip as the quarters of Florence. In the sagas, where nothing is of much importance except individual men, and where all the chief men are known to one another, a journey from Borg [in the south-west] to Eyjafjord [in the north] is no more than going past a few houses. The distant corners of the island are near each other. There is no sense of those impersonal forces, those nameless multitudes that make history a different thing from biography in other lands.[2]

The Althing was a hothouse of information, a central clearing house uniting the whole of Iceland. Along with the great-village society came a dispute dynamic that corresponds more to vendetta, which unlike tribal warfare can be characterized as personalized violence often within or touching upon village life. Vendetta tends to involve small groups and individuals rather than large corporate bodies. Peters distinguishes feud between rival tribes from vendetta killings in villages, whose residents recognize codependence and accept the need for moderation in order to live together. As he points out, killings occur in vendetta, but 'villages are residential units from which feud must be excluded . . . Vendetta, akin to feud in the forms of the behaviour which characterize hostility, is distinctly different, and appears where feuding relationships cannot be tolerated.'[3]

Viewing Iceland as a great village leads to further observations. Although the chieftaincies could not provide the refuge areas so important to blood feud and internal cohesion among tribes, all Iceland, right from its inception, was a safe haven. In many ways the country was formed as a Viking Age immigrant sanctuary, and the generations following the land-taking expanded this concept. In the Icelandic cultural mindset the 'us' was the Icelanders themselves and the 'them' meant the Norwegians.[4] As is well expressed in many sagas, Icelanders came to see the Norwegians as having lost to kings their freemen's rights. Abroad in Norway, Icelanders, who believed they retained these rights, are frequently portrayed as falling foul of the Norwegian system.

The production of Icelandic farms, like households in villages,

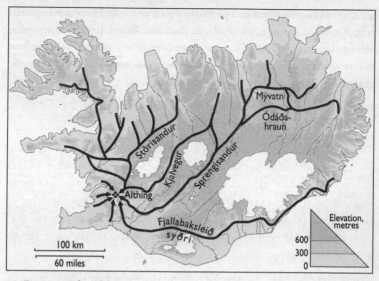

18. Routes to the Althing.

depended upon cooperation. During the summer, the sheep roamed the high pastures freely, intermingling in the mountains. The crucial moment for subsistence was the autumn round-up. Then the herds were located in the mountains and brought down to the valleys, where they were separated and returned to their owners. Throughout this harvest-like process, with its many opportunities to settle old scores, and possibilities for new dispute, feud was barred. *The Saga of the People of Weapon's Fjord* recounts an episode where a man named Thorkell planned to break the peace and attack his cousin Bjarni in the common lands up in the highlands during the autumn round-up. A farmer named Thorvard the Doctor learns of Thorkel's plans, and although he has had no part in the feud, Thorvard intervenes (Chapter 14):

Bjarni was accustomed every autumn to go up to the mountain pastures, just as his father had done, and at such times no one ventured to attack anyone else. But Thorvard the Doctor learned that Thorkel was getting ready to set out for the mountains and had picked out men who could be trusted to assist him. Thorvard warned Bjarni about this, and Bjarni remained at home, getting others to go in his place. Now came the time when men went up into the mountains, and Thorkel's intended meeting with Bjarni did not take place. They remained peaceful over the winter.

Peer pressure to maintain the peace also existed in the fisheries. *Laxdæla saga* (Chapter 14) tells us:

There was a fishery in Broad Fjord [Breiðafjord] called the Barn Isles. There are many small islands in this group, and they were rich producers. In that time people used to go there in great numbers for the fishing, and many stayed there all year round. Wise people thought it very important that in such fishing stations men should get on well together. It was believed that fishing-luck would turn against them if there were quarrels. Most people were careful to respect this.

In Iceland's broad community, honour, profit and safety could be found in ways other than in continued vengeance killing. This point is made in *Bandamanna saga* when a sly old father explains the principle of Icelandic feuding to his naive son who has just become a *goði*: 'It seems unwise for a person to let his honour depend on having the larger band of followers.' At times conflicting forces were at work. If vengeance could be taken on any member of an opponent's extended kin, Icelandic institutions nevertheless fostered solutions whereby its families and kin networks avoided much of the blood-letting of feuding societies. Vengeance-seeking, influenced by the strategies of private entrepreneurial leadership, was routinely conducted through arbitrations bounded by legal precedent. Whereas the language of the sagas and feud is one of honour, for the chieftains it was mostly a business.

Wergild, the payment of blood money and related assessments of material compensation, is known in almost all feuding societies. In some systems payments are downplayed as unacceptably dishonourable, but in Iceland the acceptance of blood money carried little stigma. Because of the emphasis on avoiding a public condemnation of immoderation, wergild and compensation became routine. They provided restitution for damages rather than fines to authorities.

The tradition of wergild in Iceland was inherited from Norway and from Scandinavian society in general. A difference between Iceland and contemporaneous Scandinavia was that in Iceland compensation operated without forceful overlords who could take sides and command settlement. Icelanders, both individuals and groups, worked out by themselves all the elements of a settlement. The competitive and entrepreneurial nature of Icelandic political and governmental life was a central factor in the financial transactions of feud settlement. *Goðar* gained prestige and increased their honour through brokering. They also found ways to take a share for themselves.

The *goðar*, who transferred wealth, worked through a country-wide series of networks that reinforced the great-village milieu. Much of the boisterous and at times threatening nature of Icelandic court cases and negotiated settlements, both inside and outside the courts, turned on fixing suitable sums. Wealth is often institutionalized into power when individuals find ways of converting it into control over sectors of the economy. The early *goðar* found their role in the management of feud and the maintenance of an island-wide society. The goals of such leaders were to prosper repeatedly through participation in feuds, and not to get killed. We can ask ourselves whether these men were deeply enmeshed in the type of hatred that is so essential to the continuance of blood feud.

The Language of Feud

The core of the feuding system is exposed by tracing the role of advocacy and other forms of third-party intervention. Establishing a complex and well-conceived apparatus of local and national courts with fixed dates and responsibilities provided the Icelanders with forums for negotiating. The legal standards that evolved from Viking Age beginnings not only strengthened and legitimated the roles of moderator and advocate but also added prestige to these undertakings. The social order, reinforced by the advocacy system, made possible Iceland's controlled type of feuding. The shift from violent 'self-help' (a term in legal anthropology meaning to take matters into one's own hands) to publicly condoned displays of moderation diminished the need to exact blood and reinforced the acceptability of compromise.

As might be expected, the vocabulary of the system was extensive. The Icelanders had many words to describe conflicts between individuals and among groups. These words included *fæð* (related to the English word 'feud'), *thykkja, kali, dylgjur, úfar, úlfúð, viðrsjá, óthykkja, óthykkt, óthokki, misthokki, misthykkja, óvingan, sundrlyndi, sundrthykki, illdeildir* and *deildir*. They describe situations and the various degrees of dispute and feud. There are also words for the participants themselves. Certain aspects of different cultures show a linguistic density that is in keeping with a cultural focus of a particular society. In Iceland many of these words refer to states of conflict whose gradations may be difficult to distinguish today. Most of them connote states of dispute that do not or need not involve violence. The principal point is that there is animosity, and people can no longer trust each other to act in good faith. Crucial for the Icelandic situation, these words signify that compromise is no longer possible, hence a movement toward feud.

One of the most commonly used of these words is *deila*, meaning a disagreement or a contest. It is also a verb, *at deila* (to quarrel, dispute, engage in hostilities, feud). As a legal term it is part of numerous compound words, including dispute at law (*laga-deila*), and at the thing (*thing-deila*). A quarrel was a *deilu-mál* and a quarrelsome person was called *deilu-gjarn* (eager to dispute or quarrelsome). Many compounds are also formed with the related word *deild* (often used in the plural *deildir*), meaning dealings or dispute. When preceded by the prefix *ill* (bad), *deild* connotes violence. Once it was clear in the minds of the hearers that the 'dealings' in question constituted a feud (*illdeildir*), the word was often shortened to *deildir*. Many of the above words or phrases employing *deild* take on the meaning of serious dispute or blood feud. An example is a confrontation over the farm at Tunga in Borgarfjord in the *Saga of Hvamm-Sturla*. It later became known as Deildartunga (Dispute-Tunga). In the family and Sturlung sagas *illdeildir* is spelled out in full several times (*'menn deili illdeildum við einhverja* [men contested in a blood feud with someone]'). For example, in Chapter 49 of *Njal's Saga*, Hallbjorn the White asks Otkel: 'What do you expect to gain by contesting with Gunnar in a blood feud [*deila við Gunnar illdeildum*]?' In its shortened form *deildir* is used formulaically, meaning that people quarrelled or engaged in feuds with others.

Norms of Restraint

Icelandic leaders may have acted tough, but ultimately they proved their mettle in court and in arbitrations. Most settlements were reached out of court, but the availability of courts with fixed locations and times served both as an impetus to arbitrate and settle as well as a deterrent to escalating a dispute into a feud. The threat by one party to take the issue in dispute to court was a major step. It served as a warning that matters would be taken from the hands of the feuding parties and placed into the hands of the community. At this stage many reasonable people chose to settle their differences themselves or through their advocates.

In the late tenth and early eleventh centuries the courts evolved in such a way as to facilitate settlements. The Fifth Court of Appeal was created, and the duel (*hólmganga*) was outlawed.[5] These changes reflect the restraining norms of Icelandic feud. Early Icelanders readily participated in disputes, including perhaps a killing or two, but they engaged less readily in blood feuds. Manslaughters resulted from many motivations. These could be as varied as insult, theft, greed, politics, seduction, temper, passion, insanity, depression or wilful cruelty. A killing was often enough to start a blood feud, but it did not always do so.

One element of restraint also in force during the Viking Age was the distinction between manslaughter (*víg*) and murder (*morð*).[6] *Víg* was a killing publicly acknowledged by the perpetrator shortly after the act, and could be atoned for through compensation. It was a step in the disputing process which opened the way to settlement in court or by outside arbitration. *Morð* was a concealed and unacknowledged slaying, a shameful act that brought disgrace to the perpetrator. It could seldom be kept secret, and led to reprisal killings. Its discovery meant ostracism and usually led to death or outlawry.

It was also shameful to harm women and children. Although at times women might goad within the family structure, they were shielded from the violence of Icelandic feud by being excluded from participation in court cases and public life. As for protection, removing women from the arenas of dispute and settlement seems to have worked. It is rare in the sources for armed men purposefully to harm women. The cost of this arrangement for women was that they were barred from taking part in legal processes. It was also a characteristic feature of Icelandic feud that defenceless children were not to be purposely harmed. This unwritten rule apparently was observed even in instances where young boys stood to inherit rights to vengeance-taking, with a feud having a good chance of reigniting.[7]

Iceland exhibits many aspects of a shame society, in which the conviction of members of the peer group and public opinion at large carried significant influence. Praiseworthy conduct was clearly distinguished from conduct that brought disgrace. In the great-village environment, everyone knew, or thought they knew, everything. The earlier example of Hrut and Mord the Fiddle (Chapter 1) reveals much about the norms of behaviour. After all these centuries, their restraining influence on an action such as Hrut's challenging of the much older Mord to a duel can still be felt. However justified and legal the action may have been, it brought Hrut little if any praise. On the contrary, (in Chapter 8) when returning

home from the Althing, Hrut and Hoskuld rode west to Reykjardale. They stayed overnight at Lund, the home of Thjostolf the son of Bjorn Gold-Bearer. It had rained heavily that day; the travellers were soaked, and long-fires [down the centre of the hall] were lit for them.

Thjostolf sat between Hoskuld and Hrut. Two boys, who were under his care, were playing on the floor with a little girl; they were chattering loudly with the folly of youth.

One of the boys said, 'I'll be Mord and divorce you from your wife on the grounds that you couldn't have intercourse with her.'

The other boy replied, 'Then I'll be Hrut and invalidate your claim to the money if you don't dare to fight me.'

They repeated these statements several times, and the household burst out laughing. Hoskuld [Hrut's brother] was furious, and he hit the boy who was calling himself Mord with a stick. It struck him on the face and drew blood.

'Get outside,' said Hoskuld, 'and don't try to ridicule us.'

'Come over here to me,' said Hrut. The boy did so. Hrut drew a gold ring from his finger and gave it to him.

'Go away now,' he said, 'and never provoke anyone again.'

The boy went away, saying, 'I shall always remember your noble-mindedness.'

Hrut was highly praised for his conduct. Later he and his party rode off home to the west, and so ends the episode of Hrut and Mord the Fiddle.

Though Hrut is the object of the joke and is shamed by the children's antics, he is able to prevent utter disaster to his reputation by demonstrating both restraint and generosity. With a sense of graciousness and a largeness of spirit, which he is wise enough to know will be held in high regard and spoken of long after the event, he gives the boy a fine gift.

We see the culture of restraint in the law. Repeatedly, as in the following two passages from the 'Manslaughter Section [*Vígslóði*]' of *Grágás*, the law gave people the right to take vengeance and to defend their person and their honour, but only within limitations. It is not clear, and in my view it is doubtful, that these laws were ever much followed. Written law was more fixed and extreme than the portrayal of applied law given in the sagas. Yet in presenting such a well-developed concept of restraint, the law book entries agree with the general thrust of the sagas, showing a consensus among the population for allowing vengeance-taking but only within the limits of acceptable windows of opportunity.

It is prescribed that a man on whom injury is inflicted has the right to avenge himself if he wants to up to the time of the General Assembly at which he is required to bring a case for the injuries; and the same applies to everyone who has the right to avenge a killing. Those who have the right to avenge a killing are the principals in a killing case. The man who inflicted the injury falls with forfeit immunity at the hands of a principal and at the hands of any of his company, though it is lawful for vengeance to be taken by other men within twenty-four hours.

It is prescribed that if a man shields or gives help to a man who at that same place of action has killed or wounded someone, the penalty is outlawry; and further, such a man forfeits his immunity in respect of injuries received from any men trying to help the other side unless it was his wish to separate them in a lawful way and that was why he gave help to the one side, and such helping carries no penalty. And he separates them in a lawful way if he can get a panel verdict that he would have separated them in the same way if the wounded man had inflicted such injuries on the other man as he had now received from him.[8]

Restraint is widely expressed in the sagas. When the power-broker and sage Njal Thorgeirsson counsels Iceland's finest warrior, his friend Gunnar, Njal's advice is, 'Never kill in the same family more than once, and never break a settlement that good men make between you and others' (Chapter 55). Not killing more than once in the same family virtually rules out blood feud. Gunnar's flaw in terms of both Icelandic storytelling and social ethics was ignoring this warning. Despite the thirteenth-century saga's characteristically Christian rendering of events, Njal did not oppose a killing, just more than one in a family. Such a slaying was manslaughter, a political act to be disputed, judged, arbitrated, compensated for and, most importantly, reconciled.

When an individual committed too many manslaughters, the effect was that of murder. That was Gunnar's downfall; he disregarded the restraining rules. Instead of stopping after a manslaughter or two, he continued to kill, hence conducting blood feud even after a legal settlement had been negotiated. Njal understood the political system, whereas Gunnar, however heroic, did not.[9] By breaking the settlement (grið) of three years' outlawry from Iceland, Gunnar, like many tragic saga characters, dishonoured the system on which the peace depended. The system in turn ejected him from its protective cover.

The Tale of Snegla Halli[*][10] provides a glimpse of the dishonour caused by breaking a reconciliation. It calls a settlement-breaker a *níðingr*, the strongest legal term of abuse, normally reserved for villains, cowards, traitors, and individuals who committed wanton cruelty. In the presence of the King of Norway, Halli was accused by an opponent of having failed to avenge his father's death. In response to this accusation the King asked:

'Is it true, Halli, that you have not revenged your father?'
'True it is, lord,' answered Halli.
'With this situation, why did you travel to Norway?'
'It is this way, lord,' replied Halli. 'I was a child when he was killed, and my kinsmen took up the case. They arranged a settlement on my behalf, and among us it does not sit well to be called by the name of *griðníðingr* [settlement-breaker].'

The saga puts Halli, an Icelander, in the position of stoutly defending the honour accorded this custom of restraint, revealing a cultural contrast that Icelanders perceived to lie between their own and Norwegian society.

---

* Halli's nickname, 'Snegla', could mean several things. In modern Icelandic *snegla* means a sheep that is stubborn and hard to manage, but also the kind that survives when left out in the winter. The adjective *sneglinn* means hot-headed, bad-tempered. The word also means a weaver's shuttle; less probable is the meaning 'snail'. In Norwegian the word can mean a thin, weak man.

Bluffing and Violence

One aspect of competition that led to violence in medieval Iceland was bluffing. Not all bluffers are losers, but many of them are, and Iceland had its share of losers. Known everywhere in feuding societies where warriorship contributes to status, such individuals are aggressive prestige-seekers against whom the odds are stacked from the beginning. Often at the bottom of the prestige heap, they have, at least for a while, the most to gain by stirring up trouble. If the benefit to such people is momentary success, the cost to society is large and the effects often long-term. Practising self-deception, bluffers pump themselves up to the point where their rash claims prove attractive to the young and alarming to the more experienced, not least because the best bluffers are often those who come to believe in their own importance. For a time they deter opponents who would surely be victorious against them in a conflict that turned violent. Without being put to the test, they elevate their status and enjoy respect for being regarded as warriors. In the Icelandic context, they are people who participate in decision-making without having to learn the law. Eventually their bluff is called and they are often killed. By that time, however, they have inspired others and have set feuds in motion.

The sagas often speak of prestige-seeking bluffers, and sometimes Icelanders encounter them abroad. Grettir the Strong runs into such a man in Norway, while staying the winter with a prominent local leader named Thorkel. According to *Grettir's Saga*:

A man named Bjorn was staying at Thorkel's. He was by nature an aggressive, pushy sort, but he came from a good family and was distantly related to Thorkel. He was not popular with most people on the farm because he would falsely accuse some of those in Thorkel's service; many of them left because of his trouble-making. He and Grettir began to dislike each other. Bjorn found Grettir of little worth compared to himself, whereas Grettir stood his ground. Animosity developed between them. Bjorn was a loud man, who liked to act as if he were important. Because of this, many young men followed him, and they often gathered in the evening outside the farmhouse.

During the winter Bjorn taunted Grettir relentlessly, but Grettir, who was anxious to avoid killing his host's kinsman, repeatedly gave way. Later the two met when they were no longer the guests of Thorkel. Grettir called Bjorn's bluff and challenged him to a duel. At first Bjorn claimed the dispute was forgotten and then offered to pay compensation. Refusing the payment, Grettir quickly killed Bjorn. This killing started a blood feud. One by one Bjorn's brothers attacked Grettir, seeking vengeance, and Grettir was forced to kill them all. The conflict did not end there. It grew, eventually drawing in large numbers of people and involving Grettir's friends and family in Norway. In the end Grettir was driven out of Norway.

Outlawry

Individuals who failed to observe the rules of feud and settlement were outlawed. The legal process of banishing people from the island served to guarantee the integrity of the great-village environment, removing those who could not or would not abide by its rules. Once outlawed, a person could be killed with impunity, that is, with no vengeance expected, but this rule was sometimes broken. Outlawry provided Icelandic society with an efficient and cost-effective means of doing away with troublemakers. Dependence on outlawry simplified the role of Icelandic corporate groups, most importantly by exempting them from the need to maintain a policing body to oversee the imposition of corporal punishment, execution or incarceration. The laws name two types of outlawry: *fjörbaugsgarðr*, lesser outlawry, and *skóggangr*, full outlawry (literally 'forest-going').[11] Both punishments included the confiscation of property. Lesser outlawry brought a sentence of a three-year exile abroad. If a lesser outlaw, a *fjörbaugsmaðr*, failed to leave the country within three years, he became a full outlaw, a *skógarmaðr*. A full outlaw was denied all assistance in Iceland; he was not to be harboured by anyone, nor could he be helped to leave the country. In effect, this punishment was tantamount to a death sentence, for a *skógarmaðr* could be killed with impunity. The *lögrétta*, the legislative council at the Althing, could mitigate the sentence of full outlawry, allowing a *skógarmaðr* to leave Iceland for life. In such instances the outlaw travelled abroad without enjoying the rights of an Icelander. Removal of those rights jeopardized the safety and the status of an individual, especially of one who wanted to stay in Norway. From the early eleventh century Iceland and Norway maintained a treaty guaranteeing the rights of each other's citizens. A third type of outlawry, not mentioned in the laws, was district outlawry. Named *héraðssekt*, it was a judgement limited to a local district (*hérað*).

Because of the seriousness of the penalty and because it often resulted from arbitrated settlement, an outlawry judgement required substantial consensus. Outlawries served as political statements, signalling that the defendant's family and friends were either unwilling or unable to muster a defence.

13

Friendship, Blood Feud, and Power:
The Saga of the People of
Weapon's Fjord

Each of the wise should wield his power in moderation;
He will find that no one is foremost when stout men gather.

The Sayings of the High One (Hávamál), 64

Vápnfirðinga saga (The Saga of the People of Weapon's Fjord) is a
tale set in the eastern part of the island that gives a detailed picture
of the means by which power was regulated and political ambition
was contained. The saga focuses on a power struggle between two
young chieftains, Brodd-Helgi Thorgilsson, who lived at Hof, and
Geitir Lytingsson, whose farm was at Krossavík, and follows the
feud until it is finally resolved by the succeeding generation. The
contest, which begins in Vápnafjord (Weapon's Fjord), a series of
low-lying green valleys, eventually engages people spread widely
throughout the East Fjords as well as leaders from the Northern
Quarter. As the feud progresses it touches the political nerve of a large
area, and additional farmers and chieftains are frequently drawn into
the conflict through contractual friendship arrangements, or *vinfengi*.
Both Brodd-Helgi and Geitir rely on *vinfengi*, and ultimately their
survival depends on their skill in establishing new ties of friendship
and maintaining old ones. Through *vinfengi* arrangements Geitir and
Brodd-Helgi, who themselves were fast friends in the beginning,
acquire the supplementary power necessary to influence court
decisions.

Like Arnkel goði in *Eyrbyggja saga,* Brodd-Helgi is a man who wins most of the lesser engagements along the way but loses the larger contest. Geitir, like Snorri goði, typifies the Icelandic hero who not only succeeds in destroying an overbearing rival but also manages to survive with his power intact. Indicating the interests of saga author and audience, accounts of such rivalries detail the political behaviour of the opponents. The relative merits of moderation (*hóf*) are weighed against lack of restraint (*ójafnaðr*).

Although he is aggressive, Brodd-Helgi is careful to remain within the law. His well-controlled offensive actions and Geitir's defensive responses show that both individuals understand and abide by the rules of a sophisticated political game. To his own disadvantage, however, Brodd-Helgi does not maintain his restraint. Just as he has nearly succeeded in destroying Geitir's authority, he loses his self-control. His conduct becomes so immoderate and overbearing that chieftains and farmers in other regions adopt a more friendly attitude toward Geitir. Brodd-Helgi's ultimate failure and death are attributable in part to his abuse of *vinfengi* in his relations with farmers and with other chieftains. For his part Geitir, in a display of political acumen, establishes a network of *vinfengi* ties that protects him from disastrous legal consequences.

Geitir and Brodd-Helgi are both capable leaders, but they differ widely in their approach to problems. Brodd-Helgi, with marked skill at arms, is courageous and willing to expose himself to danger. Early in the saga he is described as 'a tall man, strong, and early matured, handsome and imposing, not talkative in his youth, stubborn and harsh from an early age. He was cunning and capricious' (Chapter 1). In contrast, Geitir is not a fighter, and as he ages he becomes 'a man of great wisdom' (Chapter 3). As their feud progresses, Brodd-Helgi acknowledges the difference between the two men and characterizes his opponent: 'It has always been true that Geitir is the wiser of us, though he has time and again been overcome by sheer force' (Chapter 8).

Two distinct types of chieftain and two distinct operational methods are presented. Brodd-Helgi, like Arnkel, assails his rival openly and is a dangerous opponent. Geitir, like Snorri goði, avoids fighting back until he feels that local *bændr* and more distant *goðar* have reached a consensus that his opponent must be stopped. A chieftain like Geitir or Snorri goði can turn another chieftain's abuse of privilege to his own advantage, but he must be subtle about it. The defensive leader must maintain his composure over long periods of time until his rival becomes overconfident and extends himself too far. He plays on the fears of *bændr* whose lands and lives have been jeopardized by his more aggressive opponent. Despite desertions as the feud wears on, Geitir's strength becomes concentrated in a small band of trusted followers. These faithful thingmen are aware of their own self-interest and, like their chieftain, fear the rise of an openly aggressive local leader. They know that a concentration of power and wealth in the hands of one chieftain, if not counterbalanced, will erode the status of landowners like themselves.

The points of contention between the two *goðar* govern the progression of the saga and serve as the framework for the following discussion. The first incident between the chieftains concerns a foreign trader's goods; in the second, the foreigner's Icelandic partner is persecuted by Brodd-Helgi; the third incident deals with the dowry of Brodd-Helgi's wife, who is also Geitir's sister; the fourth is a clash over land between two farmers, Thord and Thormod Steinbjarnarson; the fifth concerns Brodd-Helgi's attempt to buy the allegiance of one of Geitir's *bændr*; and the sixth catalogues Brodd-Helgi's breach of *vinfengi* with Gudmund the Powerful, a power-broker from the Northern Quarter. The threads of the *vinfengi* relationships that both Brodd-Helgi and Geitir establish with Gudmund run through the whole story of the feud.

More so than the feud between Arnkel goði and Snorri goði, which concentrates on the control of land, the contest between Geitir and Brodd-Helgi focuses on the control of people, especially through *vinfengi*. Again the differences between the two *goðar* become apparent. Brodd-Helgi, unlike Geitir, is careless with his power. He shows a self-destructive need to avenge insults, real or perceived. As the dispute between the two *goðar* develops, the affairs of secondary characters become increasingly involved in it.

Inheriting a Foreigner's Goods

The first quarrel between Brodd-Helgi and Geitir concerns a wealthy Norwegian merchant called Hrafn who arrives in Vápnafjord with an Icelandic partner who goes to his own farm at Krossavík in Reyðarfjord, farther down the coast.* Hrafn takes lodgings with Geitir for the winter. Apparently (the saga is not explicit), Brodd-Helgi and Geitir plot to kill Hrafn because, as is all too clear, they covet the foreigner's wealth.

Besides his supply of trade goods stored at Geitir's farm, the Norwegian has other valuable possessions. He always wears a gold arm-ring and always carries with him a small strongbox, reputedly filled with gold and silver. Because Hrafn presses people hard on their debts, he is soon unpopular. Without Icelandic family and with no alliance such as fosterage or sworn brotherhood, he is virtually unprotected. He is found dead outside the farmhouse during a winter feast. No one takes responsibility for the killing, which thus becomes murder. The Norwegian's gold arm-ring and strongbox are not found with the body. None of the local *goðar* shows any inclination to search out the killer or to prosecute the case. As no other Icelanders have a claim to Hrafn's possessions, conveniently secure in Geitir's storehouse, Brodd-Helgi and Geitir agree to split them equally. The two *goðar*, however, decide to wait out the winter and to legalize their agreement at the local spring assembly.

Then a dispute arises to disturb the *vinfengi* between the chieftains. Both of them are privy to some secret information about the murder and are concerned about the disappearance of Hrafn's valuables. Brodd-Helgi suggests that Geitir made off with the dead merchant's strongbox, and Geitir asks Brodd-Helgi about the arm-ring. Meanwhile, there is a new development which the *goðar* had not counted on. Hrafn's partner, Thorleif the Christian (*inn kristni*), determines

---

* Thorleif's farm at Krossavík in Reyðarfjord is not to be confused with Geitir's farm at Krossavík in Vápnafjord.

that Hrafn's family in Norway shall inherit his goods. Thorleif is an unusually honest and courageous man whose moral stature is understood to be connected with his religion.[1] The story, set in the period before the conversion but written several centuries after it, was probably slanted to disparage non-Christian values.

While the two chieftains are away at the local Sunnudalr *várthing*, Thorleif removes the goods from Geitir's storehouse, loads them on his ship, and waits off the coast for a favourable wind to take him to Norway. The chieftains discover their loss when they return from the assembly. Although they have only small boats, Brodd-Helgi pushes for an immediate attack on Thorleif's ship. Geitir, however, sees the danger in this venture and suggests that they wait and let the wind drive the ship on to the shore. When the winds shift and Thorleif escapes to the open sea, Brodd-Helgi blames Geitir for their tactical error. The trust between the two leaders diminishes and their friendship cools. In Norway, Thorleif gives Hrafn's goods to the merchant's heirs, thus vitiating any accusation of robbery the chieftains might make against him.

Brodd-Helgi's Revenge against Thorleif

When Thorleif returns to Iceland, Brodd-Helgi desires revenge against him. His motivation is mostly hatred, pure and simple, with little gain in wealth or power. Although lacking grounds for prosecution, he patiently waits for an opportunity to lay a claim against Thorleif. The outlook is not promising, for Thorleif's farm, Krossavík, unlike the holdings of Brodd-Helgi and Geitir, is not in Vápnafjord but in Reyðarfjord, farther to the south and down the coast. Moreover, Thorleif is not a rash man and seems to have no obvious enemies. If Brodd-Helgi is to seek vengeance, he must operate at a considerable distance from home. To do so, he devises a means of attack that is bound by the legalistic rules of Icelandic feuding.

Thorleif is in a much more secure position than the foreigner Hrafn had been. A *bóndi*, he enjoys his full rights and prerogatives. Should

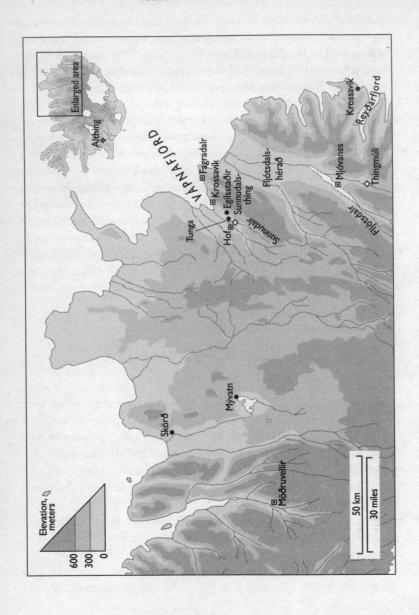

19. The Arena of Conflict between Geitir and Brodd-Helgi in Vápnafjord. The exact sites of the farms at Fljótsdalr, Mývatn and Tunga are not known. The site of the springtime assembly in Sunnudalr was probably close to the farms of Hof and Tunga.

Brodd-Helgi Thorgilsson (chieftain)	Hof
Stout Ketil	Fljótsdalr
Egil Steinbjarnarson	Egilsstaðir
Geitir Lytingsson (chieftain)	(1) Krossavík in Vápnafjord
	(2) Fagradalr
Gudmund the Powerful (chieftain)	Möðruvellir
Ofeig Jarngerdarson	Skörð
Thord	Tunga
Thorleif the Christian	Krossavík in Reyðarfjord
Thormod Steinbjarnarson	in Sunnudalr
Olvir the Wise	Mývatn

Brodd-Helgi kill a *bóndi* without cause, it would be difficult and expensive for him to defend himself in the courts against an alliance of enemies. A skilfully handled prosecution would certainly set him back and perhaps even destroy him.

Despite his rash temper and overbearing manner, Brodd-Helgi funnels his thirst for vengeance into socially acceptable channels. Determined to stay within lawful bounds, he waits for an opportunity to entrap Thorleif. The opportunity soon opens up. Steinvor, a priestess in charge of collecting dues for a local temple, complains to her relative Brodd-Helgi that Thorleif has, as a Christian, refused to pay the temple tax. Brodd-Helgi, hoping to escalate this refusal into a legal judgement against Thorleif, initiates a series of complicated manoeuvres. The saga's detailed description provides a good deal of information concerning tactics.

Our understanding of this new cluster of events would be clearer if we knew whose thingman Thorleif was. The Icelandic scholar Jón Jóhannesson suggests that Thorleif may have been a thingman of Steinvor, the temple priestess.[2] At that time a woman could inherit a *goðorð*, although she had to empower a man to act on her behalf. Because Thorleif is known from other extant sources, among them *Kristni tháttr* in *Óláfs saga Tryggvasonar en mesta*, it is possible that the author left out this information on the assumption that his audience had prior knowledge of the *bóndi*.

Brodd-Helgi's first tactic is to form an alliance with a farmer living closer to Thorleif. Travelling inland to Fljótsdalr (River Valley), he pays an unexpected visit to Stout Ketil (*Digr-Ketill*), a *bóndi* described as a most worthy person. The meeting is politically advantageous to both men. They are not related by blood, and although they hardly know each other, they soon swear *vinfengi*. Once the pact is established, Brodd-Helgi moves quickly. He requests Ketil to implement their new agreement by prosecuting Thorleif for failing to pay his temple tax. Brodd-Helgi's scheme is this: Thorleif, summoned only by Ketil, will think he is merely facing another *bóndi*. Put off his guard by this ruse, Thorleif will be unprepared in court when he suddenly finds himself confronted by a powerful chieftain with his armed thingmen.

Surprised and perhaps angered by Brodd-Helgi's devious request, Ketil protests, but nevertheless he honours the agreement: 'I would not have sworn *vinfengi* with you, had I known what was at the bottom of it, because Thorleif is a man with many friends [*maðr vinsæll*]. Still, I won't refuse you this first time' (Chapter 5). Ketil rides to Krossavík in Reyðarfjord. His heart is not in Brodd-Helgi's scheme and at first he tries to persuade Thorleif to pay the nominal temple fee. When Thorleif flatly refuses, Ketil summons him, probably to the Fljótsdalr-district spring assembly.

After the summons is issued a violent storm prevents Ketil from leaving; Thorleif offers him and his men hospitality for several days. As he leaves, Ketil gratefully pledges his friendship to Thorleif and promises to invalidate the case against him. Thorleif tells Ketil that 'your *vinfengi* is of great value to me, but it does not matter to me whether or not the case holds up' (Chapter 5).

Brodd-Helgi arrives at the thing with a large following, but Ketil keeps his promise and the case against Thorleif comes to nothing. Finding his plans frustrated, Brodd-Helgi reproaches Ketil for deceiving him and announces that 'our *vinfengi* is over'. The saga tells us that Brodd-Helgi is unable to get a 'hold on Thorleif, and Thorleif is now out of this saga'.

After leaving the thing Brodd-Helgi bitterly reproaches Geitir for the humiliation of the failed legal suit. Although it is by no means certain that Geitir had anything to do with the fiasco, Brodd-Helgi's view is clouded by hatred. At this point, the rift between the two chieftains widens into a conflict that will develop into a blood feud.

Struggle to Claim a Dowry

Just as Brodd-Helgi earlier avoided committing a random act of violence against Thorleif, so he now adopts the same cautious approach to Geitir. As the tale develops, Brodd-Helgi is guided not only by malice toward Geitir but also by his desire for political gain. To achieve his end Brodd-Helgi uses the law at every opportunity.

He seizes on any claim, however spurious, to entrap his enemy and backs it with all his strength. In aiming for the destruction of Geitir, Brodd-Helgi, like Arnkel goði in *Eyrbyggja saga*, is challenging the tradition of consensual order. If Geitir is eliminated as a viable force, Brodd-Helgi will dominate the area and might be able to destroy the system of non-territorial leadership. The rights of the farmers are in danger. On a wider scale, by disturbing the political balance he would pose a threat to other, more distant, chieftains.

A new point of contention arises when both chieftains, Brodd-Helgi and Geitir, lay claim to the dowry of Halla. Both men have claims: Halla is Geitir's sister and Brodd-Helgi's wife. Halla, dying of a lingering illness, has graciously allowed her husband to replace her in the household, but she is humiliated by Brodd-Helgi's immediate engagement to a young widow. Halla is well liked, and the saga tells us that this act by Brodd-Helgi is widely condemned in the district.

At first Brodd-Helgi persuades Halla to remain at Hof until his new wife arrives, but Geitir and his brother send men to bring her home to Krossavík. The separation raises a series of questions. As a party to the dissolved marriage Halla has the right to repossess her dowry, perhaps adding to it a share of the profit that has accrued from its use during the union. Brodd-Helgi, however, has no intention of dividing up the property. His plan shows how cunning he is: he simply ignores Halla's intention to separate from him before her death. As she is removing her personal possessions, 'Helgi stood outside the doorway and acted as if he did not know that Halla was leaving' (Chapter 6). When Brodd-Helgi refuses to honour Geitir's demand that he pay Halla a sum equal to the value of her remaining property, Geitir regards the refusal as an insult.

Geitir's subsequent attempts to obtain a money payment (*penninga*) for the value of his sister's property are equally fruitless. Brodd-Helgi refuses to relinquish his control of Halla's property, saying that he hopes she will yet return to Hof. As a negotiated settlement is not possible the next step would be a legal case, but here too Brodd-Helgi shows his ability to thwart Geitir. Brodd-Helgi's reasoning is simple: he is in possession of the lands, and thus he will be risking their loss if he allows the issue to go to court. Geitir, on the other hand, has a strong legal case when, and if, he can get to court.

To block Geitir, Brodd-Helgi seeks to deny him access to the legal process. In the spring, when Geitir summons Brodd-Helgi to the local Sunnudalr Thing, he has the ablest men on his side. But Brodd-Helgi, with a larger group of thingmen, manages to bar Geitir from the site of the court. When Geitir summons his adversary to the Althing, Brodd-Helgi, backed by Gudmund the Powerful, is once again successful in having Geitir's case voided. The dispute has still not been resolved after two attempts. As the conflict continues, the animosity between the two *goðar* understandably deepens.

The contention over Halla's dowry is more serious than the earlier disputes between the two leaders. Dowries consisted of heirlooms, farm implements, livestock, land, and perhaps a portion of a family's known monetary wealth. In the social context of a family's control over its destiny, the dowry had a value higher than its monetary worth. Seizing on the importance of the issue, Brodd-Helgi has chosen to make the retention of Halla's dowry a test of his ability to humiliate his opponent and to ignore due process. In the eyes of the community, Brodd-Helgi's refusal to accept the customary way of settling disputes is a signal that reveals his intention to strip Geitir of his authority and gain control over the local region for himself.

Skirmishes over a Woodland

Brodd-Helgi, having thwarted Geitir's efforts to settle the dowry issue legally, now seeks to end Geitir's role as a leader of local *bændr*. His opportunity comes in a dispute over a wood between two neighbouring farmers, Thord from Tunga in Sunnudalr and Thormod Steinbjarnarson, one of Geitir's thingmen. Brodd-Helgi assumes Thord's part-ownership of the woodland. Then he ruthlessly harasses and finally kills Thormod and several of his companions, all thingmen of Geitir, who had gone to Hof in order to summon Thord for having cut down Thormod's trees. In a deliberately insulting gesture, Brodd-Helgi will not allow Geitir to retrieve the bodies of his thingmen for burial at their homes. Geitir loses face because of this, and he is eventually reduced to using a ruse to reclaim the bodies. Brodd-Helgi adds to the shame when he refuses to pay compensation for these killings. With the killings and the subsequent actions, Brodd-Helgi's quarrel with Geitir has escalated from a simple difference between two friends to a deadly struggle for regional power. Within the Icelandic context, the matter has become a blood feud, involving the thingmen of the two chieftains.

Seeking a Thingman's Allegiance

The saga next tells us that a ship skippered by Thorarin Egilsson arrives in Vápnafjord. At this point some of the genealogical information supplied by the saga-teller at the start of his story becomes significant. Thorarin is one of the promising younger members of a prominent family of local *bændr* who are Geitir's thingmen. Thorarin's father, Egil from Egilsstaðir, is the brother of Thormod from Sunnudalr, the farmer whom Brodd-Helgi killed in the dispute over the woodland at Tunga and for whom he never paid compensation. Thorarin's sister, Hallfrid, was the first wife of Geitir's son Thorkel.

Brodd-Helgi now directs his attention to the newly returned trader Thorarin. Should Brodd-Helgi succeed in entering into a *vinfengi* relationship with Thorarin, he might be able to detach Thorarin and perhaps other members of his family from Geitir. Such a shift in allegiance would endanger Geitir, for these *bændr* are among his most able thingmen. In describing the contest for Thorarin's allegiance (in Chapter 11) the saga-teller plays on divisions in the community caused by a competition between chieftains:

Brodd-Helgi rode to the ship and invited Thorarin, and as many of his men as he wanted to bring along, to lodge at his farm. When Thorarin said that he would accept the invitation, Helgi went home to announce that his household should expect Captain Thorarin as their guest.

Geitir also went to the ship to meet Thorarin, and asked if he intended to go to Hof. Thorarin said that the matter had been spoken of but had not been decided upon. Geitir told Thorarin that it would be better for him to come to Krossavík 'because, as I see it, few of my men do well for themselves in accepting Helgi's hospitality'. The result was that Thorarin decided to go to Krossavík.

Brodd-Helgi, hearing of this arrangement, immediately rode to the ship with horses already saddled, intending to take Thorarin home with him. Thorarin told Helgi that things had now been decided differently. And Helgi replied, 'I wish to show you that I invited you to my house without deceit and that I will bear you no animosity if you go to Krossavík.' The next day Helgi rode to the ship again and gave Thorarin five stud horses, all dandelion yellow, for the sake of his *vinfengi*.

Geitir went to fetch Thorarin and asked the trader whether he had received the stud horses from Brodd-Helgi. Thorarin said that he had. 'Then I counsel you,' said Geitir, 'to return those stud horses.'

Thorarin did so, and Helgi took back the stud horses. Thorarin stayed with Geitir through the winter and went abroad the following summer.

Still operating within the law, Helgi is a more eager competitor for the *vinfengi* of Thorarin here. Geitir, showing his wisdom and restraint, nevertheless wins: Thorarin stays at his house over the winter.

Brodd-Helgi Breaks Vinfengi

Beginning with the death of a foreigner and continuing through a quarrel between two local farmers, the saga has chronicled the growing feud between the two *goðar*. With each stage the story has come closer to disturbing the fragile relationship between *goðar* and *bændr*. From this point on the quarrel penetrates more deeply into the community, forcing local farmers and also distant chieftains to take sides.

The saga suggests that Brodd-Helgi is disadvantaged not so much by his basic greed as by the method that he chooses to satisfy it. As the story progresses he begins to ignore the norms of reciprocity which govern *vinfengi* relationships. Arrogantly disregarding the danger inherent in provocative conduct, Brodd-Helgi breaks *vinfengi* agreements and makes new enemies. On one occasion at the Althing (Chapter 10), he refuses to keep a bargain made with his 'friend' Gudmund the Powerful:

One summer Brodd-Helgi lacked support at the Althing, and he asked Gudmund the Powerful for assistance. But Gudmund said he was not inclined to help Helgi at every thing meeting, thereby putting himself on unfriendly terms [*óvinsæla sik*] with other chieftains and getting no benefit from Helgi in return. Whereupon they settled the matter, Gudmund promising to aid Helgi in return for half a hundred of silver.[3]

When the court was dismissed and Helgi's case had gone well he and Gudmund met at the booths, and Gudmund claimed the payment from Helgi. But Helgi said that he had no obligation to pay; moreover, he added, he did not see why he should have to pay within their *vinfengi* relationship. Gudmund answered, 'It is poorly done on your part always to be in need of others, but not to pay what you have promised. And your *vinfengi* seems worth little to me. I will never ask for this money again; nor will I ever help you again.' Then they parted, with their *vinfengi* at an end.

When Geitir heard about this dispute he went to meet with Gudmund, offering him payment in return for his *vinfengi*. Gudmund refused to take Geitir's money, saying that he had little desire to help men who were resigned to losing out in all their dealings with Helgi.

Although less violent than Brodd-Helgi, Geitir is not averse to scheming to increase his own wealth and power. He shows no remorse for having helped to kill the Norwegian; indeed, his desire to acquire Hrafn's goods was obvious. But as a leader Geitir avoids bullying tactics. And, in contrast with Brodd-Helgi, he is not willing to risk his life in violent confrontation, whatever its guise of legality, Geitir's strength lies in his ability to manipulate the defensive aspects of the legal system. Each of the two rival leaders, in his own way, pushes the definition of acceptable action to its limits. The struggle between them reveals the faults and the dangers in their respective positions.

By his aggressiveness in his feud with Geitir, Brodd-Helgi forces the local *bændr* to divide into two camps. Whether enticed or threatened, many of Geitir's thingmen desert their leader and align themselves with Brodd-Helgi. Geitir's remaining thingmen are in an increasingly difficult position. They are like Snorri goði's faithful followers, the sons of Thorbrand in *Eyrbyggja saga*, in that they must either make their *goði* act or seek other alliances.

Geitir Establishes Vinfengi

Upon his return from his next voyage, Thorarin Egilsson finds that Geitir has timidly moved from Krossavík to a remote and inaccessible farm called Fagradalr, farther away from Brodd-Helgi.[4] This farm, located at the mouth of a fjord, is surrounded by unusually high mountains. Access to it is either by sea or by one small path leading down from the mountains, and in both cases an attacker would be visible from a long distance. Safe from physical danger, Geitir waits. Many thingmen have left him, and the Vápnafjord region is almost completely under the fist of Brodd-Helgi.

Geitir's loyal followers choose to protect their rights and property by inciting their defensive leader to act. As spokesman for Geitir's thingmen, the trader Thorarin Egilsson presents Geitir with an ultimatum (Chapter 11):

The thingmen of Geitir took counsel together and decided they could no longer tolerate Brodd-Helgi's domineering ways [*ójafnaðr*]. They travelled to meet Geitir. Thorarin asked, 'How long is it going to go on like this? Until everything comes to a bad end? Many men are leaving you now, and they all

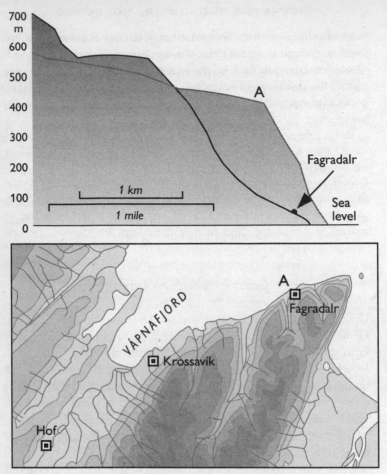

20. Fagradalr, Geitir's Retreat. Threatened by Brodd-Helgi, Geitir moves his farm to Fagradalr. The arrow indicates the location. The mountain, marked A, descends precipitously to the sea, making Fagradalr impossible to reach by land along the coast. The surrounding mountains, unusually high for an Icelandic coastal region, make the small valley a natural fortress. Within Fagradalr, the one small path leading down from the mountains could be watched from a long distance and easily blocked. Serious attack was possible only from the sea, but here, too, Geitir could easily post lookouts. Free from surprise attack, Geitir waits.

attach themselves to Helgi. We consider your timidity the sole reason you hold back from going against Helgi. You are the more clever of the two and, moreover, you have no fewer brave men with you than he has with him. And now, for our part, there are two choices: either you travel home to your farm at Krossavík, never move from it again, and take action against Helgi should he henceforth do you any dishonour, or we will sell our farms and move away, some from the country, and some from the district.'

The thingmen of Geitir have the courage and the motivation to attack and kill an aggressive *goði*. They are unwilling, however, to become tragic characters in the manner of the hero of *Gisli Sursson's Saga*, who acted intemperately and killed a chieftain when his sense of honour was violated. Recognizing their legal impotence, the few farmers who remain loyal to Geitir force the burden of action to shift from the aggressive Brodd-Helgi to their defensive leader. It is the latter who must seize an opportunity to attack and kill his rival and yet avoid disaster in the courts. The attack, to be successful, must catch his rival off guard.

Both Geitir and Snorri goði show their greatness in their ability to blunt the legal counter-claim after killing a fellow chieftain. They play a waiting game. Both manage to convince their peers that the killing was the best alternative for them and for their district. Snorri's pre-court political dealings are not detailed in *Eyrbyggja saga*. Instead, the saga-teller simply recounts Snorri's success in defending himself and his thingmen after the killing of Arnkel. *Vápnfirðinga saga* describes Geitir's journey through the north-eastern part of the country before he moves back to Krossavík. The journey enables Geitir to test the waters and to see whether there is enough support from the other *goðar* for the killing of Brodd-Helgi. One result of Geitir's new offensive posture is that Gudmund the Powerful from Möðruvellir is now willing to support him. Another factor in Geitir's favour is Brodd-Helgi's repeated lack of *hóf* (Chapter 12):

Geitir prepared for a trip and went north to Skarð in Ljósavatn,[5] to Ofeig Jarngerdarson. Gudmund the Powerful came [to Ofeig's farm] to meet Geitir and the two sat the whole day in conversation. Later they parted, and Geitir took lodgings with Olvir the Wise at his farm in Mývatn. Olvir questioned Geitir carefully about Brodd-Helgi. Geitir spoke well of him, saying that Brodd-Helgi was a most important person, stubborn and harsh but a good man in many ways. 'Is he not an aggressively unjust man [*ójafnaðarmaðr*]?' asked Olvir. 'Helgi's overbearing ways [*ójafnaðr*],' Geitir answered, 'affect me most in that Helgi finds it disagreeable to have the same sky over me as over him.' Olvir responded, 'Shall all this, then, be tolerated?' 'It has been until now,' said Geitir. Thus they ended their talk, and Geitir travelled home. Now all was quiet for the rest of the winter.

The saga moves quickly to a resolution of the contest. Although the manuscript of the saga is damaged at this spot, the outlines of the action seem clear. Geitir, with his trusted thingmen, ambushes and kills Brodd-Helgi while the latter is on his way to the thing with only a few men. In the ensuing court case Geitir, supported by his new friend Gudmund the Powerful, reaches an advantageous settlement with Brodd-Helgi's son Bjarni.* By its terms Geitir retains his *goðorð*. He pays Bjarni an honourable compensation and a few of his followers are banished for a time – a small price to pay for the demise of Brodd-Helgi. Geitir resumes his position as a respected *goði* of the district and treats his nephew Bjarni well. Eventually Bjarni's stepmother incites him to kill Geitir, an act which he regrets immediately and which causes him to be ineptly pursued by Geitir's son Thorkel. After several near confrontations, they battle each other and each loses four thingmen. After this Bjarni makes overtures of friendship, which Thorkel accepts on the counsel of his wife. The two cousins eventually resolve their differences honourably.

Like *Eyrbyggja saga*, *Vápnfirðinga saga* illustrates ways in which wealth changed hands and in which power was dependent upon a network of kin, thingmen, advocacy and *vinfengi* ties. When a single leader attained hegemony in a region, it caused farmers in this lateral

---

* The son of Brodd-Helgi and Halla, Geitir's sister.

society more unease than a similar situation might have done in European societies dominated by territorial lordship, where loyalty and control were often defined by the location of one's land. Farmers in Iceland often had more alternative courses of action than did farmers elsewhere in northern Europe for several reasons. One is that shifting intrigues of power were not bound by territorial constraints, and another is the consensual nature of decision-making in Iceland. *Eyrbyggja saga* and *Vápnfirðinga saga* suggest that Icelandic *bændr* had the responsibility to find their own solutions when faced with an infringement of their rights by an overly aggressive individual (*ójafnaðarmaðr*).

14

The Obvious Sources of Wealth

There was neither public revenue nor public expenditure, neither exchequer nor budget. No taxes were levied by the Republic, as indeed no expenses were incurred on its behalf.

James Bryce, *Studies in History and Jurisprudence*

Icelandic sources speak of many chieftains in the early centuries, but just how these leaders acquired their wealth during this formative period remains unclear. Yet the answer to this question is the key to understanding how the different elements in Iceland's complex medieval society operated as a cohesive body politic. In this chapter I seek to fill this gap. Rather than a relationship based on an extraction of payments by leaders from their followers, Iceland's system of consensual arrangements saw leaders acting entrepreneurially and competing among themselves to offer services. *Goðar*, for their support of farmers and other chieftains in lawsuits and feuds, expected to be paid in the wealth that was in limited supply in Iceland.

The major historical writings, *Landnámabók* and *Íslendingabók*, give little specific economic information about the sources of a *goði*'s wealth in the early period. *Grágás* is only slightly more informative. The legally prescribed taxes and other sources of income allotted to a chieftain in *Grágás* are noticeably small and irregular. They could not have enabled a *goði* to amass the wealth necessary to purchase support, pay compensation awards, exchange gifts, make loans, and provide feasts and hospitality.

Wealth in early Iceland's farming economy was land-based, and the methods by which leaders acquired land had a decidedly predatory stamp. Perhaps more than in other societies with more extensive resources and additional opportunities, an increase in the size of an individual's landholdings often depended on taking a neighbour's property. As a result, the success of one Icelander routinely signalled the impoverishment of another. With this factor in mind, the question asked in this and the next chapter is how best to define Iceland's system of wealth exchange in the early centuries, in particular the means by which land was acquired.

This chapter begins with a discussion of the income that a chieftain derived from his position as a governmental leader. This privileged income included revenues generated by the few taxes, profits from carrying out official services, and advantages reaped from the exclusive right to set prices on imported goods. The second part of the chapter considers sources of wealth which were not controlled solely by the *goðar* but were available to all prosperous farmers in the community. These non-privileged sources include trade and profit from the rental of livestock and land. The tithe, introduced in 1096, often went to *goðar* who controlled churches. It is discussed in Chapter 18, as is the income which prominent landowners gained from control of Church farmsteads called *staðir* (sing. *staðr*).

SOURCES OF INCOME AVAILABLE
ONLY TO CHIEFTAINS

Early Taxes

Because the historical and legal sources say so little about income for the early *goðar*, students of medieval Iceland have usually assumed that chieftains in the early centuries found little financial advantage in their official position. In keeping with this view, a disproportionate share of the comparatively small space given to the discussion of wealth exchange in current historical writings is devoted to the thing-travel-tax (*thingfararkaup*) and the temple tax (*hoftollr*). *Thingfararkaup*, which means the 'fee' or 'bargained price' (*kaup*) for 'travelling' ('faring') to the Althing, was the most lucrative assessment a *goði* could legally impose. Upon demand, if he did not attend the Althing, each farmer who possessed a minimum amount of property – a cow, a boat or a net, for example – for each person in his household had to pay the thing tax to his *goði*. *Thingfararkaup* is an old tax, but the specifics are not completely clear in *Grágás*.[1]

As mentioned in Chapter 3, Bishop Gizur Isleifsson's census (c. 1096) determined that there were approximately 4,560 thing-tax-paying farmers,[2] a figure that suggests the political importance of this broad landowning group of farmers. Again we are not completely sure of the specifics, but it appears that at the local spring-time assembly a chieftain was permitted to require each ninth *thingfararkaup* farmer among his thingmen to accompany him to the coming Althing. The *goði* then collected the tax from the thingmen who stayed at home and used the funds to compensate those who accompanied him to the Althing. This payment to the farmers was also called *thingfararkaup*. Poorer freemen not liable to the tax were also entitled to attend the assemblies. While a *goði* might have such thingmen, propertyless men were sometimes barred from serving as jurors (or judges) and in some instances they were ineligible to serve on panels giving evidence.

The size of the *thingfararkaup* varied, probably in accordance with the distance from home to the Althing. Although we lack specific information, it seems doubtful that a chieftain could set the tax above the amount assessed by competing local leaders and still retain the support of his thingmen. Because a *goði* incurred heavy expenses on a trip to the Althing, any revenue from *thingfararkaup* might be, and probably was, cancelled out by the costs he incurred.

The only other major tax available to the early *goðar* was *hoftollr*, the temple tax. Most of the little that is known about *hoftollr* comes from sagas. We have already, in the last chapter, seen one reference to *hoftollr* in the discussion of the temple priestess in *The Saga of the*

People of Weapon's Fjord. According to Chapter 5 of the saga, 'all the farmers were required to pay to the temple a temple tax'. *Eyrbyggja saga*, which, like all the family sagas, was written in later Christian times and therefore is not a trustworthy source for information about specific pre-conversion religious practices, describes the temple tax thus (in Chapter 4): 'All people were required to pay a tax to the temple priest on all his trips, in the same manner that thingmen now must accompany their leaders. But at his own expense the *goði* [who was also the temple priest] was required to oversee the upkeep of the temple so that it did not deteriorate and to hold in it sacrificial feasts.' This passage suggests that the profit from *hoftollr* was limited. In return for dues, the chieftain bore the expense of maintaining the temple and holding the feasts.

Again as with *thingfararkaup*, if one *goði* in collecting the temple tax raised his demands, the interests of other *goðar* would have been served by their asking less from their thingmen. Because *thingfararkaup* and the temple tax brought chieftains little surplus wealth, scholars have long postulated that a *goði* realized little or no income from the possession of a *goðorð*. This older view, which does not answer the question of how the *goðar* survived from the 900s until the 1200s when potentially remunerative taxes first developed, is the product of a long and interesting scholarly tradition of inquiry. I have placed discussion of this issue in the notes, where it is available for readers interested in such matters.[3] I take a different view: that possession of a chieftaincy offered significant financial rewards, although not through taxation.

Price-setting

Besides taxes the chieftains had certain other privileged sources of wealth, such as the right to set prices on wares that foreign merchants brought into Iceland. Ostensibly the purpose of this practice was to control the greed of foreign merchants, as suggested in *Grágás*, though neither the date nor the enforceability of the clause is known:

'It is said in our laws that men shall not buy expensive Norwegian goods from merchants at their ships until those three men who set the rate within each district boundary have done so.'⁴

Although some windfall profits might have accrued from price-setting, it was not as lucrative as one might expect because, in most instances, the Norwegian merchant retained the advantage. If dissatisfied with a chieftain in a particular region, the merchant could try to find a more compliant *goði* in that area or he could sail to another place on the coast. In only a few years a *goði* could acquire a bad reputation if he pressed the merchants too hard for a price advantage or demanded more than a small share in the profits. For a *goði* the value of the privilege probably was that it gave him first choice of imported goods. This advantage was significant in a society in which gift-giving, loans of precious items⁵ and displays of hospitality were used to increase political stature. At the expensive feasts and offerings of hospitality that figure prominently in the literature, the quality of relationships was judged by noting whether the host sent his guest off with 'good gifts'.⁶ These expenses were incurred on special occasions and purchased political ties. Unlike chieftains in many other parts of Northern Europe, Iceland's *goðar* did not maintain a warrior retinue within their households and hence cut their costs dramatically.

Only a few sagas narrating events before the thirteenth century – for example, *The Saga of the People of Weapon's Fjord*, *Hen-Thorir's Saga* and *The Saga of Ljosavatn* – mention price-setting. The account from *Vápnfirðinga saga* of Hrafn, the murdered Norwegian merchant (discussed in the preceding chapter), offers insight into the significance of high-status foreign goods. The following episode takes place when Hrafn first landed his ship and sought lodgings for himself and storage for his goods over the coming winter. The passage (from Chapter 4) also gives a sense of the competition among the local chieftains for housing the Norwegian:

Brodd-Helgi rode to the ship and invited the captain to lodge with him. The Norwegian answered that he would not lodge with Helgi, as 'it has

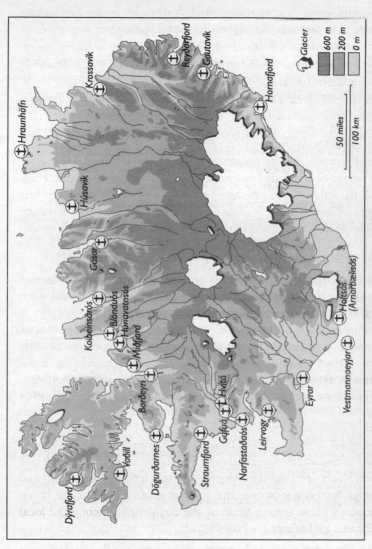

21. Principal Ship Landing Sites and Harbours from the Settlement Period until c. 1180. In this early period Icelanders still owned ocean-going ships. There were many landing sites; often these were close to the individual shipowner's farm.

been said to me that you are arrogant and greedy for money. But I am humble and a man of few needs, and the two do not go together.'

Brodd-Helgi tried to buy some valuable objects from the merchant because he was a man given to lavish display. But Hrafn replied that he had no wish to sell goods on credit.

Brodd-Helgi said, 'You have made my journey here a wasted endeavour, refusing my lodgings and refusing my trade.'

Geitir came next to the ship and found the captain, telling him that it was unwise to have fallen out with the most notable man in the district.

The Norwegian answered, 'It had been my intention to lodge with some farmer [*bóndi*], but will you now see to my needs, Geitir?'

Geitir did not quickly agree, but in the end he took the Norwegian in.

The crew also found lodgings for themselves. Rollers were put under the keel and the ship was dragged ashore and set up for the winter. The Norwegian was given a storage shed for his wares; he sold his goods slowly.

The saga depicts the Norwegian preferring to lodge with a farmer rather than with a *goði*. As the story develops, Hrafn would have been better served in following his first instincts.

In 1215 Saemund Jonsson of Oddi and Thorvald Gizurarson of Hruni, two powerful leaders, dangerously overstepped the bounds of tradition by imposing terms that the Norwegian merchants found unfair. A dangerous conflict ensued, and the foreigners' indignation suggests how unusual the chieftains' demands were. Earlier, in 1203,

22. Ship Landing Sites and Harbours in Use from *c.* 1190. By the end of the eleventh century, few Icelanders owned ocean-going ships, and foreigners, especially Norwegians, took over the Iceland trade. The number of landing sites diminished significantly, with foreign merchants arriving at specific harbours, to which the Icelanders came expecting to trade. At such a site, called a *kaupstaðr*, merchants camped alongside their ships, offering their wares. The most important of these harbours were Eyrar in the south, Hvítá in the west, Gásar in the north, and possibly Gautavík in the east. Beginning in about 1300 many new harbours were established in response to the growing stockfish trade.

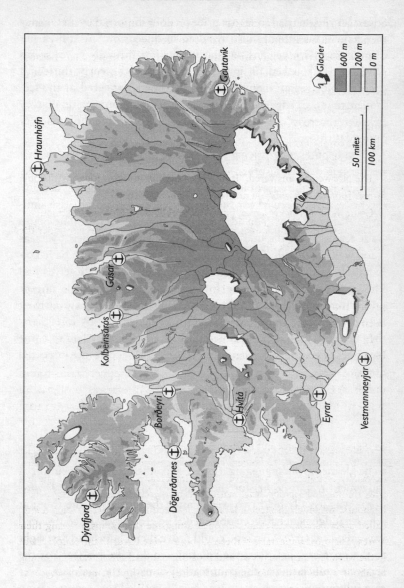

Snorri Sturluson tried to set the price on flour imported by an Orkney merchant. This attempt also resulted in dissension.[7] A still earlier dispute with Norwegians, lasting from 1170 through 1180, seems also to have touched on issues of trade.[8] By the early thirteenth century, Norwegian merchants had become so angered at the Icelanders that they engaged Norwegian rulers in planning a retaliatory invasion that was only narrowly averted through the diplomacy of Snorri Sturluson.[9]

That disputes over pricing should arise around 1200 may in part be attributed to widespread inflation in Europe. For the Icelanders the increase in the cost of imports was especially distressing because the prices they received for their exported goods did not rise similarly. Nor were they in an advantageous position to negotiate better trade terms. After the mid twelfth century almost all their overseas trade was handled by Norwegians, who seem at times to have colluded on fixing the prices of goods. The Icelanders themselves had little direct contact with the foreign markets where their import goods were purchased and their export goods sold. Whatever their temporary resistance to paying the prices demanded by foreigners, they really had no other options. In the long run, they had to come to terms with the Norwegian merchants or receive no imported goods.

Additional Privileged Sources of Wealth

Another irregular source of wealth available to a *goði* was the assets to be gleaned from managing a court of confiscation or execution of judgement (*féránsdómr*) for the benefit of claimants.[10] The *féránsdómr* was usually held two weeks after the closing of the thing at which a judgement had been obtained. The property to be confiscated was called *sektarfé*. Men who could prove their claims had first right to the property, and then the chieftain could take his fee. For the service of officiating at the confiscation of property against a lesser or a full outlaw, the chieftain was legally entitled to a remuneration of one cow or one ox four winters old. The remaining property was divided among the men of the district or of the quarter.

In itself the chieftain's fee was small, especially in view of the dangers inherent in leading a prosecution for someone else and then confiscating the defendant's property. Should a *goði* be in the position of confiscating the property of an outlaw with himself as the injured party, however, he would receive not only his fee but also a claim to a substantial part of the remaining property. Furthermore, he would be in a favourable position to determine the specific allotments. The possibility of combining roles made the practice of buying the claims of others a potentially profitable source of wealth for chieftains.

Several other irregular sources of income were available. For instance, when a foreigner died without an heir or a partner, certain rights of inheritance accrued to chieftains.[11] So too there was income in assuming the role of trustee (*fjárvarðveizlumaðr*). Chieftains at times settled issues of inheritance and sometimes managed the property rights of widows, minors and unmarried women. Although the *goður* were advantageously placed to undertake such tasks, they did not monopolize the administration of guardianships or inheritance cases. The right of each family to manage its own affairs was a basic tenet of Icelandic law.

The Sheep Tax

In order to understand Iceland's political economics, it is important to note that a tax designed specifically for the maintenance of governmental leaders was not imposed until near the end of the Free State. This new levy, the sheep tax, called *sauðakvöð* or *sauðatollr*, is mentioned several times in *Sturlunga saga*.[12] That this tax designed for the support of an over-class came so late in the history of the Free State is a clue that helps identify the earlier system of wealth extraction by which the chieftains maintained themselves. *Sauðakvöð* developed in conjunction with several lesser taxes, including a form of thing dues called *thingtollr*[13] (not to be confused with *thingfararkaup*, the thing travel tax imposed on thingmen not attending the Althing). *Kvöð* means a 'claim' or 'demand', and *tollr* a 'duty' on commodities, or sometimes 'dues'.

All the references to the *sauðakvöð* or *sauðatollr* appear toward the middle of the thirteenth century, and *sauðakvöð* seems to have been a forced tax rather than a regularly collected one;[14] it was employed most often as an expedient by chieftains in dire need of funds. An extreme example of the rapaciousness of the later chieftains is the brutal collection methods of Snorri Sturluson's ambitious son Oraekja in the West Fjords.[15]

The introduction in the thirteenth century of a tax on farmers such as *sauðakvöð*, as well as the aggressive stance that some *goðar* took at this time against foreign merchants, may be as much connected with economic conditions in Europe as with contemporaneous Icelandic political arrangements. Around 1200, when Icelandic leaders were becoming more ruthless, Europe was experiencing inflation. Those in power in many places in the medieval West were squeezing everyone within their reach.

SOURCES OF INCOME AVAILABLE
TO ALL FREEMEN

The *goðar* shared access to certain sources of wealth with all prosperous landholders. Two of these, trade and the rental of land and livestock, were available from the first years of the settlement. Another source of income, the revenue generated by ownership of the Church farmsteads called *staðir* (related to the English word 'steads') became available only after the introduction of the tithe in 1096. Both *staðir* and the tithe are discussed in Chapter 18, but here it can be said that in the twelfth and thirteenth centuries, control of Church farmsteads became increasingly concentrated in the hands of prominent leaders. *Staðir*, however, were only one kind of productive property. The more fundamental issue is to unearth the processes by which ambitious individuals acquired valuable property.

Trade

During the time of the Free State, Iceland imported staples such as barley, wheat, timber and linen, as well as all manner of luxury goods. A number of Icelanders, among them Gizur Isleifsson (later a bishop), Hall Thorarinsson from Haukadalr, and Thorhall Asgrimsson, are known to have participated at times in trading voyages, but few Icelanders devoted themselves entirely to overseas trade. Although trading voyages may have benefited individuals, they never gave rise to a merchant class or supported a governing group. As Bruce Gelsinger commented, 'What is remarkable about the Icelandic Commonwealth's foreign trade is not that it ended in failure but that it persisted, despite limitations, for almost four centuries.'[16]

Because Icelandic sheep were especially long-haired and their wool rich in lanolin, Icelandic cloth and cloaks made from it were highly water repellent. Icelanders, from early on, specialized in the exploitation of sheep by-products, and their exports were chiefly raw wool, different grades of homespun cloth (vaðmál), and a type of rough woollen cloak (vararfeldr) that provided protection from the rain. There were two types of vaðmál, a division which was based on quality.[17] Both were woven cloth, as knitting had not yet been introduced. By far the most common type was called vararvaðmál. It is frequently referred to in the written sources and is sometimes called 'standard vaðmál', because its quality was recognized throughout Iceland. Standardization meant that third parties were not needed to judge the quality of the goods, an important feature for a medium of exchange. Standard vaðmál was coarse, strong cloth. It was relatively cheap, and working clothes, gloves, stockings, and so on were sewn from it. It was often exported to Norway as unsewn cloth and there made into items. The higher grade was a finer and rarer cloth called hafnarvaðmál ('harbour vaðmál'). The best grades of hafnarvaðmál were used for sailcloth. There were several grades of *hafnarvaðmál*, with prices that varied accordingly.

Woollen goods were produced by a widespread cottage industry, and woollen products became a useful vehicle of exchange within the country. Along with merchandise derived from sheep farming, some export trade was conducted in other farm products, for example, horses, hides, and sometimes cheese. There was also a limited trade in sulphur and exotics such as white falcons.

Internally there was small-scale trade in foodstuffs, particularly dried cod for the inland districts, that was neither controlled nor taxed by the *goðar*. The self-made man Hen-Thorir is portrayed as the troublemaker in *Hen-Thorir's Saga* (*Hænsa-Thoris saga*). Although the saga author has little sympathy for how Thorir acquired his wealth, the following description gives an idea of the opportunity open to enterprising individuals:

There was a man by the name of Thorir, hard up for cash, and not much liked by people in general. He made it his practice to go travelling round, district by district, with his summer's wages, selling in one place what he bought in another, and soon made a lot of money by his peddling. On one occasion when he set off from the south over the heath, he took poultry with him on his trip to the north country, and sold it along with his other wares, by reason of which he got nicknamed Hen-Thorir. Now he made so much money that he bought himself the place known as Vatn, up from Nord-Tunga; and he had not been keeping house many winters before he became so rich a man that he had large sums out on loan with practically everyone. Yet though he made so much money, his unpopularity remained unchanged, for there could hardly be a more detestable creature alive than Hen-Thorir was known to be.[18]

The *Saga of Gudmund the Worthy* tells us about another enterprising trader, this time a man named Thorvard kamphund who used a ship to transport heavier foodstuffs. His farm at Siglunes on the sea to the west of the mouth of Eyjafjord was well suited for fishing. We know little about Thorvard kamphund beyond his being an independent *bóndi* who moved freely up and down the coast of the fjord, landing and trading. As far as can be seen, he conducted his business without any financial connections with chieftains. When he wanted, he pitched his tent at Gásar, the major port in the region, where during the summer Norwegian merchants came to trade. We only learn of Thorvard because he takes into his household a young woman named Gudrun from Arnanes. She is the former wife of Thorvard's drowned son and has run away from her second husband. Gudrun travels freely with Thorvard, and at Gásar meets her future lover:

Each summer it was Thorvard kamphund's custom to load a coastal ferry with Lenten fish and transport the cargo down the fjord from where the fish could be sold to farmers farther inland. He continued to do so, taking Gudrun with him as he sailed the fjord, making for the harbour at Gásar where a [foreign] merchant ship was berthed. There Thorvard pitched his tent, and Gudrun stayed with him.

Coastal ferries such as Thorvard kamphund's were small ships. The lack of wood of sufficient quality to build larger, ocean-going ships was from the start an almost insurmountable obstacle to the development and maintenance of a competitive merchant fleet. The *landnámsmenn* brought with them many ships, but later generations were unable to replace them; as the centuries passed the number of seagoing vessels steadily decreased. By the thirteenth century it was rare for Icelanders to own large ships. In one example of rare ownership, Snorri Sturluson received a ship as a gift from the Norwegian Jarl Skuli in 1220.[19] Most of the Icelanders who became full-time international merchants moved abroad, operating principally out of Norway. Often working in conjunction with Norwegian partners, they seem not to have confined themselves to trade with Iceland but to have operated in many northern European seaports. Some of these traders returned to Iceland. Although merchants from throughout the Norse lands, including the Orkneys, traded in Iceland, most of them came from Norway. The apparatus supporting the Iceland and the Greenland trade, including credit arrangements, merchant guilds or brotherhoods, and trade towns with warehouses and workshops, was centred in that country.

Even for well-equipped foreign merchants, trade with Iceland was a difficult and time-consuming venture. The seas were unpredictable, and shipping was threatened by the strength and coldness of the winter winds and the drift ice, which in some years came far south. Thin hulls were no match for even small chunks of drift ice, a factor that restricted routine sailing and enforced a seasonal rhythm in trading activities. Foreign traders arrived in Iceland in June and July and traded during the summer and autumn. They had to stay there for the long northern winter, spending almost a whole costly year in Iceland before spring and the sure retreat of the drift ice made it safe to leave.

Once in Iceland a foreign merchant needed a base from which to trade, and a chieftain's or a big farmer's home was the logical choice. In return the Icelander probably received some payment. Such arrangements, which provided entertainment, news of the outside world, access to prestige goods, and foreign contacts, added to the stature of individuals within the local community. Nevertheless, the chieftains' income from trade should not be overemphasized. Although better able to compete than their fellow Icelanders for the modest gains of trade, the chieftains played only a passive part in controlling the flow of goods or in regulating prices when compared with the role played by foreign merchants. The schedule of trading and the choice of goods, as well as the quantity and quality of articles traded, were in the main determined by the merchants. Only in the early fourteenth century, when the trade in stockfish (*skreið*, dried cod) was first developed, did Europe discover in Iceland a product of great commercial value.[20] Because of stockfish, Europeans with sufficient means – Norwegians until 1410–30(?), then English and German merchants – made the capital investment necessary to establish a lively trade. The specifics of the financing are not known, but the German Hanseatic League merchants in particular, with their connections throughout northern Europe, were in an advantageous

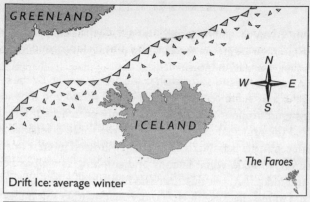

Drift Ice: average winter

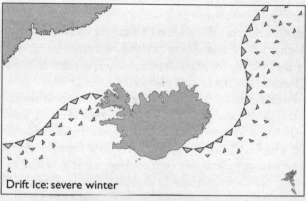

Drift Ice: severe winter

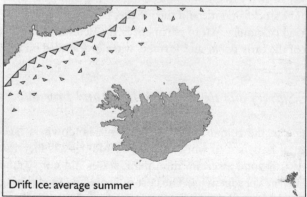

Drift Ice: average summer

23. The Range of Drift Ice.

position to finance export of Iceland's fish, the demand for which seems to have increased as stockfish became a staple food, especially during the long Lenten fast.

Once started, Iceland's stockfish trade grew rapidly. By the second half of the fourteenth century the export of *skreið* and the industry that grew up around it had become firmly entrenched. Dried cod remained the principal export, although the trade diversified in the fifteenth century when English merchants showed interest in acquiring fish oil, *vaðmál*, white falcons and sulphur, as well as perhaps wool and hides.[21] About this time the English also began to fish the Icelandic waters. Because the Icelanders had neither salt mines nor a sufficiently warm climate to produce salt by evaporation, they lacked the large quantities of salt necessary for curing and for making brines. This absence left them unable to expand their trade by exporting fish that were unsuitable for wind-drying, including salmon, herring and trout. (Smoked fish does not travel well.)

The development of the stockfish trade introduced into Iceland a new source of income and new forms of employment, which may have led in the fourteenth century to some social and economic changes. The Black Death epidemic certainly brought change. The plague arrived in Iceland in 1402, causing an upheaval of property ownership and sharp changes in people's circumstances. The epidemic lasted two years, killing more than a third of Iceland's population. The stockfish trade and the plague, however, are well beyond our period of inquiry. More pertinent is the determination that the wealth of the early *goðar* and farmers was not founded on trade.

Slavery and the Rental of Land and Livestock

Beginning in the colonization period, large landowners faced the problem of how best to work their new holdings. As mentioned in Chapter 5, beyond a certain minimum, slaves did not significantly add to a farm's productivity. The cost of providing food through the winter for additional slave labour was too high. Historically, slavery tends to be an efficient institution chiefly in countries where field agriculture allows for economies of scale and where work can easily be supervised.[22] In Iceland, with its mixed economy of coastal hunting, gathering and fishing, and inland livestock farming, the efficient use of slave labour was not possible. Shepherding and other routine tasks connected with the main enterprise of animal husbandry called for a wide dispersal of the work force and required a high degree of personal initiative. In the eleventh century slavery all but ceased. Tenant farming, a more feasible alternative, took the place of slavery.

The sagas frequently speak of farmers and chieftains renting out livestock. Certainly the practice existed, but we have almost no sure information on the specifics before 1300. After 1300 the frequency of livestock rental increased dramatically. The expansion accompanied both the extension of tenant farming and the widespread acceptance of tenants renting out parcels of their rented property together with fixed numbers of livestock. (Before 1300 livestock was rented separately from property.)

Because we have so little information, it is hard to judge how profitable livestock rental was in the earlier period. Along with profit motivation, insurance was a factor that rendered loans and rentals in livestock beneficial. In many pastoral societies, livestock loans are made less to earn interest than to reduce the risk of loss. In early Iceland with its bad year economics and its dependence on livestock farming, livestock rental functioned as investment and insurance for the well-off farmer with a surplus of animals. By dispersing stock over several geographical regions and at different farms, he could prevent the loss of all his animals from localized disease or other catastrophes.

It is apparent that the renting of land was a widely established practice by the late eleventh century, when the sources become more reliable. As Björn Thorsteinsson notes, the status of the *goðar* must have been connected with landownership and rents: 'It was not large households and important groups that secured power and reputation for the chieftains over the centuries, but the ownership of land and the income from rental property.'[23] *Grágás* supports this observation.

It contains a detailed entry on renting (*fjárleigur*) which treats matters such as contracts of sale, hire or loan, settlement of debts, found property, livestock, and so on.[24] A longer entry in *Grágás* concerns matters of landownership (*landbrigða-tháttr*), stipulating rights connected with different types of land, buying and selling property, joint interests, hunting and fishing, and others.[25]

Extensive tenant farming was possible because many sizeable family holdings included rentable property, especially outlying lands (*útjörð*, pl. *útjarðir*). In particular, a main or head farm, termed *aðalból* in *Grágás* and *höfuðból* in the later, part-Norwegian law book *Jónsbók*, played a pivotal role in the Icelandic system of land distribution. These farms existed because the original landholdings from the settlement days were not continually being divided as the years passed. In many instances they were solidified into *aðalból*, which had a prescribed minimum size. Information about the exact size and value of these patrimonial holdings is known only from documents dating from the fifteenth century. At about that time, though probably much earlier, the minimum was set at sixty hundreds (a hundred was equivalent to the value of one cow). *Jónsbók*, with its mixture of Norwegian and Icelandic law, stresses the retention of the land by the original kin group, though we cannot be sure that the relevant entries were operative during the earlier Free State.

Many scholars have connected the Icelandic *aðalból* with allodial landholding,[26] a tradition of ownership common in Norway whereby certain land was the possession of a patrilineal descent group, that is it was handed from father to son, or the next most direct descendant of a specific male ancestor who was a landholder.[27] Allodial property (the Old Norse word is *óðal*) was land held in absolute ownership, without obligation or service to any overlord. It was this ancient tradition of ownership that King Harald Fairhair (*c.* 885–930) was seeking to change in Norway at the same time as the settlement of Iceland. Without doubting that a form of family landholding is being dealt with, one should, nevertheless, point out that in *Grágás*, at least as it is preserved in the thirteenth-century texts, the term *óðal* itself is never used. On the other hand, the term *aðalból* (head farm) is spoken of in connection with matters of inheritance in a way that demonstrates acceptance of the proprietary claims of kin groups.[28] Unlike Norwegian allodial land, however, an Icelandic *aðalból* was not the exclusive possession of a patrilineal descent group. Icelandic heirs seem to have been mostly drawn from immediate kinsmen related through either the mother or the father. Potential heirs at each generation were defined by their relationship to the present holder or to the immediately preceding holder. Normally the property was inherited by an eligible male; other family members, including women, divided the chattels, the outer farms, and any land beyond the accepted minimum size of an *aðalból*.

An *aðalból* tended to remain under the management of a family member, or at least it could be neither sold nor rented without specific agreement by the legally responsible male heir. Thus land could technically be alienated from a family only if the heirs agreed to a transfer. Such an agreement, unless well compensated, would be disadvantageous to the heirs, and their consent was undoubtedly difficult to obtain. The practice of maintaining *aðalból* ensured the presence of many substantial farmers whose outlying rental farms (*leiguból*) provided their owners with an important source of income.

15
Lucrative Sources of Wealth
for Chieftains

> In a certain sense it may be said that feuds play the same
> role in family sagas as love plays in novels. But a very
> essential difference between the role of feuds in family sagas
> and the role of love in novels lies in the fact that feuds really
> were the most important happenings of that time in Iceland
> – content dictated by life itself – while romantic emotions
> have hardly been the most important occurrences in Europe
> since the novel became predominant in European literatures.
>
> M. I. Steblin-Kamenskij, *The Saga Mind*

Important as it is to say that land was the basic constituent of wealth, we need to know how chieftains acquired it. Certainly a chieftain could inherit parcels of land, or obtain them by marriage, but neither of these possibilities explains how leaders such as Snorri goði around the year 1000 and Hvamm-Sturla in the mid twelfth century obtained the wealth necessary to exercise power. This chapter focuses on the underlying system of wealth acquisition by which aspiring *goðar* amassed property, including valuable Church farmsteads.

By the end of the tenth-century settlement period, all usable free land had been claimed, and in the later centuries much of the island's valuable property remained under family ownership. The *bændr* were never a servile peasant class. They owned property, valued it, and guarded it carefully. In this society that never saw the introduction of town life, livestock farming, and thus land, remained the single most important source of wealth. Farms were cherished family possessions which determined their owners' status. How, then, did chieftains as the governing group profit from this state of affairs? The answer is found in the ties of mutual dependence which bound together chieftains and farmers. Years ago Sigurður Nordal eloquently summed up the complex and unusual character of the Icelandic arrangement, conceiving of the interplay between *goði* and *bóndi* as analogous to the finesse involved in salmon fishing. The Icelandic farmer, like the strong and agile salmon, fights the fisherman's line, while the *goði* uses the skills of a fly fisherman in knowing when to play out the line. (In mainland Europe, by contrast, Nordal saw the relationship between lord and follower as less subtle: he described the vassal as similar to a heavy cod, easily caught in a net.)[1]

The essential problem a farmer faced, either in defending or in pushing for his rights, was his exclusion from the legal privileges enjoyed by chieftains. Individually or in a band, farmers may have had the physical ability to defend their rights or even to kill their opponents (including chieftains), but when such action was undertaken without a chieftain's protection a farmer exposed himself and his family to potentially devastating consequences. The *bóndi* might lose both status and land. In important matters, law in medieval Iceland operated principally on the *goði* level. If a *goði* brought or supported a case against a farmer, the farmer could hardly defend himself without the aid of another chieftain.

Something more than simple strength was at issue. The presence of chieftains was indispensable to the negotiations and compromises that characterized the settlement of disputes and the judicial process in early Iceland. Although the law gave farmers the right as individuals to bring cases before the courts, custom and procedure placed restrictions in their way. There is a visible parallel with our theoretically more equitable modern societies. Today any citizen may bring a case to court, just as any medieval Icelander could, but if the lawsuit is complex, the claimant's action will almost certainly be fruitless without the guidance of a specialist (in these days, a qualified lawyer). So it was in medieval Iceland, especially with issues serious enough to merit consideration in the courts of the national assembly. Once disputes had been turned over to advocates, especially *goðar*, each side built a case within the parameters of legally acceptable action, whether the intention was to settle in or out of court.

In Iceland's world of confrontation, of claim and counter-claim, the resolution of a dispute depended not only on the strength and justice of the case but also on the power and prestige of the *goði* who was presenting it. A freeman who could not resolve a dispute by himself approached a chieftain, just as a disputant today might enlist the services of a lawyer. Just as in the modern judicial system, it was the 'lawyer' who decided whether or not he would take a case and what his fee would be. As in medieval Iceland, the modern claimant may win his point, but his legal advocate often reaps a significant financial benefit.

After the verdict is given a modern lawyer's task is usually finished; in medieval Iceland a chieftain's responsibility did not necessarily end at that point. Without executive structures, the courts had no mandate to carry out a sentence. Because there was no apparatus to enforce a judicial decision, the plaintiff had to see to it that the legal victory became an actual victory. If the plaintiff was strong enough, or if he could count on friends or kin, he might try to carry out the sentence on his own. Most freemen, however, turned to chieftains for this service, a service that reinforced the need for advocates. At times a chieftain's task may have been the easy collection of a few farm animals; on other occasions he may have had to enforce a judgement of outlawry. Such a job, requiring manpower and time, might expose the *goði* to attacks from either the defendant or his kin group.

THE ACQUISITION OF PROPERTY
IN THE FAMILY SAGAS

Disputed Property in the East Fjords:
The Saga of the People of Weapon's Fjord

An incident like the one described below is familiar to any reader of the sagas. Taken from *Vápnfirðinga saga* (Chapter 7), it has to do with local feuds in the East Fjords. The conflict, beginning over a piece of wooded land owned jointly by neighbouring farmers, is one in a series of disputes that originated among *bændr* but in the end involved chieftains. (This incident was discussed in Chapter 13 within the larger context of the power struggle described in the saga; see also Map 19.) The next few pages trace the evolution of this seemingly trivial incident up to the point where two rival local chieftains position themselves for a confrontation.

The incident begins when Thord and Thormod, each the thingman of a different local chieftain, quarrel over grazing and tree-cutting rights in a wood they own jointly. Woods were a rare and coveted commodity in Iceland. Thord, threatened by his more aggressive neighbour Thormod, goes to his chieftain Brodd-Helgi, tells him about the problem, and asks him for aid. But Brodd-Helgi, an overbearing man, drives a hard bargain. He refuses to help his thingman unless the latter hands over his wealth and land and comes to live on Brodd-Helgi's farm: 'Brodd-Helgi said he didn't have a mind to quarrel over his [Thord's] property and would have no part of it unless he assigned him all his property by *handsal* and moved to Hof with all his possessions.' In a tight spot, Thord accepts Brodd-Helgi's offer; he legally assigns his patrimony to his *goði* by *handsal*, thus increasing Brodd-Helgi's wealth and power in the area.

The use of the term *handsal* (verb *at handsala*) is important in this exchange. The word refers to a handshake that formalized or sealed an agreement. To be recognized as legally binding, a *handsal* had to be witnessed. *Handsal* agreements could be entered into for many reasons: to arrange a marriage and dowry, to transfer land, to bind a resolution of a feud. A transfer of land by *handsal*, in which one man gave over his land, perhaps to a *goði* in return for protection, sometimes violated Iceland's inheritance laws.

It may seem far-fetched that a farmer would deed his land away just because he was threatened by his neighbour, but Thord has very few options: he can stay on his farm and risk losing his life to his bullying neighbour, or he can secure the protection of a powerful man. By handing over his land, Thord gains security and, perhaps, peace of mind for himself and his family; on the other hand, he loses both for himself and his heirs the autonomy and status that go with being a *bóndi*.

Honour, as it so often does in the sagas, invigorates the issue of choices, providing an intellectual as well as an emotional bridge between otherwise patterned and repetitive social actions.[2] Here, in the bargain between *goði* and *bóndi*, honour plays a crucial background role.[3] The medieval audience would surely note, and probably comment upon, Thord's small victory, for if this poor farmer loses his land, he nevertheless does so in a manner that partly assuages his honour: he gets the last bitter laugh in his dealings with his neighbour Thormod. In choosing to transfer his land to Brodd-Helgi, Thord, for a brief instant, takes control of the direction of the action. He exits from the quarrel with the knowledge – shared by the community – that his opponent Thormod is now embroiled in contention with a powerful antagonist. Thormod, in return for his determination to bully a neighbour, will now have to defend his person and property against Brodd-Helgi, a dangerous and motivated *goði*.

Honour, in fact, has been in the background the whole time. Despite the danger, honour made it difficult for Thord to do nothing. Faced with a humiliating situation, he would have been scorned and probably goaded by others into challenging and perhaps even attempting to kill Thormod – a risky venture. Instead, Thord turns to an advocate, proving himself a difficult man to humiliate. Once Thord has transferred his land, he cannot be intimidated into dropping his claim. On the contrary, he is relieved of responsibility. The rights of prosecution that come with ownership have been assumed by Brodd-Helgi. With the *schadenfreude* that we so often see in the Icelandic texts, Thord can enjoy, from a distance, the dangers (and death) that await Thormod in the escalating feud between the *goðar*, Brodd-Helgi and Geitir.

Brodd-Helgi also has choices. As a *goði* he wants to increase his wealth and power, and thus his influence, but he must weigh against those advantages the costs of taking the farmer's case. Geitir, Thormod's chieftain and a more peaceful man than Brodd-Helgi, is already embroiled in a feud with Brodd-Helgi. Local farmers will watch carefully to see which chieftain gains the prestige of keeping Thord's land and gaining the advantage over his rival.

Of significance in the relationship between Brodd-Helgi and Thord is the clear awareness of the difference in power between *goði* and *bóndi*. Each man has something that the other desires. The farmer has a sound claim to half-ownership in a parcel of disputed land, but he lacks the strength to support his claim. The chieftain has no valid right to the land but does have the power to assert a claim because of his role as supporter of his thingman; each has something of value with which he can bargain. The thingman receives a service and the chieftain receives a payment that benefits him financially or politically or both. Integral to the exchange is the fact that the chieftain, Brodd-Helgi, is in the right place at the right time and has enough power to act both in his own and in Thord's interest.

After the negotiations between Brodd-Helgi and Thord are completed and the claim to the land is transferred, Thord and his family go to live on Brodd-Helgi's farm. Having given up his rights to the land, the most Thord can hope for is that Brodd-Helgi will protect him for life and that his enemy Thormod will also lose his right to the land. We never learn of Thord's fate; after this incident he disappears from the saga. Thord's opponent Thormod soon finds Brodd-Helgi to be a difficult man with whom to share land. Thormod in his turn loses the use of the wood and calls on his *goði*, Geitir Lytingsson, for aid (see Chapter 13).

Decisions like the one facing Brodd-Helgi have much to do with a chieftain's ultimate success or failure. If a chieftain presses his thingmen too hard he loses their support, which is vital to his position. If he misjudges his power and abuses his position too often, his thingmen seek other means of maintaining themselves and protecting their families and property. If he is not aggressive enough in supporting his thingmen, he may similarly lose vital support.

Disputed Property in the Salmon River Valley: Laxdæla saga

Another example of a farmer calling upon a *goði* to act as his advocate and paying the chieftain generously for the service is found in Chapter 16 of *Laxdæla saga*. In this instance, however, a feud is cut off before it can escalate because the advocates engaged settle the case quickly out of court. A farmer, Thord goddi, has an argument with his wife, the strong-willed Vigdis. The wife wants Thord to harbour her outlawed distant kinsman, a vagrant. When Thord betrays the outlaw Vigdis declares herself divorced. She goes to her kinsman, the powerful chieftain Thord the Bellower (*gellir*), and together they plan to claim half of the farmer's estate. Thord goddi, who is described as rich though ineffectual, turns for support to the local chieftain, Hoskuld Dala-Kollsson.

Again, as in *Vápnfirðinga saga*, the meeting between *goði* and *bóndi* becomes a business negotiation. Farmer Thord goddi is in a weak position. In order to face Thord the Bellower, he needs the support of an equally powerful chieftain. But Hoskuld is in no rush to offer his protection. In fact, he taunts the *bóndi* with the seriousness of his position: 'You have often been scared before but never with better reason.' In this incident Hoskuld is in a position similar to that of Brodd-Helgi in *Vápnfirðinga saga*, although the motivation and the fate of these two leaders are quite different. Known as an upright and proud man, Hoskuld is presented in *Laxdæla saga* and in other sagas as intelligent, capable and successful. In temperament, he is

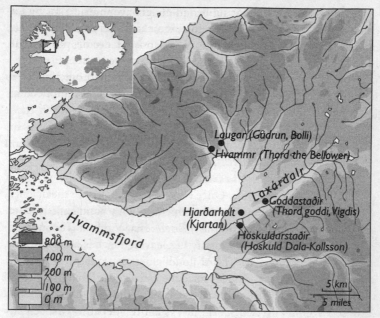

24. Chieftains and Farmers from *Laxdœla saga* Involved in the Dispute over the Farm at Goddastaðir.

almost the exact opposite of the brash and violent Brodd-Helgi. *Laxdœla saga* makes it clear (in Chapter 7) that Hoskuld's success is attributable in large part to his restraint and sagacity.

Thord goddi, realizing that Hoskuld wants something in return for his aid, offers to pay handsomely: 'Thord then offered Hoskuld money for his support and said he would not be stingy with it.' Still Hoskuld is reluctant to help. Thord goddi is known to be tight with his money, and both parties are aware that the *bóndi* is in a very precarious position. Faced with this reality, farmer Thord sweetens the offer: 'I would like you to manage all the property through a *handsal* agreement. Then I would offer to foster your son Olaf and leave it all to him when I'm gone, as I have no heirs here in Iceland.' Because the childless Thord has no close relatives in Iceland, the farmer's land is especially valuable to the chieftain, as it is not subject to possible counter-claims by Icelandic heirs; Hoskuld will have to contest only the wife's claim. The proposition is so advantageous that Hoskuld decides to support Thord, and the two men enter into a binding agreement.

Hoskuld is certain to reap a windfall profit without having to scheme for it. Moreover, the fee will include an inheritance for his illegitimate and favourite son Olaf, later called the Peacock (*pái*). Thus far Hoskuld's major contribution to the deal has been his potential as an advocate. He assesses the plight of the farmer and bases his fee on the depth of Thord goddi's desperation.

Ironically, the *bóndi* has from the start a strong legal case, but it is the chieftain who profits. Once Hoskuld is in charge of the defence, he seeks to placate the opposing chieftain with handsome gifts; at the same time he tells Thord the Bellower that Vigdis has brought no charges that would legally justify her leaving her husband. Further, as Hoskuld points out, Thord goddi's actions that prompted the marital split were reasonable, since the farmer was attempting to rid himself of his wife's outlawed relative. Although this effort had aroused Vigdis's ire and scorn, it was entirely legal. In a succinctly narrated passage, Hoskuld shows his skill as a broker by defending his bastard son's promised inheritance through a knowledge of law and an understanding of men:

Hoskuld sent handsome gifts to Thord the Bellower and asked him not to take offence at what had happened, for he and Vigdis had no legal claim on Thord goddi for the money. He pointed out that Vigdis had not brought any valid charges against her husband which could justify her desertion: 'Thord was none the worse a man for seeking some means of ridding himself of someone who had been thrust upon him and was as prickly with guilt as a juniper bush.'

This incident from *Laxdæla saga* has a thematic purpose beyond the problem of farmer Thord. Hoskuld is aware that legitimate sons seldom appreciate their father's love for the offspring of a concubine, and that Olaf's legitimate half-brothers will probably try to stop the boy (as they do) from inheriting a substantial share of Hoskuld's property. Whether a traditional tale or a pure invention of the saga-teller, Thord goddi's story offers a reasonable explanation of how Hoskuld causes valuable lands to come into Olaf's possession.[4] Thord goddi emerges from his trials much better off than Thord in *Vápnfirðinga saga*. He fosters the son of an important figure and thereby acquires a chieftain's protection. Unlike farmer Thord in *Vápnfirðinga* saga, Thord goddi lives out his life on his own land.

In *Laxdæla saga* the narrative section on Hoskuld and his sons is a lengthy introduction to the core of the saga: the famous love triangle of Kjartan, Gudrun and Bolli. Before the tale reaches that point, however, sufficient background must be presented. Not only does the saga-teller unravel the genealogy of the families, both legitimate and illegitimate; he also thoroughly catalogues the passage of property through generations. In this story of people and land, Olaf the Peacock and his property play an important role. Kjartan is Olaf's son and Hoskuld's grandson. The land deal made with Thord goddi forms the initial underpinning of the fortune of the great family that stems from Hoskuld's illegitimate line. This wealth plays a significant part in the later tragic killing of Kjartan.

Farmer Thord goddi in *Laxdæla saga* and farmer Thord in *Vápnfirðinga saga* both provide opportunities for chieftains to profit quickly and bloodlessly from their service as advocates. This practice, which has its roots in the political and economic realities that shaped Iceland's early development, was not always so painless.

INHERITANCE CLAIMS IN THE STURLUNGA SAGAS

Over the centuries, the *goðar* consistently managed to win out over other farmers in gaining control of valuable lands, prizes that within the spirit of Icelandic law were available to all freemen. The family sagas portray the *goðar* as advocates who frequently profited from the troubles of others. The early sagas in the Sturlunga compilation present a similar picture. In particular, they repeatedly show leaders manoeuvring to obtain the property of farmers, behaviour familiar from the family sagas.

The following pages present examples taken from three sagas of the Sturlunga compilation: *The Saga of Hvamm-Sturla*, *The Saga of Gudmund the Worthy* and *The Saga of the Icelanders*. These three sagas recount events from the late twelfth century, and all three examples concern valuable land. In one instance the property in question, Helgastaðir, is a Church farmstead. As frequently happened in Iceland, disputes over these properties begin with contentions among farmers. Again we see chieftains manoeuvring to gain a foothold on someone else's land by acquiring a legal claim, often of a tenuous nature. Once that has been done, the determination of ownership becomes a matter of political negotiation, dependent more on power than on the justness of the claim. The detail with which the saga authors describe these instances may reflect the concern of the contemporary twelfth- and thirteenth-century audiences over the increasing wealth of successful leaders.

In the give-and-take of the Icelandic court system, a compromise solution was the usual outcome of a lawsuit. This reality made the advancement of a questionable legal claim a potentially profitable venture. It gave an ambitious individual, even one who had no previous claim to another's property, reasonable hope of at least some success in acquiring a part of the wealth. In some instances, as in the manoeuvre employed by the chieftain Einar Thorgilsson in his efforts to gain possession of the farm of Heinaberg, an aggressor might allege an infraction of the law by the property owner and begin a prosecution. The lawsuit might cause the defendant not only to lose his property but also to be made an outlaw, a judgement that could cost him his life.

The Struggle to Inherit Helgastaðir: The Saga of Gudmund the Worthy

Set in the Eyjafjord region, The Saga of Gudmund the Worthy opens with a dispute over land. Members of the family of Gudmund Eyjolfs-son, a wealthy farmer, are in disagreement as to who will inherit his property, Helgastaðir, in Reykjadalr (see Map 13). Gudmund had willed the land to his son before retiring to a monastery, but the son unexpectedly predeceases the father. The son's wife prudently leaves Helgastaðir after recovering her dowry and agreeing to a settlement that divides her property from that of her dead husband.

The young man's early death raises a difficult question of inherit-ance within the family. Gudmund has two poor brothers who want to inherit their nephew's property. 'It was the opinion of many men,' according to the saga, 'that his [the son's] father should be his heir and receive the inheritance, but Gudmund's brothers, Bjorn and Halldor, said the Gudmund could neither inherit the property nor take care of it because he was a monk. Then men divided into opposing groups, and there were many on each side.' (Chapter 1)

As the debate about inheritance continues, another farmer, the priest Eyjolf Hallsson, begins to scheme on his own behalf. He has two sons and wants to set each one up independently. The acquisition of Helgastaðir would provide Eyjolf with the additional inheritance he needs to achieve his goal. Although he is an outsider, Eyjolf rides over to the monastery at Thverá to bargain with Gudmund. As a result, he buys the land and the inheritance for little more than half the market value, with the proviso that he will be 'answerable himself, if it should come before the law' (Chapter 1). By doing so, Eyjolf gains a presumption of ownership in the tangled negotiations that follow. Gudmund's brothers, who deem the property to be their own, are angry when they hear the news. They swear that Eyjolf will not be permitted to benefit from his deal while they themselves are in need. Carrying out their oaths will not be easy for the brothers, as

Eyjolf is a strong opponent. Descended from several law-speakers, he is a man who has many friends and kinsmen.

The account of Eyjolf's actions gives an insight into the manner in which important churchmen were integrated into Iceland's operating systems of wealth and power, for after the events described here this same Eyjolf Hallsson was briefly (c. 1201) a candidate for the bishopric of Hólar and from 1206 to 1212 was abbot of the monastery of Saurbær. Eyjolf is the warden of Grenjaðarstaðir, one of the richest *staðir* in the country. Like the brothers, he is a *bóndi*, and as a father he is on the lookout for the welfare of his sons. Now that Eyjolf has a claim to Helgastaðir, the issue is no longer who ought to inherit the land but which contestant – he or the blood heirs – is more powerful.

In their claim to ownership, the brothers are supported by the law; *Grágás* specifies that land may not be transferred without consent of the heirs; to do so is *arfskot*, cheating on an inheritance.[5] Gudmund failed to consult the brothers when he sold the property to Eyjolf. According to *Grágás* the brothers have the right to prosecute Gudmund, the testator, who is liable to a sentence of three years' outlawry or to lose control of his property. Such a prosecution would be fruitless, however, for Gudmund no longer has possession of the property.

Violence is an option. The brothers might simply try to kill Eyjolf, who is clearly interfering with their rights to family land. There is no suggestion, however, that they ever seriously consider taking so drastic an action, which would be dangerous and probably self-defeating. They might get themselves killed in the attempt, or, if they did succeed in killing Eyjolf, they would probably be outlawed and hunted down by Eyjolf's sons or kinsmen. The brothers' decision to shun violence follows a perceived pattern of behaviour: *hóf*, or restraint, gains the upper hand. It is a socially conditioned response of men who understand their society well enough not to overextend their reach.

The angry brothers seek support of their rights through the advocacy of their *goðar*. Each brother is the thingman of a different *goði*, and when the brothers turn to their respective chieftains for support, it is not hard to guess the result. The chieftains are apparently unsympathetic, and the saga laconically tells us that each *bóndi* makes over to his *goði* by *handsal* his entire claim to the 'wealth': '*hvárr handsalaði sínum goðorðsmanni heimting fjárins*' (Chapter 1). In return, the powerless *bændr* get only the satisfaction of seeing their position vindicated by Eyjolf's being denied the use of the land. After they have transferred their legal claims, the brothers drop out of the saga. Their *goðar*, Onund Thorkelsson and Thorvard Thorgeirsson, if successful, will keep all the fruits of the coming legal action. The contest over Helgastaðir is now between Eyjolf, backed by his powerful family and friends, and the allied chieftains of the two brothers.

Before it is brought to an end, the dispute over Helgastaðir develops into a major confrontation. At least four local chieftains, Thorvard Thorgeirsson, Onund Thorkelsson, Einar Hallsson and Gudmund the Worthy become involved in the contest. The saga does not indicate the exact site of the two brothers' farms, but it tells us they lived in this region. The process of settlement begins when the *goði* Gudmund the Worthy enters the case as a *góðviljamaðr* (man of goodwill), separating the threatening sides. As neither party is able to force its rival to withdraw or is willing to risk an all-out attack, a stalemate ensues. Having succeeded in keeping the two sides apart, Gudmund becomes a neutral arbitrator of the opposing claims. In the end, through arbitration, the property is awarded to a father and son who are closely related to both sides by alliance, kinship or marriage. This compromise solution is agreeable to everyone, as it gives all parties a future interest in the land. Each claimant can assume that the property may eventually come into his family.

Inheritance Rights to Heinaberg: The Saga of Hvamm-Sturla

The second Sturlunga example of property changing hands between farmers and chieftains is of special interest because it concerns two well-known and powerful *goðar*. One is Hvamm-Sturla, the progenitor of the Sturlungs; the other is Einar Thorgilsson (1121?–85) from Staðarhóll, one of Sturla's major rivals. The incident, from Chapter 28, takes place in western Iceland and begins in the 1170s. A wealthy *bóndi* named Birning Steinarsson lives on a small farm called Heinaberg on Skarðsströnd. Birning is married and has a daughter named Sigrid. The marriage is not happy. The *bóndi* and his wife divorce and each subsequently remarries. By his new marriage Birning has a son, Thorleik, whom he now names as his heir. He neglects his daughter from the first marriage, and she fares poorly. Eventually she becomes the mistress of a Shetlander. Even though she has no power or position and is ignored by her father, Sigrid does possess one valuable attribute: an inheritance claim that can and will undermine Birning's control of his farm.

Why did important leaders like Sturla and Einar contend over Birning's small property? The farm of Heinaberg, only a narrow strip of land along the coast and with cliffs at its back, is itself of little value. In terms of geography, however, the reason for Einar's and Sturla's keen interest becomes clearer. A few metres off the shore below the farm buildings lie several tiny, flat islands which appear only on detailed local maps. Because of their size these islands would have been relatively valueless if they had not been, as they remain in modern times, one of the best seal-hunting spots along that stretch of coast.* As this information would have been well known to the local audience, it did not need to be included in the saga narrative.

Perceiving a way to gain possession of Birning's valuable property, Einar buys from Sigrid the expectation of her inheritance. Without

---

* I appreciated Björn Thorsteinsson's good company on our trip to Heinaberg.

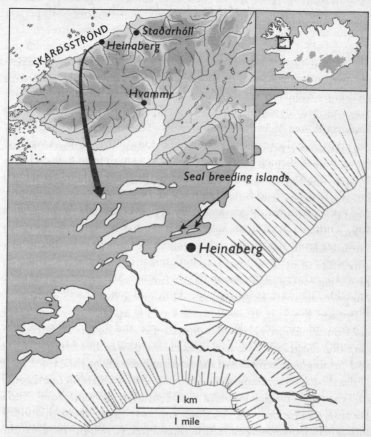

25. **The Farm of Heinaberg and the Nearby Seal Breeding Islands on Skarðsströnd.** The farm, situated on a narrow strip of poor coastal land beneath cliffs, is in itself of little value. Below the farm buildings, however, just off the coast, lie several very small, flat islands, which are often unrecorded on even large-scale modern maps. In the Middle Ages, as now, these islands were one of the most productive seal breeding and hence hunting spots along the coast.

the purchase, the *goði* would have been guilty of robbery if he had seized Birning's land; now its ownership is a legal matter. As a person with an interest in the disposition of the property, Einar uses the law to attack and accuses Birning of having contracted an unlawful second marriage. He intimates that Birning can escape the repercussions of this legal infraction by moving over to Einar's estate with his goods, though he does agree to share the rest of Birning's property with the second wife and her son 'according to what he finds advisable'.

Einar, an overbearing and sometimes violent man, is thus threatening Birning, but the *bóndi* faced with so ruinous a demand refuses to yield. In an effort at further intimidation, Einar responds to Birning's intransigence by sending one of his men to collect Birning's geldings from the heath. When the man returns to Einar's farm with seventy beasts, Einar has them slaughtered. Although he has not yet taken Birning's land, Einar's first move has been highly profitable. When cured, the meat from seventy geldings will go a long way towards providing for the large winter establishment of a wealthy and generous *goði*; alternatively, it can be sold or given away.

Birning, however, chooses not to knuckle under. Instead, he seeks aid from Einar's rival, Hvamm-Sturla, a *goði* who has an interest in checking the growth of Einar's wealth and power. In addition, Sturla and Birning are members of the Snorrungar family; they trace their descent back to a common ancestor, the crafty chieftain Snorri goði (d. 1031). If Birning expects preferential treatment from Sturla because of kinship ties, enabling him to emerge from this affair unscathed, he is mistaken. Sturla does agree to help Birning, but he arranges matters to his own advantage; the two men make a *handsal* agreement whereby Birning conveys all his property to Sturla. The agreement also specifies that Birning is to live out his life on Sturla's farm at Hvammr and that Birning's second wife, Gudbjorg, is to remain at Heinaberg.

For the moment at least, a stalemate has been reached. Neither Einar nor Sturla wants to confront the other openly over the land. Each *goði* has gained from the property of a farmer, and for a while

they are content to let the matter drop. Sturla will not prosecute
Einar for the robbery 'as long as Einar voices no displeasure with
Sturla's and Birning's *handsal*'. Each chieftain settles for what he has
received and the matter remains uncontested for a number of years.
Sturlu saga ends with the dispute over Heinaberg unresolved.

Resurgence of the Dispute over Heinaberg: The Saga of the Icelanders

The status of Birning's property, Heinaberg, turns up again at the
opening of *Íslendinga saga* after Sturla dies of old age. At the time of
Sturla's death in 1183, Birning is living on Sturla's farm. His second
wife Gudbjorg and their young son Thorleik have, under Sturla's
watchful eye, continued to live at Heinaberg. In 1185 Einar rides to
Heinaberg with seven men and, in the presence of Gudbjorg, lays
claim to Birning's property. When Gudbjorg refuses to give up the
land, Einar and his men ride off to round up the livestock on the
farm and drive the animals away with them. Seeing what the men
are doing, Gudbjorg and the other women rush out of the house,
followed by Birning's son Thorleik and his foster-brother Snorri.

Einar must feel that he and his men are in complete control of
the situation, as only women and boys are living at Heinaberg.
Gudbjorg's son Thorleik is described as still not quite twenty years
old and 'slight of stature', and Snorri, the foster-brother, is even
younger. But these young farmers have been pushed to their limit,
and Einar is about to receive the surprise of his life.

While her women chase the cattle away from Einar's men,
Gudbjorg and the boys turn on Einar: 'Gudbjorg grabbed his cloak
with both hands and held it behind him, and both boys struck him
at the same time' (Chapter 2). After inflicting a severe wound on
Einar, the boys run away before the chieftain's men can get at them,
and 'Einar and his followers went home but left the animals behind'.
The boys make good their escape and take shelter with Sturla's family
at Hvammr. Einar lies ill with his wounds for a while and then dies.

The killing of a *goði* by farmers without the aid or sanction of chieftains was an unusual event. Einar, who was not noted for his political acumen, was killed because he miscalculated in his dealings with farmers. This saga portrays the checks and balances of the social order functioning in such a way that everyone faced some kind of danger. Birning's son has vindicated his father's honour, but his deed will eventually cost him the property.

Birning's son Thorleik and his foster-brother Snorri remain with Sturla's family until the case comes to trial at the Althing. In the meantime Einar's sisters, who are his heirs, settle his estate and then prepare a lawsuit against the killers and those who have aided them. A relative of Einar's, Thorvald Gizurarson, takes charge of the case. He seeks out the advice and help of Jon Loftsson, the most powerful chieftain of his day. Jon was known as a wise and just man; his words carried weight and his views elicited respect throughout Iceland. As the modern saga scholar Einar Ól. Sveinsson has noted, 'For all his ambition he was a man of moderation, and as he was also the most equitable of men, he was the greatest peacemaker in the country in his time.'[6]

It is interesting, then, to note the reason given in the saga for Jon's decision to come to the aid of the prosecution against Einar's young killers. The saga makes clear that in their lifetimes Jon and Einar had little in common and did not like each other. With Einar's death, however, the issue is not friendship but the guarding of privilege. In reply to the request for aid in the prosecution, Jon states that he was not in a *vinfengi* relationship with Einar which would make him feel any obligation in this case. Nevertheless, it seems to Jon that 'things have come to a dangerous pass if there is no attempt to right matters when men of little regard strike down chieftains'. Therefore Jon pledges his word to support the prosecution.

When the case comes to court at the Althing, both Thorleik and Snorri are outlawed. Rather than allowing them to be hunted down as outlaws, members of Sturla's family arrange passage out of the country for their young kinsmen. Although he has saved his own life and upheld his personal honour, Birning's son has lost all claim to his land. As an example to other farmers, the outcome of the case satisfies Jon Loftsson. As to the final ownership of Heinaberg, *Sturlunga saga* gives no indication. The story of the feud over Heinaberg was apparently included in the sagas because it explained the death of Einar Thorgilsson. With the political connection gone, the disposition of this property is not of importance to the author of *Íslendinga saga*, Sturla Thordarson, Hvamm-Sturla's grandson and namesake.

The ambitions of chieftains such as Einar Thorgilsson called for aggressive tactics. Such tactics, including the use of trumped-up legal claims to acquire property, by their very nature alienated the farmers and chieftains whose property rights were being challenged. Set in the historical context of the late twelfth century, Einar's death is an example of how acquisitive actions could produce a deadly reaction.

16

A Peaceful Conversion:
The Viking Age Church

It will prove true that if we divide the law we also divide the peace.

The Book of the Icelanders

Even a clerical mind was compelled to accept much of the pagan heritage in order not to become alienated from the native culture. This acceptance had to be reconciled, in some way or another, with Christian doctrine.

Lars Lönnroth, *Njál's Saga: A Critical Introduction*

Information about the conversion to Christianity and the Icelandic Church is found in a number of different kinds of sources.[1] Beyond the family and Sturlunga sagas and Ari Thorgilsson's *Book of the Icelanders* (*Íslendingabók*), the principal sources are Icelandic annals, diplomatic texts and Church writings, the last including special sagas written about Icelandic churchmen. The earliest extant annals are relatively late sources, written at the end of the thirteenth century.[2] Their secondhand information about the first two centuries is sparse and inaccurate. *Diplomatarium Islandicum*, the nineteenth- and twentieth-century scholarly collection of medieval documents, judgements, contracts, church inventories, and other writings, contains only a few reliable documents for the first centuries following the conversion.[3] This extensive assemblage of sources is, however, an invaluable tool for the study of medieval Iceland after the twelfth century.

Around 1200 the first bishops' sagas (*byskupa sögur*) were written about Iceland's two saintly bishops, Thorlak Thorhallsson and Jon Ogmundarson.[4] Probably the lives of these men were originally written in Latin, but all that remains is a number of fragments from an early saga about Thorlak. The lives of the first bishops are treated in *Hungrvaka*, a brief Church history written in the very early 1200s whose title means 'hunger-waker'. Its unknown author tells us that his intention is to awaken the readers' hunger for more learning about his subject.[5] *Hungrvaka* reports events from the first half of the eleventh century until 1176. The lives of nine of the Skálholt bishops and three of the Hólar bishops were written down in the thirteenth and early fourteenth centuries. Some of them, such as Pal Jonsson, Bishop of Skálholt at the turn of the thirteenth century, merited separate sagas. Almost all these writings were in the vernacular.

The bishops' sagas and other Church writings focus on the lives, turmoils and joys of Iceland's prominent churchmen and saints. They provide a wealth of information about selected topics such as the conversion, the establishment of Iceland's two bishoprics, the manner of choosing Iceland's bishops, and the role of priests in the society. Church texts touch on the functioning of the early secular society only in passing. For the later period, beginning in the twelfth century but especially in the thirteenth century and in the first half of the fourteenth, the bishops' sagas and other Church documents offer information on a wide variety of subjects, including Church finances.

Concerning the earliest Christian observance, we know that a few of the *landnámsmenn* had converted to Christianity before coming to Iceland. Others among the settlers possessed at least a passing knowledge of the new religion, an acquaintance which derived from the meeting of cultures which occurred in the Viking outposts in northern Europe, especially those in the British Isles. The majority of the settlers were believers in the old gods, and organized worship among the relatively few Christian immigrants probably died out within a generation or two. Probably some individuals and a few families maintained a belief in the Christian God. A distinction here is that belief may have been relatively easy, but maintaining Christian observance was much more difficult.

Pagan Observance

In the tenth century, as the island's new social order evolved, most Icelanders worshipped the traditional Norse gods. Called collectively the *Æsir*, a name that includes the small number of fertility deities named the *Vanir*, the gods, and the goddesses (*ásynjur*) are chiefly known from Iceland's later written sources. The most important of these sources are the *Elder Edda* or *Poetic Edda*, anonymous folk poetry with origins in the Viking Age, and the *Prose Edda*, written in the early thirteenth century by the famous chieftain Snorri Sturluson. By far the most important deity for the early Icelanders was Thor, the god of farmers and seafarers. His name is connected with large numbers of personal and place names. Frey, the god of fertility, also seems to have been popular. Odin, the god of warriors and aristocrats, was worshipped to a far lesser extent. Little reliable information about actual belief has survived, but it appears that people also believed in land spirits, including guardian spirits called *landvættir*. Personal attachment to the Norse gods varied with the individual, but seasonal observances and public rites, such as the hallowing of assemblies, were important formal ceremonies. As noted earlier, the *goðar* seem to have carried out most of the priestly functions in such ceremonies.

Archaeology offers tantalizing hints of pagan religious practices, including several instances of providing a dead person with a boat for the journey to the other world. This description of a tenth-century boat grave from the West Fjords was written by Thórr Magnússon, the archaeologist who led the excavation. It describes one of the most extensive pagan burials found in Iceland and gives an idea of the difficulty in piecing together from different sources an accurate picture of religious beliefs in the period before the conversion.

In the spring of 1964 a boat grave from the Viking Age was discovered on the premises of the farm Vatnsdalur on the south coast of Patreksfjord, Western Iceland ... It proved to be one of the richest and most varied Viking Age burials hitherto excavated in Iceland, even though its worth was somewhat reduced by the obvious traces of the activity of grave robbers in former times.

The grave boat had been dug into a sand dune quite near the beach and then covered by a low mound and a layer of stones on the top. The orientation is E–W, the stern almost certainly in the west end. Of the boat itself nothing was left except the iron nails, of which a great number were found. They lay in rows, and even though they were to some extent brought out of order by the bulldozer they allow a fairly accurate estimate of the size and proportions of the boat. It was 6 m long and about 1 m wide, obviously very shallow. It was made from larch (or spruce), six strakes on each side, the boards assembled with iron nails. On one side near the stem two peculiar whalebone pieces with cuts in the top were fastened with iron nails on to the inside of the gunwale. The anchor-line or a tow-line must have been intended to rest in the cut, and the function of the whalebone pieces is thus to protect the gunwale against the friction of the line.

In the boat there were bones from seven people, three males and four females, all young people. The bones lay in a disorderly heap and it is out of the question that all these people had been buried in the boat. Originally only one person, probably a young woman, was buried there, but the other skeletons must have been collected from other graves in the same graveyard and placed in the boat grave, very likely by grave robbers or anyway by people who for some reason or other dug up the bones and grave goods from the ancient cemetery. There can hardly be any doubt that this locality, situated at the beach about 400–500 metres from the farm buildings, was a graveyard in pagan times, but of the graves, apart from the boat grave, no traces are visible except a single stone-lined grave in which a whetstone and a horse tooth were found. Otherwise the grave had been emptied.

The following objects were found in the boat grave: *30 beads*, 2 of amber, 28 of glass of different colours, usual Viking Age style; *Thor's hammer* of silver, 3.55 cm long, very likely an amulet which was worn as a pendant along with the string of beads; *Bronze bell*, fragmentary, height 2.2 cm (the bell is similar to two such bells previously found in Icelandic Viking Age graves; such bells in all probability are of either Anglo-Saxon or Celtic origin and had been brought to Iceland from north-west England); *Fragment of a Kufic* [Arabic] *coin*, a dirham, probably from the period AD 870–930; *A pendant of gilt bronze*, very fragmentary; *Two parts of a bronze chain*, probably from some personal ornaments; *A bronze pin* of uncertain use; *A piece of lead* with an inlaid cross with green colour, probably of enamel; *Two bracelets of bronze*, of precisely the same kind, plan and open, without ornaments, widest in the middle and tapering off towards the ends; *A finger-ring of bronze*, very plain and simple; *Two bone combs and fragments* of a third one as well as parts of bone-cases for combs, all made in the usual Viking Age fashion and decorated with simple engraved ornaments; and *13 balance-weights of lead*, of different kinds, the biggest one weighing 24.605 g.

. . . When the skeletons from the other graves were removed from them and put into the boat grave the grave goods originally accompanying them must have been taken away by the people at work, no matter who they were and why they did this bone-digging.

This is the fifth boat grave found in Iceland. Since Viking Age graves are rather scarce there, this figure is sufficiently high to show that the custom of boat burials was well known. Otherwise the find does not add much to what was already known of the general burial customs in pagan times in Iceland, i.e. the tenth century approximately.

Most of the artifacts are of kinds previously known from Icelandic finds, the most remarkable exception being the Thor's hammer. It is interesting to find this heathen symbol side by side with the bell, which must be looked upon as a Christian symbol, and maybe also the cross inlaid in the piece of lead. This reminds us that some of the early settlers of Iceland, even if they were heathen Norsemen, had stayed for some time in the British Isles and become acquainted with Christianity. A few had been baptized. The bell seems to indicate connections with England. According to *The Book of Settlements* the land in Patreksfjord and its immediate neighbourhood was settled by people who came to Iceland from the Viking settlements in the British Isles.[6]

A Viking Age Conversion

Assessing the impact of the conversion on a society such as Iceland's is difficult; Church practices in Iceland, often irregular in the light of accepted Roman procedure, may be interpreted in different ways. In forming a view, there are several key factors to consider. First, the conversion to Christianity was unusually peaceful and rapid, considering the long and bloody conversion in Norway. Second, the Church expanded the cultural horizon of the Icelanders by introducing new ideas from the Latin West. Third, Iceland's new Church developed for almost two centuries with little external supervision, and during this stage of development it does not make much sense to talk about the Icelandic Church as if it was a full-fledged institution. Economics is a fourth factor. Until well after the end of the Free State the Icelandic Church reaped only a small portion of the revenue from the land it ostensibly owned, because laymen controlled most of the property. Additionally, one must reckon with the nature of the Icelandic priesthood. Icelandic priests did not form a caste distinct from the society. Their behaviour was dominated by secular norms, and they included among their ranks chieftains and influential farmers who had no desire to lose their family lands to Church control.

A major question for understanding Iceland's Church and the transition following the conversion is: did the Church significantly alter the basic patterns through which members of the secular society acquired wealth and power? The indications are that the Church did not supplant Iceland's long-established traditions of secular self-governance. G. Turville-Petre and E. S. Olszewska succinctly described the situation that prevailed after the conversion:

Just as their pagan ancestors had built temples to Thor and Frey, so the Christian *goðar* built churches upon their lands, and maintained these churches as their private property. Until the question of patronage became acute, towards the end of the twelfth century, and until the Icelandic Church, under foreign influence, began to press for separate jurisdiction for the clergy, there were scarcely grounds for a quarrel between Church and state. Isleif, Iceland's first bishop in 1056, was not only a bishop, he was also a *goði*, and, it seems, his son Gizur (died 1118) succeeded him in both these offices.[7]

Iceland's acceptance of Christianity[8] is traditionally ascribed to the year 1000. Ari the Learned's account of the conversion appears to be reliable. Ari, who wrote around 1120–40, was born in 1067, sixty-seven years after the event. A careful historian, Ari names his major sources and had the opportunity to hear even first-hand accounts. He was brought up at Haukadalr by Hall Thorarinsson, who lived to the age of ninety-four and who remembered being baptized as a child of three by the missionary Thangbrand. Ari was also the student of Teit Isleifsson. Teit was the son of Iceland's first bishop, Isleif, who was the son of Gizur the White, a participant in the events of the conversion. Other information about the transition is contained in a number of overlapping, often late, and sometimes divergent sources.[9] Nevertheless, the basic progression of events as reported in the sources has a certain logic. Beginning approximately in 980, the island was visited by several missionaries. Among the first was an Icelander returning from abroad, Thorvald Kodransson, called the Far Traveller (*inn víðförli*).[10] Thorvald was accompanied by Fridrek, a German bishop who had previously baptized him and about whom we know very little.[11] Thorvald met with little success. He became the subject of lampoons and, with Fridrek, was forced to leave after being involved in disturbances in which two men were killed.

During the reign of Olaf Tryggvason (995–1000), Norway's proselytizing warrior king, the effort to convert Iceland suddenly intensified. Early in his reign, King Olaf sent an Icelander named Stefnir Thorgilsson home to convert his countrymen.[12] Stefnir is said to have used so much violence in destroying the sanctuaries and images of the old gods that he was outlawed from Iceland. In response to such missionary probes, the so-called 'kin shame' (*frændaskömm*) legislation was passed at the Althing. It called upon families to prosecute Christians within their ranks if they blasphemed the old gods or committed other impious offences.

After the failure of Stefnir's mission, King Olaf next sent to Iceland a German, or perhaps Flemish, priest named Thangbrand. He was an experienced missionary already known for his proselytizing work in Norway and in the Faroes. His mission to Iceland (*c.* 997–9) is mentioned in many sources.[13] Not only was Thangbrand a preacher but, according to later stories, he was skilled in the use of weapons. His efforts were only partly successful; he converted several prominent Icelanders but also killed two or three men who had composed mocking verses about him. *Njáls saga* gives a lively, although probably exaggerated, account of Thangbrand's methods of conversion. According to the saga, the priest, accompanied by his converts, traversed the countryside, pausing here and there to preach. At one such stop at Fljótshlíð in the south, where Thangbrand and his group extolled the faith, 'Vetrlidi the poet and his son Ari spoke most strongly against it, so they killed Vetrlidi'.[14]

Thangbrand returned to Norway around 999 without having converted Iceland. In retaliation, King Olaf became more aggressive toward the Icelanders. He closed Norwegian ports to Icelandic traders and took hostage a few Icelanders who were then in Norway. In this way the King banned Icelanders, as long as they remained pagan, from trading with Norwegians. Among the captives taken by the Norwegians were sons or relatives of prominent Icelandic pagans, whom the King threatened to maim or kill unless Iceland accepted Christianity. The King's hostile actions soon had the desired effect in Iceland, for several reasons. A tenet of the Free State's otherwise limited foreign policy was to preserve good relations with Norway. Many Icelanders retained family ties with Norwegians, and Norway was the major trading partner. Emboldened by the King's actions, the Christians in Iceland grew more determined to convert the entire country and to do away with religious traditions offensive to Christians, such as the hallowing of assemblies by pagan rites.

Adherents of the two rival religions formed antagonistic groups, and events moved swiftly. A delegation of important Christians journeyed to Norway and rescued the hostages by promising King Olaf that they would try to convert the country. At home the Christian chieftains moved towards establishing separate courts and a government distinct from the pre-existing system, which was controlled by believers in the old faith. The issues raised by these developments presented a dilemma to thoughtful Icelanders, as the division of the country into separate camps raised the danger of civil war.

Matters came to a head the next summer at the Althing, as those believing in the Norse gods skirmished with the Christians. When a major warlike encounter appeared imminent, a typical Icelandic scenario developed: mediators intervened, and the dispute, which was treated as a feud ripe for settlement, was submitted to arbitration. The law-speaker, Thorgeir Thorkelsson, a *goði* from the farm of Ljósavatn in the Northern Quarter, was selected for the delicate job of settling the dispute. Thorgeir, who as law-speaker had been constitutionally elected, was acceptable to both sides and it may be that each side thought that they had him in their pocket as their advocate. This was because he was a pagan yet seemed to have strong ties with members of the Christian camp.

According to Ari's account in *Íslendingabók*, Thorgeir sequestered himself, lying under a cloak for part of a day and through the following night. Then, before announcing his decision, he received assurances that both sides would abide by his ruling since it 'will prove to be true that if we divide the law we also divide the peace'. Ari relates Thorgeir's decision (Chapter 7):

Then it was made law that all people should become Christian and that those who here in the land were yet unbaptized should be baptized; but as concerns the exposure of infants, the old laws should stand, as should those pertaining to the eating of horseflesh.[15] If they wished, people might sacrifice to the old gods in private, but it would be lesser outlawry [*fjörbaugsgarðr*] if this practice were verified by witnesses. But a few years later this heathen custom was abolished, as were the others.

Within the brief period of the meeting of the national assembly in the summer of the year 1000, the menacing problem of changing religions was resolved, and Iceland averted civil war. Given the decades of strife (roughly from 990 to 1040) both before and after the conversion in neighbouring Norway, the peaceful manner in which the Icelanders adopted the new faith has long been considered remarkable, even miraculous. But was the manner of conversion so strange in light of the methods of channelling and resolving disputes which the Icelanders had developed in the preceding seven decades? The process of resolving the antagonisms attendant upon the conversion dispute followed the pattern by which important feuds were settled: third parties intervened and through arbitration a compromise was reached. By the year 1000 the procedure for conflict resolution in Iceland was so well established that even an issue as potentially disruptive as a change in religion could be resolved with little violence.

With this skilful compromise the Icelanders peacefully accepted the conversion, avoiding a sharp break with the past. Although the pagans were in the majority, they joined the Christians in legislating for the adoption of Christianity. We may guess that they feared social upheaval more than they disliked religious change. This supposition is reinforced by the fact that Iceland continued to abide by Thorgeir's ruling, even though, with King Olaf's death that same year (1000), Norway partly reverted to paganism. The sense of compromise and political expediency underlying the conversion may be glimpsed in the decision by many of the participants as to when and where they would accept baptism. Some chose not to do so in the cold waters at the Althing; instead, they put off formal acceptance of the faith until they reached hot springs on their way home.

Geography and the Church

The irregular and difficult communications that distanced Icelandic churchmen from their foreign superiors fostered the independent evolution of Iceland's Church. The relative unimportance of Iceland in the eyes of continental churchmen may also have been a factor. From the conversion until the beginning of the twelfth century Iceland fell within the archiepiscopal see of Hamburg-Bremen. The archbishop and his chapter were preoccupied with the events taking place in the neighbouring kingdoms of Norway, Sweden and Denmark, as well as in their own north German locality, and paid little attention to distant Iceland. The situation did not change significantly for Iceland when, in 1104, a new archbishopric for all Scandinavia was established at Lund, in the Danish kingdom. Communications with Lund, which today is in southern Sweden, were irregular. The archbishops in Lund were friendly and helpful to the Icelanders, but Iceland was not a primary or even a particularly important concern of these archbishops, involved as they were in the affairs of Denmark and its surrounding countries.

In 1153 a separate archiepiscopal see was established in Norway at Niðaróss (Trondheim). The archbishop of Niðaróss was given jurisdiction over the dioceses of Norway as well as over the Orkneys, Hebrides, Faroes, Iceland and Greenland. Communications with Norway were usually good, but the archbishops' influence on Iceland's lay society was limited. In the late twelfth century the Niðaróss archbishop and Norway's King Sverrir Sigurdarson (1184–1202) were locked in a deadly struggle, during which the King was excommunicated, Norway was placed under an interdict, and its bishops were exiled. It was not until well into the thirteenth century that the archbishops and the Norwegian Crown, particularly under Sverrir's grandson, King Hakon Hakonarson (1217–63), were able to work together effectively in order that both Church and Crown might extend their authority to Iceland.

Early Bishops, Priests and Nuns

During the seven or so decades following the conversion, Icelanders had only a limited knowledge of the new religion. A large part of the training they did receive came from an assortment of foreign priests and itinerant missionary bishops who travelled to the newly converted country. Among them were three foreign teachers, Peter, Abraham and Stephen, who Ari tells us called themselves Armenian (*ermskir*) bishops.[16] In order to facilitate the observance of Christianity, many chieftains and farmers built churches on their farms at their own expense and considered themselves their 'owners'. From 1030 to 1153 there were many similarities between the Icelandic and Norwegian Churches, in particular, this private control of churches.[17] Many *goðar* exchanged their pagan priestly role for that of a Christian priest, and they seem to have suffered no diminution in their status and power. Perhaps their authority even grew. Among the individuals who were both chieftains and priests in the century and a half following the conversion were Ari the Learned, Saemund the Learned from Oddi, Teit (Bishop Isleif's son) from Haukadalr, and Teit's son Hall.

When the church owner or warden did not himself become the priest, he could arrange to have a priest serve in his church. One way he could do this was to enter into a contractual agreement with an impoverished young man willing to be trained for the priesthood. In return for the training and the provision of the necessary books and vestments, the youth would remain throughout his life at the owner's church. Such a priest, who was called a *kirkjuprestr*, probably enjoyed little respect. If he ran away, the landowner, whether farmer or chieftain, could demand him back as though he were a runaway slave. Not very much is known about this type of priest, and in any event the practice seems to have diminished sharply in the twelfth century.

The other type of priest, at times called a *thingaprestr*, functioned in the manner of a private chaplain. Such individuals were freemen with clerical training who undertook employment as priests. For a fee including room and board, they would look after one or more churches. These priests normally became members of the household of the church owner, leaving some doubt as to the degree of independence with which they managed their churches. Among them were Thorlak Thorhallsson and Gudmund Arason, both of whom later became bishops.

Six nuns can be identified in Iceland before 1300, and all became hermit nuns after full secular lives. One of these six nuns was Groa (died 1160), the daughter of a bishop, wife of another bishop, and mother of a priest.[18] We met Groa earlier, at the end of Chapter 4, when her extra-marital affair, the source of a quarrel, was discussed. Groa was the wife of Ketil (later a bishop), the man who by recounting his story persuaded the feuding chieftain Haflidi to compromise. So also we met in Chapter 10 Gudrun Osvifrsdottir, in the story of the goading women from *Laxdæla saga*. This was the Gudrun who planned the death of her lover, Kjartan, and was the feuding opponent of Kjartan's vengeful mother, Thorgerd. In later life, Gudrun, after four marriages, became Iceland's first hermit nun.

Gudrid Thorbjarnardottir is another of these hermit nuns. According to the sagas, she too enjoyed a full life before becoming a hermit in old age. Married three times, she travelled from the Greenlandic–Icelandic colony in Vínland (North America) to the Mediterranean. The outline of her travels as recounted in the sagas is given in Appendix 4.

The Beginnings of a Formal Church Structure

Iceland lay far from the centres of Roman authority, and in few places in medieval Europe, especially in the twelfth and thirteenth centuries, did laymen exercise as much control over the Church as they did in this distant land. Beginning with the conversion and continuing into the thirteenth century, chieftains and influential farmers met at the assemblies, where through consensus they regulated almost all points of contention between the Church and lay society. From early on, the Icelandic Church was vulnerable to secular interference because of its inability to exercise control over its property. The Icelanders looked on their society as a Christian one, and Christian observance was built into the secular law in a fairly thorough fashion. Nevertheless, they had their own ideas about Church organization. More than 200 years after Iceland's conversion, the wealth and the authority of the Icelandic Church were still largely administered by laymen. As on the Continent, the Church in Iceland claimed ownership of large tracts of land. The difference was that in Europe the Church often enjoyed the social, economic and political advantages derived from control of valuable property. In Iceland the claim to such control was mostly hollow because families granted land to the Church in the name of a saint but retained control over the land by acting as 'wardens', that is guardians of the property. Through such arrangements much of the Church's property remained under secular control until a compromise was finally arranged in 1297 which granted a portion of the lands to the Church.[19]

The lack of friction between the early Icelandic Church and secular society was owing in part to the financial benefits that the Church brought to many chieftains and prominent farmers. These benefits, which increased after the tithe law was introduced in 1096, fuelled the move toward a more stratified society by altering to some degree the distribution of wealth. Possession of farmsteads with churches on them became an important new source of income for the chieftains and farmers who owned them. Donations in honour of saints increased the value of many of these churches, and owners could acquire several churches, each with one or more farms attached. Revenue from such property contributed to the success of many of the six chieftain families whose power became so important in the thirteenth century.

A formal Church structure had begun to take shape in the mid eleventh century. Gizur the White (*inn hvíti*), a prominent Christian *goði* who had played an important role in the conversion, sent his son Isleif (born *c.* 1006) to study the new religion at the monastic school in Herford, Westphalia. Isleif, one of the first Icelanders to be educated and ordained abroad, returned home to Iceland, married, and became a chieftain like his father. At the Althing some years later, about 1055, Isleif was elected Iceland's first bishop. After his election he again went abroad and in 1056 was consecrated by the archbishop of Hamburg-Bremen.

We do not know very much about Isleif's episcopate, but it seems that he enjoyed only limited success in making his authority felt. *Hungrvaka*, a major source for information about Isleif, says (in Chapter 2) that Bishop Isleif 'encountered many serious difficulties during his episcopate stemming from people's disobedience. As an example of the kind of problem caused by lack of faith, disobedience and immorality among his subjects, the law-speaker married two women – a mother and her daughter.' We are not told whether these unions were concurrent or whether one followed the other. Apparently Isleif was not appointed to a specific see, and *Hungrvaka* tells us that he suffered because people showed him little respect or obedience. From his farm at Skálholt in the Southern Quarter he seems to have acted much like the missionary bishops with whom he competed. Possibly referring to the Armenians or to other missionaries from the Eastern Church, *Hungrvaka* says that in 'Bishop Isleif's day bishops who preached a more lenient doctrine than Bishop Isleif came from other countries to Iceland. They therefore became popular with wicked men until Archbishop Adalbertus [archbishop of Hamburg-Bremen, 1043–72] sent a letter to Iceland prohibiting people from accepting any of their services and said that some had been excommunicated and that all of them had gone out to Iceland without his permission.'

Isleif's eldest son, Gizur Isleifsson, succeeded his father as bishop of Skálholt in what appears to have been a smooth transition. Like his father, Gizur was elected bishop at the Althing. *Hungrvaka* (Chapter 4) reports that Gizur sought to remedy the problem of disobedience which his father had experienced. Before accepting the office, he received pledges from all the chieftains in the country that they would accept those ordinances that he would enforce. Gizur went abroad and was consecrated Iceland's second bishop in 1082 in Magdeburg. During his long episcopate (1082–1118) Gizur was deeply respected and worked to set the Church on a more secure footing. He was responsible for the introduction of the tithe in 1096 and provided the Icelandic Church with a fixed episcopal seat by willing his farm at Skálholt to the Church. Transferring land out of family control usually required the approval of potential heirs, a process that might lead to disputes, but we are not told whether Gizur encountered any such difficulties. At the time of his episcopate people in the Northern Quarter were feeling the need to have their own bishop, and at the beginning of the twelfth century an episcopal seat was established at Hólar in Hjaltadalr. The bishop at Skálholt retained jurisdiction over the inhabitants of the Western, Southern and Eastern quarters. Jon Ogmundarson was selected first bishop of Hólar by the clergy and laymen of the Northern Quarter. He was consecrated in 1106 by the archbishop of Lund.

It seems wise to agree with the Icelandic historian Jón Jóhannesson, who wrote that Bishop Gizur 'saw to it that there were no clashes between the Church and the secular leaders, even if it meant that he had to bypass the letter of ecclesiastical law. His Church policies remind us of the compromise at the Althing in the year 1000.'[20] Little changed with the establishment of the northern bishopric, and the Icelandic Church assumed the basic form that it was to retain throughout the remaining century and a half of the Free State. With this start, the bishops set the example for the integration of the clergy into Icelandic life. Except for the stormy episcopates of Thorlak Thorhallsson in the Skálholt diocese at the end of the twelfth century and Gudmund Arason in Hólar at the beginning of the thirteenth century (see Chapter 18), all Icelandic bishops until 1238 (when Norwegians first filled the two offices) followed Gizur's example of pursuing a national Church policy.

17
Grágás: *The 'Grey Goose' Law*

Among them [the Icelanders] there is no king, but only law.

Adam of Bremen, *History of the Archbishops of
Hamburg-Bremen* (11th century)

Iceland has a rare treasure in its law books. Collectively the extant
Free State laws are called *Grágás*, meaning 'grey goose'.[1] The origin
of the name is unknown: it first appears in an inventory taken in
1548 at the bishop's seat at Skálholt, but it may be much older. Unlike
other Scandinavian law, *Grágás* was compiled without concern for
royal justice or prerogatives. Its resolutions and rulings illustrate the
limits and precedents of a legal system that operated without an
executive authority. Knowledge of the law is often essential to understanding medieval Iceland, especially the events portrayed in its sagas.
Grágás contains much customary law. It was the law of a society in
which order was maintained principally through negotiation and
compromise and in which the upholding of an individual's rights
through legal proceedings and extralegal arbitrations; prosecution
and the exaction of penalties was a private responsibility. Together
the sagas and the laws reflect the medieval Icelanders' conception of
how their society worked. The law was not a unified corpus, and the
name *Grágás* refers to as many as 130 codices, fragments and copies
written down over the centuries. *Grágás* was not a set code that
everyone was expected to obey, but a group of rules that individuals
could use to their advantage or turn to the disadvantage of others.

The sagas show characters routinely breaking the law when they thought they could get away with it, and it may well be that people acted in this way.

Manuscripts and Legal Origins

The heart of *Grágás* is two large manuscripts. One is called *Konungsbók*, the king's book, so named because in later years it was owned by the Danish Crown and kept in the Old Royal Library in Copenhagen. The other, *Staðarhólsbók*, is named after the farm in western Iceland where it was found in the sixteenth century. The leaves of these manuscript volumes are, like most other medieval Icelandic books, made of calfskin. Dating from the mid thirteenth century, they are well-preserved large folios, skilfully written and ornamented with polychrome initials.[2] Their production must have been extremely expensive, but we do not know for whom the work was done. Neither *Konungsbók* nor *Staðarhólsbók* is an official codex. Rather, they are private law books that cover, even if somewhat haphazardly, the breadth and depth of Iceland's constitutional and judicial systems.

In addition to the two main components of *Grágás*, a number of diverse vellum fragments have survived from early volumes, one of them dating perhaps from as early as 1150. A few otherwise unknown entries, as well as many sections of the law which repeat provisions recorded earlier, are found in various fourteenth- and fifteenth-century manuscripts.

Grágás preserves many laws that far predate the extant thirteenth-century manuscripts. The writing down of various legal provisions probably began as early as the late eleventh century, and scholars often assume that the tithe laws of 1096, as well as an earlier treaty (see Chapter 7) between the Icelanders and Norway's King Olaf the Saint, were among Iceland's first written legal documents. The process of transcribing and codifying the laws was formalized in the winter of 1117–18, when a commission headed by the chieftain

Haflidi Masson was, according to Ari's *Íslendingabók* (Chapter 10), empowered by the *lögrétta*, the legislative council at the Althing, to undertake the work:

The first summer that Bergthor [Hrafnsson, law-speaker 1117–22] recited the law, a new law [*nýmæli*, sing. and pl.] was passed that the laws should be written out in a book at Haflidi Masson's farm during the following winter according to the speech and consultation of Haflidi, Bergthor and other wise men who were selected for the task. They were to put into the laws all the new provisions [*nýmæli*] that seemed to them better than the old laws. The laws were to be said aloud the following summer in the law council [*lögrétta*] and would all take effect if a majority did not oppose them. And that was how the Manslaughter Section [*Vígslóði*] and much else in the law came to be written down and read aloud in the law council by clerics the following summer.

This first writing of *Vígslóði* is now lost, although a later version is found in *Grágás*.

According to *Grágás*, the function of the law council (*lögrétta*), the central legislative institution of the Free State, was to amend old laws (*rétta lög sín*) and to initiate new legislation (*gera nýmæli*).[3] The precise meaning of this entry has stirred much debate.[4] Although there is no doubt that the *lögrétta* enacted new laws, *Grágás* says nothing as to the procedure by which they were to be adopted. We know that only chieftains had the right to vote in the *lögrétta*, but did a simple majority suffice to pass legislation or was a unanimous vote required? This question has been debated for a century.[5] The ability to formulate new laws, however, was not limited to the *lögretta*. According to *Íslendingabók* (Chapters 4 and 5), private individuals could also introduce legislation at the Law Rock (*lögberg*) at the Althing. Further, a disputant who questioned the interpretation of a law, or who believed that no existing ruling applied to a specific situation, could initiate legislation by bringing a case before the *lögrétta* for clarification by vote. The legislative council's determination might reinterpret or supersede old law, thereby establishing new legislation. The *lögrétta* was thus able to adapt Icelandic law to meet prevailing needs. It is probable that in the course of time the rules of voting and procedure in the *lögrétta* and at the courts were altered to some extent.

Public access to law-making in the *lögrétta* and at the Law Rock may have brought innovations to Icelandic law. It may also have been responsible for the proliferation of enactments on matters of minor significance, a notable feature of *Grágás*. *Nýmæli* has long been a troublesome aspect of *Grágás*. To be valid in all or part of the country, new law required ratification, principally by acceptance over a period of time.* Unfortunately, the law books seldom specify whether ratification had or had not occurred.

The writing down of the laws ensured the transmission into the thirteenth century of many older legal provisions. For example, although slavery had almost certainly died out by 1117, the thirteenth-century texts record many rules concerning slavery. Legal scholars such as Lúðvík Ingvarsson have argued with good reason that provisions regarding the underlying structure of the Icelandic government – for example, those specifying the composition of the quarter courts, the springtime assemblies and the Fifth Court – closely approximate the provisions of the original tenth- and eleventh-century laws.[6] In a number of areas – for instance, the ownership of land – there seems little reason to doubt that the burden of the entries is conservative and old.[7]

Laws pertaining to the Christian faith and institutions, including those concerned with the offices of bishops and priests, baptism, burial, witchcraft, feast and holy days, fasting, and sorcery, are principally contained in the Christian Law Section (*Kristinna laga*

---

* *Grágás* 1852a: 37 (Ch. 8) and 1883: 443. These two entries are not in agreement. *Grágás* I (1852) requires that a new law will be in force for no more than three years, after which time it will lose its validity if it is not publicly recited every third summer thereafter. *Grágás* III (1883) calls for *nýmæli* to be recited publicly at the Law Rock every summer for three years following the initial enactment. If this regulation is observed the law is thereafter fully established. The two entries probably stem from different periods.

tháttr) of *Grágás*.[8] This special group of laws, which governed relations between the Church and temporal society, was written sometime between 1122 and 1133. Often called the 'Old Christian Laws' (*Kristinréttr forni*), these laws contain provisions that may go back as far as the conversion to Christianity at the beginning of the eleventh century. They also include revisions of later eleventh-century enactments as well as new laws from the twelfth century pertaining to religion.

The Christian Law Section was adopted at a time when the secular legal system had matured. No separate ecclesiastical jurisdiction was permitted in matters touching lay society, and there were no provisions for an independent Church. Christian enactments accepted hereditary private control of churches and, for the most part, were adapted to the already centuries-old Icelandic traditions of law and legal procedure. In general, throughout the history of the Free State and beyond, the Old Christian Laws defined the rights and prerogatives of the Icelandic Church. Their provisions remained in force in the southern diocese of Skálholt until 1275, when the 'New Christian Laws' (*Kristinréttr nýi*) were introduced.[9] This new code of Christian law, which established the principle that the Icelandic Church had the right to control its property and to govern itself, was not accepted in the northern diocese of Hólar until 1354. Even at this late date not all the new provisions were enforced.

Although *Konungsbók* and *Staðarhólsbók* are basically similar, they differ from each other in order, word choice, and to some extent in content. Of the two, *Konungsbók* is the more important. It contains several sections missing from *Staðarhólsbók*, among them the Assembly Procedures Section (*Thingskapatháttr*), the Compensation List (*Baugatal*), the Law-speaker's Section (*Lögsögumannstháttr*) and the Law Council Section (*Lögréttutháttr*). For its part, *Staðarhólsbók* preserves a number of provisions that are not in *Konungsbók*, and it is generally more detailed in the sections that appear in both manuscripts. It is not unusual to find in *Konungsbók* only the beginning or, occasionally, the beginning and the ending of an entry. The missing part may sometimes be found elsewhere, especially in *Staðarhólsbók*, which also has a number of similarly abridged entries. This peculiar method of entry may have arisen because, when the books were written or copied, their owners possessed other manuscripts in which the provisions in question were written out in full. Truncating the entries thus would have saved the cost of labour and parchment.

Grágás differs from other Scandinavian collections of laws in almost all respects. There are no provisions for defence or other military arrangements, and the constitution that it proposes is without parallel elsewhere in Scandinavia. Even basic matters like the rules of court procedure, including rules of proof and strictures governing the presentation of cases before the court, show an independent development. The penal code also has its peculiarities. The laws, when dealing with offences committed by freemen, contain no provisions for government officers to carry out corporal punishment or imprisonment, or to enact a death penalty.

In keeping with Iceland's cultural focus, vengeance killings, a central aspect of private feud, were incorporated into the law. This incorporation, as well as the general proliferation of legal sanctions, compensated for the absence of executive institutions. If private parties were sanctioned to undertake privileged vengeance, such actions were, nevertheless, restricted. The Manslaughter Section specifies both on whom and when vengeance may be taken:

It is the law that a man who has been injured is entitled, if he wishes, to avenge himself up to the time of the Althing where he is required to pursue the case for the wounds; it is the same for all those who have the right to avenge a killing. Those who have the right to avenge a killing are the principals in a manslaughter case. The man who inflicted the injury can be killed, having forfeited immunity [hence compensation] if killed by the principal or any of his followers, and it is also lawful for other men to avenge him [the person killed] within twenty-four hours if they want to.[10]

Private parties were also responsible for restraining violent individuals in their midst:

If a man goes berserk, the penalty is lesser outlawry. The same penalty applies to those men who are present except if they restrain him. But if they succeed in restraining him then the penalty falls on none of them. If it happens again, lesser outlawry applies.[11]

Its bulk is another distinctive feature of *Grágás*. *Konungsbók* alone is three and a half times the size of the Danish King Erik's Sjælland Laws, the largest of the Scandinavian provincial law books.[12] Furthermore, the Icelandic provisions have a sober and straightforward style, in contrast with the alliterative, formulaic diction of other Scandinavian laws. The direct style of *Grágás* may result from the manner in which the oral laws were revised when first written down, although, as Peter Foote has suggested, the diction of *Grágás* may simply reflect the original oral character of the laws.[13]

Grágás provides a wealth of detail about Old Icelandic society. For example, the legal entries often give a precise picture of the formal rights and duties of freemen and outline the composition and arrangement of assemblies and courts. Nevertheless, reliance on written law has its limitations. Although *Grágás* gives much information about Icelandic governmental and social institutions, it rarely specifies how these elements fit together. It is one thing to know the proposed composition of a court or an assembly; it is quite another to understand how bodies and gatherings actually worked when they met in open fields in medieval Iceland. Alongside the provisions in *Grágás* there surely existed a body of customary rule and law whose operation we at times witness in the sagas. At times, *Grágás* entries appear to be more the product of the wishes of the law-making elite than the society at large, whose operating concepts of law are often better displayed in the family and Sturlunga sagas.

Konungsbók and *Staðarhólsbók* are compendia of the law, not treatises on legal procedure and application. The individuals who used these extensive compilations understood the ways in which their society functioned. They did not require their law books to give instructions in the essential arts of posturing, negotiating and arbitrating; instead, they kept the detailing of such social behaviour for the sagas. In its entries concerned with situations from everyday life, *Grágás* often makes minute distinctions. It provides a mass of frequently lengthy rulings on a wide variety of issues in daily life, often specifying penalties of fines or outlawry. For example, in a section concerning horse riding, entitled '*Um hross reiðir*', the following provisions form only a small portion of the complete entry on this subject:[14]

If a man climbs on the back of a man's horse without permission, he incurs a fine of six ounces.* Now if he rides away, then he incurs a payment of three marks. There are three ways of riding a horse away which constitute outlawry. One is if a man rides so that three farms are on one side and he rides past them. The second is if a man rides past those mountains that divide the watersheds between districts. The third is if a man rides between quarters. There is an option to summon for a lesser offence even if a larger distance be ridden. If a man summons another man for horse riding, charging that he has ridden his horse past three farms, then he causes fines to be incurred along with outlawry. A jury of twelve shall preside when outlawry is to be determined. Now if the verdict is against him, it is up to him to ask for acquittal based on whether he had ridden so near to those three farms all lying on one side that a man with good eyesight could see him riding in daylight from all those farms if one were to check and there must not be hills or ridges blocking the line of sight. If a man lends a man a horse . . .

Fines together with outlawry were the major penalties under the laws

---

* The precise value of this fine is not clear, as standards and values varied considerably during the Free State period. The medieval Icelanders never minted their own coins, but the early settlers brought with them silver and foreign coins, as well as the Norwegian units of currency: the *mörk* (mark) – nearly half a pound – equalling 8 *aurar* (ounces, sing. *eyrir*). The ounce and mark began as units of weight but over the course of the eleventh century evolved into units of value. Pure silver was replaced by alloys, and *vaðmál*, homespun cloth, became the basis of the currency. Although there was little gold in Iceland, as a unit of value a mark of gold equalled eight marks of silver. The fine of six ounces would be equivalent to 36 ells of homespun; its value in silver would depend on the current rate of exchange. See the discussion of medieval Icelandic standards and values in Chapter 3.

of the Free State. A large part of *Grágás* is devoted to cataloguing the fines that could be levied for different infractions. The imposition of fines was clearly intended as an important method of restraining violence, insult and aggression. Fines were levied in settlements made in and out of court, but private settlements remained subject to approval at the *lögrétta*. Such settlements, often mentioned in the family and Sturlunga sagas, seem to have been common elements of dispute resolution. The sagas consistently imply that an individual could not expect to settle more cases against him than he could pay for.

Women and the Law

Feuding and lawsuits were primarily carried on by men, and consequently *Grágás* discusses women primarily in relation to men. Nevertheless, the law gives considerable information about freeborn women (though much less about female slaves). Investigating what the legal status of freeborn women was exactly also leads us to the critical issue of sources. Despite the fact that a freeborn woman could legally run a farm and make economic decisions as a *bóndi*,[15] *Grágás* clearly indicates that women took no part in the overt workings of the judicial system. There is no reason to doubt the reliability of this information.[16] Only men served as judges in the local springtime assemblies (*várthing*) or in the Althing courts.[17] Likewise, it seems that women did not participate as members of the panels of neighbours called *kviðir* (sing. *kviðr*) that were a vital element in legal administration and local government.*

Being barred from participation in *kviðir* had serious repercussions. It meant that a woman, even when acting as the head of a household, had fewer formal rights than hired workmen. Even men who owned no land could serve on a panel: the requirements for a

---

* Numerous panels carried the name of *kviðr*, the underlying concept being that a panel of neighbours (a form of local jury) should influence verdicts.

male to participate in *kviðir* were a minimum age of twelve years and an ability to earn his own keep.[18] Probably women were also barred from serving as witnesses in court, because almost all the discussions in *Grágás* concerning the eligibility of witnesses turn on descriptions of freemen (*karlar*).[19] Women were not allowed to participate personally in prosecutions for manslaughter (*vígsök*), yet when wronged a woman could legally claim the right to prosecution.[20] The sources are in general agreement that if a woman was an aggrieved party and owned a right of prosecution, she was to put her claim into the hands of a man. Women could also pursue their desires for vengeance by pushing their male kinfolk into action or by restraining them (see Chapter 10). The same was true in the case of a defence. Whatever the initial purpose of such regulations, they distanced women from a good deal of violence as prosecutions moved through stages of threat and sometimes force. Shielding women meant removing them completely from armed political life, and in *Grágás* women are barred from carrying weapons.[21]

Although shielded from extra-familial violence, women still retained the right to make many decisions. According to *Grágás*, a maiden (*mær*) who had reached the age of twenty (sixteen in some instances) could control her choice of residence,[22] while grown women were held accountable for their actions and bore the same responsibility as men for all infractions of the law: 'A woman is to be punished the same as a man if she kills a man or a woman, or causes injury, and this procedure is followed for all breaches of the law.'[23] The sagas do not show much evidence of this rule being enforced, however.

In its treatment of women, *Grágás* shows particular concern for the protection of a woman's person, as can be seen in the following opening sentences in the five-page entry[24] on seduction, itself only a part of a far larger section on 'chargeable offences concerning women'. The passage is formulated in terms of possible offences perpetrated by men against women, and generally a man brings charges against another man:

If a man kisses a woman in secret, away from other men, and with her approval, it is a penalty of three marks, and he [the aggrieved] has the right of prosecution as in a case of seduction. But if she is offended, then she herself has the right of prosecution, and it is then lesser outlawry. If a man gives another man's wife a secret kiss, it is a penalty of lesser outlawry even if she permitted him to do so, but also if she forbade it, and nine neighbours shall be called to a panel [kviðr] at the assembly. If a man proposes to have sexual intercourse with a woman, there is a penalty of lesser outlawry. These are summoning cases and a panel [kviðr] of nine neighbours shall be called at that thing where the case is prosecuted. If a man goes into a woman's bed with the intention of having sex with her, it is a penalty of lesser outlawry. If a man puts on a woman's headdress in order to seduce her, there is a penalty of lesser outlawry. If a man entices a woman and goes to bed with her in order to have sex with her, there is a penalty of full outlawry, and a panel [kviðr] of nine neighbours shall be called at that thing where the prosecution is taken.[25]

Beginning with kisses and continuing through propositions to full seductions, the full entry lays out penalties that escalate according to the severity of the offence. In its entirety the entry is eight times the length of this extract and considers almost every possible form of seduction.[26]

Were such stipulations enforced? The probable answer is that many of the specific provisions of *Grágás* were applied only loosely, if at all. Numerous entries on the pages of the different Icelandic law books, having outlived their usefulness, would simply have been ignored. Further, scribes acting on their own initiative may have added many clauses, fleshing out entries in order to satisfy their own personal, and probably clerically oriented, views.* As noted earlier in this chapter, Iceland's copious medieval law was a series of often extensive entries relating to most aspects of life. Rather than being hard and fast, these rules served instead as guidelines for limiting and judging the parameters of permissible action. Both women and men

---

* Although scribes are largely anonymous, they probably had a Church education.

used the sometimes contradictory rules of *Grágás* to their advantage. That was the nature of the legal game.

The Church was deeply involved in the formulation of laws concerning women. Especially after the eleventh century, the *goðar* gave churchmen the final say in most legal matters involving women, even if the *goðar* themselves and the population in general had little inclination to follow such laws. A practical aspect of the Althing's system of consensual governance was that making laws was one matter, while enforcing them was quite another. Like the social relationship between *goðar* and *bændr* which guaranteed the rights of freemen, the rights of women were upheld not by legal enforcement but through the give and take of the advocacy system. Additionally, *Grágás* frequently focuses on the privileges of sanctioned marriage with regard to women, giving the impression that other options were consistently degrading.

The important economic role played by women is recorded only scantily in both saga and law book. The historian Ólafía Einarsdóttir proposes that a woman's importance in running the farm may have given her a high social standing.[27] Helgi Thorláksson and Nanna Damsholt have also explored different sides of the economic issue, drawing attention to women's central role in the production and management of *vaðmál*, the homespun wool cloth that was Iceland's major export during the Free State period.[28] Nevertheless, economic production does not always translate into social importance. In 1862, J. Ross Browne travelled to Iceland from California and, observing one group of women, reported that:

Like all Icelandic women I saw, they fulfill all the tasks at hand, tend to the cows, make cheese, cut the grass, carry a heavy load and usually work all heavy labor. Sometimes men help them, but they would rather ride about the country or lounge at home.[29]

Marriage and the Church

Marriage in pre-Christian Iceland was a rather straightforward agreement, a mutual linking of families. We have only a vague knowledge of the specifics, but we do know that the bride brought a dowry, settled in advance. This was called a *heimanfylgja*, meaning property that 'followed' the bride from home. Betrothal was called *festar* or attachment, and the terms used to describe marriage itself speak of a bargain. The actual event was called a 'bride purchase' (*brúðkaup*),* and at the marriage the groom paid the 'bride price' (*mundr*), an agreed-upon sum for the bride. The whole transaction of arranging and paying the bride price[30] was called the 'bride-price matter' (*mundar-mál*). Originally the legal guardian of the woman (*lögráðandi*) probably kept the bride price, but by the time of *Grágás*, both the bride price and the dowry were counted as the woman's personal possessions. For instance, one of the entries in the section on divorce says: 'If a man initiates divorce, then the woman has the right to retrieve her bride price and dowry.'[31] Women, too, could initiate divorce. The permissible reasons were varied, and included: when a husband wanted to take a wife's property out of the country against her will; when violence had been committed by either party against the other; incompatibility; or when the husband wore feminine clothing.[32] When a wife initiated divorce, the return of the bride price was less certain than when the husband began the proceedings.[33]

Although the specific event described may not be historical, the nature of the marital agreement as a transaction between families is made clear in the following passage from *Njáls saga* (Chapter 97).[34] In this instance Njal, as head of his household, is acting for his foster-son Hoskuld, whose father is dead. Flosi speaks for his niece Hildigunn, a proud young woman, who states her views plainly:

* The related term *brullaup* (bride jump or journey) is popular in later manuscripts. The common law practice of marriage in England was to jump over a broomstick. Divorce involved jumping the other way.

One day Njal said to his foster-son Hoskuld, 'I want to find a good match for you and provide you with a wife.'

'I leave it in your hands,' said Hoskuld. 'Where are you thinking of seeking a match?'

Njal replied, 'There is a woman called Hildigunn, the daughter of Starkad, the son of Thord Frey's-Priest. She is the best match I know of.'

'You decide, foster-father,' said Hoskuld. 'I shall accept whatever choice you wish to make.'

'That is the match we shall try for, then,' said Njal.

A little later Njal asked the Sigfussons, his own sons, and Kari Solmundarson to accompany him. They rode east to Svínafell, where they were well received. Next day Njal and Flosi went aside to talk, and eventually Njal said, 'The purpose of our visit is to make a proposal of marriage, to link our family with yours, Flosi. We are asking for the hand of your niece, Hildigunn.'

'On whose behalf?' asked Flosi.

'For Hoskuld Thrainsson, my foster-son,' replied Njal.

'This is a good offer,' said Flosi. 'On the other hand there are dangerous flaws in your family relationships. What can you tell me of Hoskuld?'

'Nothing but good,' replied Njal, 'and I am prepared to settle as large a sum on him as you think proper, if you care to consider the matter at all.'

'We shall send for Hildigunn,' said Flosi, 'and see what she thinks of the man.'

Hildigunn was sent for. When she arrived Flosi told her of the proposal.

'I have my pride,' said Hildigunn, 'and I am not sure whether this proposal suits me, considering the type of people involved – particularly since this is a man without authority. You made me a promise that you would never marry me to a man without the rank of chieftain.'

'If you don't want to marry the man, that in itself is sufficient reason for me to refuse the offer,' said Flosi.

'I am not saying that I do not want to marry Hoskuld – if they provide him with a chieftainship,' said Hildigunn. 'But otherwise I will not consider it.'

Njal said, 'Give me three years' grace to deal with the matter.'

Flosi agreed to this.

'I want to stipulate,' said Hildigunn, 'that we settle here in the east if the marriage takes place.'

Njal said that he would rather leave that to Hoskuld to decide.

Hoskuld said that he trusted many men, but none so well as his foster-father Njal. With that they rode back west.[35]

Hildigunn, the daughter of a prominent family, is portrayed as having the power of refusal. She had set her sights on marrying a *goði*, a desire that her family supported and one which was to have considerable ramifications in the saga.

Marriage in Iceland changed somewhat as the Christian period developed, especially toward the end of the twelfth century. Such change was not peculiar to Iceland, as the historian Georges Duby notes:

The entire history of marriage in Western Christendom amounts to a gradual process of acculturation, in which the ecclesiastical model slowly gained the upper hand, not over disorder – as is too often claimed by those who blindly espouse the point of view of churchmen whose testimony is almost all that has come down to us – but over a different order, one that was solidly entrenched and not easily dislodged. The real problem is not to find out why the victory of the ecclesiastical model was so slow and so precarious, but why this model was able to gain as much ground as it finally did. The fact is that the lay model was gradually infiltrated and eventually absorbed. The priests became involved in the marriage ceremony, adding certain acts of benediction and exorcism to all the solemn rites, whose climax they imperceptibly shifted from the house to the entrance gate of the church, and eventually to its interior. The priests were also able to gain control over marriage by taking over its jurisdiction. This enabled them to institute reforms, to establish the rules, and to impose their own system of prohibitions.[36]

Grágás contains many laws from the later centuries of the Free State concerning marriage. These were mostly written in the twelfth and thirteenth centuries and suggest that marriage was not an option for everyone. For example, a couple could not marry unless they owned in common 120 legal ounces of silver (*lögaurar*, i.e., 720 ells' worth), plus their everyday clothes, and had no dependants.[37] If these laws were enforced, as some may have been because they appealed to individuals in local positions of power, they would have severely limited the number of marriageable people. Gunnar Karlsson, principal editor of the 1992 edition of *Grágás*, estimates that if the economic restrictions concerning marriage were ever enforced, landless workers would have needed almost twenty years to amass just the minimum amount of wealth required as a precondition for legal marriage.[38] Most women and men did not, of course, wait that long to form unions.

Other restrictions on marriage affected more than the poor. According to the dictates of the Church in Rome, parties to a marriage could not be more closely related by blood than the seventh degree. In Iceland this restriction was never more than the fifth degree, that is sharing a great-great-great-grandfather.[39] The situation was even more complicated if either or both of the parties had been married to others earlier or had children. In such instances neither their previous spouses nor a parent of their children might be closer than the fifth degree to the new spouse.[40] Compliance with such strict rules was problematic in many lands, and the Fourth Lateran Council of 1215 consequently lowered the limits of consanguinity to the fourth degree. The Althing quickly adopted this change in 1217, but in a small society like Iceland's the restrictions still made it difficult for some to find partners, especially the children of prominent landowners wishing to marry among equals.

18

Bishops and Secular Authority:
The Later Church

The men from Fljót could see that they would not have their
full rights vindicated in a lawsuit against Onund unless they
could depend upon the support of others. So they went
to Bishop Brand [Saemundarson, d. 1201] and sought his
advice. The Bishop told them that Gudmund the Worthy's
assistance had determined the outcome of the most important lawsuits that had come to the Althing during the preceding summer. The Bishop advised them to seek a meeting
with Gudmund to see if they could get him to take on their
case.

The Saga of Gudmund the Worthy, Chapter 4

The conversion Church showed itself highly adaptable. The following centuries saw the roles and demands of the Church integrated
into an island culture, dominated by law and restrained feuding, and
without urban centres.

Bishops

In the status-driven world of early Iceland, chieftains depended on
the wisdom of their advisers to maintain their position. Bishops
forged a role for themselves as nominally impartial semi-advocates
to whom laymen in need could turn. The position of the Icelandic

bishops has parallels in other decentralized societies in which feuding played a large role. Consider, for example, the ambiguous role of the bishop, the *vladika*, in Montenegro's more warlike, tribal society:

The *vladika* in Cetinje himself had to earn most of the respect he received as bishop. He found himself in a curious position: he was a political leader without any real coercive power who was also the chief representative of a religious ideology that the tribesmen resisted in many of its facets. In trying to resolve blood feuds, a *vladika* had to work against the indigenous Montenegrin code of honour, as he upheld the specific values of the Church. From an outside perspective this was useful, in that the feuding tribesmen themselves were virtually prisoners of their own warlike secular moral code, and therefore needed the moral leverage of a milder, competing set of values in trying to settle their feuds. Indeed, tribesmen who were not directly involved in the feud saw their *vladika* as someone who, through force of persuasion, might be able to help a tribal community out of these difficulties. But pacification was made very difficult by the fact that the participants themselves were at best extremely ambivalent about setting aside their feuds and frequently would ignore supernaturally based threats made by their *vladika*.[1]

Like the Christian Montenegrins, the Icelanders accepted the primacy of their religion, but they faced a dilemma. Participation in feud was a way of life in Iceland. Feuding regulated wealth and status, a situation reinforced by the courts and the focus on law. Advocacy, brokerage, 'friendship' agreements and arbitration were the accepted ways that people implemented their social and political relationships. The Icelandic Church evolved in a way that complemented what already existed rather than setting itself at odds with expected social behaviour. The role of peacemaker was an integral part in the operation of Icelandic consensual governance, and bishops often participated in arranging settlements. Just as some chieftains were adept at this role, so too were some bishops. Bishop Brand Saemundarson of Hólar (1163–1201) was such a leader, and many turned to him for advice.

From the days of Bishop Gizur in the eleventh century, the office of bishop was highly prestigious. The two bishops sat in the law council, where they enjoyed full voting rights and where, we may guess, their views were respected. In spiritual matters the bishops possessed great authority. Although we do not have much information on the subject, it is reasonable to assume that as mediators between the corporeal world and eternal life, the clergy in general enjoyed strong spiritual influence. The Icelandic Church was also highly influential in cultural matters. Clerics played an important role in introducing educational and literary concepts. Both sees maintained schools where the sons of chieftains and farmers were educated. These schools, together with other centres of learning such as those maintained in the homes of prominent chieftain families (for example, the Haukdaelir from Haukadalr and the Oddaverjar from Oddi), enlarged the intellectual world of twelfth- and thirteenth-century Icelanders.

Even though the *bændr* respected their bishops, they seem to have been careful not to surrender to them too much authority, especially when potential patronage was involved. The *bændr* did not grant their bishops the opportunity to be responsible for distributing alms to the poor, an otherwise traditional function of the Roman Church. Instead the farmers, through their self-governing communal units or *hreppar* (see Chapter 7), retained for themselves the right to collect and to disburse locally the part of the tithe (*tíund*) which was designated for the poor. Called the tithe for those in need (*thurfamanna-tíund*), this portion was substantial, amounting to a quarter of the tithe collected locally. In retaining control over the distribution of poor relief, the *bændr* seem to have been reinforcing their status.

The Tithe and Church Farmsteads

The introduction of the tithe brought about a marked change in both the state of the Church and the chieftains' flow of revenue. Iceland's was the first national tithe in all Scandinavia; it also was the first tax in

Iceland's history which assessed an individual's economic circumstances, thus providing a basis for graduated taxation. An important feature of the tithe law was that a chieftaincy – an otherwise marketable commodity that could be bought or sold – was declared to be 'power, not wealth' (*Velldi er þat en ægi fé*) and thus tax-exempt.[2] Possessions of the Church, including many farms on which stood churches or private chapels nominally owned by the Church, were exempt from the tithe. This tax-exempt status, advantageous to landowners, had important consequences. Families in the twelfth century often donated large parts of their landholdings to the Church under agreements allowing them to become hereditary wardens of the property, thus retaining administrative rights for themselves and their heirs.

The tithe, which did not discriminate between men and women, was required of all heads of households who qualified as thing-tax-paying farmers or *thingfararkaupsbændr*. People holding less property than the *thingfararkaupsbændr* were required to tithe only when they had no dependants. As the historian Jón Jóhannesson points out, 'This regulation is noteworthy because of its implicit leniency towards people in the lower income categories.'[3]

The tithe was divided into four parts: one for the bishop (*biskupstíund*), the second for the priest's services (*preststíund*), the third for the upkeep of the church building (*kirkjutíund*), and the fourth for the poor (*fátækratíund* or *thurfamannatíund*). The person in control of the farm on which the church stood received the part set aside for the maintenance of the church. A person who controlled or owned a farmstead with a church on it, whether or not the farm was a *staðr* (the most important of the Church farmsteads), was often in a position to collect two quarters of the tithe. For example, the proprietor of the farm naturally kept the *kirkjutíund*, and he could also get the *preststíund* if he had himself, a family member or a servant ordained as a priest. The advantages that the tithe offered chieftains suggest that from the first many *goðar* perceived this tax as a means of increasing their wealth. The chieftains gave their consent to the tithe through the law council at the Althing and then manipulated its operation in their favour.

If the chieftains were indeed instrumental in introducing the tithe, they did not create the situation that made the new law agreeable to them as well as to many farmers. The custom of lay administration or hereditary wardship of churches was a continuation of the pagan practice of having a temple on one's property. In its Christian form, the custom granted a level of control almost equivalent to ownership. It began shortly after the conversion, when landowners, both *bændr* and *goðar*, built churches on their property. Churches, after being consecrated in the name of the deity or of his saints, were returned to the guardianship of secular individuals and their heirs. This agreement was almost a form of enfeoffment, resembling a feudal contract: land in return for the services of upkeep and management. Theoretically, the ownership of the property passed to the Church when the building was consecrated. In practice, the control of the land, along with the added benefits that came from the presence of a church building, was regarded by secular landholders as a hereditary administrative right. Yet there were some limitations on the owner of a *staðr*: the church building had to be properly maintained; the land could not be sold; and the owner was required to keep a list (*máldagi*) of all church property.

Besides tithe payments, some church owners could also collect dues, called *tollar* and *skyldir*, from churchgoers. These small payments may have become standard in the thirteenth century, and some of them, such as the church candle tax (*ljóstollr* or *lýsitollr*), may well have been fairly lucrative.[4] Unfortunately, little is known about these minor taxes.[5] Added together, the different church-related payments formed an important source of wealth for owners of churches and Church farmsteads.

Many studies have stressed the control of *staðir* as the principal source of wealth for the 'big' chieftains or *stórgoðar* who emerged in twelfth- and thirteenth-century Iceland.[6] This conclusion is sound in certain respects, but when accepted as a general rule it becomes misleading. The tithe did not establish the *goðar* as leaders. Traditions of leadership were firmly in place when in the late eleventh century the chieftains used their legislative power to reap benefits from a new form of revenue, one that also offered a non-taxable shelter for existing wealth. On the other hand, some chieftain families, particularly the Oddaverjar and the Haukdaelir in the south, profited to an inordinate degree from their management of *staðir*. The increased wealth such families derived from their control of Church property hastened the evolution toward increased social complexity.

The effect of *staðir* ownership was not the same throughout the country. Especially in the West Fjords and in Eyjafjord in the north, gaining control of *staðir* was not an absolute prerequisite for power. Attempts by individuals or families to achieve hegemony over local areas had been a feature of the Icelandic body politic long before the effect of tithing and *staðir* was felt. In the pre-conversion tenth century, for instance, Gudmund the Powerful from Eyjafjord in the Northern Quarter probably controlled two *goðorð* (hence his name). Likewise, the chieftain Haflidi Masson in the north-west had become very powerful by the early twelfth century, before the tithe became a factor. Neither of these men depended on Church-related wealth.[7]

Bishops and Priests in the Later Free State

The episcopal seats at Hólar and Skálholt were often filled by members of the most powerful families, especially by the Haukdaelir and the Oddaverjar in the south. Only on a very few occasions were the elections sources of major controversy, and almost never of feud or other violence. For example, by 1174 Bishop Klaeng of Skálholt, having become old and sickly, received permission from Archbishop Eystein Erlendsson (1161–88) in Norway to arrange for a successor. The subsequent selection in 1174 of the new Skálholt bishop was carried out in a highly political manner.[8] Klaeng went to the Althing where, after consultations, three candidates were selected. Each of the three regions that together formed the diocese, the west, the south and the east, put forward an aspirant. After further negotiations the old bishop was asked to choose from among the nominees. Klaeng selected Thorlak Thorhallsson, a priest noted for his virtue and financial acumen. A good business sense was a helpful quality since the see of Skálholt was in poor financial condition as the result of Klaeng's having built at Skálholt a large cathedral using imported timber. Thorlak, who had been a founder and abbot of the first Augustinian monastery in the country at Thykkvibær, was the candidate of the Oddaverjar, led by the chieftain Jon Loftsson. Klaeng died in 1176, and in accordance with the normal procedure, the candidate-elect went abroad for consecration.

The consistent lack of conflict in the filling of high Icelandic Church positions is a factor that may help us evaluate the relative political and economic importance of the Icelandic bishops. Had the office been one of significant power, the choice of a new bishop would surely have led to fierce contention among leading families, ever on the lookout for more authority. The Christian Law Section of *Grágás* gives no rules as to how Icelandic bishops were to be elected. Until 1237, when the archbishop and the cathedral chapter at Niðaróss (modern Trondheim) in Norway finally refused to consecrate the two Icelandic candidates, one because he was a *goði* (the Church had by now banned chieftains from the priesthood) and the other because he was illegitimate, the Icelanders elected their own Church leaders according to their own criteria. When one of Iceland's two bishops died or became too infirm to carry out his functions, the normal procedure was for the other bishop to suggest a politically acceptable candidate to the chieftains assembled at the Althing, a practice of secular interference which would have been generally unacceptable on the European mainland even before the Second Lateran Council in 1139 forbade such interference. Gudmund Arason's election to the seat at Hólar in 1201 by an assembly of laymen and clergy from the Northern Quarter was one of the most controversial during the life of the Free State, yet even in that instance the open competition for the office caused no violence.

The lack of confrontation over the control of Iceland's two bishoprics stands in contrast to the fierce rivalries that otherwise characterized power struggles among Icelandic leaders. With so much of the Church's wealth in secular hands, and thus already committed to the political process, there was little inducement for leaders to fight over control of the remaining resources of the Church. Whatever the reasons, conditions in Iceland were at variance with those in many parts of Europe, where the elaborate political machinations often preceding the selection of high churchmen underscored the political, economic and governmental role of the Church there. Icelandic bishops were handicapped by the nature of Icelandic diocesan administration. At least until 1267 neither Hólar nor Skálholt had a cathedral chapter of canons (the *kórsbræðr*, choir brethren, of Norwegian cathedrals). In 1267, that is, after the end of the Free State, Bishop Jorund of Hólar (1267–1313) received permission to institute a chapter, but it is not clear how quickly the chapter came into being. Thus during the life of the Free State in the period after the Second Lateran Council (1139), the Icelandic episcopal centres operated not only differently from but also less effectively than most of their European counterparts. Probably no chapters existed because the bishops lacked the economic means to support them.

The Church's Struggle for Power in the Later Free State

The first Icelandic bishop who tried to lessen secular influence on his diocese was Thorlak Thorhallsson of Skálholt (1178–93, later canonized). Thorlak attempted to gain control over Church property and to enforce on the laity the Church's views on the sanctity of marriage, demanding that laymen give up their concubines and end marriages to which he found impediments.[9] During his contests with the chieftains of his diocese he received no assistance from his colleague, Bishop Brand Saemundarson of Hólar. When Thorlak died after years of bitter disputes with various *goðar*, most of which he lost, the chieftains at the Althing displayed their power over the governance of the Church by electing as his successor the *goði* Pal Jonsson (1195–1211). Pal was the illegitimate son of the *goði* Jon Loftsson and Thorlak's sister, Ragnheid. Jon, who first seems to have been a strong supporter of Thorlak, became the bishop's chief opponent and, in spite of the bishop's vehement objection, for years kept Ragnheid as his concubine. Jon had also successfully refused to relinquish to the bishop control over his Church property.

In keeping with the long-standing custom by which temporal Icelandic leaders took Church orders, both Jon Loftsson and Pal Jonsson were deacons. Pal was a learned man and, although a reasonable Icelandic choice for bishop, he was a highly unusual candidate for high Church office in view of the standards of the Roman Church.[10] Contrary to Roman procedure, he was not elected by the 'greater and sounder part' of a cathedral chapter, because there were no such chapters in Iceland, and his illegitimate birth was an irregularity that, under standard Church rules, could be remedied only by a papal dispensation. Further, Pal was married. His wife was the daughter of a priest, and the couple had four children. Pal's marriage was another irregularity that should have been remedied by consultation with Church authorities before his election. Technically, in fact, because he was ineligible on at least two counts, he should have been 'requested' (*postulatus*) rather than 'elected' (*electus*).[11] Nevertheless, the Norwegians were accustomed to the practices of the Icelanders. According to his saga (*Páls saga biskups*, Chapters 3–4), when Pal came to Norway King Sverrir, who had enemies among his own churchmen, treated him with manifest friendship. After Pal's ordination by Bishop Thorir, he returned home and ended his Uncle Thorlak's experiments with Church reform. He returned the diocese of Skálholt to the older, insular traditions of the Icelandic Church.

A notable exception to the failure of the Church to institute its claims for diminished secular control occurred in 1190. At this time the Norwegian Archbishop Eirik Ivarsson prohibited the ordination of Iceland's *goðar* as priests, thus lessening the control of secular leaders over the Church.[12] Although this prohibition was never officially made part of Icelandic law, no sure evidence that any new priests were ordained from among the chieftains emerges after 1190. Yet even here change came slowly. Previously ordained chieftain-priests retained their dual function. Temporal leaders continued to assume lower clerical orders, and their sons occasionally assumed higher orders. Further, even after 1190 *bændr* who were allied with chieftains continued to serve as ordained priests.

Reform of the Icelandic Church was difficult because it was not a semi-independent state-within-a-state, as in many other countries. It was a not clearly defined organization that was, from the start, largely subject to lay supervision. The Church's acceptance of the norms of the secular community was formalized in the period 1122–33 when the laws governing Christian observances, including those modified for Icelandic conditions, were written down.* These laws, contained in the Christian Law Section (*Kristinna laga tháttr*) of *Grágás*, together with the separate tithe entries,[13] served to define the relations between Church and temporal society. As noted in the previous chapter, on *Grágás*, *Kristinna laga tháttr* remained in force in Skálholt until 1275 and in Hólar until at least 1354. Beyond governing the internal life of the Church and supervising the moral and marriage practices of their flocks, the Icelandic bishops had relatively little legal authority. Even when laws from the Christian Law Section of *Grágás* were broken, the bishop had no right to prosecute. Judicial matters stemming from breaches of Christian laws or cases involving a cleric were handled by secular courts. The bishops exercised judicial authority only when a priest was disobedient to his superior. Even in such instances the Church's inability to execute any of its judgements made it advisable, at times, to turn the matter over to the secular courts.

The demand that the bishop be given independent judicial power over his clergy and control over Church property was taken up by Iceland's other reform bishop, Gudmund Arason of Hólar (1203–37). Like Thorlak, Gudmund was in the end unsuccessful in achieving

---

* There is an irony in the date: in 1122 the papacy concluded an agreement – the Concordat of Worms – with the Holy Roman Emperor Henry V. The concordat guaranteed a degree of autonomy to the Church in the elevation of bishops within Germany and, especially, Italy.

his goals. Also like Thorlak, he was not the leader of a united Church party. During Gudmund's long conflict with secular leaders, he received no support from Skálholt, either during the episcopate of Pal Jonsson or during that of Magnus Gizurarson (1216–37). Unlike Bishop Thorlak's contest, however, Gudmund's turned violent. Gudmund early showed a predilection toward gathering unruly men about him. In the autumn of 1208 some of the bishop's followers killed Kolbein Tumason, Gudmund's main opponent, in a skirmish. Kolbein had been the most prominent chieftain in the north, and despite his later opposition, he was the man responsible for Gudmund's election.

Gudmund's victory was short lived, for after the spring of 1209 his efforts were continually blocked by a series of alliances among chieftains living in many parts of the country. On several occasions the bishop was driven from Hólar and forced to wander about the countryside. This situation did not please churchmen in Norway, and twice Gudmund obeyed summonses by the archbishop to come to Norway. Although he spent a total of eight winters there, he seems to have received little support. When he returned to Iceland in 1218, after his first stay, his goals had changed. He no longer advanced his earlier claim for increased judicial authority; instead he became a champion of the poor.

Gudmund's episcopate came during a period when the ideals of poverty and humility had gained popularity in medieval Europe. Among the ideas circulating which may have influenced him were those that motivated the mendicant friars and inspired the rebellious, puritanical Waldensian movement in France. Gudmund now lived in poverty, often surrounded by a following of men and women including clergy, weapon-bearing men, vagrants, beggars and thieves. According to Jón Jóhannesson, the years around the beginning of the thirteenth century were times of famine, and 'the great number of beggars in Bishop Gudmund's day has no parallel in Icelandic history, either before or after.'[14] When he was able to do so, Gudmund allowed most of the revenues of his diocese to go to charitable causes. Here again he clashed with *goðar* and *bændr*, who saw the depletion of the episcopal treasury as a demonstration of the bishop's irresponsibility.

Secular leaders repeatedly dispersed Gudmund's following, and at times he was held in confinement. The struggle, which continued for well over a decade, helped the rise of some leaders who have become known as 'big' goðar (stórgoðar) to increase their authority at the expense of the farmers' traditional independence. Many bændr opposed the bishop; they seem to have particularly disliked his demand that they provide hospitality for his following. Íslendinga saga (Chapter 37) tells us that Gudmund, accompanied by 120 followers, spent the summer of 1220 moving about in Reykjadalr, a region east of Eyjafjord. When Gudmund came for the second time to the farm called Múli, the local bændr, forty strong, barred the way. After declaring that the bóndi at Múli was possessed by an unclean spirit, the bishop moved on without a fight. The farmers, nevertheless, must have felt threatened. They sent for assistance from two stórgoðar who lived outside the region, Sighvat Sturluson from Eyjafjord and Arnor Tumason from Skagafjord. Seizing the opportunity, Sighvat and Arnor quickly gathered men and came east to Reykjadalr; eventually they came to blows with the bishop's followers.

Although Gudmund did not win any lasting victories for the Church, his stormy three decades as bishop of Hólar marked a turning point in Icelandic affairs. The controversy that surrounded his actions gave the archbishop and later the Norwegian king their first prolonged opportunity to intervene in Icelandic affairs. At different times during the controversy, these foreign lords summoned both Icelandic bishops and many chieftains to their presence. Although the bishops and chieftains chose frequently to ignore these summonses, the door for interference from abroad had been opened. From the 1240s to the 1260s the Norwegian king increasingly intervened in Iceland's internal affairs, undermining Icelandic autonomy. The turmoil that surrounded Thorlak's and Gudmund's attempts to institute in Iceland the claims of the Universal Church tends to overshadow the otherwise peaceful role the bishops assumed in Icelandic society.

Priests

The Icelandic priesthood was a major impediment to more centralized Church control, in part because the priests did not form a united religious caste. Some were loyal followers of their bishops while others, perhaps the majority, participated as self-interested freemen in the acquisitive manoeuvrings that characterized Icelandic life. Most priests married, saw to their children's inheritances, and adapted their responsibilities as churchmen to the dominant codes of Icelandic society. They regularly took part in the incessant disputes and feuds as partisan advocates, arbitrators, and supporters of their kinsmen and political allies. When in 1208 Bishop Gudmund Arason of Hólar placed the chieftains opposing him under a Church ban, his position was undermined by the lack of support from the Skálholt episcopacy but also from many priests of his own diocese, who continued to associate with the excommunicates. These priests held religious services for Gudmund's enemies and continued to do so after they themselves had been placed under the ban. This state of affairs continued for many years.

The situation of the Icelandic clergy had already, by the late twelfth century, troubled the Norwegian archbishop in Niðaróss. In 1173 Archbishop Eystein Erlendsson wrote in a letter 'to the Bishops in Iceland, the Chieftains, and all the people':

Now, all those clergymen from the lowest orders to the highest, those who have killed men, to them I forbid the performing of religious services. And, from this time on, I forbid all clerics to undertake the role of prosecutor in lawsuits except when they act on the behalf of disabled relatives, fatherless children or defenceless poverty-stricken women. These prosecutions must be assumed for God's sake and for no other reason, irrespective of any recompense.[15]

In 1180 Archbishop Eystein, who was having his own troubles with Sverrir (who claimed the Norwegian throne), was forced by him to leave Niðaróss. His injunction against Icelandic priests participating in lawsuits apparently was not heeded. In 1190 Archbishop Eirik Ivarsson wrote to the Icelanders reminding those in orders, beginning with subdeacons, 'not to undertake prosecutions that would have to be pursued with valour and weapons'.[16]

The participation of Icelandic priests in legal disputes is confirmed by *Sturlunga saga*, which shows many priests taking part in feuds. A detailed example of the manner in which a decidedly peaceful cleric was drawn into a feud is found in *The Saga of Hvamm-Sturla* (*Sturlu saga*, *Sturl. 1*, Chapters 30–36). One of the conflicts the saga narrates was a big feud from the last part of the twelfth century whose action swirls around Pal Solvason, a wealthy priest and *goði* from Reykjaholt in the Western Quarter. According to *The Saga of Bishop Thorlak* (Chapter 9), Pal was famed for his skill in managing his property; he was also one of the three candidates considered at the Althing in 1174 for the office of bishop of Skálholt. The feud, called the *Deildartungumál* (the Tunga affair) after one of the main properties, started when someone contested Pal's, and hence his legitimate sons', right to inherit all the valuable property claimed by Pal after the death of his widowed and childless daughter.[17]

Two other examples from *Sturlunga saga* of priests actively engaged in lawsuits and feuds are considered in this book. One (discussed in Chapter 10) concerns Gudmund Arason, who in the early thirteenth century became bishop of Hólar. At the time of the saga account, Gudmund was a priest of illegitimate parentage who took on the prosecution of a killer. The other example (in Chapter 15) concerns the turmoil resulting from attempts by the priest Eyjolf Hallsson to acquire additional inheritances for his legitimate sons. For a short time he was an unsuccessful candidate for bishop of Hólar when Gudmund Arason was elected to that position in 1201. A few years later, in 1206, Eyjolf became abbot of the short-lived monastery of Saurbær.

Monasteries

Monastic holdings did not significantly alter the economic or political position of the early Icelandic Church, though monasteries did play an active role in Iceland's cultural life. Modern writings about Iceland's sagas have frequently included assumptions that these religious communities were more important than the verifiable information suggests. In fact, the sources give little information about them. Probably this was because monasteries were so few and small. Einar Ól. Sveinsson notes that 'the monastic population was, to be sure, not large, from five to ten members to a house, and we have no information that before 1300 there were in any Icelandic monastery more than five monks at one time.'[18] Communities of monks in Iceland followed the rules of either the Benedictine or the Augustinian order, but were not branches of specific international houses. Instead they seem to have relied heavily on native cultural traditions. This reliance was perhaps owing to the Icelandic custom whereby monasteries were often founded and maintained through the participation of *goðar* and prominent *bændr*, a number of whom retired to these communities at the end of their lives.

Icelandic monasteries served as centres of learning and probably of instruction, although information about the latter is scant. We probably know most about the Benedictine monastery at Thingeyrar in the northern diocese. It was Iceland's first monastery to survive and it was perhaps the most scholarly. Its monks were particularly interested in hagiographical works. They wrote early sagas of Norway's missionary kings, Olaf Tryggvason and Olaf the Saint, and promoted the saintly reputation of the northern diocese's first bishop, Jon Ogmundarson. In 1185–8 Karl Jonsson, Thingeyrar's abbot, visited Norway. There, with the participation of King Sverrir, he

26. (*right*) **The Monasteries and the Two Bishoprics during the Period of the Free State.** Later in the Middle Ages, three more monasteries were founded: Reynistaðr (1296) and Möðruvellir (1296) in the north, and Skriðuklaustr (1493) in the east.

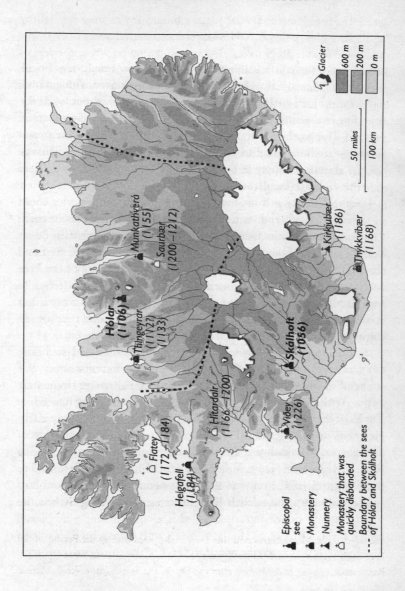

Glacier

600 m
200 m
0 m

50 miles
100 km

Munkaþverá
(1155)
Saurbær
(1200–1212)

Kirkjubær
(1186)
Þykkvibær
(1168)

Hólar
(1106)
Þingeyrar
(1122)
(1133)

Skálholt
(1056)

Hítardalr
(1166–1200)

Viðey
(1226)

Flatey
(1172–1184)

Helgafell
(1184)

† Episcopal see
▲ Monastery
♠ Nunnery
⌂ Monastery that was quickly disbanded
- - - Boundary between the sees of Hólar and Skálholt

wrote the beginning of *Sverris saga*, a biography of the King, telling of the struggles of this Faroese claimant, who after years of civil war had come to rule all Norway. No one knows who wrote the rest of *Sverris saga*, but it is possible that this and a few family sagas were written at Thingeyrar. The scholarly production of Thingeyrar's monks was aided by their monastery's exceptional prosperity. At the founding of this first religious community, Bishop Jon Ogmundarson granted Thingeyrar a portion of Hólar's tithes. Thingeyrar's own property provided good trout and salmon fishing, fertile pasturage and an abundant supply of seabirds' eggs. The monastery also held valuable rights to the gathering of driftwood.

Despite Thingeyrar's prosperity, few Icelandic monasteries could be considered rich and, with only a handful of members in each, these tiny communities faced grave difficulties in keeping their doors open. Those that failed early left almost no trace. The late start and slow growth of the monastic movement during the life of the Free State contributed to the limited role of Icelandic monasteries in non-cultural spheres. Thingeyrar may have been started in 1112, but it was not formally established until 1133.[19] The second one, also in the northern diocese of Hólar, was founded at Munkathverá in 1155. A third monastery established in the north, at Saurbær, lasted only from 1200 to 1212. In the Skálholt diocese the first monastery was founded at Hítardalr in about 1166 and lasted to approximately 1200. Within the diocese other monasteries were established at Thykkvibær in 1168, on the island of Flatey in 1172 (moved to Helgafell in 1184), and on Viðey in 1226. The establishments of Thingeyrar, Munkathverá and Kirkjubær followed the Benedictine Rule; Thykkvibær, Flatey, Viðey and probably Saurbær belonged to the Augustinian. The only nunnery to operate during the period of the Free State was founded at Kirkjubær in 1186. Probably because of inadequate financial resources, this establishment was placed under the control of Skálholt in 1218 and apparently was soon disbanded. It was revived toward the end of the thirteenth century.

19

Big Chieftains, Big Farmers and their Sagas at the End of the Free State

> Then that decree [to submit and pay tribute to the Norwegian king] was sent to Iceland on the advice of the Cardinal [William of Sabina], since he called it beyond belief that the land was not subject to some king, as were all the others in the world.
>
> *The Saga of King Hakon Hakonarson* (13th century)

In the twelfth and thirteenth centuries Icelandic society experienced changes in the balance of power. As part of the evolution to a more stratified social order, the number of chieftains diminished and the power of the remaining leaders grew. By the thirteenth century six large families had come to monopolize the control and ownership of many of the original chieftaincies. The destabilizing effect of this increase in the power of individual leaders was especially evident in the period 1220–60, which is often referred to in modern studies as the Age of the Sturlungs[1] because it was typified by the success of that family.

From our vantage point it is clear that these men (called *stórgoðar* – big chieftains – or *stórhöfðingjar* – big leaders – in modern studies) were in the process of forming a new social class, though they often continued to use the more modest term *goðar* in reference to themselves. The thirteenth century was a time of transition. The earlier two-tiered system of *goðar* and *bændr* was enlarging with an additional top layer, a change supported to a significant degree by wealth garnished from the control of Church farmsteads (staðir).[2] But if rank was hardening and stratification increasing, the extent of the change brought on by the development of this overlord level in the social order is difficult to quantify. The difficulty exists because the movement was much less of an upheaval than it might have been; the rise in social complexity was evolutionary rather than revolutionary. The stórgoðar did not overthrow an existing governing elite; instead, as the historian Gunnar Karlsson notes in his pioneering study on the subject, they simply moved up the ladder.[3]

Abandoning much of the goðar's previous focus on local leadership and administration, stórgoðar of the late twelfth and early thirteenth centuries gained control over whole regions. The development continued during the most troubled years of the Sturlung period (c. 1230–62), as the more ambitious of the stórgoðar attempted to extend their sphere of influence over ever larger geographical areas. At the same time other social transformations were at work. In conjunction with the development of the stórgoðar elite, the most successful among the bændr also moved up a rung on the social ladder, becoming 'big farmers' or stórbændr.

For the stórbændr the rise of the stórgoðar presented a time of opportunity, and big farmers became the middlemen in the new three-tiered system of big chieftains, big farmers and farmers.[4] Becoming a big farmer or stórbóndi was a mark of success for ambitious bændr. At the same time, descendants of some of the older, unsuccessful goðar families carved out a niche for themselves in the new order, adapting to a stórbóndi role. In many ways the stórbændr operated as local big men or small-scale chieftains, much as earlier goðar did. They led interest groups of local farmers and offered protection and legal services. The stórbændr were cut from the same cloth as the ambitious bændr, typified by successful farmers of the twelfth century such as Thorgils Oddason from Staðarhóll (d. 1151) and Thord Gilsson from Staðarfell, who had gained control of chieftaincies. Thord Gilsson, for example, was active in the first half of the twelfth century. He was the father of the goði Hvamm-Sturla (d. 1181), who became influential in the mid twelfth century. Sturla in turn was the father of three sons called the Sturlusons – Thord, Sighvat and Snorri – the *stórgoðar* who gave their name to the thirteenth-century Age of the Sturlungs.

When *stórgoðar* devoted their attention to the control of large regions, called *ríki* (sing. and plural), dominating the Althing, and maintaining intra-regional political alliances, big farmers filled the local power vacuum by adapting the hardening structures to their advantage. Because they offered services to a mostly regional constituency, big farmers were more closely connected with a defined local area than were earlier *goðar*, who as a group participated in the workings of the national Althing. And here we can draw a distinction: whereas earlier *goðar* were middlemen between farmers and the operation of the law, the thirteenth-century *stórbœndr* added the role of serving as middlemen between farmers and *stórgoðar*.

Big Farmers and the Family Sagas

In filling the place of earlier *goðar*, the *stórbœndr* of the twelfth and thirteenth centuries kept alive much of Iceland's earlier social and political culture. The competition between these big farmers and the emerging *stórgoðar* over power and resources was sometimes public, as can be seen in *The Saga of Gudmund the Worthy*, which documents the contest for power in Eyjafjord at the turn of the thirteenth century. The overt nature of this contest almost obscures from our view an important element of narrative rivalry. *Stórbœndr* are most probably the answer to the central question of who were the patrons of many, though it should be stressed not all, of the family sagas. Important and prosperous local leaders, the *stórbœndr* and their *bœndr* followers were politically and often by blood the direct descendants of the earlier *goðar* and *bœndr* who fill the pages of the family sagas. In the thirteenth century, *stórbœndr* and *bœndr* were still engaged in the conduct and settlement of local disputes and feuds. To a large extent, the *stórgoðar* had other interests. The affairs of these new 'lords' are described elsewhere, in the later sagas of the

Sturlunga compilation, which monitor the rise and fall of great leaders and their families in the thirteenth century. They rarely give personal information about *stórbændr* or local farmers except where they affect the careers of *stórgoðar*.

The production of literature in medieval Iceland was a costly enterprise. In the modern discussion of the sagas, it has routinely been forgotten that the patronage of medieval books often had political as well as aesthetic goals. *Stórbændr* used the family sagas to verify the local history of their families and districts. In this way the family sagas served as tools for laying historical claims to local leadership. The common farmers were the constituencies of the *stórbændr*, and the family sagas bear witness to the interests and story-telling of this broad group of landowners, some of whom surely also had a hand in their composition.

The two leadership elites, *stórbændr* and *stórgoðar*, shared the same cultural base, reaching back to the years of Iceland's settlement. In the thirteenth century the divergence between the two emerging over-classes was a question of each group focusing on its particular sphere of authority, as they opportunistically divided up the leadership pie. Both *stórgoðar* and *stórbændr* used, enjoyed and probably delighted in each other's texts.

Advantages Enjoyed by the Stórbændr

As the first half of the thirteenth century advanced, the contest between *stórgoðar* and *stórbændr* subtly intensified. Perhaps surprisingly in an age where free farmers in other parts of Europe were often losing ground, Iceland's *stórbændr*, as leaders of local farmers, had certain advantages. Not least was the fact that they were locally based, often territorial, and hence continually available. The opportunity for *stórbændr* to assume the roles of the earlier *goðar*, including solving disputes between neighbouring farmers, increased during the Sturlung period. At that time, as Gunnar Karlsson notes, a region 'could be without a *stórgoði* for years, either because he was staying in Norway or because he had been killed and no one had the authority to succeed him'.[5] So too, *stórbœndr* could often rely on the ingrained strength of their culture's continuity with its past, and the concept of reciprocity and consensus among farmers and their local leaders remained operative until, and well past, the end of the Free State. The settlement pattern from the earlier centuries also remained intact, reinforcing a traditional way of life and leadership. Without towns or even villages, farmers remained scattered across the landscape. Of equal importance, the population still supported itself by decentralized, mostly subsistence production. A large number of small farmers retained dominion over their property, and as a group the *bœndr* and their local leaders continued to control the majority of the society's labour and resources.

Additionally, farmers in the twelfth and thirteenth centuries, and perhaps earlier, controlled entrepreneurial sources of income. As depicted in several of the family sagas, including *Bandamanna saga* and *The Saga of Hen-Thorir*, farmers engaged in small-scale regional trading.[6] This activity provided an essential local network for producing, warehousing and distributing food that remained outside *stórgoðar* control.

Because of the importance of *stórbœndr* in gathering consensus and resources from the farmers, contests for power among *stórgoðar* were in many ways competitions to sway or coerce the allegiance of *stórbœndr*. In the background to these contests, rudimentary military structures were developing. In the last decades of the Free State, *stórgoðar* such as Thord kakali and Gizur Thorvaldsson (later Jarl), formed small military contingents called *gestasveitir* to police and coerce the farmers. Such units, however, proved almost too costly for the *stórgoðar* to maintain and became, at times, a danger to them.[7]

Costs remained a problem for the new class of leaders because farmers at the end of the Free State often successfully resisted the new taxes imposed by the *stórgoðar*. Later sagas in the Sturlunga compilation tell us that in the 1240s and 1250s the farmers were often reluctant to accept the new taxes of the *stórgoðar*. At times, as in the *Saga of Thorgils Skardi*, the *bændr* openly refused to furnish these leaders with supplies. For example, Thorgils skarði and Thord kakali, two *stórgoðar* who claimed control over large regions, faced strong opposition from the *bændr* when they tried to levy taxes; in the end both succeeded only to a limited extent. Even when his power was finally assured, Thord's right to tax the farmers in his territory was not well established. When Thord and his rich enemy Kolbein ungi agreed to travel to Norway and lay their case before the king, part of the arrangement was that Thord's travel expenses should be paid by Kolbein, since Thord's thingmen apparently refused to pay taxes to defray the costs.[8]

The weakness of *stórgoðar* in controlling resources is indicative of the problem that in the end brought down this elite. Whereas *stórgoðar* dominated the upper ends of the social and political systems, they could only marginally exploit an economic system dependent on decentralized modes of production. The import trade in luxury and status goods at a few seasonal ports, such as Gásar, supplied a few *stórgoðar*, including Gudmund the Worthy and for a time the Oddaverjar in the south, with modest wealth but only limited control over the distribution of imports. Whereas the *stórgoðar* with hopes of being local lords wanted to set prices, tax the imports and reserve the best terms and goods for themselves, they were, as mentioned in Chapter 14, unable to coerce the merchants to agree. The Norwegian merchants wanted to set their own prices and trade freely with the more numerous *stórbændr*. The advantage always lay with the foreign merchants, who could choose where to land, thus resisting the demands of specific Icelandic *stórgoðar* and forcing competition among the Icelandic elites to offer traders low costs, including lodgings. As the thirteenth century advanced, the resources under the control of *stórgoðar* proved too fragile and too fragmented to support this group's increasingly complex social and political aspirations.

Attempts by *stórgoðar* at establishing overlordship can be seen as an experimental phase of social development in Icelandic history. With dreams of ruling princely domains, they tried to establish new positions of executive authority, positions that for centuries had been only remote possibilities in Iceland's kingless society. Although *stórgoðar* sometimes modelled their claims to authority and hopes for titles on European thirteenth-century feudal examples,[9] their *ríki* (areas of regional control) never developed into cohesive chiefdoms, small states or operational feudal polities. Instead the *ríki*, many of which had collapsed by the mid thirteenth century, were weak 'paramount structures', that is a type of regional chieftaincy in which a *stórgoði* became a 'paramount *goði*', exercising increased but ill-defined territorial authority by taking control over several of the older *goðorð*. The *ríki* in around 1260 were much the same as they had been in 1200: fragile, patched-up arrangements almost without a supporting infrastructure.

By the 1250s *stórbændr* and their followers had grown weary of the *stórgoðar* and their quarrels. In the end *bændr*, as a broad class, proved adept at holding on to their privileges. The farmers had by then a long history of honing the tools necessary to maintaining themselves in the face of chieftains seeking to extend their power at the expense of the farmers.

The Saga of the Icelanders *in the Sturlunga Compilation*

The most serious strife of the troubled Sturlung years lasted little more than a generation, and despite the fact that leaders turned against each other with unusual ferocity, the extent of the disruption is probably exaggerated in the contemporary sources. The Sturlunga saga collection, the major source for this period, is not the story of a contented people. It dwells on the violence and the greed for political power which characterized the lives of thirteenth-century leaders. The picture is made particularly clear in *The Saga of the Icelanders* (*Íslendinga saga*), the central and longest saga in the Sturlunga compilation. *Íslendinga saga* recounts events from 1183 to 1264, and its author, Sturla Thordarson, was himself a member of the Sturlung family. As an important leader he played an active role in the events of the last decades of the Free State. A man whose fortunes as a leader alternately rose and fell, Sturla had first-hand experience of the dangers and treacheries about which he wrote.

Sturla Thordarson probably wrote *Íslendinga saga* near the end of his life, in the years 1271–84, the period after the Icelanders had submitted to Norwegian overlordship. Sturla's work is not a general history of the Sturlung Age but a retrospective description of the power struggles among the country's most powerful leaders. Although he mentions many *bændr* and their leaders the *stórbændr*, his interests are elsewhere. As a historian Sturla is concerned principally with the activities and the fate of the new *stórgoðar* group of leaders to which he himself belonged. In particular he recounts the fortunes of members of his large and quarrelsome family. This focus on major leaders and their families is also representative of the other sagas that make up the Sturlunga compilation. Neither Sturla Thordarson nor the authors of other sagas in the compilation try to hide or to soften the cruel realities of political intrigue. The result makes the whole of *Sturlunga saga* a selective political history, a collection of stories that together sweep over more than a century.

The Stórgoðar, *Not Quite Rulers*

The *stórgoðar*, because of their political importance and the wealth of contemporary thirteenth-century sources documenting their quarrels, assume centre place in studies about the last period of the Free State. Without doubting the importance of this leadership group, especially in the years from the 1220s to the 1250s, it is nevertheless wise to ask the underlying question: Did the actions of the *stórgoðar* uproot the continuity in Icelandic culture that began with the Viking Age settlement? The answer would seem to be no. Despite obvious changes, the *stórgoðar* were an evolutionary development. They were a rising elite in a troubled thirteenth-century society whose norms and values remained rooted in the freeman's rights and family landownership institutionalized during the century following the *landnám*.

Especially in the last decades of the Free State, the careers of the *stórgoðar* tended to be short, and their hold on power became insecure as their feuds increased. Rather than setting up effective administrations dependent on sheriffs, bailiffs and other functionaries of a central political hierarchy, individual leaders among this new elite usually did not have the time or the authority to replace older forms of government. Instead, more often than not they remained dependent on often fickle *stórbændr* as their local representatives. Those *stórgoðar* who succeeded in exercising regional control usually did so through the expedient, but inefficient, means of owning or controlling several older chieftaincies (*goðorð*).

Families were also a problem for many *stórgoðar*. The custom of prominent men openly keeping concubines diversified the kin group, making the degree of relatedness of kin at the same generational level problematic. For example, Snorri Sturluson (d. 1241) had two legitimate children, Jon Murti (d. 1231) and a daughter Hallbera. His best-known son, Oraekja (d. 1245), was illegitimate.[10] Snorri's brother Thord Sturluson (d. 1237) was separated from his first wife and had a son and a daughter by his second wife. In between the two marriages, he had several concubines. With one of these, named Thora, he had three daughters and three sons, one of whom was Sturla Thordarson, the *stórgoði* who wrote *Íslendinga saga*.

Stórgoðar families usually had no pre-established system of hierarchy and no well-defined system of inheritance, and they were not cohesive political groups. If one family, or one group within a family, did gain control of several chieftaincies, these *goðorð* were often distributed among relatives, including half-siblings, both legitimate and illegitimate. Such kinsmen might be uncooperative and might even be inimical, as often happened with the Sturlungs. The resulting confusion made Iceland in the mid thirteenth century fertile ground for the expansionist policies of the Norwegian Crown.

Iceland's Jarl

Not sufficiently powerful to overturn the conservative old order, ambitious *stórgoðar* turned to Norway's King Hakon for assistance. Hakon, however, was an uncertain ally. More interested in furthering his own ambitions than advancing the aims of Icelanders, the King throughout his long reign from 1217 to 1263 stood back, allowing one Icelandic leader to weaken another, a method that eventually assured his own success.[11] Only at the very end of the Free State in 1258 did King Hakon appoint Gizur Thorvaldsson a jarl (earl), thus distinguishing Gizur from the other contesting *stórgoðar*. The concept of an Icelander holding a noble title was not new. Norwegian rulers had for decades manipulated *stórgoðar* with the possibility. Sturla Thordarson reports in *Íslendinga saga* that in a secret meeting with the Norwegian Duke (*Hertogi*) Skuli Bardarson in 1239, Snorri Sturluson received the title of jarl. The next year the Duke's attempt to seize power from King Hakon ended with his death. In Iceland, nothing came of Snorri's jarldom (earldom), if in fact it ever existed. Earlier, between 1218 and 1220, King Hakon had made Snorri a *lendr maðr*, a 'landed man', a noble title equivalent to a baron. Several other Icelandic leaders of the Sturlung Age entered the King's retinue with the hope of acquiring his support for bringing Iceland under royal control. These included Thord kakali, Thorgils skarði, Finnbjorn Helgason and Gizur Thorvaldsson. King Hakon was so successful in interjecting uncertainty into the Icelandic political situation that leaders such as Jarl Gizur and his rival Hrafn Oddsson contested with each other at a time when both claimed to be acting in the King's interest.

Gizur Thorvaldsson's career is instructive for understanding the patient, destabilizing role played by Hakon in ending the Free State. As early as perhaps 1230, Gizur had become a Norwegian courtier, placing himself under obligation to do the King's bidding. When Sturla Sighvatsson set out to seize control of the whole country in the late 1230s, it was Gizur who thwarted his ambition and wiped out a large part of the Sturlung family, including Sighvat Sturluson and his son Sturla (in 1238) and Snorri Sturluson (in 1241). As a jarl, Gizur succeeded for a short time at the very end of the Free State in gaining control over almost all of the country. According to *Íslendinga saga* the King placed under the management of this most successful of *stórgoðar* all of the Southern Quarter, the Northern Quarter and all of Borgarfjord in the west. Gizur, whose seat of authority was at Hruni in the south, quickly set out to establish a feudal political structure based on vassalage; however, as seen from a modern vantage point, his options were limited from the beginning. Despite granting Gizur honours, the King seemed to allow his Icelandic jarl little independence. Hakon had no intention of losing his growing authority in Iceland to a native lord.

1262–4: The Covenant with Norway's King and the End of the Free State

Gizur's jarldom proved to be only a temporary political experiment. It brought about no fundamental rearrangement of the social or political order, and its authority was never extended over the whole country. King Hakon seemed to have little trust in Gizur, and in the early 1260s sent his own representatives to Iceland. Aided by Norway's archbishop, the King effectively bypassed the jarl's authority and sent royal messengers to talk in person to Iceland's farmers. At a series of local assemblies from 1262 to 1264, the King's representatives offered the Icelanders an alternative to the turmoil caused by the quarrels of the *stórgoðar*, and the *stórbœndr* and the few remaining *stórgoðar* accepted the offer. Hakon rapidly used this consensus to put an end to the *stórgoðar* as a class by abolishing all *goðorð*. Likewise the influence of the jarl was quickly overshadowed by the submission of the Icelanders to the King. After Gizur's death in 1268 Norwegian kings appointed no more jarls exercising power in Iceland.[12]

In turning to a king who resided an ocean away, the farmers and their big farmer leaders were able to preserve many rights, including many belonging to the older *goðar*, that had been threatened by the ambitions of the *stórgoðar*. During the first decades of Norwegian control, Iceland fared reasonably well, largely because the acceptance of Norwegian suzerainty caused little social dislocation. If not fully independent, Iceland nevertheless functioned as a semi-autonomous region with respect to law. The formal agreement, by which representatives from the northern and southern regions swore allegiance to the King in 1262–4, was called the Old Covenant (*Gamli Sáttmáli*). The rest of the Icelanders swore allegiance to the King soon after, using this or a similar covenant.[13] The Old Covenant guaranteed that the King would show deference to the Icelanders: 'In return the King shall let us enjoy peace and the Icelandic laws.'[14] The last phrase seems not to have precluded the right of Norwegians to alter the existing Free State laws; it suggests that the Icelanders would have the right to accept or reject new legislation. Thus much of the traditional legislative power remained with the Icelanders, even though the King was free to modify older laws or to propose new ones.

After the strong-willed empire builder King Hakon Hakonarson died in 1263, his son Magnus the Law Mender (*lagabœtir*, d. 1280) became king. Magnus showed himself to be a wise and conciliatory ruler, who usually avoided offending the Icelanders. He allowed them a measure of autonomy and was willing to replace *Járnsíða* ('Ironsides'), the unpopular Norwegian-inspired law book introduced in 1271. In 1280 a second Norwegian law code, called *Jónsbók*, was submitted to the Icelanders, who initially opposed it, even though it retained many traditional features of *Grágás*. After much debate among Icelanders and royal pressure, *Jónsbók* was accepted in 1281 at the Althing by a majority vote of the law council.

In the decades immediately following the introduction of *Jónsbók*, the King normally refrained from repressive use of his new powers, and Iceland enjoyed a period of peace and relative prosperity. This was a time when some of the family sagas were written, illustrating a rich understanding of *Grágás* and traditional procedure and governmental structure. With an, at first, mild Norwegian administration, many of the social, political and legal traditions, whose roots lay in the first centuries following the *landnám*, slowly slipped away. By the early fourteenth century, Iceland had been incorporated into a foreign kingdom for a couple of generations.

The fourteenth century also saw basic economic and environmental changes. Beginning around 1320 the large-scale export of dried cod introduced a new source of wealth and employment. Pockets of prosperity developed in coastal regions opposite the best fishing grounds. Most other areas did not fare so well. Erosion continued and in the fourteenth century, the climate, which had already begun to grow colder, rapidly worsened. By 1350 Iceland had entered a 'little Ice Age' which was to last for several centuries. In this time of hardship, ice, which further lowered the temperature, capped even low-lying mountains during the summers. Large floes of drift ice now routinely appeared off the northern and eastern coasts. Sometimes the chilling ice came far south. The colder climate forced the abandonment of even small-scale growing of barley and other crops, and the grass-growing season was often cut short. Throughout this period of hardship the landholdings and powers of the Church increased.

The herds of sheep and cattle also diminished, and many farmers abandoned livestock farming, falling back for survival on the more dangerous work of fishing and seal-hunting. The numbers of seals increased as these animals rode southward from the Arctic on the drifting sea ice. In the fourteenth and fifteenth centuries large numbers of destitute farmers abandoned their farms, giving up their independence to increasingly powerful local leaders and churchmen. In 1402, fifty years after it first appeared in Europe, the plague came to Iceland. The effects were devastating. The death rates are only estimates, but perhaps a third or more of the population died. By then the Viking Age was long past.

APPENDIX I

The Law-speakers

1	Ulfljot	
2	Hrafn Haengsson	*c.* 930–49
3	Thorarin Ragi's Brother Oleifsson	*c.* 950–69
4	Thorkel Moon Thorsteinsson	970–84
5	Thorgeir the *goði* from Ljósavatn Thorkelsson	985–1001
6	Grim Svertingsson	1002–3
7	Skafti Thoroddsson	1004–30
8	Stein Thorgestsson	1031–3
9	Thorkel Tjorvason	1034–53
10	Gellir Bolverksson	1054–62
11	Gunnar the Wise Thorgrimsson	1063–5
12	Kolbein Flosason	1066–71
13	Gellir Bolverksson, second term	1072–4
14	Gunnar the Wise Thorgrimsson, second term	1075
15	Sighvat Surtsson	1076–83
16	Markus Skeggjason	1084–1107
17	Ulfhedin Gunnarsson	1108–16
18	Bergthor Hrafnsson	1117–22
19	Gudmund Thorgeirsson	1123–34
20	Hrafn Ulfhedinsson	1135–8
21	Finn Hallsson the Priest	1139–45
22	Gunnar Ulfhedinsson	1146–55
23	Snorri Hunbogason the Priest	1156–70
24	Styrkar Oddason	1171–80
25	Gizur Hallsson	1181–1202

26	Hall Gizurarson the Priest	1203–9
27	Styrmir the Wise Karason the Priest	1210–14
28	Snorri Sturluson	1215–18
29	Teit Thorvaldsson the Priest	1219–21
30	Snorri Sturluson, second term	1222–31
31	Styrmir the Wise Karason the Priest, second term	1232–5
32	Teit Thorvaldsson the Priest, second term	1236–47
33	Olaf the White Poet Thordarson	1248–50
34	Sturla Thordarson	1251
35	Olaf the White Poet Thordarson, second term	1252
36	Teit Einarsson	1253–8
37	Ketil Thorlaksson the Priest	1259–62
38	Thorleif the Noisy Ketilsson	1263–5
39	Sigurd Thorvaldsson	1266
40	Jon Einarsson	1267
41	Thorleif the Noisy Ketilsson, second term	1268
42	Jon Einarsson, second term	1269–70
43	Thorleif the Noisy Ketilsson, third term	1271

APPENDIX 2
Bishops During the Free State

For the whole country:

1	Isleif Gizurarson	1056–80
2	Gizur Isleifsson	1082–1106

In Skálholt:

1	Gizur Isleifsson	1106–18
2	Thorlak Runolfsson	1118–33
3	Magnus Einarsson	1134–48
4	Klaeng Thorsteinsson	1152–76
5	Thorlak the Saint Thorhallsson	1178–93
6	Pal Jonsson	1195–1211
7	Magnus Gizurarson	1216–37
8	Sivard Thettmarsson (Norwegian)	1238–68

In Hólar:

1	Jon the Saint Ogmundarson	1106–21
2	Ketil Thorsteinsson	1122–45
3	Bjorn Gilsson	1147–62
4	Brand Saemundarson	1163–1201
5	Gudmund the Good Arason	1203–37
6	Botolf (Norwegian)	1238–46
7	Heinrek Karsson (Norwegian)	1247–60
8	Brand Jonsson	1263–4

APPENDIX 3
Turf Construction

Two kinds of turf can be used for building: marsh turf from swampy ground and dry grassland turf. Marsh turf is much better than grassland turf because its slowly decomposing and matted roots produced dense, tough pieces with a thick grass surface. Marsh turf, found only in cold, damp climates, is common in Iceland and Greenland. The drier grassland turf is also found widely in Iceland but was seldom used because its root material is not densely matted, and walls built from grassland turf shrink and settle considerably.

Icelandic turfs were cut into several shapes for building. Most common were long, flat rectangular strips (*strengur*) and blocks (*hnaus*). In *strengur* walls the strips were placed one on top of the other, forming strong, well-knit walls more than a metre thick. These were, however, costly to build because they required a large supply of cut turfs, which all had to be transported to the site, and which took considerable time to lay. Blocks and shaped pieces of turf were easier to manipulate. Walls built from them consisted of two rows of blocks, one on the inside and one on the outside, with the gap between them infilled with soil, which could be dug on the spot. The blocks that made up the inside and outside wall facings were often arranged into patterns, including some that resembled herringbone. These patterns added strength to the construction as the sod settled. Flat stones were used for some flooring and paving, especially at the farmhouse entrance and in the cowsheds, but most buildings had hardened dirt floors.

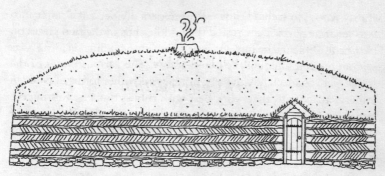

11. **Eiríksstaðir (Eirik's Stead) from the Mid Tenth Century.** Eirik's Stead is mentioned in the *Book of Settlements* and *The Saga of Eirik the Red*. Eirik the Red is said to have lived at Eirik's Stead before voyaging to Greenland in the 980s. The drawing is based on a reconstruction by the archaeologist Guðmundur Ólafsson and the architects Grétar Markússon and Stefán Örn Stefánsson.

Finding the archaeological remains of turf buildings can be quite difficult. This is especially so when the remains are covered by wind-blown soil from Iceland's considerable erosion; when the walls have melted back into the surrounding earth as a result of exposure to wind, rain and snow; or if the builders did not use foundation stones under the walls, as was sometimes the case in early and inexpensively built structures. Once located, the trained eye can often easily distinguish the lower parts of turf walls, and if a simple trench is cut into the site, see evidence of cultural layers.

Roofs and Rafters

Faced with northern gales, Icelanders had to make their roofs sturdy and heavy. How they and the Greenlanders did this with the resources available to them, while building large, comfortable houses, is a story of technical innovation. One issue was the quality of roof rafters. In mainland Scandinavia, with ample softwood in the north and hardwood in the south, rafters could be made from one piece of long, sturdy wood. In Iceland, however, builders divided each rafter into two separate parts. They rested the middle ends of the two pieces on two rafter-bracing beams. As elsewhere in Scandinavia, iron was seldom used in building the house-frame. The various pieces of the frame were connected with pegs, notches and other forms of wooden joinery, all systems that work best with robust timbers. Resting the lower end of the upper rafter piece and the top end of the lower rafter on horizontal rafter-bracing beams was a solution that permitted the rafters to be made from short pieces of driftwood and the thin local birch.

The cutaway drawing of Grelutótt shows how the upper rafters and the short cross beams connected the ridge beam and the two rafter-bracing beams into a rigid triangular structure. At the point of greatest stress, where the rafters would otherwise have been bent inward by the weight of the sod roof, the two rafter-bracing beams

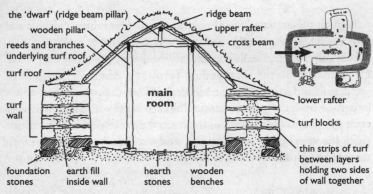

12. Cross-section of Grelutótt, Looking into the Main Room after Entering.
The upper part of the roof is supported by a rectangular frame structure, resting on two rows of pillars or vertical staves. The roof is not steeply pitched, and its lower part is supported on the turf walls. This small longhouse seems to have been built quickly and inexpensively, its walls made of turf blocks and earth fill. The inside and outside walls were bonded together by thin strips of turf. There was no panelling along the inside of the interior walls.

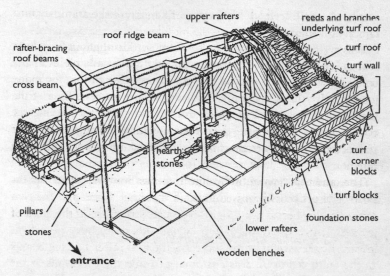

13. Cutaway of Grelutótt, Illustrating the Interior Construction. This reconstruction shows the division of upper and lower rafters. Branches and reeds placed on top of the rafters allowed air to circulate under the turfs, thus protecting the rafters and roof beams from rot. Such roofs tended to leak in heavy rains, however.

(stiffened by cross beams) pushed back the thrust. At the centre of each upper cross beam was a short vertical stave that supported the ridge beam. This short pillar was aptly called the dwarf (*dvergr*), referring to Norse mythology, where dwarfs held up the vault of the heavens.

The weight of the roof divided into upper and lower roof loads. The triangular upper roof-support system rested on long vertical pillars called staves (*stafar*). These pillars carried the upper roof loads down to the dirt floor, where a flat stone was placed under each post. The stones protected the wood from moisture and rot while also allowing the use of shorter timbers, since the pillars were not sunk into the ground. The remaining weight load from the lower roof moved on to the lower rafters. Their bottom ends pushed down on to the turf walls, which also served to buttress the frame against lateral movement.

This system of supporting the roof, known throughout Scandinavia, had its limitations. In some instances it barred adding internally connected new rooms to a turf longhouse because cutting too many passageways through the load-bearing walls weakened their structural integrity. Icelanders addressed this problem by relieving the roof weight from the turf walls. They added a double row of outer pillars to the wooden frame. In the eleventh century when the Stöng longhouse was built there were four rows of internal supporting pillars, and this type of frame structure was known as early as the settlement period.

Innovation and the Expansion of Living Quarters

In the tenth century it was customary to line the turf walls at the back of the benches with wooden planks, which resembled what is called in English wainscotting or panelling. (Wainscotting and panelling are usually understood to be attached to the wall, whereas the panelling in an Icelandic turf house was a part of the timber frame.) A set of short outer pillars or staves was built into this wooden 'stave' wall and the lower roof rafters were attached to the tops of these wall pillars. In this way, the weight of the lower roof was lifted off the turf walls.

The outer support pillars at the back of the benches are illustrated in the cutaway drawing of the Stöng longhouse. The Stöng illustrations were drawn by the architect Hörður Ágústsson, who followed archaeologist Aage Roussell's floor plan. In several instances I have reworked the original drawings on the computer, making some changes. Almost no wood from the upper structure survived, and this reconstruction is based on careful analysis of the well-preserved foundations and lower walls. The reconstruction employs a sampling of building techniques known from excavations in other parts of Iceland as well as Greenland. The main hall was encased in wood panelling, and rows of inner and outer vertical staves ran the length

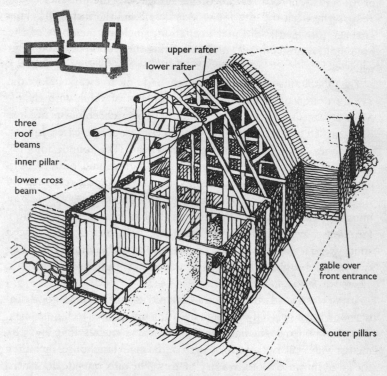

14. Cutaway of the Eleventh-century Longhouse at Stöng in Southern Iceland.
Much valuable wood was used in the construction, and some of the larger
timbers may have been imported. There is an expanded frame structure with
inner and outer pillars. Turf roofs, which had to resist high winds, were thick
and heavy. They were often built in three layers. The bottom layer was turf
with the grass turned inward. Next came a compressed layer of soil, topped
by an additional layer of turf with the grass facing upward. Pitching the
roof steeply, as in the drawing, aided the water run-off and lessened snow
accumulation, but it also increased the roof's size and weight.

of the hall. A crucial feature of the design was the presence of an airspace between the interior wooden wall and the turf walls. This airspace provided additional insulation, shielding members of the household from dampness and protecting the wood panelling from rot.

The inhabitants of Stöng apparently had time to escape before the 1104 eruption of Hekla and to take objects of value with them.[1] Most artifacts that have been found there by archaeologists are lost or discarded objects, including broken combs, needle-cases, knives, whetstones, a spearhead and an arrowhead. The foundations lay buried under thick layers of white volcanic ash and pumice until excavated in 1939 by a Scandinavian archaeological team led by Aage Roussell.[2] This excavation and more recent ones provide an unusually clear picture of farm life in the late Viking Age. The large farmhouse, whose walls were from 1.3 to 2 metres thick, faced south-west. It was surrounded by a cluster of outbuildings, including two smithies, a small church, and a cowshed with stalls for ten cows. There was also a graveyard.

Stöng was a costly building that offered its inhabitants a good deal of room, but it was only average size for a prosperous Icelandic farm. The wood-lined main hall (*skáli*) was 12.25 metres long by 5.85 metres wide. The full interior length of the main longhouse, including the large entrance room, was 17 metres. The only outside door was, in traditional longhouse fashion, in the front at one end of the main hall. The secondary longhouse, measuring 8 by 4.3 metres, was called a *stofa* (living hall). Two smaller back houses were attached at right angles to the back of the main hall. One was the pantry or food-storage room; the other was a large latrine. The area in front of the outside door and the passageway through the wall were paved with flat stones.

The foundations of the *stofa* were well preserved. Such a living hall probably had several uses. The name *stofa*, related to the English word 'stove' (Scandinavian *stue / stuga*), originally meant a heated room. At times the *stofa* may have been used for cooking and eating as well as for a family sitting room in the evenings. The

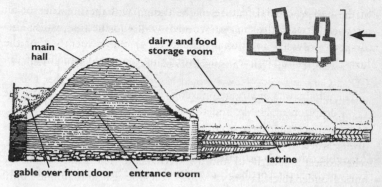

15. Side View of the Longhouse at Stöng. The roof is steeply pitched to aid rain run-off and lessen snow accumulation. The walls were built on top of a foundation of rough, uncut stones, which facilitated drainage. This reconstruction shows walls built with two different techniques. The main hall is built with flat strips, whereas the back rooms used turf blocks in a herringbone pattern with alternating strips of flat turf for added strength.

fireplace was a partly sunken stone box, different from the long-fire in the *skáli*. The wall benches, much narrower (50 cm) than those in the main hall, were not for sleeping, and the room was certainly used as a fine feasting hall. At the far end was a raised wooden platform called a *pallr*. It was on these platforms, which are mentioned in the written sources, that the women worked. Loom weights, spindle whorls and other evidences of wool-working were found in the room.

The Saga of Gunnlaug Serpent-Tongue gives a brief description of a *stofa* in use, bringing together the human side of farm life and the factors of conflict. Early in the saga, a young man named Gunnlaug runs away to Borg, where he is taken into the home of Thorstein Egilsson. Thorstein, the grandson of Skallagrim (whose land-take was described at the beginning of Chapter 2 above), has a young daughter named Helga. She and Gunnlaug amuse themselves playing a board game called *tafl* (tables), a kind of chess or draughts, and fall in love. Chapter 4 relates:

One time when people sat in the living hall (*stofa*) at Borg, Gunnlaug spoke to Thorstein: 'There is still one part of the laws that you have not taught me: how to make a match with a woman.'

Thorstein, saying, 'That is not much of a matter', taught him the procedure.

Then Gunnlaug said, 'Now I would like to show you whether I have understood, and I would like to take your hand and act as though I am betrothing your daughter Helga.'

The trick does not fool Thorstein, and the scene becomes a harbinger of trouble. Although probably fictional, it is a medieval account of a family in their *stofa*, probably not very different from the one at Stöng.

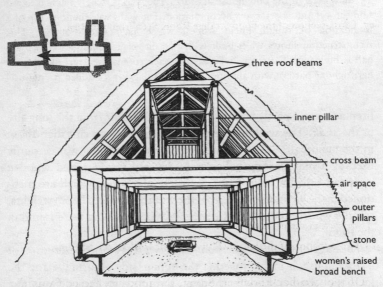

16. The Living Hall (*Stofa*) at Stöng. This large room was built differently from the main hall. The inner pillars or staves supporting the three horizontal roof beams did not go straight down to the floor. Instead they rested on cross beams whose ends were attached to outer beams built into the interior wooden wall. This structural arrangement formed a room with far more usable floor space than the traditional longhouse design.

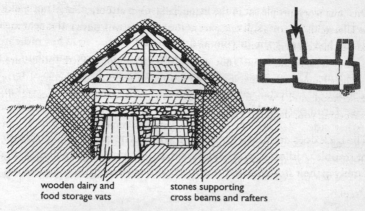

wooden dairy and
food storage vats

stones supporting
cross beams and rafters

17. Cross-section of the Food Storage Room Seen from the Rear.

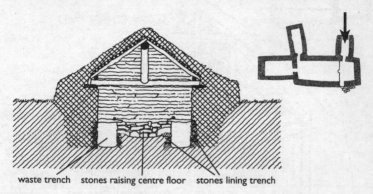

waste trench   stones raising centre floor   stones lining trench

18. Cross-section of the Latrine Seen from the Back of the Building.

Of the two backrooms at Stöng, the food-storage one was the
larger. Impressions in its floor reveal the placement of three very
large wooden vats, each measuring 1.44 metres in diameter. The vats
were sunk into the earth in order to keep them cool. They were used
to store protein-rich curdled milk (*skyr*), and possibly meat pickled
in sour whey.

The remains of an indoor latrine are well preserved at Stöng. It had deep, stone-lined waste trenches, or gutters, along both side walls, with openings for waste removal that ran under the rear turf wall. The size of the latrine and the length of the trenches indicate that a substantial number of people could be accommodated at one time. Throughout Scandinavia, visiting the latrine was often a communal undertaking. One saga reveals that the latrine of a Viking Age farmhouse in Norway had room for 'eleven people to sit on either side'. Because the wooden fixtures have not survived, it is unclear whether people at Stöng sat over holes on long wooden benches, as in the example from Norway, or whether they rested on a horizontal wooden pole running just above and parallel to the trench.

APPENDIX 4

A Woman Who Travelled from Vínland to Rome

Gudrid, who lived at the turn of the first millennium and journeyed across the then known world, stands out as one of the most widely travelled Viking Age Icelanders about whom we have information. She is known mainly because she was a respected ancestor of later Icelanders, including three twelfth-century bishops. Gudrid's travels are described both in *Grænlendinga saga* (*The Saga of the Greenlanders*) and in *Eiríks saga rauða* (*The Saga of Eirik the Red*).[1] Although the two texts are different in numerous ways, they are in general agreement about Gudrid's journeys, with *Grænlendinga saga* recounting additional travels after Gudrid leaves Greenland.

Gudrid's North Atlantic journeys, a mixture of entrepreneurial trading voyages and pioneering attempts at colonization, are a medieval picture of the long-range sailings undertaken by medieval Scandinavians. According to *Grænlendinga saga*, Gudrid arrived in Greenland with her husband Thorir in about the year 1000. The couple may have been married in Norway, but it is more likely that Thorir, a Norwegian, first sailed to Iceland and there met and married Gudrid. With his wife on board, Thorir continued his journey to Greenland, where his luck ran out. The couple were shipwrecked on the Greenland coast and lost their boat. After they were rescued, Thorir died of an illness during the winter in the Eastern Settlement.

A widow, Gudrid now marries a man named Thorstein Eiriksson. He is the son of Eirik the Red (*inn rauði*), the settlement's leader. With her new husband, Gudrid moves north up the Greenland coast to a farm in the Western Settlement, but then Thorstein dies of

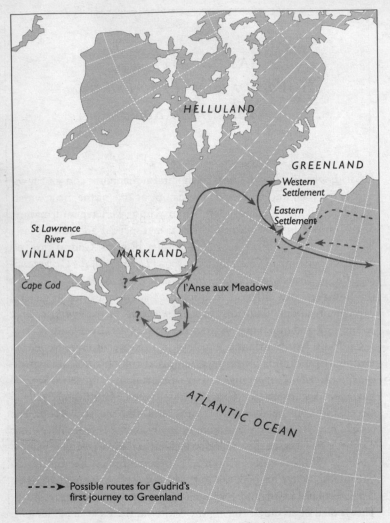

Helluland

GREENLAND

Western
Settlement

Eastern
Settlement

St Lawrence
River

VÍNLAND   MARKLAND

Cape Cod

?

l'Anse aux Meadows

?

ATLANTIC OCEAN

- - - ▶ Possible routes for Gudrid's
first journey to Greenland

27. The Travels of Gudrid Thorbjarnardottir. This map is drawn according
to information in *The Saga of the Greenlanders* and *The Saga of Eirik the
Red*.

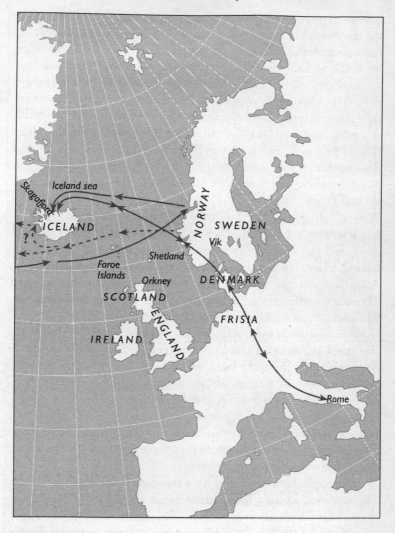

sickness. The young widow returns to the Eastern Settlement, where she stays with her brother-in-law Leif the Lucky (*inn heppni*), at the farm Brattahlíð. Not long afterward, Gudrid marries Thorfinn Karlsefni, an Icelander recently arrived from Norway. The next year (*c.* 1010) the couple set out in Karlsefni's ship in an ambitious attempt to settle in Vínland. Accompanied by men and women in two other ships, they sail west to the North American continent and then south along the coast. Reaching Vínland, they settle in, some using the cabins (*búðir*) built by Leif Eiriksson on his earlier Vínland voyage. Gudrid gives birth to a son named Snorri, the first European child born in North America. After a few years, the Vínland settlement fails. Gudrid and Thorfinn sail back to Greenland, spending the winter in the Eastern Settlement. The following spring the couple sail east to Norway. They sell the cargo they acquired in Vínland and Greenland and spend the winter in Norway. In the spring, they sail back to Iceland, presumably with a shipload of valuable Norwegian goods. According to *Grænlendinga saga*, the couple land in Skagafjord,[2] Thorfinn's home region. There they buy a farm called Glaumbær and after a successful life together, Thorfinn Karlsefni dies.

Eiríks saga rauða stops at this point. *Grænlendinga saga*, however, says that Gudrid, again a widow, managed the farm with the help of her son Snorri, the child born in Vínland. When Snorri marries, Gudrid, now a woman of advanced age, sets off on a pilgrimage south to Rome. Surviving this arduous and dangerous journey, she returns to Iceland. There she lives out the rest of her life in solitude as one of Iceland's first Norse anchorites, or independent nuns, dying about the year 1050. She outlived three husbands and saw the world from Vínland to the Mediterranean.

Other Icelandic women may have travelled to the Mediterranean. The medieval visitors' book at the Swiss monastery of Reichenau hints about the travels of other Icelandic women. This register, used mainly to record names of pilgrims heading south, contains a page with the heading *Hislant terra* (Iceland). It lists eight Icelandic men and four Icelandic women. These, Vigdis, Vilborg, Kolthera and Thurid, probably stopped at the monastery in the eleventh century.

Notes

A short reference system has been followed, with full details for each work cited being given in the Bibliography. So 'Tomasson 1980: 25' refers to 'Richard F. Tomasson. 1980. *Iceland: The First New Society*. Minneapolis: University of Minnesota Press, p. 25'.

References to the family sagas are mostly to the standard editions in Old Icelandic, the *Íslenzk fornrit* (published from 1933 on), abbreviated *Íf.* (A modern Icelandic edition is *Íslendinga sögur* 1985.) The standard edition of the Sturlunga sagas is *Sturlunga saga* 1946, abbreviated *Sturl.* 1 and 2. Articles in the 22-volume *Kulturhistoriskt lexikon för nordisk medeltid* are cited as *KLNM* 1, 2, etc.

Chapter 1

1. Mord the Fiddle (Mörðr gígja) is mentioned in several places in the *Book of Settlements* as well as in several sagas. Lúðvík Ingvarsson 1970: 208.

2. Bryce 1968 1: 263. First published in 1901.

3. Hermann Pálsson 1996; Gísli Sigurðsson 1988.

4. *Íslendingabók* (*The Book of the Icelanders*) 1968: Ch. 1.

5. It may be because Denmark was one of the first of the Scandinavian lands to become a powerful, centralized kingdom, and the speech of the influential Danish court became for a time the accepted standard.

6. Olsen 1966.

7. Because of uncertainty as to what calendars the medieval Icelanders used at different times, a controversy exists as to whether the conversion should be dated by our modern calendar to 999 or 1000. Since the precise date is in doubt, and probably will remain so, I have chosen the traditional year of 1000. Ólafía Einarsdóttir 1964: 72–90 argues for the year 999. Jakob

Benediktsson in his introduction to *Íslendingabók* 1968 reviews in detail the question of dating, including the views of Ólafía Einarsdóttir 1964: xxix–xv.

8. With slight modifications these passages are from *Njal's Saga* 1960: 52–5.

9. *Grágás* 1852b: 42–3 (Ch. 150).

10. Ciklamini 1963; Bø 1969; Byock 1993a, 'Hólmganga'.

11. Fentress and Wickham 1992: 134 and 163–172; Byock 1984–5, 1998.

12. I list modern translations of the sagas in the Bibliography under their individual titles.

Chapter 2

1. Amorosi *et al.* 1997.

2. Iceland's ecosystem and the effects of the settlement have been the subject of extensive research, including Amorosi *et al.* 1997; Arnalds 1987; Buckland *et al.* 1991a and b; Dugmore and Simpson 1999; Sturla Friðriksson 1972; Margrét Hallsdóttir 1987; McGovern 1990; McGovern *et al.* 1988; Sveinn Runólfsson 1987; Guðrún Sveinbjarnardóttir 1992; Thórarinn Thórarinsson 1974. See also *Jarðvegsrof á Íslandi* 1997.

3. There is no doubt about the core holdings of Skallagrim's land-take, but the claims of control over areas far from Borg may be a later exaggeration.

4. Guðrún Sveinbjarnardóttir 1992; Adolf Friðriksson and Orri Vésteinsson 1998.

5. The excavation in the *tún* or home meadow at Hrísbrú in the summer of 1999 was undertaken as part of the Mosfell Valley Project. Trenches showed that resting directly above the *landnám* tephra layer (volcanic pumice and ash from an eruption in about the year 871) was a widespread thin layer of organic ash, almost certainly the remains of the initial woodland that was cleared by burning.

6. Enormous work appears to have been devoted to maintaining them. *Grágás* 1852b: 91.

7. My thanks to colleagues and friends who aided me in researching this section and Appendix 3 on turf houses. Guðmundur Ólafsson lent me the Grelutótt floor plan. Hörður Ágústsson (1974, 1987, 1989) also discussed turf-house structure with me and lent me drawings. Grétar Markússon and Stefán Örn Stefánsson helped with several architectural illustrations. Robert

Guillemette and Lori Gudmundson provided graphics. Hjörleifur Stefánsson and Harold Zellman offered expert advice.

8. Parts of south-western Norway were an exception. Over the centuries the different regions of Iceland developed characteristic styles of turf construction, but in southern Iceland the basic Viking Age longhouse remained a common building type until the eighteenth century.

9. Wallace 1991.

10. Guðmundur Ólafsson 1979.

11. Bjarni Einarsson 1995; *Archaeologia Islandia* 1998.

12. Guðmundur Ólafsson 1979: 73.

13. Sigríður Sigurðardóttir 1996–7.

14. Grönvold 1994. Grönvold dates the abandonment to the 1104 eruption using tephrochronology and ice core analysis. He questions the hypothesis that Stöng was abandoned later.

Chapter 3

1. Internally the situation was different. By 1250–60 cod fisheries that provided for internal consumption had become widespread, corresponding to increases in population and the expansion of tenant farming at the time (Helgi Thorláksson 1991).

2. Jón Haukur Ingimundarson 1995; Helgi Thorláksson 1991.

3. Páll Zóphóníasson 1914: 52–4.

4. The word *almenning* also means 'the people'.

5. The line refers to eggs, seals, and all that was useful along the coast.

6. A *drápa* was a formal poem of praise. Fifteen stanzas of Thorgeir's *drápa* are preserved in *The Saga of the Foster-Brothers.*

7. The eating of horse meat was forbidden in the early Christian centuries, after the year 1000, and stopped for a time.

8. Bio-archaeological analysis of kitchen middens will add more data in the coming years. The North Atlantic Biocultural Organization (NABO) has been especially active in this area.

9. Bjarni Einarsson 1994.

10. Jón Jóhannesson 1974: 292.

11. Helgi Skúli Kjartansson 1975.

12. My thanks to Ian Simpson for explaining this process to me at a North

Atlantic Biocultural Organization (NABO) conference in Akureyri in July 1999.

13. Páll Bergthórsson 1987; Gerrard 1991; Grove 1988; Grove and Switsur 1994; Lamb 1995; Ogilvie 1984 and 1990.

14. Halstead and O'Shea 1989: 1–7.

15. This incident and the quarrel that follows are discussed in Byock 1982: 39–46.

16. Storm 1888.

Chapter 4

1. Although their limitations are obvious, typologies, when used in a careful way, remain useful for comparative purposes, especially in the instance of Iceland, a hybrid, immigrant society that does not fall into any standard category.

2. For the classic formulation of cultural focus, see Herskovits 1970: 542–60.

3. Friedman 1979; Solvason 1991.

4. Byock 1986b.

Chapter 5

1. Tomasson 1980: 4.

2. Hartz 1964: 6.

3. Ibid.: 4.

4. Andersen 1977: 84–91.

5. *Íf* 26, Ch. 6: 98.

6. Margrét Hallsdóttir 1987; Sturla Friðriksson 1972; Dugmore and Simpson 1999.

7. Gerrard 1991; Maizels and Caseldine 1991.

8. Ólafur Halldórsson 1978 discusses the relationship between *Eiríks saga rauða* and *Grænlendinga saga*. He finds both the product of independent oral traditions.

9. Orri Vésteinsson 1998: 24.

10. Durrenberger 1991: 15; Gelsinger 1981.

11. Sigurður Thórarinsson 1981; Guðrún Larsen 1996; Dugmore and Simpson 1999.

12. Grönvold 1994; Grönvold *et al.* 1995; Guðrún Larsen 1996.

13. Buckland *et al.* 1995; Dugmore and Simpson 1999.

14. Smith and Parsons 1989: 186.

15. Orri Vésteinsson 1998.

16. Family grouping was traditionally an important concept in Norse society, and in the *Grágás* law books, kinship is reckoned out to the fifth degree, to the *þriðjabræði*, or fourth cousin. *Grágás* 1852a: 173–4 (Ch. 97), 194 (Ch. 113); *Grágás* 1852b: 25–6 (Ch. 143); *Grágás* 1879: 75 (Ch. 61), 113 (Ch. 87), 341 (Ch. 300); *Grágás* 1883: 450.

17. Sigurður Nordal 1942: 111–19; see also Sørensen 1977: 19–20.

18. Líndal 1969: 5–26.

19. Jakob Benediktsson 1974a: 171. See also *Grágás* 1980: 8–10.

20. Jakob Benediktsson 1974a: 172; Wimmer 1899–1901 2: 346–51, 352–61, 368–83; Magerøy 1965: 31–3.

21. The standard editions of *Íslendingabók* and *Landnámabók* were edited by Jakob Benediktsson in *Íslenzk fornrit* 1.

22. Björn Sigfússon 1944.

23. For the textual history of *Landnámabók* see Jakob Benediktsson's introduction to *Landnámabók* 1968; Jón Jóhannesson 1941; Sveinbjörn Rafnsson 1974: 13–67.

24. The reliability of *Landnámabók* and *Íslendingabók* has been questioned by numerous scholars. Olsen 1966 argues that much information concerning pagan practices and sanctuaries in *Landnámabók* is of late origin, probably culled from the sagas. Other aspects of the story of Iceland's settlement and state-building given in these books have been questioned by Líndal 1969: 5–26; and Sørensen 1974: 20–40. Bekker-Nielsen 1965: 35–41 emphasizes, perhaps too strongly, the continental influences on those twelfth- and thirteenth-century sources about Iceland's earlier periods. Sveinbjörn Rafnsson 1974 has reconsidered the purpose of *Landnámabók*. He argues that the information was altered to support twelfth- and thirteenth-century claims to landownership. For a discussion of Sveinbjörn Rafnsson's views see Jakob Benediktsson 1974b: 207–15. See also Jakob Benediktsson's introductions to *Íslendingabók* 1968 and *Landnámabók* 1968, and Jakob Benediktsson 1969: 275–92.

Chapter 6

1. Further ramifications are described in Chapter 63, when Thorolf returns from the grave to take vengeance on Thorodd, one of the sons of Thorbrand (Vésteinn Ólason 1971: 11; see also Byock 1982: 131–3).

2. Sections of this chapter appeared in Byock 1988.

3. Matthías Thórðarson 1932.

4. The narrative progression in Chapters 30–31 of *Eyrbyggja saga* is discussed in Byock 1982: 152–4; see also Miller 1984.

5. *Fé* in this instance has the legal meaning of both land and chattels, as in *Grágás* 1852a: 15 (Ch. 4): '*þar er maðr leggr fe til kirkio. hvartz þat er i londom eða bv fe. eða lausom avrom . . .*' See also *Grágás* 1879: 17 (Ch. 13); 1883: 15 (*Skálholtsbók*, Ch. 5).

6. *Grágás* 1852a: 247–9 (Ch. 127).

7. *Grágás* 1852a: 227 (Ch. 119); 1879: 72 (Ch. 60). An apparent exception occurs when the manumitter is himself the freedman's slayer. See Lúðvík Ingvarsson 1970: 316; *Grágás* 1852a: 172 (Ch. 96).

8. *Grágás* 1852a: 247 (Ch. 127); 1879: 85 (Ch. 66).

9. *Grágás* 1852b: 17 (Ch. 134); 1879: 126 (Ch. 93).

10. Hastrup 1985: 116.

11. *Grágás* 1852a: 190–91 (Ch. 111); 1879: 395–7 (Ch. 379).

12. *Grágás* 1852a: 185 (Ch. 109).

13. *Grágás* 1852a: 247 (Ch. 127); 1879: 84 (Ch. 66).

14. The laws apparently imposed a time limit on challenges to the transfer of inheritance rights, although the exact provisions are unclear. See *Grágás* 1852a: 249 (Ch. 127).

15. This passage agrees with entries in *Grágás* 1852a: 167–9 (Ch. 94); 1879: 334–6 (Ch. 297).

Chapter 7

1. On arbitration see Heusler 1911: esp. 40–41, 73–95; and Heusler 1912: 43–58; Lúðvík Ingvarsson 1970: 319–80; Miller 1984; Byock 1982: 102–6, 260–65.

2. For example, Ólafur Lárusson 1958a: 61, writes: 'The Icelandic republic was at all times a kind of federation. The dominion of the Icelandic chief-

taincies, the *goðorð*, corresponds to small Norwegian kingdoms.' See also Byock 1986b: 20. Icelandic arrangements are also not easily compared with modern democratic ones. See Gunnar Karlsson 1977.

3. Jochens 1985. As mentioned earlier, during much of the Free State's early history chieftaincies could be bought, shared, traded or inherited, *Grágás* 1852a: 141–2 (Ch. 84).

4. '*Betra að vera góðs manns frilla en gefin illa.*' Auður G. Magnúsdóttir (1988: 8) draws attention to this Icelandic folk expression in her pioneering article on *frillur*. But there are also distressing stories, such as that of Yngvildr fagrkinn (Fine Cheek) Ásgeirsdóttir from *Svarfdæla saga*, who was treated badly after being given as a *frilla* to Ljótr, a 'friend' of her father, in order to implement a *vinfengi* alliance.

5. Auður G. Magnúsdóttir 1988: 4. On concubines in the Sturlung period, see also Agnes S. Arnórsdóttir 1990. Karras 1990: 141–62 gives a wide view of the practice.

6. '*Um rettarfar manna*' section of *Den ældre Gulathings-Lov* in *Norges gamle love* 1846 1: 71. Variations among the classifications of rank existed in the different Norwegian regions with their diverse laws.

7. *Grágás* 1852a: 155 (Ch. 88); 1879: 202 (Ch. 169), 313–14 (Ch. 282), 390 (Ch. 375); 1883: 434.

8. Jón Jóhannesson 1974: 109–17.

9. *Grágás* 1852b: 195–7 (Chs. 247–8); 1883: 463–6.

10. Bøe, *KLNM* 6: 'Hauld'.

11. *Den ældre Gulathings-Lov* in *Norges gamle love* 1846 1: 71.

12. *Grágás* 1883: 464.

13. *Grágás* 1852a: 140–41 (Ch. 83); 1879: 277–8 (Ch. 245).

14. *Grágás* 1852a: 137 (Ch. 81). See also *Grágás* 1879: 273 (Ch. 242).

15. *Grágás* 1852a: 140 (Ch. 83). See also *Grágás* 1879: 277–8 (Ch. 245).

16. *Grágás* 1852a: 141 (Ch. 83). See also *Grágás* 1879: 278–9 (Ch. 247); 1883: 426–7.

17. *Sturlunga saga* offers many examples of farmers moving in the later centuries of the Free State, a time when the territorial authority of the *goðar* was increasing (*Sturlu saga*, Chs. 3, 6, 9, 23, 26; *Guðmundar saga dýra*, Ch. 4; *Hrafns saga Sveinbjarnarsonar*, Ch. 13; *Íslendinga saga*, Chs. 6, 13, 18, 32, 33, 52, 53, 56, 59, 81, 83, 146, 166).

18. Magnús Már Lárusson, *KLNM* 7: '*Hreppr*'; Jón Jóhannesson 1974: 83–9.

19. Jón Jóhannesson 1974.

20. Solvason 1993: 105.

21. Foote 1977b.

22. Karras 1988.

23. Hastrup 1985: 107–18 may overemphasize class distinctions.

24. *Grágás* 1852a: 136 (Ch. 81). A line from the document '*Skipan Sæmundar Ormssonar*' (1245) corroborates that the chieftains drew their thing-tax-paying followers from both landowners and tenant farmers: 'each *bóndi* who . . .' (*Diplomatarium Islandicum* 1, Pt 2: 536). A tenant farmer's exercise of his rights must have varied according to the reasonableness (*hóf*) of the landowner.

Chapter 8

1. Byock 1982 and 1984–5. See also Hallberg 1985: 71–2; Vésteinn Ólason 1984.

2. In Byock 1982 I term these action particles of a saga story 'feudemes'. By analogy with linguistic terminology, the role of these indivisible units of action in saga feud is similar to the role of morphemes in language. See also Byock 1985b.

3. Magerøy 1978: 167.

4. The sagas and tales included in the 1946 edition are as follows: *Sturlunga saga* 1 contains *Geirmundar tháttr heljarskinns*, *Thorgils saga ok Hafliða*, *Haukdæla tháttr*, *Sturlu saga*, *Prestssaga Guðmundar góða*, *Guðmundar saga dýra*, *Hrafns saga Sveinbjarnarsonar* and *Íslendinga saga*. *Sturlunga saga* 2 includes *Thórðar saga kakala*, *Svínfellinga saga*, *Thorgils saga skarða*, *Sturla tháttr* and *Arons saga*.

5. A description of this manuscript (*Reykjafjarðarbók*) and a picture of a leaf cut to serve as a pattern for a waistcoat are found in Jón Helgason 1958: 44–5.

6. *Sturl.* 2, pp. v–li.

7. See, for example, Gunnar Karlsson 1972 and 1980b; Helgi Thorláksson 1979a and 1979b.

8. Different aspects of the Icelandic school's 'bookprose' concept, as well as views on the long debate in the first half of the twentieth century between bookprosists and freeprosists (believers in the oral origins of the sagas), are reviewed by Andersson 1964 and Scovazzi 1960. See also Hallberg 1962:

49–69; Holtsmark 1959; Byock 1982: 7–10. Two collections of older articles pertinent to the debate are Baetke 1974 and Mundal 1977. See also Mundal 1975. Stephen A. Mitchell 1991 (Chapter 1) provides an overview of the effects of the controversy.

9. For an example of an extreme bookprose position see Clover 1982. Vésteinn Ólason 1984: 179 notes that Clover's book is 'an attempt to strengthen the foundations of the bookprose theory'. Vilhjálmur Árnason 1991 grapples with the issues in the light of custom and philosophy.

10. Nordal 1957.

11. Óskar Halldórsson 1976, for example, disputes on folkloristic and archaeological grounds many of Nordal's statements about *Hrafnkels saga*.

12. Nordal 1957: 14.

13. Weibull 1911 and 1913. For further discussion see Arvidsson 1972; Moberg 1974.

14. For a discussion of the academic side of these debates see Andersson 1964: 41–50.

15. See Björn Thorsteinsson 1970.

16. *Mannfjöldi, mannafli og tekjur* 1984: 9.

17. Gísli Gunnarsson 1983.

18. *Iceland* 1946: 43.

19. *Iceland* 1966: 27.

20. Ibid.

21. Laxness 1934–5; Vésteinn Ólason 1983.

22. The title *Independent People* is probably ironic. A more determinedly nationalistic work by Laxness is *Íslandsklukkan* (1957).

23. Byock 1990a and 1992, expanded in Byock 1994b. See also Gunnar Karlsson 1984.

24. Jón Helgason 1926: 181, 195. The original is contained in Jón Ólafsson frá Grunnavík, 'Historiam Litterariam Islandicam' (1740). See *Katalog over de oldnorsk-islandske håndskrifter* 1900, vol. 1: 425–6.

25. Finnur Jónsson 1921: 141.

26. Laxness 1948; English translation by Magnus Magnusson, 1982: 58–9.

27. Nordal 1958: 57.

28. Nordal 1957: 29.

29. Continuity is discussed by Gunnar Karlsson 1972: especially p. 35; Byock 1985a.

30. Einar Ól. Sveinsson 1953; Byock 1986a.

31. Scandinavian scholars have grappled with these issues. Some influential review articles are Hallberg 1985 and Helgi Thorláksson 1987.

32. See, for example, Olrik 1909, whose laws distinguishing between oral and written narrative periodically haunt saga studies.

33. Ong 1982.

34. *The First Grammatical Treatise* 1972.

35. Ibid.: 209.

Chapter 9

1. Solvason 1993.

2. According to *Heimskringla* (Chs. 124–5), the Norwegian king (later the saint) Olaf Haraldsson in the early eleventh century showed some interest in controlling Iceland, but the matter came to nothing. *Íslendinga saga* (*Sturl.* 1, Ch. 38) speaks of the threat of Norwegian military aggression becoming a serious possibility in the thirteenth century (especially *c.* 1220), though an attack was never undertaken. See Magnús Már Lárusson 1967.

3. *Grágás* 1852a: 140 (Ch. 82); 1879: 277 (Ch. 245).

4. Ólafur Lárusson 1958a: 76.

5. In *Íslendingabók*, Ch. 5, Ari reports that Hen-Thorir (Hænsa-Thórir) was outlawed at the Althing (*c.* 965), indicating that a judicial court also sat there. Nothing is known about this court, which would have existed before the reforms.

6. *Grágás* 1852a: 216 (Ch. 117).

7. *Grágás* 1852a: 209 (Ch. 116).

8. The confrontation between the two men is reported with somewhat differing details in *Íslendingabók* and in the *Saga of Hen-Thorir* (*Hænsa-Thóris saga*; *Íslenzk fornit* 3): 1–47.

9. For a discussion of the different types of *goðorð* see Björn Sigfússon 1960: 48–53.

10. '*Nokkrar athugasemdir um fjórðungaþingin*' in Ólafur Lárusson 1958a: 110–118, esp. 117–18.

11. *Grágás* 1879: 356 (Ch. 328).

12. Jakob Benediktsson 1974a: 180; Jón Jóhannesson 1974: 66.

13. *Grágás* 1852a: 38 (Ch. 20).

14. *Grágás* 1852a: 77 (Ch. 43).

15. Bø 1969; Ciklamini 1963.

16. Heusler 1911: 103.

Chapter 10

1. For advocacy and its occurrence in saga narrative, see Byock 1982: 37–8, 74–92.

2. Sørensen 1977: 48.

3. *Grágás* 1852a: 193–207 (Chs. 113–15).

4. In Byock 1982: 38–46, a part of this specific *bóndi–goði* confrontation from *Droplaugarsona saga* is examined in the light of advocacy and narrative structure.

5. *Grágás* 1852b: 206 (Ch. 255); 1879: 47 (Ch. 37); 1883: 44 (Ch. 28).

6. *Grágás* 1879: 350 (Ch. 318).

7. *Grágás* 1852a: 38–9 (Ch. 20).

8. *Grágás* 1852a: 161 (Ch. 89); 1879: 322 (Ch. 289).

9. *Grágás* 1852a: 142.

10. Women in early Iceland are the subject of a large and growing literature: Agnes Arnórsdóttir 1990; Damsholt 1984; Ólafía Einarsdóttir 1984; Frank 1973; Heller 1958: 98–122; Guðrún Ingólfsdóttir 1994; Jochens 1995 and 1996; Gunnar Karlsson 1986; Helga Kress 1977; Lunden 1980; Auður Magnúsdóttir 1988; Mundal 1982; Ross 1992; Anna Sigurðardóttir 1981. For a wide view of women in the Viking world see Jesch 1991; Mundal 1992; and Øye 1990.

11. *Grágás* 1852a: 193–207 (Chs. 113–15). See also the discussion of kinship and *Baugatal* (the laws of wergild) earlier in this chapter.

12. *Laxdæla Saga*, trans. Magnusson and Pálsson 1969: 177.

13. On Kjartan's lack of moderation, see Byock 1982: 146–8.

14. With changes, this passage follows *Laxdæla Saga*, trans. Arent 1964: 138.

15. See, for example, Victor W. Turner's idea of the sagas as social drama (Turner 1971).

16. Byock 1982: 87–90.

17. Sverrir Jakobsson 1998a: 17–19.

18. Bragg 1997 discusses Thorgils skarði as well as Einar Thorgilsson from Staðarhóll.

Chapter 11

1. There is a large literature on this subject. See, for instance, Black-Michaud 1975; Boehm 1984; and Peters 1967.

2. A classic example of squeezing Iceland into such an ill-fitting shoe by relying on models of feuding and concepts of honour taken from warring tribal societies is William Miller 1990. Helgi Thorláksson 1994a: 394 in his important article on Icelandic feud, '*Hvað er blóðhefnd?*' ('What is Blood Feud?'), considers this issue of ill-fitting models, observing that 'Miller compares incidents from the Icelandic sagas with anthropological studies about other feuding societies, placing the emphasis on showing similarities. One may ask, however, whether he does not go too far in basing his understanding of Icelandic feud on comparisons with foreign societies which are so unlike Iceland that the comparison will be faulty, if not completely wrong [*að samanburðurinn verði villandi, ef ekki beinlínis skakkur*].'

3. Peters in his foreword to Black-Michaud 1975: xxvi.

4. Boehm 1984: 5.

5. Lord 1960.

6. I have selected this group because research on feud in the South Slavic region and especially among Montenegrins is well known.

7. Boehm 1984: 3.

8. *Egil's Saga* 1976.

9. In his foreword to Black-Michaud 1975: xxvi.

Chapter 12

1. Byock 1994d, esp. p. 166, where Icelandic political life is likened to the operation of ward politics in a modern American city.

2. Ker 1958: 200–201.

3. Peters in Black-Michaud 1975. Without thinking of Iceland, Peters describes (xiii) a situation close to that in Iceland, where the duty of blood-taking was converted to the routine acceptance of compromise necessary for economic production: 'It is possible to envisage a condition of things in which quarters of, say, a village are sufficiently detached to permit feud to occur, without at the same time wrecking the basis of ordinary, day-to-day, economic pursuits.' See also Knudsen 1985; Helgi Thorláksson 1994a: 403–6; and Wilson 1988. Thorláksson points out the similarity between Icelandic

and Corsican groups, which 'are formed ad hoc as in Iceland and composed of unrelated neighbours as well as kinsmen'.

4. Sverrir Jakobsson 1999 considers Icelanders and Norwegians in the medieval period.

5. Bø 1969; Byock 1993a, 'Hólmganga'; Ciklamini 1963.

6. Grágás 1852a: 154–7 (Ch. 88); 1879: 348–9 (Ch. 315). See 1964: 21–2.

7. Sverrir Jakobsson 1998b.

8. Grágás 1980.

9. Vilhjálmur Árnason 1991 has grappled with the possibility that some of modern Iceland's favourite saga heroes were in their original environment politically inept.

10. The Tale of Snegla Halli (Sneglu Halla tháttr) is found in Íf 9: 278.

11. Lúðvík Ingvarsson 1970: 94–173; 339–48; Magnús Már Lárusson, KLNM 4: 'Fredløshed: Island' cols. 603–8; Grágás 1980: 7–8; and Byock 1993a, 'Outlawry': 460–61.

Chapter 13

1. For a discussion of Thorleif's Christianity, see Walter 1956: 44–50. Berger 1978–9: 72–5 also discusses this episode in the light of the saga author's use of the law.

2. Introduction to Íf 11: 33, n. 1.

3. 'hálft hundrað silfrs': a 'hundred' was actually 120, so Brodd-Helgi is offering 60 silver coins or their equivalent weight of silver.

4. Icelandic readers like to correct Fagradalr to Fagridalur, but the name seems to have originally been spelled Fagradalr.

5. The saga says Skarð, but Ofeig lived at Skörð in Reykjahverfi. Skörð is the plural of Skarð (a mountain pass), and both words are place names. Skarð in Ljósavatn (Ljósavatnsskarð) is the name of a wide gap in the mountains about midway between the farms Skörð and Möðruvellir.

Chapter 14

1. Grágás 1852a: 159 (Ch. 89); 1879: 320 (Ch. 287); 1883: 173, 431–2. See Sveinbjörn Rafnsson 1974: 135–6, especially note 9.

2. According to Ari in Íslendingabók (Ch. 10).

3. The concept that a chieftaincy was not remunerative, but instead a drain

on a chieftain's resources, was argued by Maurer 1852: 102, who found that a *goðorð* 'demanded monetary sacrifices'. The idea survived well over a century without being seriously challenged. In 1883 the Arnamagnæan Commission included in the *Grágás* III index: 'In accepting the [thing] tax it does not appear that the chieftain had an income' (*Grágás* 1883: 702). Numerous scholars have commented on the chieftains' limited financial prospects. Sigurður Nordal 1942: 124, wrote: 'But even if the chieftain had employed the magnificence and authority [of the *goðorð*] to its full extent, then his position would in general have been an expense for him rather than a profit.' Jón Jóhannesson 1974: 62 remarked that chieftains enjoyed a small income from maintaining the temple and from levying certain dues (*lausatekjur*). Finding information about *thingfararkaup* unclear, he concluded: 'The office of a chieftain does not appear to have been a lucrative position, considering the many expenses involved.' Ólafur Lárusson 1958a: 71 suggested most *bændr* avoided *thingfararkaup* by following their chieftain to the Althing, and that the chieftaincy was 'not especially remunerative'. Jakob Benediktsson 1974a: 174 pointed out the dual nature of the thing tax: 'The *goðar* seem both to have received payment of *thingfararkaup* from those who stayed home and at the same time compensated those who went to the thing, and it cannot be seen whether they had any profit from these transactions.'

Björn Thorsteinsson 1953: 101 found little revenue from temple dues and from *thingfararkaup*: 'These payments were rather low and covered little more than the cost of sacrifices and of travel to the thing.' He later, 1966: 85, maintained a similar view of *thingfararkaup*. His major treatment of chieftains' wealth was directed to the twelfth and thirteenth centuries, when chieftains along with big farmers controlled Church property. Concerning the early period, he (1978: 52) notes briefly: 'The chieftains had their main source of income in the control of the law', but does not elaborate. Kirsten Hastrup 1985: 13, 118–21 also stresses the importance of the law, giving no indication of how the *goðar* used the law to their financial benefit: 'Just as it is difficult to extract from the sources information about the economy and about the nature of the relations of production, so is it also difficult to get a clear picture of actual political power and political actions'.

Sveinbjörn Rafnsson notes that '*thingfararkaup* went through a chieftain's hands', and attempts an additional connection between *thingfararkaup* and taxes introduced late in the Free State (1974: 134). He suggests *thingfararkaup* may have set a precedent for the thirteenth-century *sauðakvöð*. The two levies are, however, dissimilar: *thingfararkaup* was payment by specific individuals for a specific purpose; *sauðakvöð* was a general levy providing leaders with income. *Thingfararkaup* may have smoothed the way for the later taxes, but tenth- and eleventh-century farmers were not so primitive that they did not know how taxes worked.

4. *Grágás* 1852b: 72 (Ch. 167).

5. *Gísla saga Súrssonar* (Ch. 15) mentions a valuable imported tapestry which was lent for a feast.

6. Gurevich 1968; Miller 1986; and Helgi Thorláksson 1979b.

7. *Sturl.* 1, *Íslendinga saga*, Ch. 15.

8. See Jón Jóhannesson 1974: 181–2.

9. Jón Jóhannesson 1974: 242.

10. *Grágás* has many references to *féránsdómr*. See for instance: *Grágás* 1852a: 83–88 (Chs. 48–51), 108 (Ch. 59), 112–116 (Ch. 62), 118–119 (Chs. 66–67), 120 (Ch. 69), 125 (Ch. 77).

11. *Grágás* 1852b: 197–8 (Ch. 249); Berger 1978–9: 72–5.

12. *Sturl.* 1, *Íslendinga saga*, Ch. 79, in 1230; *Sturl.* 2, *Thórðar saga kakala*, Ch. 37, in 1245; *Sturl.* 2, *Thorgils saga skarða*, Chs. 14, 55 and 58, in 1252 and 1255. See also Björn Thorsteinsson 1953: 101.

13. *Thingtollr* is mentioned, for example, in *Diplomatarium Islandicum* 1, Pt 1: 276. For a listing of the different *tollr* see Björn Thorsteinsson, 'Tollr', *KLNM* 18: Cols. 452–4.

14. The editors of *Sturlunga saga* infer from Ch. 37 of *Thórðar saga kakala* that *sauðatollr* might have been collected yearly (*Sturl.* 2: 299, note 1). This conclusion is only a guess; the source on which it is based is unclear and does not specify a regular collection.

15. *Sturl.* 1, *Íslendinga saga*, Ch. 93.

16. Gelsinger 1981: 180. For export and import trade, see Jón Jóhannesson 1974: 305–17; Helgi Thorláksson 1991; Björn Thorsteinsson, 'Handel: Island', *KLNM* 6.

17. Helgi Thorláksson 1991.

18. *Eirik the Red and other Icelandic Sagas* 1980: 4.

19. *Sturl.* 1, *Íslendinga saga*, Ch. 38.

20. Björn Thorsteinsson, 'Fiskhandel, Island', *KLNM* 4; Kurlansky 1997; Gelsinger 1981: especially 181–94.

21. Björn Thorsteinsson 1969: 32–5.

22. Rader 1971: 40–42.

23. Björn Thorsteinsson did not pursue the issue (1966: 123).

24. *Grágás* 1852b: 140–61 (Chs. 221–6); 1879: 210–90 (Chs. 171–262).

25. *Grágás* 1852b: 76–139 (Chs. 172–220); 1879: 408–538 (Chs. 389–460).

26. Magnús Már Lárusson, *KLNM* 12: 'Odelsrett: Island', and Lárusson 1971. Sveinbjörn Rafnsson 1974: 142–51 discusses the issue of land-ownership, emphasizing the importance of *aðalból* and *höfuðból*. In part three of his book he argues that the purpose of *Landnámabók* was to verify the actual twelfth- and thirteenth-century possession of land. See also Jakob Benediktsson 1974b; Magerøy 1965: 24–8. Björn Thorsteinsson 1978: 34–6 describes the different types of landholdings. See also Gurevich 1968: 126–7; and Chapter 8, 'The Importance of Land in Saga Feud', in Byock 1982. Hastrup 1985: 72–5 emphasizes the importance of the *ætt* (kin group). She connects *ætt* land with *óðal* land (190–92, 201–4), suggesting that the right of potential heirs to influence a legitimate claim to 'major economic transactions in which the present owner might engage himself was to be seen as a modification of the idea of private ownership according to a latent principle of *ætt*-ownership' (190).

27. Björn Thorsteinsson and Sigurður Líndal, for example, stress the import-ance of family landholding. They point out that from the *landbrigða-tháttr* section of *Grágás*, one may unequivocally determine that the *landnámsmenn* understood the fundamental concept of Norwegian allodial landholding. Björn Thorsteinsson and Sigurður Líndal 1978: 77–9.

28. *Grágás* 1852b: 78 (Ch. 172), 150 (Ch. 223); 1879: 226 (Ch. 185), 415 (Ch. 389).

Chapter 15

1. Nordal 1942: 120.

2. Bauman 1986 considers honour in the sagas in the light of performance.

3. See Vilhjálmur Árnason 1991 for a discussion of saga morality, honour and ethics; and Byock 1995a.

4. A similar arrangement, though one not involving the complication of illegitimacy, is found in *Hænsa-Thóris saga* 1938: Ch. 2.

5. *Grágás* 1852a: 247, 249 (Ch. 127); 1879: 84 (Ch. 66), 100 (Ch. 76), 127

(Ch. 95). *Arfskot* is discussed in more detail in Chapter 6, which focuses on *Eyrbyggja saga*.

6. Einar Ól. Sveinsson 1953: 25.

Chapter 16

1. Much has also been written in modern times about the Icelandic Church. See for example the essays in *Saga Íslands*: Líndal 1974, including a bibliography; and Magnús Stefánsson 1975 and 1978, both of which include bibliographies. See also the section 'Church and Religion' in Jón Jóhannesson 1974, and Cormac 1994.

2. Jónas Kristjánsson 1980; Storm 1888.

3. *Diplomatarium Islandicum*, 16 vols., 1857–1952.

4. *Jóns saga* was most probably written between 1201 and 1210. The bishops' sagas are contained in three major editions: 1858–78, 1938 (Part 1) and 1978 (Part 2), and 1953, ed. Guðni Jónsson. The Guðni Jónsson edition, although more popular in presentation, remains a highly serviceable text. Because it is more readily available than any of the other editions, I have cited it where possible.

5. See *Byskupa sögur* 1953, 1: 1–31.

6. Thórr Magnússon 1966: 31–2.

7. *The Life of Gudmund the Good, Bishop of Hólar* 1942: xi.

8. See Strömbäck 1975; Jón Jóhannesson 1974: 118–144; Jón Hnefill Aðalsteinsson 1978; and Foote 1984.

9. One account is found in the *Historia de antiquitate regum Norwagiensium* written about 1180 by the Norwegian monk Theodoricus monachus. An Old Icelandic translation of the lost Latin *Saga of King Olaf Tryggvason* by the monk Odd Snorrason of Thingeyrar gives an account of the Christianization of Iceland which is largely based on *Íslendingabók*. Another lost Latin *Saga of King Olaf Tryggvason* by the monk Gunnlaug Leifsson of Thingeyrar seems to have been highly credulous and unreliable; it formed the basis for the remaining sources on the Christianization of Iceland. These are *Kristni saga* 1953; *Ólafs saga Tryggvasonar en mesta* 1958–1961; and the account of the conversion in *Njáls saga*, Chs. 100–105. A number of other family sagas such as *Laxdæla saga* contribute additional accounts.

10. Thorvald's mission is reported only in *Kristni saga* and in the *Kristni*

tháttr section of *Ólács saga Tryggvasonar en mesta*, two not altogether trustworthy sources.

11. *Íslendingabók* (Ch. 8) mentions a Bishop Fridrek who came to Iceland during the heathen period but gives no further information.

12. Like Thorvald's mission, Stefnir's is reported only in the *Kristni tháttr* section of *Ólács saga Tryggvasonar en mesta* and in *Kristni saga*.

13. Sveinbjörn Rafnsson 1977b discusses this missionary.

14. *Íf* 12, Ch. 102. The killing of Vetrlidi is mentioned in *Heimskringla*, *Kristni saga*, *Landnámabók* and *Ólács saga Tryggvasonar en mesta*. The *Njáls saga* account is probably derived from one of these.

15. Eating horse meat was thought to be connected to rituals of the old religion, but it was a staple food for the poor.

16. *Íslendingabók* (Ch. 8). See Magnús Már Lárusson 1960.

17. Stutz 1895 discusses private chapels (*Eigenkirchen*).

18. Groa was the daughter of Bishop Gizur Isleifsson of Skálholt, the wife of Bishop Ketil Thorsteinsson of Hólar (1122–45), and mother of the priest Runolf; see Frank 1973: 482.

19. Magnús Stefánsson 1978: 222–6; Jón Jóhannesson 1974: 89–109.

20. Jón Jóhannesson 1974: 148.

Chapter 17

1. The standard edition of *Grágás* was edited by Vilhjálmur Finsen and published in three volumes (1852, 1879 and 1883). A modern Icelandic edition is *Grágás. Lagasafn íslenska þjóðveldisins* 1992. An English translation of sections 1–117 of volume 1 appeared in *Laws of Early Iceland: Grágás I* (see *Grágás* 1980).

2. *Konungsbók* (*Codex Regius*) is usually dated to around 1250 and *Staðarhólsbók* to the years between 1260 and 1270. The two law books are now found in the Stofnun Árna Magnússonar (Árni Magnússon Manuscript Institute) in Reykjavík.

3. *Grágás* 1852a: 212 (Ch. 117).

4. Líndal 1984: 124.

5. Ibid. 139–41. Líndal argues for a unanimous vote.

6. Lúðvík Ingvarsson 1970: 18.

7. Dennis 1973: 3 notes that in addition to rules of constitution and procedure the original laws 'would have dealt with such matters as: homicide, assault,

theft, wergild, family law, inheritance, land, drift, negotiable currency, and commerce'.

8. *Grágás* 1852a: 3–37 (Chs. 1–19); 1879: 1–62 (Chs. 1–55); 1883: 1–376, 502–7.

9. *Norges gamle love indtil 1387*, 1895 5: 16–56.

10. *Grágás* 1852a: 147 (Ch. 86); 1879: 303–4 (Ch. 275). Men had the right to kill for certain offences against women (1852a: 164–6 [Ch. 90]). Aspects of vengeance in the sagas and *Grágás* are considered by Ólafur Lárusson 1958b: 146–78, in the section 'Hefndir'; Lúðvík Ingvarsson 1970: 62–93; and Miller 1983.

11. *Grágás* 1852a: 23 (Ch. 7).

12. Ólafur Lárusson 1958a: 86.

13. Foote 1977a: 54–5.

14. *Grágás* 1852b: 61–5 (Ch. 164).

15. *Grágás* 1852b: 206 (Ch. 255) and 1852a: 161 (Ch. 89).

16. The later *Jónsbók*, the Norwegian law adopted in 1281, likewise asserts that women took no part in the overt workings of the judicial system. *Jónsbók* 1970, Vol. 1: Ch. 4.

17. *Grágás* 1852a: 38–9 (Ch. 20).

18. *Grágás* 1852a: 38 (Ch. 20) and 161 (Ch. 89). My thanks to Gunnar Karlsson who shared with me his '*sérstaða kvenna*' from his typescript 'Drög að fræðilegri námsbók í íslenskri miðaldasögu' (1996b).

19. *Karlar* twelve years of age or older (*karlar tólf vetra gamlir eða eldri*), *Grágás* 1852a: 153 (Ch. 87).

20. *Grágás* 1852a: 170–71 (Ch. 95). As noted earlier, in Chapter 6, *Eyrbyggja saga* (Ch. 38) maintains that women did at one time participate in prosecutions. There is, however, no other source verifying this report, and it may be no more than a supposition by the author of *Eyrbyggja saga*.

21. *Grágás* 1852b: 47 (Ch. 155). See also Agnes S. Arnórsdóttir 1986: 25.

22. *Grágás* 1852a: 129 (Ch. 78) and 226 (Ch. 118).

23. *Grágás* 1879: 350 (Ch. 318).

24. Printed pages in the 1852b volume.

25. *Grágás* 1852b: 47 (Ch. 155). If one reads further it becomes clear that the protection varied, depending upon the social status of the woman concerned.

26. In the sagas, cases of seduction frequently turn on issues of honour.

Compensation is often demanded for the abasement of a kinswoman and conflict sometimes results. For example in *Vatnsdæla saga* (Ch. 37), a conflict ensues over Ingolf Thorsteinsson's seduction of the daughter of Ottar of Grímstunga and his composing love songs to her. In *Ljósvetninga saga* (A text, Ch. 21; C text, Ch. 22), a series of disputes follows the *bóndi* Isolf's request to his chieftain Eyjolf Gudmundarson to take a case against Brand Gunnsteinsson for seducing and impregnating Isolf's daughter.

27. Ólafía Einarsdóttir 1985: 82 and 1984. For a contrary view, see Gunnar Karlsson 1986: 45–7.

28. Nanna Damsholt 1984; Helgi Thorláksson 1991: 298–318 and 1981; see also Anna Sigurðardóttir 1985.

29. Browne 1862. According to Browne, 'The women are really the only class of inhabitants, except the fleas, who possess any vitality.'

30. *Grágás* 1879: 66 (Ch. 58); 162 (Ch. 126); 204 (Ch. 171).

31. *Grágás* 1852b: 42–3 (Ch. 150).

32. Taking property: *Grágás* 1852b: 44 (Ch. 151); 1879: 172 (Ch. 134). Violence committed: 1852b: 40 (Ch. 149); 1879: 168 (Ch. 134). Incompatibility: 1879: 168 (Ch. 134); 170 (Ch. 135); 1852b: 39, 41–3 (Ch. 150). Wearing feminine clothing: 1852b: 203–4 (Ch. 254).

33. *Grágás* 1852b: 43 (Ch. 150). *Jónsbók* gives a detailed listing of the circumstances under which a woman forfeited her bride price, *Jónsbók* 1970, Sect. 5: Ch. 5.

34. For a discussion of such transactions and arrangements see Schulman 1997. I am grateful to Professor Schulman for drawing my attention to numerous points of law concerning women.

35. *Njal's Saga* 1960: 207–8.

36. Duby 1978: 17–18; see also Johnsen 1948. The New Christian Laws of 1275 (*Kristinréttr nýi – Kristinréttr Árna Thorlákssonar*) formalized many of these changes.

37. Gunnar Karlsson 1986: 53. *Jónsbók* makes it clear, however, that poor people could in many instances legally marry, albeit with certain restrictions. *Jónsbók*, Sect. 5: Ch. 4.

38. Gunnar Karlsson 1986: 53.

39. The fifth degree seems to have been a special provision for Iceland. In Norway it was the sixth degree until 1215. Iceland's special status was probably due to the extreme difficulties which would have resulted from

restricting marriage to the sixth or seventh degree among such a small population.

40. Neither could people have spiritual kinship, for example having sponsored the other at baptism or confirmation. *Grágás* 1852b: 31 (Ch. 144).

Chapter 18

1. Boehm 1984: 68.

2. *Grágás* 1883: 44 (*Skálholtsbók*, Ch. 28). See also *Grágás* 1852b: 206 (Ch. 255); 1879: 47 (Ch. 37).

3. Jón Jóhannesson 1974: 173.

4. *Grágás* 1883: 144 (*Belgsdalsbók*, Ch. 32), 191 (*Arnarbælisbók*, Ch. 17). See Magnús Már Lárusson, *KLNM* 4: 'Fabrica: Island'; Jón Jóhannesson 1974: 176. For examples of *lýsitollr*, see *Diplomatarium Islandicum* Vol. 1: Pt 1, 276; Pt 3, 597.

5. Magnús Stefánsson 1975: 77.

6. Björn Thorsteinsson drew attention to the importance of *staðir* for those chieftains often called 'church chieftains' (*kirkjugoðar*). He emphasizes class 1966: 207–8. Gunnar Karlsson 1980b notes that both big farmers and big chieftains owned *staðir* and that possession of *staðir* alone did not assure the authority of a big chieftain; see especially 9–11.

7. Björn Sigfússon 1960 argues with good reason that Church influence, whether direct or indirect, has been considerably exaggerated in modern scholarship. He specifically takes issue with scholars such as Jón Jóhannesson, who stressed the importance of the Church in altering the conditions in the twelfth and thirteenth centuries.

8. *Thorláks biskups saga hin elzta*, Ch. 9: 98–9; *Thorláks biskups saga hin ýngri*, Ch. 10: 272–3 (*Biskupa sögur* 1858, Vol. 1). See also *Byskupa sögur* 1953, Vol. 1: 49–51.

9. Marriage and the sexual behaviour of laity and clergy are discussed by Jochens 1980 and Frank 1973.

10. See, for example, Pope Innocent III's decretal, '*Innotuit nobis*', written in 1200 to the archbishop of Canterbury, in which Innocent states the recognized procedure and established standards for ecclesiastical election (*Liber extra* 1.6.20 in Friedberg 1881: 2, cols. 61–3). An excellent account on the procedure of ecclesiastic election from the eleventh to the thirteenth century is Benson 1971.

11. See *Liber extra* 1.5, containing six decretals '*De postulatione praelatorum*', in Friedberg 1881: 2, cols. 41–8.

12. *Diplomatarium Islandicum*, Vol. 1: Pt 1, 291.

13. *Grágás* 1852b: 205–218 (Chs. 255–268).

14. Jón Jóhannesson 1974: 212.

15. *Diplomatarium Islandicum*, Vol. 1: Pt 1, 222.

16. Ibid., 291.

17. For a summary of the Tunga affair see Byock 1982: 154–60.

18. Einar Ól. Sveinsson 1953: 112, especially note 1.

19. Magnús Már Lárusson, *KLNM*: 'Kloster: Island'; Hermann Pálsson 1970: 92–102. The official date for the opening of the Thingeyrar monastery is 1133; the earlier date is more hypothesis than fact (Magnús Stefánsson 1975: 82–3; Jón Jóhannesson 1974: 192–200).

Chapter 19

1. Byock 1986a; Gunnar Karlsson 1972 and 1994a; Jón Víðar Sigurðsson 1989; Einar Ól. Sveinsson 1953; Helgi Thorláksson 1979b, 1982, 1994b.

2. Byock 1986a. As noted earlier, the economic hierarchy was more extensive and included at the lower levels slaves (in the early period), free labourers and tenant farmers. There were also gradations of wealth among landowners.

3. Gunnar Karlsson 1972: 42–3.

4. Aspects of this emerging class of territorial leaders are discussed by Gunnar Karlsson 1972 and 1994a; Jón Víðar Sigurðsson 1989; and Helgi Thorláksson 1979b. See also Byock 1986a; Einar Ól. Sveinsson 1953; and Helgi Thorláksson 1994b.

5. Gunnar Karlsson 1977: 368.

6. *Bandamanna saga* 1936; *Hænsa-Thóris saga* 1938.

7. Orning 1997: especially 479–82.

8. *Thorgils saga skarða*, Ch. 14. The question of whether or not Thorgils skarði and other *stórgoðar* were affluent is debated by Helgi Thorláksson 1979b and Gunnar Karlsson 1980b. Helgi Thorláksson 1979b: 229 doubts that Thorgils skarði was in great need. Gunnar Karlsson 1972: 43–4 and 1980b: 14–19 takes the opposing view, arguing that Thorgils was for years troubled by a lack of funds.

9. Breisch 1994.

10. *Íslendinga saga* 1946, Ch. 16.

11. Ármann Jakobsson 1995.

12. Two other men are later called Icelandic jarls in the sources, but it is doubtful that either really were jarls in Iceland. One was a well-known Norwegian baron named Audun Hugleiksson hestekorn. He was the principal adviser to Eirik Magnusson (1280–1299). The other was an Icelander named Kolbein Bjarnason the Knight (*riddari*). Kolbein's title may have been a nickname. Both men were killed in the early 1300s.

13. For different manuscript versions of the covenant see *Diplomatarium Islandicum*, Vol. 1: Pt 3: 619–25; Vol. 9: 1–4; Vol. 10: 5–8. I cite the A version of the covenant (Vol. 1: 620–21).

14. 'Hier j mot skal konungr lata oss naa fridi og jslendskum laugum', *Diplomatarium Islandicum*, Vol. 1: 620.

Appendix 3

1. Grönvald 1994. The only known person connected to Stöng is the hero Gaukr Trandilsson. Called Gaukr á Stöng (from Stöng), he lived around the year 1000 and is mentioned in the *Book of Settlements* and *Njal's Saga*. There was once a whole saga about Gaukr, but it is now lost.

2. Kristján Eldjárn 1971; Grönvold 1994; Roussell 1943.

Appendix 4

1. *Grænlendinga saga* is found only in *Flateyjarbók*, a large manuscript from c. 1390. *Eiríks saga rauða* is preserved in two manuscripts: the *Hauksbók* compilation from the beginning of the fourteenth century and *Skálholtsbók* from c. 1420. Although *Hauksbók* is older, the text in *Skálholtsbók* may be closer to an original. Such dating is very imprecise. Ólafur Halldórsson 1978 discusses the relationship between *Eiríks saga rauða* and *Grælendinga saga*, finding both products of independent oral tradition. More speculatively, the meteorologist Páll Bergthórsson 1997 explores possible routes of the different sailings. For English translations see *The Vinland Sagas* 1965.

2. *Eiríks saga rauða* also places Thorfinn Karlsefni and Gudrid in Skagafjord, but at a place named Reynines (probably the farm later called Reynistaðir).

Bibliography

Aðalsteinsson, Jón Hnefill. 1978. *Under the Cloak: The Acceptance of Christianity in Iceland with Particular Reference to the Religious Attitudes Prevailing at the Time.* Acta Universitatis Upsaliensis, Studia Ethnologica Upsaliensia 4. Stockholm: Almqvist and Wiksell.

Aðalsteinsson, Stefán. 1991. 'Importance of Sheep in Early Icelandic Agriculture'. *The Norse of the North Atlantic*, ed. Gerald F. Bigelow. *Acta Archaeologica* vol. 61: 285–291.

Adam of Bremen. 1959. *History of the Archbishops of Hamburg-Bremen.* Trans. Francis J. Tschan. Columbia University Records of Civilization 53. New York: Columbia University Press.

Agnarsdóttir, Anna and Ragnar Árnason. 1983. 'Þrælahald á þjóðveldisöld'. *Saga* 21: 5–26.

Ágústsson, Hörður. 1974. *Hér stóð bær: Líkan af Þjóðveldisbæ.* Reykjavík: Þjóðhátíðarnefnd.

——— 1987. 'Íslenski torfbærinn'. *Íslensk þjóðmenning* 1: 227–344.

——— 1989. 'Húsagerð á síðmiðöldum'. *Saga Íslands* 4: 259–300.

Amorosi, T., P. Buckland, A. Dugmore, John H. Ingimundarson and T. H. McGovern. 1997. 'Raiding the Landscape: Human Impact in the Scandinavian North Atlantic'. *Human Ecology* 25/3: 491–518.

Andersen, Per Sveaas. 1977. *Samlingen av Norge og kristningen av landet 800–1130.* Handbok i Norges historie 2. Bergen: Universitetsforlaget.

Andersson, Theodore M. 1964. *The Problem of Icelandic Saga Origins: A Historical Survey.* Yale Germanic Studies 1. New Haven: Yale University Press.

Archaeologia Islandia. 1998–.

Arnalds, A. 1987. 'Ecosystem Disturbance and Recovery in Iceland'. *Arctic and Alpine Research* 19: 508–13.

Árnason, Vilhjálmur. 1985. 'Saga og siðferði: Hugleiðingar um túlkun á siðfræði Íslendingasagna'. *Tímarit Máls og menningar* 46: 21–37.

——— 1991. 'Morality and Social Structure in the Icelandic Sagas'. *Journal of English and Germanic Philology* 90/2: 157–74.

Arnórsdóttir, Agnes S. 1986. 'Viðhorf til kvenna í *Grágás*'. *Sagnir* 7: 23–30.

——— 1990. *Kvinner og 'Krigsmenn': kjønnens stilling i det islandske samfunnet på 1100–1200 tallet*. Bergen: Universitetet i Bergen. Translation into Icelandic 1995. *Konur og vígamenn: Staða kynjanna á Íslandi á 12. og 13. öld*. Sagnfræðirannsóknir – *Studia Historica XII*. Reykjavík: Sagnfræðistofnun.

Arvidsson, Rolf. 1972. 'Source-Criticism and Literary History: Lauritz Weibull, Henrik Schück and Joseph Bédier: A Discussion'. *Mediaeval Scandinavia* 5: 96–138.

Baetke, Walter (ed.). 1974. *Die Isländersaga*. Wege der Forschung 151. Darmstadt: Wissenschaftliche Buchgesellschaft.

Bagge, Sverre. 1986a. 'Borgerkrig og statsutvikling i Norge i middelalderen'. *Historisk tidsskrift* 65: 145–97.

——— 1986b. 'The Formation of the State and Concepts of Society in 13th Century Norway'. *Continuity and Change: Political Institutions and Literature in the Middle Ages*, ed. Elisabeth Vestergaard, 43–59. Proceedings of the Tenth International Symposium Organized by the Centre for the Study of Vernacular Literature in the Middle Ages. Odense: Odense University Press.

——— 1996. *From Gang Leader to the Lord's Anointed. Kingship in Sverris saga and Hákonar saga Hákonarsonar*. The Viking Collection, vol. 8. Odense: Odense University Press.

Bandamanna saga (The Saga of the Confederates). 1936. Ed. Guðni Jónsson. *Íslenzk fornrit* 7. Reykjavík: Hið íslenzka fornritafélag.

Bárðarson, Hjálmar R. 1971. *Ice and Fire: Contrasts of Icelandic Nature*. Reykjavík: Bárðarson.

Bauman, Richard. 1986. 'Performance and Honor in 13th-Century Iceland'. *Journal of American Folklore* 99: 131–50.

Beck, Heinrich. 1977. '*Laxdæla saga* – A Structural Approach'. *Saga-Book of the Viking Society for Northern Research* 19: 383–402.

Bekker-Nielsen, Hans. 1965. 'Frode mænd og tradition'. *Norrøn fortælle-kunst: kapitler af den norsk-islandske middelalderlitteraturs historie*, ed. Hans Bekker-Nielsen, Thorkil Damsgaard Olsen and Ole Widding, 35–41. Copenhagen: Akademisk forlag.

Benedictow, Ole Jørgen. 1992. *The Medieval Demographic System of the Nordic Countries*. Oslo: Middelalderforlaget.

Benediktsson, Jakob. 1969. '*Landnámabók*: Some Remarks on Its Value as a Historical Source'. *Saga-Book of the Viking Society for Northern Research* 17: 275–92.

―――― 1974a. 'Landnám og upphaf allsherjarríkis'. *Saga Íslands* 1: 153–96.

―――― 1974b. 'Markmið Landnámabókar: Nýjar rannsóknir'. *Skírnir* 148 (1974): 207–15.

Benson, Robert L. 1971. 'Election by Community and Chapter: Reflections on Co-responsibility in the Historical Church'. *The Jurist* 31: 54–80.

Berger, Alan. 1978–9. 'Lawyers in the Old Icelandic Family Sagas: Heroes, Villains, and Authors'. *Saga-Book of the Viking Society for Northern Research* 20: 70–79.

Bergthórsson, Páll. 1987. 'Veðurfar á Íslandi'. *Íslensk þjóðmenning* 1: 195–225.

―――― 1997. *Vínlandsgátan*. Reykjavík: Mál og menning.

Bigelow, Gerald F. (ed.). 1991. *The Norse of the North Atlantic. Acta Archaeologica* vol. 61. Copenhagen: Munksgaard.

Bishops' Sagas: see *Biskupa sögur* and *Byskupa sögur*.

Biskupa sögur (*Bishops' Sagas*). 1858–78. Ed. Hið íslenzka bókmentafélag. 2 vols. Copenhagen: S. L. Möller. See also *Byskupa sögur*.

Black-Michaud, Jacob. 1975. *Cohesive Force: Feud in the Mediterranean and the Middle East*. Oxford: Basil Blackwell. Foreword by E. L. Peters.

Bø, Olav. 1969. '*Hólmganga* and *Einvígi*: Scandinavian Forms of the Duel'. *Mediaeval Scandinavia* 2: 132–148.

Bøe, Arne. *Kulturhistoriskt lexikon för nordisk medeltid*: 'Hauld', *KLNM* 6, cols. 251–254.

Boehm, Christopher. 1984. *Blood Revenge: The Anthropology of Feuding in Montenegro and other Tribal Societies*. Lawrence: University Press of Kansas.

The Book of the Icelanders: see *Íslendingabók*.

The Book of Settlements: see *Landnámabók*.

Boyer, Régis. 1967. 'L'évêque Gudmundr Arason, témoin de son temps'. *Études Germaniques* 3: 427–44.

―――― 1994. 'Were the Icelanders Good Christians, According to Samtíðarsögur?' *Samtíðarsögur: The Contemporary Sagas*, vol. I. Níunda Althjóðlega Fornsagnaþingið, pp. 111–22. Reykjavík: Stofnun Árna Magnússonar.

Bragg, Lois. 1997. 'Generational Tensions in *Sturlunga saga*'. *Arkiv för nordisk filologi* 112: 5–34.

Bredsdorff, Thomas. 1996. *Kaos og kærlighed: En studie i islændingesagaers livsbillede*. Copenhagen: Gyldendal, 1971, 2nd edn. 1996.

Breisch, Agneta. 1994. *Frid och fredlöshet: Sociala band och utanförskap på Island under äldre medeltid. Studia Historica Upsaliensia*, no. 174. Stockholm: Almqvist & Wiksell.

Browne, J. Ross. 1862. 'A Californian in Iceland'. *Harper's New Monthly Magazine* 26: 292.

Bryce, James. 1968. *Studies in History and Jurisprudence*. 2 vols. 1901. Freeport, New York: Books for Libraries Press.

Buckland, Paul C., Andrew Dugmore and Jon Sadler. 1991a. 'Faunal change or taphonomic problem? A comparison of modern and fossil insect faunas from south-east Iceland'. J. Maizels and C. Caseldine (eds.), *Environmental Change in Iceland: Past and Present*. Dordrecht: Kluwer Academic Publishers, 127–46.

Buckland, Paul C., Andrew J. Dugmore, D. Perry, D. Savory and Guðrún Sveinbjarnardóttir. 1991b. 'Holt in Eyjafjallasveit, Iceland: A palaeoecological study of the impact of the *Landnám*'. *Acta Archaeologica* 61: 267–71.

Buckland, Paul C., K. J. Edwards, J. J. Blackford, Andrew J. Dugmore, Jon P. Sadler and Guðrún Sveinbjarnardóttir. 1995. 'A question of *Landnám*: Pollen, charcoal and insect studies on Papey, Iceland'. R. Butlin and N. Roberts (eds.), *Ecological relations in historical times*. London: Blackwell, 245–65.

Byock, Jesse L. 1982. *Feud in the Icelandic Saga*. Berkeley, Los Angeles, and London: University of California Press.

―――― 1984–5. 'Saga Form, Oral Prehistory, and the Icelandic Social Context'. *New Literary History* 16: 153–73.

——— 1985a. 'Cultural Continuity, the Church, and the Concept of Independent Ages in Medieval Iceland'. *Skandinavistik* 15/1: 1–14.

——— 1985b. 'The Narrative Strategy of Small Feud Stories'. *Les Sagas de Chevaliers (Riddarasögur)*, ed. Régis Boyer, pp. 404–15. Civilisations 10. Paris: Presses de l'Université de Paris-Sorbonne.

——— 1985c. 'The Power and Wealth of the Icelandic Church: Some Talking Points'. *The Sixth International Saga Conference 1985*, vol. 1, pp. 89–101. Copenhagen: Det arnamagnæanske Institut.

——— 1986a. 'The Age of the Sturlungs'. *Continuity and Change: Political Institutions and Literary Monuments in the Middle Ages*, ed. Elisabeth Vestergaard, pp. 27–42. Proceedings of the Tenth International Symposium Organized by the Centre for the Study of Vernacular Literature in the Middle Ages. Odense: Odense University Press, 1986.

——— 1986b. 'Governmental Order in Early Medieval Iceland'. *Viator* 17: 19–34.

——— 1986c. '"Milliganga": Félagslegar rætur Íslendingasagna'. *Tímarit Máls og menningar*: 96–104.

——— 1987. 'Inheritance and Ambition in *Eyrbyggja saga*'. *The Sagas of the Icelanders: Essays in Criticism*, ed. John Tucker. New York: Garland Press.

——— 1988a. *Medieval Iceland: Society, Sagas, and Power*. Berkeley and Los Angeles: University of California Press.

——— 1988b. 'Vinfengi og valdatafl'. *Skírnir* 162: 127–37.

——— 1990a. 'Íslendingasögur og kenningar um formgerð frásagna: Munnleg hefð og bóksögur í ljósi samfélagsgerðar'. *Tímarit Máls og menningar* 2: 21–39.

——— 1990b. 'Sigurðr Fáfnisbani: An Eddic Hero Carved on Norwegian Stave Churches'. *The Seventh International Saga Conference*, ed. Theresa Pàroli, 619–28. Spoleto: Centro Italiano di Studi Sull'Alto Medioevo.

——— 1992. 'History and the sagas: The effect of nationalism'. *From Sagas to Society: Comparative Approaches to Early Iceland*, ed. Gísli Pálsson. London: Hisarlik Press, 44–59.

——— 1993a. 'Althingi', 'Bóndi', 'Goði', 'Hólmganga' and 'Outlawry'. *Encyclopedia of Old Norse Studies*, ed. Philip Pulsiano. New York: Garland Publishers.

——— 1993b. 'The Skull and Bones in *Egils saga*: A Viking, A Grave, and Paget's Disease'. *Viator: Medieval and Renaissance Studies* 24: 23–50.

—— 1993c. 'Þjóðernishyggja nútímans og Íslendingasögurnar'. *Tímarit Máls og menningar* 1: 36–50.

—— 1994a. 'Hauskúpan og beinin í Egils sögu'. *Skírnir* (Vor): 73–109.

—— 1994b. 'Modern nationalism and the medieval sagas'. *Yearbook of Comparative and General Literature* 39 (1990–91): 62–74. Enlarged in *Northern Antiquity: The Post-Medieval Reception of Edda and Saga*, ed. Andrew Wawn, 163–87. London: Hisarlik Press.

—— 1994c. 'Narrating Saga Feud: Deconstructing the fundamental oral progression'. *Sagnaþing: Helgað Jónasi Kristjánssyni sjötugum 10. apríl 1994*, ed. Gísli Sigurðsson, Guðrún Kvaran and Sigurgeir Steingrímsson, pp. 97–106. Reykjavík: Hið íslenska bókmenntafélag.

—— 1994d. 'State and Statelessness in Early Iceland'. *Samtíðarsögur: The Contemporary Sagas*, vol. I. The Ninth International Saga Conference (Níunda Althjóðlega Fornsagnaþingið), 155–69. Reykjavík: Stofnun Árna Magnússonar.

—— 1995a. 'Choices of Honor: Telling Saga Feud, *Tháttr*, and the Fundamental Oral Progression'. *Oral Tradition* 10/1 (1995): 166–80.

—— 1995b. 'Egil's Bones: A Viking Warrior and Paget's Disease'. *Scientific American* 272/1 (January, 1995): 82–7. Translated as: 'Die Egil-saga und das Paget-Syndrom', *Spectrum der Wissenschaft* (März, 1995); 'Les os d'Egil, héros viking', *Pour La Science* 209 (Mars, 1995): 52–8; 'Le ossa di Egill', *Le Scienze* 319 (Marzo, 1995): 74–9; 'Kości Egila', *Świat Nauki* (Marzec, 1995): 72–7; *Archaeology: Annual Edition 96/97*. Guildford: Brown and Benchmark Publishers, 1996, pp. 80–85.

—— 1995c. *Evidence of the Vikings*. BBC documentary film, *see* Ereira, Alan.

—— 1997. 'Excavation Report: Mosfell and Hrísbrú in Mosfellssveit'. *Sagas and the Norwegian Experience: (Sagaene og Noreg)*. Tenth International Saga Conference, Trondheim, 3–9 August, 1997. Trondheim: Center for Middelalderstudier, University of Trondheim.

—— 1998. 'Egilssaga og samfélagsminni'. *Íslenska söguþingið 28.–31. maí 1997. Ráðstefnurit I*. Ed. Guðmundur J. Guðmundsson and Eiríkur K. Björnsson. Reykjavík: Sagnfræðistofnun Háskóla Íslands & Sagnfræðingafélag Íslands, 379–89.

—— 1999. *Island í sagatiden: Samfund, magt og fejde*. Copenhagen: C. A. Reitzel.

Byock, Jesse L. and Skia. 1992. 'Disease and Archaeology in *Egil's Saga*: A first look'. *The Haskins Society Journal: Studies in Medieval History* 4: 11–22.

Byskupa sögur (*Bishops' Sagas*). 1938. Ed. Jón Helgason for Det kongelige nordiske oldskriftselskab. Copenhagen: Munksgaard. (Now considered as Editiones Arnamagnæanæ, series A, 13, Pt. 1.) See also *Biskupa sögur*.

———— 1953. Ed. Guðni Jónsson. 3 vols. [Akureyri]: Íslendingasagnaútgáfan, Haukadalsútgáfan.

———— 1978. Ed. Jón Helgason. Editiones Arnamagnæanæ, series A, 13, Pt. 2. Copenhagen: C. A. Reitzel.

Carneiro, Robert L. 1981. 'The Chiefdom: Precursor to the State'. *The Transition to Statehood in the New World*, ed. G. Jones and R. Kautz. Cambridge: Cambridge University Press, 37–79.

Ciklamini, Marlene. 1963. 'The Old Icelandic Duel'. *Scandinavian Studies* 35: 175–94.

Cleasby–Vigfusson. 1957. See *Icelandic–English Dictionary*.

Clover, Carol J. 1982. *The Medieval Saga*. Ithaca and London: Cornell University Press.

Cook, Robert. 1993. 'Vápnfirðinga saga (The Saga of the People of Vápnafjord)'. *Medieval Scandinavia: An Encyclopedia*, ed. P. Pulsiano and K. Wolf, pp. 687–8. New York: Garland Publishing.

Cormac, Margaret. 1994. *The Saints in Iceland: Their Veneration from the Conversion to 1400*. Subsidia hagiographica 78. Brussels: Société des Bollandistes.

Damsholt, Nanna. 1984. 'The Role of Icelandic Women in the Sagas and in the Production of Homespun Cloth'. *Scandinavian Journal of History* 9: 75–90.

Dennis, Andrew. 1973. '*Grágás*: An Examination of the Content and Technique of the Old Icelandic Law Books, Focused on *Þingskapaþáttr* (the "Assembly Section")'. Ph.D. dissertation, Cambridge University.

Diplomatarium Islandicum [Icelandic documents]: Íslenzkt fornbréfasafn. 1857–1952. 16 vols. Copenhagen and Reykjavík: S. L. Möller and Hið íslenzka bókmentafélag.

Duby, Georges. 1978. *Medieval Marriage: Two Models from Twelfth-Century France*. Baltimore: Johns Hopkins University Press.

Dugmore, Andrew J. and Ian A. Simpson. 1999. '1,200 years of Icelandic soil erosion reconstructed using tephrochronology'. Unpublished paper.

Durrenberger, E. Paul. 1991. 'Production in Medieval Iceland'. *The Norse of the North Atlantic*, ed. Gerald F. Bigelow. *Acta Archaeologica* vol. 61: 14–21.

Durrenberger, E. Paul and Gísli Pálsson (eds.). 1989. *The Anthropology of Iceland*. Iowa City: University of Iowa Press.

Earle, Timothy (ed.). 1991. *Chiefdoms: Power, Economy and Ideology*. Cambridge: Cambridge University Press.

——— 1997. *How Chiefs Came to Power: The political economy in prehistory*. Stanford University Press.

Edda: Die Lieder des Codex Regius nebst verwandten Denkmälern. 1962. Ed. Gustav Neckel. 4th edn. Revised by Hans Kuhn. 2 vols. Heidelberg: Carl Winter Universitätsverlag.

Egil's Saga. 1976. Trans. Hermann Pálsson and Paul Edwards. New York: Penguin Books.

Egils saga Skalla-Grímssonar. 1933. Ed. Sigurður Nordal. *Íslenzk fornrit* 2. Reykjavík: Hið íslenzka fornritafélag.

Einarsdóttir, Ólafía. 1964. *Studier i kronologisk metode i tidlig islandsk historieskrivning. Bibliotheca historica Lundensis* 13. Stockholm: Natur och kultur.

——— 1984. 'Staða kvenna á þjóðveldisöld. Hugleiðingar í ljósi samfélagsgerðar og efnahagskerfis'. *Saga* 22: 7–30.

——— 1985. 'Om husfreyjamyndighed i det gamle Island'. *Festskrift til Thelma Jexley: Fromhed og verdslighed i middelalder og renaissance*. Odense: Odense Universitetsforlag.

Einarsson, Bjarni. 1974. 'On the Status of Free Men in Society and Saga'. *Mediaeval Scandinavia* 7: 45–55.

Einarsson, Bjarni. 1995. *The Settlement of Iceland. A Critical Approach. Granastaðir and the Ecological Heritage*. Gothenburg Archaeological Theses 4. Gothenburg.

Einarsson, Stefán. 1957. *A History of Icelandic Literature*. Baltimore: Johns Hopkins University Press.

Eiríks saga rauða (The Saga of Eirik the Red). 1935. *Íslenzk fornrit* 4. Reykjavík: Hið íslenzka fornritafélag. (See also *The Vinland Sagas* 1965.)

Eirik the Red and other Icelandic Sagas. 1980. Trans. Gwyn Jones. Oxford: Oxford University Press.

Eldjárn Kristján. 1971. *Stöng í Þjórsárdal: leiðarvísir*. Reykjavík: Þjóð-minjasafn íslands.

Elias, Norbert. 1994. *The Civilizing Process: The History of Manners and State Formation and Civilization*. Trans. Edmund Jepchott. Oxford: Blackwell.

Ereira, Alan (director) and Jesse Byock (historical consultant). 1995. *Evidence of the Vikings*. BBC film in the historical documentary series *Timewatch*.

Evans-Pritchard, Edward Evan. 1953. *Kinship and Marriage among the Nuer*. London: Oxford University Press.

Eyfirðingja sögur (The Sagas of the People of Eyjafjord). 1956. Ed. Jónas Kristjánsson. *Íslenzk fornrit* 9. Reykjavík: Hið íslenzka fornritafélag.

Eyrbyggja saga (The Sagas of the People of Eyri). 1935. Eds. Einar Ól. Sveinsson and Matthías Þórðarson. *Íslenzk fornrit* 4. Reykjavík: Hið íslenzka fornritafélag.

Fentress, James and Chris Wickham. 1992. *Social Memory*. Oxford: Blackwell Publishers.

Finsen, Vilhjálmur. 1873. 'Om de islandske love i fristatiden'. *Aarbøger for nordisk oldkyndighed og historie*, 101–250.

—— 1888. *Om den oprindelige ordning af nogle af den islandske fristats institutioner*. Copenhagen: Bianco Luno Kgl. Hof-Bogtrykkeri.

The First Grammatical Treatise. 1972. Ed. Hreinn Benediktsson. University of Iceland Publications in Linguistics 1. Reykjavík: Institute for Nordic Linguistics.

'Fiskveiðilandhelgi Íslands' (map). Landmælingar Íslands og Sjávarútvegs-ráðuneytið, 1984.

Foote, Peter G. 1974. 'Secular Attitudes in Early Iceland'. *Mediaeval Scandinavia* 7: 31–44.

—— 1977a. 'Oral and Literary Tradition in Early Scandinavian Law: Aspects of a Problem'. *Oral Tradition – Literary Tradition: A Symposium*, ed. Hans Bekker-Nielsen, Peter Foote, Andreas Haarder and Hans Frede Nielsen, 47–55. Odense: Odense University Press.

—— 1977b. 'Þrælahald á Íslandi'. *Saga* 15: 41–74.

—— 1984. 'On the Conversion of the Icelanders'. *Aurvandilstá: Norse Studies*, 56–64. Odense: Odense University Press.

Foote, Peter G. and David M. Wilson. 1970. *The Viking Achievement: The*

Society and Culture of Early Medieval Scandinavia. London: Sidgwick and Jackson.

Fóstbræðra saga (The Saga of the Foster-Brothers). 1943. Ed. Björn K. Thórólfsson and Guðni Jónsson. *Íslenzk fornrit* 6. Reykjavík: Hið íslenzka fornritafélag.

Frank, Roberta. 1973. 'Marriage in Twelfth- and Thirteenth-Century Iceland'. *Viator* 4: 473–84.

Friðriksson, Adolf. 1994. *Sagas and Popular Antiquarianism in Icelandic Archaeology.* Worldwide Archaeology Series 10. Aldershot: Avebury Books.

Friðriksson, Adolf and Orri Vésteinsson. 1998. 'Fornleifaskráning: Brot úr íslenskri vísindasögu'. *Archaeologia Islandia* 1: 14–44.

Friðriksson, Sturla. 1972. 'Grass and Grass Utilization in Iceland'. *Ecology* 53: 785–97.

Fried, Morton H. 1968. 'On the Evolution of Social Stratification and the State'. *Readings in Anthropology.* Vol. II: *Cultural Anthropology*, ed. Morton H. Fried, 462–78. New York: Thomas Y. Crowell.

Friedberg, Emil (ed.). 1879–81. *Corpus iuris canonici.* 2 vols. Leipzig: B. Tauchnitz.

Friedman, David. 1979. 'Private Creation and Enforcement of Law: A Historical Case'. *Journal of Legal Studies* 8: 399–415.

Geirmundar þáttr heljarskinns (The Tale of Geirmundr Helskinn). In *Sturlunga saga* 1946 1: 5–11.

Gelsinger, Bruce E. 1981. *Icelandic Enterprise: Commerce and Economy in the Middle Ages.* Columbia, South Carolina: University of South Carolina Press.

Gerrard, J. 1991. 'An Assessment of some of the factors involved in recent landscape change in Iceland'. J. Maizels and C. Caseldine (eds.), *Environmental Change in Iceland: Past and present.* Dordrecht, The Netherlands: Kluwer Academic Publishers, 237–53.

Gilman, Antonio. 1995. 'Prehistoric European Chiefdoms: Rethinking Germanic societies'. *Foundations of Social Inequality*, ed. Gary Feinman and T. Douglas Price, 235–51. New York: Plenum.

Gísla saga Súrssonar (Gisli Sursson's Saga). 1943. Ed. Björn K. Thórólfsson and Guðni Jónsson. *Íslenzk fornrit* 6. Reykjavík: Hið íslenzka fornritafélag.

Gisli Sursson's Saga: see *Gísla saga Súrssonar*.

Gluckman, Max. 1955. 'The Peace in the Feud'. *Past and Present* 8: 1–14.

Godelier, Maurice. 1986. *The Making of Great Men*. Cambridge: Cambridge University Press.

Godelier, Maurice and Marilyn Strathern (eds.). 1991. *Big Men and Great Men*. Cambridge and Paris: Cambridge University Press and Editions de la Maison des Sciences de l'Homme.

Grænlendinga saga (*The Saga of the Greenlanders*). 1935 and *Grænlendinga Þáttr* (*The Tale of the Greenlanders*). 1935. Ed. Einar Ól. Sveinsson. *Íslenzk fornrit* 4. Reykjavík: Hið íslenzka fornritafélag. (See also *The Vinland Sagas* 1965.)

Grágás. 1852. Ed. Vilhjálmur Finsen. Vol. I a–b: *Grágás: Islændernes Lovbog i Fristatens Tid, udgivet efter det kongelige Bibliotheks Haandskrift*. Copenhagen: Det nordiske Literatur Samfund.

——— 1879. Ed. Vilhjálmur Finsen. Vol. II: *Grágás efter det Arnamagnæanske Haandskrift Nr. 334 fol., Staðarhólsbók*. Copenhagen: Gyldendalske Boghandel.

——— 1883. Ed. Vilhjálmur Finsen. Vol. III: *Grágás: Stykker, som findes i det Arnamagnæanske Haandskrift Nr. 351 fol. Skálholtsbók og en Række andre Haandskrifter*. Copenhagen: Gyldendalske Boghandel.

——— 1980. *Laws of Early Iceland: Grágás I*. Trans. Andrew Dennis, Peter Foote and Richard Perkins. University of Manitoba Icelandic Studies 3. Winnipeg: University of Manitoba Press.

——— 1992. *Grágás. Lagasafn íslenska þjóðveldisins*. Ed. Gunnar Karlsson, Kristján Sveinsson, Mörður Árnason. 1992. Reykjavík: Mál og menning.

Grímsdóttir, Guðrún Ása 1982. 'Um afskipti erkibiskupa af íslenzkum málefnum á 12. og 13. öld'. *Saga* 20: 28–62.

——— (ed.). 1996. *Um landnám á Íslandi. Fjórtán erindi*. Vísindafélag Íslendinga. Reykjavík: Háskólaútgáfan.

Grönvold, Karl. 1994. 'Öskulagatímatalið, geislakol, ískjarnar og aldur fornleifa'. *Árbók hins íslenzka fornleifafélags*, 162–84.

Grönvold, Karl, Niels Óskarsson, Sigfús J. Johnsen, H. B. Clausen, C. U. Hammer, G. Bond and E. Bard. 1995. 'Tephra layers from Iceland in the Greenland GRIP ice core correlated with oceanic and land-based sediments'. *Earth and Planetary Science Letters* 135: 149–55.

Grove, J. M. 1988. *The Little Ice Age*. London: Methuen.

Grove, J. M. and R. Switsur. 1994. 'Glacial geological evidence for the Mediaeval Warm Period'. *Climatic Change* 26: 143–69.

Guðmundar saga biskups (*The Saga of Bishop Gudmund*). In *Biskupa sögur* 2, 1878.

Guðmundar saga dýra (*The Saga of Gudmund the Worthy*). In *Sturlunga saga* 1946 1: 160–212.

Guðmundsson, Guðmundur J. 1993. 'Keltnesk áhrif á íslenskt þjóðlíf'. *Saga* 31: 107–26.

[*Gulathing Law*] 'Den ældre Gulathings-Lov'. *Norges gamle love* 1: 1–118.

Gunnarsson, Gísli. 1983. *Monopoly Trade and Economic Stagnation: Studies in the Foreign Trade of Iceland, 1602–1787*. Skrifter utgivna av ekonomisk-historiska föreningen i Lund, 38. Lund: Studentlitteratur.

Gunnlaugs saga ormstungu (*The Saga of Gunnlaug Serpent-Tongue*). 1938. *Íslenzk fornrit* 3. Reykjavík: Hið íslenzka fornritafélag.

Gurevich [Gurevitj], Aron Ya. [J.]. 1968. 'Wealth and Gift-Bestowal among the Ancient Scandinavians'. *Scandinavica* 7: 126–38.

—— 1979. *Feodalismens uppkomst i Västeuropa*. Trans. Marie-Anne Sahlin. Stockholm: Tidens förlag.

Haasum, Sibylla. 1974. 'Vikingatidens Segling och Navigation'. Unpublished article.

Hænsa-Þóris saga (*Hen-Thorir's Saga*). 1938. Ed. Sigurður Nordal and Guðni Jónsson. *Íslenzk fornrit* 3. Reykjavík: Hið íslenzka fornritafélag.

Hagland, Jan Ragnar. 1996. 'Ingimundr prestr Þorgeirsson and Icelandic Runic Literacy in the Twelfth Century'. *Alvíssmál* 6: 99–108.

Hákonardóttir, Inga Huld (ed.). 1996. *Konur og kristmenn: Þættir úr kristnisögu Íslands*. Reykjavík: Hið íslenzka bókmenntafélag.

Hákonar saga Hákonarsonar (*The Saga of King Hakon Hakonarson*) *etter Sth. 8 fol., AM 325 VIII, 4 to og AM 304, 4 to*. 1977. Ed. Marina Mundt. Norrøne tekster 2. Oslo: Norsk historisk kjeldeskrift-institutt.

Hallberg, Peter. 1962. *The Icelandic Saga*. Trans. Paul Schach. Lincoln: University of Nebraska Press.

—— 1985. 'Forskningsöversikt: Från den norröna forskningsfronten'. *Samlaren* 106: 67–79.

Halldórsson, Ólafur. 1978. *Grænland í miðaldaritum*. Reykjavík: Sögufélag.

Halldórsson, Óskar. 1976. *Uppruni og þema Hrafnkels sögu*. Rannsóknastofnun í bókmenntafræði við Háskóla Íslands, Fræðirit 3. Reykjavík: Hið íslenska bókmenntafélag.

Hallsdóttir, Margrét. 1987. *Pollen analytical studies of human influence on vegetation in relation to the landnám tephra layer in southwest Iceland.* Ph.D. dissertation, Lund University.

Halstead, Paul and John O'Shea. 1989. *Bad Year Economics: Cultural Responses to Risk and Uncertainty.* Cambridge and New York: Cambridge University Press, 1989.

Halvorsen, Eyvind Fjeld. *Kulturhistoriskt lexikon för nordisk medeltid*: 'Dómr: Island', *KLNM* 3, cols. 217–18.

Harris, Marvin. 1978. *Cannibals and Kings.* New York: Random House.

Hartz, Louis. 1964. *The Founding of New Societies.* New York: Harcourt, Brace, and World.

Hastrup, Kirsten. 1979. 'Classification and Demography in Medieval Iceland'. *Ethnos* 44: 182–91.

——— 1981a. 'Cosmology and Society in Medieval Iceland: A Social Anthropological Perspective on World-View'. *Ethnologia Scandinavica*, 63–78.

——— 1981b. 'Kinship in Medieval Iceland'. *Folk* 23: 331–44.

——— 1985. *Culture and History in Medieval Iceland: An Anthropological Analysis of Structure and Change.* Oxford: Clarendon Press.

Haugen, Einar. 1976. *The Scandinavian Languages.* Cambridge: Harvard University Press.

Hedeager, Lotte. 1992. *Iron-Age Societies: From tribe to state in northern Europe, 500 BC to AD 700.* Oxford: Blackwell.

Heimskringla (History of the Kings of Norway by Snorri Sturluson). 1941–51. Ed. Bjarni Aðalbjarnarson. 3 vols. *Íslenzk fornrit* 1–3. Reykjavík: Hið íslenzka fornritafélag.

Heimskringla: History of the Kings of Norway. 1964. Trans. Lee M. Hollander. Austin: University of Texas Press.

Heinrichs, Anne. 1970. 'Über Blutrache auf Island in der Sagazeit'. *Kurz und Gut* 4: 20–23, 30–32.

Helgason, Jón. 1926. *Jón Ólafsson frá Grunnavík.* Safn Fræðafjelagsins um Ísland og Íslendinga 5. Copenhagen: S. L. Möller.

——— 1934. *Norrøn litteraturhistorie.* Copenhagen: Levin and Munksgaard.

——— 1958. *Handritaspjall.* Reykjavík: Mál og menning.

Helle, Knut. 1964. *Norge blir en stat 1130–1319*. Handbok i Norges historie. 1/3. Bergen: Universitetsforlaget.

Heller, Rolf. 1958. *Die literarische Darstellung der Frau in den Isländersagas*. Saga 2. Halle (Saale): Max Niemeyer Verlag.

———. 1963. 'Studien zu Aufbau und Stil der *Vápnfirðinga saga*'. *Arkiv för nordisk filologi* 78: 170–189.

Hen-Thorir's Saga: see *Hænsa-Þóris saga*.

Hermannsdóttir, Margrét. 1982. 'Fornleifarannsóknir í Herjólfsdal-Vestmannaeyjum 1971–81'. *Eyjaskinna: Rit Sögufélags Vestmannaeyja* 1: 83–127.

Herskovits, Melville J. 1970. *Man and His Works: The Science of Cultural Anthropology*. New York: Alfred A. Knopf.

Heusler, Andreas. 1911. *Das Strafrecht der Isländersagas*. Leipzig: Duncker und Humbolt.

———. 1912. *Zum isländischen Fehdewesen in der Sturlungzeit*. Abhandlungen der königlich preussischen Akademie der Wissenschaften, Phil.-hist. Klasse 4. Berlin: Verlag der königlichen Akademie der Wissenschaften, in Kommission bei Georg Reimer.

Historia de antiquitate regum Norwagiensium, by Theodoricus monachus. *Monumenta Historica Norvegiæ*, ed. Gustav Storm, 1880, 1–68. Christiania: A. W. Brøgger.

Hoebel, E. Adamson. 1971. 'Feud: Concept, Reality, and Method in the Study of Primitive Law'. *Essays on Modernization of Underdeveloped Societies*, ed. A. R. Desai, vol. 1: 500–513. Bombay: Thacker & Co.

Hofmann, Dietrich. 1982. 'Die mündliche Sagaerzählkunst aus pragmatischer Sicht'. *Skandinavistik* 12: 12–21.

Holtsmark, Anne. 1959. 'Det nye syn på sagaene'. *Nordisk tidskrift för vetenskap, kunst og industri* 35: 511–23.

Høyer, Jon. 1997. *Den glemte historie: Roman om en borgerkrig, der blev afværget i fristaten Island*. Copenhagen: Forum.

Hrólfs saga kraka: see *The Saga of King Hrolf Kraki*.

Hungrvaka (Hunger-waker). Ed. Guðni Jónsson. In *Byskupa sögur* 1953 1: 1–31.

Iceland 874–1974 (handbook published by the Central Bank of Iceland on the Occasion of the Eleventh Centenary of the Settlement of Iceland). 1975. Reykjavík: Ísafoldarprentsmiðja.

Iceland 1946 (handbook published by the Central Bank of Iceland), ed. Thorsteinn Thorsteinsson. 1946. Reykjavík: Ríkisprentsmiðjan Gutenberg.

Iceland 1966 (handbook published by the Central Bank of Iceland), ed. Jóhannes Nordal and Valdimar Kristinsson. 1967. Reykjavík: Ísafoldarprentsmiðja.

An Icelandic–English Dictionary. 1957. Ed. Richard Cleasby and Gudbrand Vigfusson. 2nd edn., with supplement by William A. Craigie. Oxford: Clarendon Press.

Ingimundarson, Jón Haukur. 1995. *Of Sagas and Sheep: Toward a Historical Anthropology of Social Change and Production for Market, Subsistence and Tribute in Early Iceland (10th to the 13th century).* Ph.D. dissertation. Tucson, Arizona: University of Arizona Press.

Ingólfsdóttir, Guðrún. 1990. 'Vísur í Íslendinga sögum'. *Skaldskaparmál* 1: 226–40.

—— 1994. ' "En mér þykir illt að láta risnu mína." Um virðingu kvenna og stöðu á heimili í Fljótsdæla sögu'. *Sagnaþing: Helgað Jónasi Kristjánssyni sjötugum 10. apríl 1994*, ed. Gísli Sigurðsson, Guðrún Kvaran and Sigurgeir Steingrímsson. Reykjavík: Hið íslenska bókmenntafélag, 257–67.

Ingvarsson, Lúðvík. 1970. *Refsingar á Íslandi á þjóðveldistímanum.* Reykjavík: Bókaútgáfa menningarsjóðs.

—— 1986–7. *Goðorð og goðorðsmenn.* 3 vols. Egilsstaðir: vols. I–II: 1986, vol. III: 1987.

Íslendingabók (The Book of the Icelanders) by Ari Thorgilsson. 1930. Ed. and trans. Halldór Hermannsson. Islandica 20. Ithaca: Cornell University Library.

—— 1968. Ed. Jakob Benediktsson. *Íslenzk fornrit* 1. Reykjavík: Hið íslenzka fornritafélag.

Íslendinga saga (The Saga of the Icelanders). In *Sturlunga saga* 1946 1: 229–534.

Íslendinga sögur (The Sagas of the Icelanders). 1985. Ed. Jón Torfason, Sverrir Tómasson and Örnólfur Thorsson. 2 vols. Reykjavík: Svart á hvítu.

Íslenskur söguatlas: Frá öndverðu til 18. aldar. 1990. Ed. Árni Daníel Júlíusson, Helgi Skúli Kjartjánsson and Jón Ólafur Ísberg, vol. 1. Reykjavík: Almenna bókafélagið.

Íslenzk fornrit. 1933–. Reykjavík: Hið íslenzka fornritafélag.

Jakobsson, Ármann. 1995. 'Hákon Hákonarson: Friðarkonungur eða fúl-
menni?' *Saga* 33: 166–85.

Jakobsson, Sverrir. 1998a. 'Friðarviðleitni kirkjunnar á 13. öld'. *Saga* 36: 7–
46.

——— 1998b. 'Griðamál á ófriðaröld'. *Íslenska söguþingið 28.–31. maí
1997. Ráðstefnurit I.* Ed. Guðmundur J. Guðmundsson and Eiríkur K.
Björnsson. Reykjavík: Sagnfræðistofnun Háskóla Íslands, 117–34.

——— 1999. 'Hvers konar þjóð voru Íslendingar á miðöldum?' *Skírnir* 173
(Vor): 111–40.

*Jarðvegsrof á Íslandi.*1997. Ed. Ólafur Arnalds, Elín Fjóla Thórarinsdóttir,
Sigmar Metúsalemsson, Ásgeir Jónsson, Einar Grétarsson and Arnór
Árnason. Reykjavík: Landgræðsla ríkisins and Rannsóknastofnun land-
búnaðarins.

[*Járnsíða*] 'Kong Haakon Haakonssøns islandske Lov'. *Norges gamle love*
5: 13–15. In *Grágás* 1883: 467–73.

Jesch, Judith. 1985. 'Some Early Christians in *Landnámabók*'. *The Sixth
International Saga Conference 1985*, vol. 1: 513–29. Copenhagen: Det
arnamagnæanske Institut.

——— 1991. *Women in the Viking Age*. London: The Boydell Press.

Jochens, Jenny M. 1980. 'The Church and Sexuality in Medieval Iceland',
Journal of Medieval History 6: 377–92.

——— 1985. 'En islande médiévale: Á la recherche de la famille nucléaire'.
Annales: Économies, Sociétés, Civilisations, 95–112.

——— 1986. 'The Medieval Icelandic Heroine: Fact or Fiction?' *Viator* 17:
35–50.

——— 1995. *Women in Old Norse Society*. Ithaca: Cornell University Press.

——— 1996. *Old Norse Images of Women*. Philadelphia: University of
Pennsylvania Press.

Jóhannesson, Jón. 1941. *Gerðir Landnámabókar*. Reykjavík: Félagsprent-
smiðjan.

——— 1958. *Íslendinga saga*. Vol. 2: *Fyrirlestrar og ritgerðir um tímabilið
1262–1550*. Reykjavík: Almenna bókafélagið.

——— 1974. *A History of the Old Icelandic Commonwealth: Íslendinga
saga*. Trans. Haraldur Bessason. University of Manitoba Icelandic
Studies 2. Winnipeg: University of Manitoba Press. (Translated from

Íslendinga saga, vol. 1: *Þjóðveldisöld*. Reykjavík: Almenna bókafélagið, 1956.)

Johnsen, Arne Odd. 1948. *Fra ættesamfunn til statssamfunn*. Oslo: H. Aschehoug & Co. (W. Nygaard).

Johnson, Alan and Timothy K. Earle. 1987. *The Evolution of Human Societies: From Hunting Band to Agrarian State*. Stanford: Stanford University Press.

Jónsbók: Kong Magnus Haakonssons Lovbog for Island. 1970. Ed. Ólafur Halldórsson. Copenhagen, 1904. Reprinted Odense: Odense Universitetsforlag.

Jónsson, Finnur. 1921. *Norsk-Islandske kultur- og sprogforhold i 9. og 10. árh*. Det Kgl. Danske Videnskabernes Selskab. Historisk-filologiske Meddelelser 3, Pt 2. Copenhagen: Bianco Lunos.

———— 1936. 'Islands mønt, mål og vægt'. *Mått och vikt*, ed. Svend Aakjær, 155–61. Nordisk kultur 30. Stockholm: Albert Bonniers förlag.

Jónsson, Kristján Jóhann. 1998. *Lykillinn að Njálu*. Reykjavík: Vaka Helgafell.

Jónsson, Magnús. 1940. *Guðmundar saga dýra: nokkrar athuganir um uppruna hennar og samsetning*. Studia Islandica (Íslensk fræði) 8. Reykjavík: Sigurður Nordal.

Júlíusson, Árni Daníel. 1997. 'Bønder i pestens tid. Landbrug, godsdrift og social konflikt i senmiddelalderens islandske bondesamfund'. Diss. University of Copenhagen.

Kaiser, Charlotte. 1998. *Krankheit und Krankheitsbewältigung in den Isländersagas: Medizinhistorischer Aspekt und erzähltechnische Funktion*. Cologne: Seltman & Hein Verlag.

Karlsson, Gunnar. 1972. 'Goðar og bændur'. *Saga* 10: 5–57.

———— 1975. 'Frá þjóðveldi til konungsríkis'. *Saga Íslands* 2: 1–54.

———— 1977. 'Goðar and Höfðingjar in Medieval Iceland'. *Saga-Book of the Viking Society for Northern Research* 19: 358–70.

———— 1980a. 'Icelandic Nationalism and the Inspiration of History'. *The Roots of Nationalism: Studies in Northern Europe*, ed. Rosalind Mitchison, 77–89. Edinburgh: John Donald Publishers.

———— 1980b. 'Völd og auður á 13. öld'. *Saga* 18: 5–30.

———— 1984. 'Saga í þágu samtíðar'. *Tímarit Máls og menningar* 45/1: 19–27.

—— 1985. 'Dyggðir og lestir í þjóðfélagi Íslendingasagna'. *Tímarit Máls og menningar* 46: 9–19.

—— 1986. 'Kenningin um fornt kvenfrelsi á Íslandi'. *Saga* 24: 45–77.

—— 1993. 'Um hagfræði íslenskra miðaldamanna. Athugun á búfjárverði og búfjárleigu'. *Ný saga* 4: 50–61.

—— 1994a. 'Nafngreindar höfðingjaættir í Sturlungu'. *Sagnaþing: Helgað Jónasi Kristjánssyni sjötugum 10. apríl 1994*, ed. Gísli Sigurðsson, Guðrún Kvaran and Sigurgeir Steingrímsson, vol. 1: 307–15. Reykjavík: Hið íslenska bókmenntafélag.

—— 1994b. Review of *From Sagas to Society: Comparative approaches to early Iceland*, ed. Gísli Pálsson. *Saga* 32: 281–5.

—— 1995. 'The Emergence of Nationalism in Iceland'. *Ethnicity and Nation Building in the Nordic World*, ed. Sven Tägil, 33–62. London: Hurst & Company.

—— 1996a. ' "Að hugsa er að bera saman." Um sagnfræði Sigurðar Nordals og Fragmenta ultima'. *Andvari* 121 (Nýr flokkur 38): 126–37.

—— 1996b. 'Drög að fræðilegri námsbók í íslenskri miðaldasögu'. Fourth draft. Reykjavík: Sagnfræðistofnun.

—— 1996c. 'Plague without Rats: The case of fifteenth-century Iceland'. *Journal of Medieval History* 22/3: 263–84.

Karlsson, Gunnar and Helgi Thorláksson (eds.). 1979. *Snorri: Átta alda minning*. Reykjavík: Sögufélag.

Karlsson, Stefán. 1979. 'Íslandsk bogeksport til Norge i middelalderen'. *Maal og Minne*: 1–17.

Karras, Ruth Mazo. 1988. *Slavery and Society in Medieval Scandinavia*. Philadelphia: University of Pennsylvania Press.

—— 1990. 'Concubinage and Slavery in the Viking Age', *Scandinavian Studies* 62: 141–62.

Katalog over de oldnorsk-islandske håndskrifter i det Store Kongelige Bibliotek og i Universitetsbiblioteket samt den Arnamagnæanske Samlings tilvækst 1894–1900. Ed. Kommissionen for det Arnamagnæanske Legat. 1900. Copenhagen: Gyldendalske Boghandel.

Kellogg, Robert. 1973. 'Sex and the Vernacular in Medieval Iceland'. *Proceedings of the First International Saga Conference, University of Edinburgh, 1971*, ed. Peter Foote, Hermann Pálsson and Desmond Slay, 244–57. London: Viking Society for Northern Research.

Ker, W. P. 1958. *The Dark Ages*. New York: Mentor Books.

Kern, Fritz. 1939. *Kingship and Law in the Middle Ages*. Trans. S. B. Chrimes. Oxford: Blackwell.

Kjartansson, Helgi Skúli. 1975. 'Spáð í Pýramiða: Um Mannfjöldasögu Íslands á 17. Öld'. *Afmælisrit Björns Sigfússonar*. Reykjavík: Sögufélagið: 120–34.

——— 1989. *Fjöldi goðorða samkvæmt Grágás*. Félag áhugamanna um réttarsögu. *Erindi og greinar 26*.

KLNM: see *Kulturhistoriskt lexikon för nordisk medeltid*.

Knirk, James. 1981. *Oratory in the Kings' Sagas*. Oslo: Universitetsforlaget.

Knudsen, Anne. 1985. 'Internal Unrest: Corsican vendetta – a structured catastrophe'. *Folk* 27: 65–70.

Krag, Claus. 1996. *Vikingtid og rikssamling 800–1300*. Aschehougs Noregs-historie, vol. 2. Oslo.

Kress, Helga. 1977. 'Ekki höfu vér kvennaskap: Nokkrar laustengdar athuganir um karlmennsku og kvenhatur í Njálu'. *Sjötíu ritgerðir helgaðar Jakobi Benediktssyni 20. júlí 1977*, ed. Einar G. Pétursson and Jónas Kristjánsson, Pt. 1: 293–313. Reykjavík: Stofnun Árna Magnús-sonar.

——— 1993. *Máttugar meyjar*. Íslensk fornbókmenntasaga. Reykjavík: Háskólaútgáfan.

Kristiansen, Kristian. 1991. 'Chieftains, states, and systems of social evol-ution'. Timothy Earle (ed.), *Chiefdoms: Power, Economy and Ideology*. Cambridge: Cambridge University Press, 16–43.

Kristjánsson, Jónas. 1975. 'Bókmenntasaga'. *Saga Íslands* 2: 147–258.

——— 1978. 'Bókmenntasaga'. *Saga Íslands*: 3: 259–350.

——— 1980. 'Annálar og íslendingasögur'. *Gripla* 4: 295–319.

——— 1986. 'The Roots of the Sagas'. *Sagnaskemmtun: Studies in Honour of Hermann Pálsson on his 65th Birthday*, 26th May 1986, ed. Rudolf Simek, Jónas Kristjánsson and Hans Bekker-Nielsen, 183–200. Philolog-ica Germanica 8. Vienna: Hermann Böhlaus Nachf.

Kristjánsson, Lúðvík. 1964. 'Grænlenzki landnemaflotinn og Breiðfirzki bát-urinn'. *Árbók hins íslenzka fornleifafélags, 1964*: 20–68.

Kristni saga (The Saga of the Conversion). 1953. Ed. Guðni Jónsson. *Íslend-inga sögur*, vol. 1, *Landssaga og Landnám*. (Akureyri): Íslendinga-sagnaútgáfan.

BIBLIOGRAPHY

Kulturhistoriskt lexikon för nordisk medeltid (KLNM). 1956–78. 22 volumes. Malmö: Allhems förlag.

Kurlansky, Mark. 1997. *Cod: A Biography of the Fish That Changed the World*. New York: Walker and Co.

Kværness, Gunhild. 1996. *Blote kan ein gjere om det berre skjer í løynd: Kristenrettane i Gulatingslova og Grágás of forholdet mellom dei*. Kult nr. 65. Oslo.

Lamb, H. H. 1995. *Climate, History and the Modern World*. New York: Routledge.

Landnámabók (The Book of Settlements). 1968. Ed. Jakob Benediktsson. *Íslenzk fornrit* 1. Reykjavík: Hið íslenzka fornritafélag.

Larsen, Guðrún. 1996. 'Gjöskutímatal og gjöskulög frá tíma norræns landnáms á Íslandi'. G. A. Grímsdóttir (ed.), *Um Landnám á Íslandi*, Ráðstefnurit V, Societas scientarum Islandica, Reykjavík, 81–106.

Lárusson, Björn. 1961. 'Valuation and Distribution of Landed Property in Iceland'. *Economy and History* 4: 34–64.

—— 1967. *The Old Icelandic Land Registers*. Lund: C. W. K. Gleerup.

Lárusson, Magnús Már. 1958. 'Íslenzkar mælieiningar'. *Skírnir* 132: 208–45.

—— 1960. 'On the So-Called "Armenian" Bishops'. *Íslenzk fræði (Studia Islandica)* 18: 23–38.

—— 1967. 'Þrístirnið á norðurlöndum'. *Skírnir* 141: 28–33.

—— 1971. 'Á höfuðbólum landsins'. *Saga* 9: 40–90.

—— *Kulturhistoriskt lexikon för nordisk medeltid*: 'Fabrica: Island', *KLNM* 4, cols. 120–22; 'Fredløshed: Island', *KLNM* 4, cols. 603–608; 'Hreppr', *KLNM* 7, cols. 17–22; 'Kloster: Island', *KLNM* 8, cols. 544–6; 'Odelsrett: Island', *KLNM* 12, cols. 499–502.

Lárusson, Magnús Már and Lars Hamre. *Kulturhistoriskt lexikon för nordisk medeltid*: 'Handarband; handsal: Island', *KLNM* 6, cols. 110–14.

Lárusson, Ólafur. 1923. *Grágás og lögbækurnar*. Fylgir Árbók Háskóla Íslands, 1922. Reykjavík: Prentsmiðjan Gutenberg, 1923.

—— 1944. *Byggð og saga*. Reykjavík: Ísafoldaprentsmiðjan.

—— 1958a. *Lög og saga*. Reykjavík: Hlaðbúð. Translated into Norwegian by Knut Helle as *Lov og ting, Islands forfatning og lover i fristatstiden*. Bergen and Oslo: Universitetsforlaget, 1960.

—— 1958b. 'On *Grágás* – the Oldest Icelandic Code of Law'. Proceedings of the Third Viking Congress, Reykjavík, 1956. *Árbók hins íslenzka fornleifafélags*, 77–89.

Laxdæla saga. 1934. Ed. Einar Ól. Sveinsson. *Íslenzk fornrit* 5. Reykjavík: Hið íslenzka fornritafélag.

Laxdæla Saga. 1964. Trans. A. Margaret Arent. American Scandinavian Foundation. New York: University of Washington Press.

—— 1969. Trans. Magnus Magnusson and Hermann Pálsson. New York: Penguin Books.

Laxness, Halldór Kiljan. 1934–5. *Sjálfstætt fólk*. 2 vols. Reykjavík: E. P. Briem, 2nd edn. Helgafell, 1952. English translation: *Independent People*. Trans. J. A. Thompson. New York: Alfred A. Knopf, 1946.

—— 1948. *Atómstöðin*. Reykjavík: Helgafell, 2nd edn. 1961. English translation: *The Atom Station*. Trans. Magnus Magnusson. Sag Harbor, New York: Second Chance Press, 1982.

—— 1957. *Íslandsklukkan*. 2nd edn. Reykjavík: Helgafell.

LeVine, Robert A. 1960. 'The Internalization of Political Values in Stateless Societies'. *Human Organization* 19: 51–8.

The Life of Gudmund the Good, Bishop of Holar (Prestssaga Guðmundar góða). 1942. Trans. G. Turville-Petre and E. S. Olszewska. Coventry: Viking Society for Northern Research.

Líndal, Sigurður. 1969. 'Sendiför Úlfljóts: Ásamt nokkrum athugasemdum um landnám Ingólfs Arnarsonar'. *Skírnir* 143: 5–26.

—— 1974. 'Upphaf kristni og kirkju'. *Saga Íslands* 1: 227–88.

—— (ed.). 1974–8. *Saga Íslands*. 3 vols. Reykjavík: Hið íslenzka bók-menntafélag, Sögufélagið.

—— 1981. 'Early Democratic Traditions in the Nordic Countries'. *Nordic Democracy: Ideas, Issues, and Institutions*, ed. Erik Allardt *et al.*, 15–43. Copenhagen: Det Danske Selskab.

—— 1984. 'Lög og lagasetning í íslenzka Þjóðveldinu'. *Skírnir* 158: 121–58.

Lipset, Seymour M. 1963. *The First New Nation: The United States in Historical and Comparative Perspective*. New York: Basic Books.

Ljósvetninga saga (The Saga of the People of Ljosavatn). 1940. Ed. Björn Sigfússon. *Íslenzk fornrit* 10. Reykjavík: Hið íslenzka fornritafélag.

Lönnroth, Lars. 1976. *Njál's Saga: A Critical Introduction*. Berkeley, Los Angeles and London: University of California Press.

Lord, Albert. 1960. *The Singer of Tales*. Harvard Studies in Comparative Literature 24. Cambridge: Harvard University Press.

Lunden, Kåre. 1980. 'Sagakvinner og sosialvictorianarar: Kvinnehistoriske observasjonar'. *Kjettarar, prestar og sagakvinner: Om historie og historie-produksjon*, 46–61. Oslo: Universitetsforlaget.

Magerøy, Hallvard. 1965. *Norsk–islandske problem*. Omstridde spørsmål i Nordens historie 3. Foreningene Nordens historiske publikasjoner 4. Oslo: Universitetsforlaget.

—— 1978. 'Kvar står sagaforskningen i dag?' *Nordisk Tidskrift för vetenskap, konst og industri* 54/3: 164–75.

Magnúsdóttir, Auður G. 1988. 'Ástir og völd: Frillulífi á Íslandi á Þjóðveldisöld'. *Ný saga*. Tímarit sögufélags 2: 4–12.

Magnússon, Thórr. 1966. 'Bátkumlið í Vatnsdal'. *Árbók hins íslenzka fornleifafélags*: 1–32.

Maizels, J. and C. Caseldine (eds.). 1991. *Environmental Change in Iceland: Past and Present*. Dordrecht: Kluwer Academic Publishers.

Mann, Michael. 1987. *The Sources of Social Power*. Cambridge: Cambridge University Press.

Mannfjöldi, mannafli og tekjur. 1984. Reykjavík: Framkvæmdastofnun ríkisins.

Marcus, G. J. 1957. 'The Norse Traffic with Iceland'. *Economic History Review*, 2nd series, 9: 408–19.

Martin, John Stanley. 1994. 'The function of bishops in the early Icelandic Church'. *Samtíðarsögur: The Contemporary Sagas*, vol. II. Níunda Alþjóðlega Fornsagnaþingið, 561–76. Reykjavík: Stofnun Árna Magnússonar.

Maurer, Konrad. 1852. *Die Entstehung des isländischen Staats und seiner Verfassung*. Munich: Christian Kaiser.

—— 1869. *Die Quellenzeugnisse über das erste Landrecht und über die Ordnung der Bezirksverfassung des isländischen Freistaates*. Abhandlungen der königlich-bayerischen Akademie der Wissenschaften, 1. Classe. Vol. 12, Pt. 1. Munich: F. Straub.

—— 1874. *Island: von seiner ersten Entdeckung bis zum Untergange des Freistaats*. Munich: Christian Kaiser.

Mazo, Jeffrey Alan. 1991. *Folk Traditions and the Emergence of Ethnic Identity in Medieval Iceland*. Ph.D. dissertation, University of California, Los Angeles.

McGovern, Thomas H. 1990. 'The Archaeology of the Norse North Atlantic'. *Annual Review of Anthropology* 19: 331–51.

McGovern, Thomas H., G. F. Bigelow, T. Amorosi and D. Russell. 1988. 'Northern Islands, Human Error, and Environmental Degradation: A View of Social and Ecological Change in the Medieval North Atlantic'. *Human Ecology* 16: 225–70.

Middleton, John and David Tait (eds.). 1958. *Tribes without Rulers: Studies in African Segmentary Systems*. London: Routledge & Kegan Paul.

Miller, William I. 1983. 'Choosing the Avenger: Some Aspects of the Bloodfeud in Medieval Iceland and England'. *Law and History Review* 1: 159–204.

—— 1984. 'Avoiding Legal Judgment: The Submission of Disputes to Arbitration in Medieval Iceland'. *American Journal of Legal History* 28: 95–134.

—— 1986. 'Gift, Sale, Payment, Raid'. *Speculum*: 18–50.

—— 1990. *Blood-taking and Peacemaking: Feud, Law and Society in Saga Iceland* (Chicago: University of Chicago Press).

Mitchell, Stephen A. 1991. *Heroic Sagas and Ballads*. Ithaca: Cornell University Press.

Moberg, Ove. 1974. 'Bröderna Weibull och den isländska traditionen'. *Scripta Islandica* 25: 8–22.

Mundal, Else. 1975. 'Til debatten om islendingasogene'. *Maal og Minne*: 105–26.

—— (ed.). 1977. *Sagadebatt*. Oslo, Bergen and Tromsø: Universitetsforlaget.

—— 1982. 'Kvinnebiletet i nokre mellomaldergenrar. Eit opposisjonelt kvinnesyn?' *Edda* 72: 341–71.

—— 1992. 'Norrønn litteratur som kjelde til nordisk kvinnehistorie'. *Kvinnospår i medeltiden*, ed. Inger Lövkrona, 93–113. Kvinnovetenskapliga studier 1. Lund: Lund University Press.

Mundt, Marina. 1973. 'Pleading the Cause of Hænsa-Þórir'. *Alþjóðlegt fornsagnaþing, Reykjavík, 1973*. Reykjavík: International Association for Scandinavian Studies.

Musset, Lucien. 1951. *Les peuples scandinaves au moyen âge*. Paris: Presses Universitaires de France.

——— 1997. *Nordica et Normannica: Receueil d'études sur la Scandinavie ancienne et médiévale.* Ed. François Dillmann, Preface by Michel Fleury. Paris: Société des études nordiques.

Njáls saga (Brennu-Njáls saga). 1954. Ed. Einar Ól. Sveinsson. *Íslenzk fornrit* 12. Reykjavík: Hið íslenzka fornritafélag.

Njal's Saga. 1960. Trans. Magnus Magnusson and Hermann Pálsson. New York: Penguin Books.

Njarðvík, Njörður P. 1978. *Birth of a Nation: The Story of the Icelandic Commonwealth.* Trans. John Porter. Iceland Review History Series. Reykjavík: Iceland Review.

Nordal, Guðrún. 1989. ' "Eitt sinn skal hver deyja." Dráp og dauðalýsingar í Íslendinga sögu'. *Skírnir* 163 (Spring): 72–94.

——— 1998. *Ethics and Action in Thirteenth-Century Iceland.* The Viking Collection. Studies in Northern Civilization 10. Odense: Odense University Press.

Nordal, Sigurður. 1940. *Hrafnkatla.* Íslensk fræði (Studia Islandica) 7. Reykjavík: Ísafoldarprentsmiðja.

——— 1942. *Íslenzk menning.* Reykjavík: Mál og menning.

——— 1952. 'Time and Vellum'. *Bulletin of the Modern Humanities Research Association* 24: 15–26.

——— 1953. 'Sagalitteraturen'. *Litteraturhistorie,* ed. Sigurður Nordal, 180–273. Nordisk Kultur 8B. Stockholm: Albert Bonniers förlag.

——— 1957. *The Historical Element in the Icelandic Family Sagas.* W. P. Ker Memorial Lecture 15. Glasgow: Jackson, Son, and Co., Norwegian translation: 'Det historiske element i islendinge sagaene'. *Rikssamling og kristendom,* vol. 1 of *Norske historikere i utvalg,* 126–43. Oslo: Universitetsforlaget, 1967.

——— 1958. *Hrafnkels saga Freysgoða: A Study.* Trans. R. George Thomas. Cardiff: University of Wales Press.

Norges gamle love indtil 1387. 1846–1895. 5 vols. Vols. 1–3, ed. R. Keyser and P. A. Munch. Vol. 4, ed. Gustav Storm. Vol. 5, ed. Gustav Storm and Ebbe Herzberg. Christiania: Chr. Gröndahl.

Ogilvie, A. E. J. 1984. 'The Past Climate and the Sea-Ice Record from Iceland: Part 1: Data to AD 1780'. *Climatic Change* 6: 131–52.

——— 1990. 'Climatic Changes in Iceland AD 865–1598'. *Acta Archaeologica* 60: 233–51.

Ólafs saga Tryggvasonar (*The Saga of King Olaf Tryggvason*), by Odd Snorrason of Thingeyrar. 1974. *Olav Tryggvasons saga: etter AM 310 qv*. Ed. Anne Holtsmark. Oslo: Selskapet til utgivelse av gamle norske håndskrifter.

Óláfs saga Tryggvasonar en mesta (*The Longest Saga of King Olaf Tryggvason*). 1958–1961. 2 vols. Ed. Ólafur Halldórsson. Editiones Arnamagnæanæ, ser. A 1–2. Copenhagen: Munksgaard.

Ólafsson, Guðmundur. 1979. 'Grelutóttir. Landnámsbær á Eyri við Arnarfjörð'. *Árbók hins íslenzka fornleifafélags*, 25–73.

———— 1982. *Torfbærinn frá eldaskála til burstabær*. Reykjavík: Þjóðminjasafnið Íslands.

Ólason, Vésteinn. 1971. 'Nokkrar athugasemdir um Eyrbyggja sögu'. *Skírnir* 145: 5–25.

———— 1983. *Sjálfstætt fólk*. Bókmenntakver Máls og menningar. Reykjavík: Mál og menning.

———— 1984. 'Íslensk sagnalist: Erlendur lærdómur'. *Tímarit Máls og menningar* 45: 174–89.

———— 1987. 'Norrøn litteratur som historisk kildemateriale'. *Kilderne til den tidlig middelalders historie. Rapporter til den XX nordiske historikerkongress Reykjavík 1987*. Ritsafn: Sagnfræðistofnunar 18: 30–47.

———— 1993a. 'Íslendingasögur'. *Medieval Scandinavia: An Encyclopedia*, ed. P. Pulsiano and K. Wolf, 333–6. New York: Garland Publishing.

———— 1993b. 'Íslendingasögur og þættir', *Íslensk bókmenntasaga I*. Reykjavík: Mál og menning.

———— 1998. *Dialogues with the Viking Age: Narration and Representation in the Sagas of the Icelanders*. Trans. Andrew Wawn. Reykjavík: Mál og menning. Translation of: *Samræður við frásagnarlíst: Íslendingasögur og fortíðarmynd*. Reykjavík: Mál og menning, 1998.

Olgeirsson, Einar. 1954. *Ættasamfélag og ríkisvald í þjóðveldi íslendinga*. Þriðji bókaflokkar Máls og menningar 5. Reykjavík: Heimskringla.

Ölkofra þáttr (*The Tale of Ale-Hood*). 1950. Ed. Jón Jóhannesson. *Íslenzk fornrit* 11. Reykjavík: Hið íslenzka fornritafélag.

Olrik, Axel. 1909. 'Epische Gesetze der Volksdichtung'. *Zeitschrift für deutsches Altertum und deutsche Literatur* 51: 1–12.

Olsen, Olaf. 1966. *Hørg, hov og kirke: Historiske og arkæologiske vikingetidsstudier*. Copenhagen: Gad.

Ong, Walter J. 1982. *Orality and Literacy: The Technologizing of the Word*. New York: Methuen.

Orning, Hans Jacob. 1997. 'Statsutvikling i Norge og på Island i høymiddelalderen belyst ut fra en analyse av Þórðr Kakali Sighvatssons og Sverre Sigurdssons vei til makten', *Historisk tidskrift* 4: 469–86.

Österberg, Eva. 1989. 'Tystnadens strategi. Miljö och mentalitet i de isländska sagorna'. *Historisk tidskrift* 2: 165–85.

―――― 1991. 'Strategies of Silence: Milieu and mentality in the Icelandic sagas'. *Mentalities and Other Realities: Essays in Medieval and Early Modern Scandinavian History*, 9–30. Lund Studies in International History 28. Lund: Lund University Press.

Øye, Ingvild. 1990. 'Middelalderkvinner i tverrfaglig belysning'. *Historisk tidskrift* 4: 435–54.

Páls saga biskups (The Saga of Bishop Pal). In *Biskupa sögur* 1: 125–48.

Pálsson, Gísli (ed.). 1992. *From Sagas to Society: Comparative Approaches to Early Iceland*. London: Hisarlik Press.

Pálsson, Heimir. 1998. *Lykill að Íslendingasögum*. Reykjavík: Mál og menning.

Pálsson, Hermann. 1970. *Tólfta öldin: þættir um menn og málefni*. Reykjavík: Prentsmiðja Jóns Helgasonar.

―――― 1996. *Keltar á Íslandi*. Reykjavík: Háskólaútgáfan.

The Penguin Historical Atlas of the Vikings. 1995. Ed. John Haywood. London: Penguin Books.

Peters, Emyrs L. 1967. 'Some Structural Aspects of the Feud among Camelherding Bedouin of Cyrenaica'. *Africa* 37: 261–82.

Pétursson, Einar G. 1985. 'Kirkjulegar ástæður fyrir ritun Landnámu'. *The Sixth International Saga Conference 1985*, vol. 1: 279–97. Copenhagen: Det arnamagnæanske Institut.

Phillpotts, Bertha S. 1913. *Kindred and Clan in the Middle Ages and After: A Study in the Sociology of the Teutonic Races*. Cambridge University Press.

The Poetic Edda. 1996. Trans. Carolyne Larrington. Oxford: Clarendon Press.

Posner, Richard A. 1983. 'A Theory of Primitive Society', *The Economics of Justice*. Cambridge, Mass.: Harvard University Press, 146–73.

Pospísil, Leopold. 1974. *Anthropology of Law: A Comparative Theory*. New Haven: Human Relations Area File Press.

Prestssaga Guðmundar góða (*The Saga of the Priest Gudmund the Good*). In *Sturlunga saga* 1946 1: 116–59. See also *The Life of Gudmund the Good*.

Rader, Trout. 1971. *The Economics of Feudalism*. New York: Gordon and Breach.

Rafnsson, Sveinbjörn. 1974. *Studier i Landnámabók: Kritiska bidrag till den isländska fristatstidens historia. Bibliotheca historica Lundensis* 31. Lund: C. W. K. Gleerup.

—— 1977a. 'Grágás og Digesta Iustiniani'. *Sjötíu ritgerðir helgaðar Jakobi Benediktssyni 20. júlí 1977*, ed. Einar G. Pétursson and Jónas Kristjánsson, Pt. 2: 720–32. Reykjavík: Stofnun Árna Magnússonar.

—— 1977b. 'Um Kristniboðsþættina'. *Gripla* 2: 19–31.

—— 1993. *Páll Jónsson Skálholtsbiskup: Nokkrar athuganir á sögu hans og kirkustjórn*. Rit Sagnfræðistofnunnar 33. Reykjavík.

Ross, Margaret Clunies. 1992. 'Women and Power in the Scandinavian Sagas'. *Stereotypes of Women in Power*, ed. Barbara Garlick *et al.*, 105–19. *Contributions in Women's Studies* 125. New York: Greenwood Press.

Roussell, Aage. 1943. 'Stöng, Þjórsárdalur'. *Forntida gårdar i Island*, Copenhagen.

Rubow, Paul V. 1936. 'Den islandske Familieroman og den islandske saga-litterature i nutiden'. *Tilskueren* 45/1 (1928): 347–57, 45/2 (1928): 170–74. Reprinted in his *Små kritiske breve*. Copenhagen: Gyldendal.

Runólfsson, Sveinn. 1987. 'Land Reclamation in Iceland'. *Arctic and Alpine Research* 19: 514–17.

Saga Íslands: see Líndal, Sigurður (ed.).

The Saga of Bishop Gudmund: see *Guðmundar saga biskups*.

The Saga of Eirik the Red: see *Eiríks saga rauða*.

The Saga of Gudmund the Worthy: see *Guðmundar saga dýra*.

The Saga of Gunnlaug Serpent-Tongue: see *Gunnlaugs saga ormstungu*.

The Saga of Hvamm-Sturla: see *Sturlu saga*.

The Saga of King Hrolf Kraki. 1998. Trans. Jesse L. Byock. London and New York: Penguin Books.

The Saga of the Confederates: see *Bandamanna saga*.

The Saga of the Icelanders: see *Íslendinga saga*.

The Sagas of the People of Eyjafjord: see *Eyfirðinga sögur*.

The Saga of the People of Eyri: see *Eyrbyggja saga*.

The Saga of the People of Ljosavatn: see *Ljósvetninga saga*.

The Saga of the People of Vatnsdal: see *Vatnsdæla saga*.

The Saga of the People of Weapon's Fjord: see *Vápnfirðinga saga*.

The Saga of the Sturlungs: see *Sturlunga saga*.

The Saga of the Foster-Brothers: see *Fóstbræðra saga*.

The Saga of the Volsungs: The Norse Epic of Sigurd the Dragon Slayer. 1999. Trans. Jesse L. Byock. London and New York: Penguin Books.

The Saga of Thorgils and Haflidi: see *Þorgils saga ok Haflíða*.

The Saga of Thorgils Skardi: see *Þorgils saga skarða*.

Sahlins, Marshall D. 1977. 'Culture and Environment: The Study of Cultural Ecology'. *Horizons of Anthropology*, ed. Sol Tax and Leslie G. Freeman, 215–31. 2nd edn. Chicago: Aldine Publishing Company.

Samsonarson, Jón Marinó. 1958. 'Var Gissur Þorvaldsson jarl yfir öllu Íslandi?' *Saga* 2: 326–65.

Sawyer, Birgit and Peter. 1993. *Medieval Scandinavia: From Conversion to Reformation circa 800–1500*. Minneapolis: University of Minnesota Press.

Schier, Kurt. 1975. 'Iceland and the Rise of Literature in "Terra Nova"'. *Gripla* 1: 168–81.

Schulman, Jana K. 1997. 'Make Me a Match: Motifs of Betrothal in the Sagas of the Icelanders'. *Scandinavian Studies* 69/3: 296–321.

Scovazzi, Marco. 1960. *La saga di Hrafnkell e il problema delle saghe islandesi*. Arona: Paideia.

Searle, Eleanor. 1984. 'Fact and Pattern in Heroic History: Dudo of Saint-Quentin'. *Viator* 15: 119–37.

See, Klaus von. 1964. *Altnordische Rechtswörter: Philologische Studien zur Rechtsauffassung und Rechtsgesinnung der Germanen*. Hermaea, 2nd series, 16. Tübingen: Max Niemeyer Verlag.

Seggewiss, Hermann-Josef. 1978. *Goði und Höfðingi: Die literarische Darstellung und Funktion von Gode und Häuptling in den Isländersagas*. Europäische Hochschulschriften Reihe 1. Deutsche Literatur und Germanistik 259. Frankfurt am Main: Peter Lang.

Service, Elman R. 1962. *Primitive Social Organization: An Evolutionary Perspective*. New York: Random House.

—— 1975. *Origins of the State and Civilization*. New York: W. W. Norton.

Sigfússon, Björn. 1944. *Um Íslendingabók*. Reykjavík: Víkingsprent.

―――― 1960. 'Full goðorð og forn og heimildir frá 12. öld'. *Saga* 3: 48–75.

―――― 1964. 'Millilanda-samningur Íslendinga frá Ólafi digra til Hákonar gamla'. *Saga* 4: 87–120.

―――― 1977. 'Gamli sáttmáli endursvarinn 1302'. *Sjötíu ritgerðir helgaðar Jakobi Benediktssyni 20. júlí 1977*, ed. Einar G. Pétursson and Jónas Kristjánsson, Pt. 1: 121–37. Reykjavík: Stofnun Árna Magnússonar.

Sigurðardóttir, Anna. 1981. 'Islandske kvinders økonomiske retslige stilling i middelalderen'. *Kvinnans ekonomiska ställning under nordisk medeltid*, ed. Hedda Gunneng and Birgit Strand, 89–104. Lindome: Kompendiet.

―――― 1985. *Vinna kvenna á Íslandi í 1100 ár*. Reykjavík: Kvennasögusafn.

―――― 1988. *Allt hafði annan róm áður í páfadóm. Nunnuklausturinn tvö á Íslandi á miðöldum og brot úr kristnisögu*. Reykjavík: Kvennasögusafn.

Sigurðardóttir, Sigríður 1996–7. 'Um Náðhús'. *Árbók hins íslenzka fornleifafélags*, 69–93.

Sigurðsson, Gísli. 1988. *Gaelic Influence in Iceland: Historical and Literary Contacts; A Survey of Research. Studica Islandica* 46. Reykjavík: Bókaútgáfa menningarsjóðs.

―――― 1994. 'Bók í stað lögsögumanns: Valdabarátta kirkju og veraldlegra höfðingja?' *Sagnaþing: Helgað Jónasi Kristjánssyni sjötugum 10. apríl 1994*, ed. Gísli Sigurðsson, Guðrún Kvaran and Sigurgeir Steingrímsson, 207–33. Reykjavík: Hið íslenska bókmenntafélag.

Sigurðsson, Gísli, Guðrún Kvaran and Sigurgeir Steingrímsson (eds.). 1994. *Sagnaþing: Helgað Jónasi Kristjánssyni sjötugum 10. apríl 1994*. Reykjavík: Hið íslenska bókmenntafélag.

Sigurðsson, Jón Viðar. 1989. *Frá goðorðum til ríkja: Þróun goðavalds á 12. og 13. öld*. Ed. Bergsteinn Jónsson. Sagnfræðirannsóknir, *Studia historica* 10. Reykjavík.

―――― 1992. 'Friendship in the Icelandic Commonwealth'. *From Sagas to Society: Comparative Approaches to Early Iceland*, ed. Gísli Pálsson, 205–15. London: Hisarlik Press.

―――― 1993. *Goder og maktforhold på Island i fristatstiden*. Diss. Historisk Institut, Bergen: University of Bergen.

Skúlason, Páll. 1981. 'Hugleiðingar um heimspeki og frásagnir'. *Skírnir* 155: 6–28.

Smith, Kevin P. 1995. 'Landnám: The settlement of Iceland in archaeological and historical perspective'. World Archaeology 26/3: 319–46.

Smith, Kevin P. and Jeffrey R. Parsons. 1989. 'Regional Archaeological Research in Iceland: Potentials and Possibilities'. E. Paul Durrenberger and Gísli Pálsson (eds.), The Anthropology of Iceland, 179–202. Iowa City: University of Iowa Press.

Sneglu Halla þáttr (The Tale of Snegla Halli). 1956. Íslenzk fornrit 9. Reykjavík: Hið íslenzka fornritafélag.

Solvason, Birgir T. Runolfsson. 1991. Ordered Anarchy, State and Rent-Seeking: The Icelandic Commonwealth, 930–1262. Dissertation. Virginia: George Mason University.

—— 1993. 'Institutional Evolution in the Icelandic Commonwealth'. Constitutional Political Economy 4/1: 97–125.

Sørensen, Preben Meulengracht. 1974. 'Sagan um Ingólf og Hjörleif: Athugasemdir um söguskoðun íslendinga á seinni hluta þjóðveldisaldar'. Skírnir 148: 20–40.

—— 1977. Saga og samfund: En indføring i oldislandsk litteratur. Copenhagen: Berlingske forlag.

—— 1993. Fortælling og ære: Studier i islændingesagaerne. Århus: Århus Universitetsforlag, 2nd edn. Oslo, 1995.

Steblin-Kamenskij, M. I. 1973. The Saga Mind. Trans. Kenneth H. Ober. Odense: Odense University Press.

Stefánsson, Magnús. 1975. 'Kirkjuvald eflist'. Saga Íslands 2: 55–144.

—— 1978. 'Frá goðakirkju til Biskupskirkju'. Saga Íslands 3: 111–257.

—— 1993. 'Iceland'. Medieval Scandinavia: An Encyclopedia, ed. P. Pulsiano and K. Wolf. New York: Garland Publishing, 311–19.

Steffensen, Jón. 1975. Menning og Meinsemdir: Ritgerðasafn um mótunarsögu íslenskrar þjóðar og baráttu hennar við hungur og sóttir. Reykjavík: Sögufélagið.

Steinnes, Asgaut. 1936. 'Mál, vekt og verderekning i Norge i mellomalderen og ei tid etter'. Mått och vikt, ed. Svend Aakjær, 84–154. Nordisk Kultur 30. Stockholm: Albert Bonniers förlag.

Storm, Gustav (ed.). 1888. Islandske annalar indtil 1578. Kristiania: Udgivne for det norske historiske kildeskriftfond.

Strömbäck, Dag. 1975. The Conversion of Iceland: A Survey. Trans. and annotated by Peter Foote. London: Viking Society for Northern Research.

Sturlunga saga (The Saga of the Sturlungs). 1946. Ed. Jón Jóhannesson, Magnús Finnbogason and Kristján Eldjárn. 2 vols. Reykjavík: Sturlungu-útgáfan.

—— 1988. Ed. Örnólfur Thorsson. 3 vols. Reykjavík: Svart á hvítu.

Sturlunga Saga. 1970–74. Trans. Julia McGrew and R. George Thomas. 2 vols. American Scandinavian Foundation Library of Scandinavian Literature 9–10. New York: Twayne Publishers.

Sturlu saga (The Saga of Hvamm-Sturla). In *Sturlunga saga* 1946 1: 63–114.

Stutz, Ulrich. 1895. *Geschichte des kirchlichen Benefizialwesens von seinen Anfängen bis auf die Zeit Alexanders III*. Reprinted 1961. Aalen: Scientia.

Sveinbjarnardóttir, Guðrún. 1992. *Farm Abandonment in Medieval and Post-Medieval Iceland: An Interdisciplinary Study*. Oxbow Monograph 17. Oxford: Oxbow Books.

Sveinsson, Einar Ól. 1953. *The Age of the Sturlungs: Icelandic Civilization in the Thirteenth Century*. Trans. Jóhann S. Hannesson. *Islandica* 36. Ithaca: Cornell University Press.

—— 1965. *Ritunartími íslendingasagna: Rök og rannsóknaraðferð*. Reykjavík: Hið íslenzka bókmenntafélag.

—— *Kulturhistoriskt lexikon för nordisk medeltid*: 'Íslendingasögur', *KLNM* 7, cols. 496–513.

The Tale of Ale-Hood: see *Ölkofra þáttr*.

The Tale of Snegla Halli: see *Sneglu Halla þáttr*.

Thirslund, Søren. 1998. *Viking Navigation: Sun-compass guided Norsemen first to America*. Skjern: Gullanders Bogtrykkeri.

Thórarinsson, Sigurður. 1974. 'Sambúð lands og lýðs í ellefu aldir'. *Saga Íslands* 1: 27–97.

—— 1981. 'The application of tephrochronology in Iceland'. S. Self and R. S. J. Sparks (eds.), *Tephra Studies*, 109–34. Dordrecht: Reidel.

Thórarinsson, Thórarinn. 1974. 'Þjóðin lifði en skógurinn dó'. *Ársrit skóg-ræktarfélags Íslands* 74: 16–29.

Þórðar saga kakala (The Saga of Thord Kakali). In *Sturlunga saga* 1946 2: 1–86.

Thórðarson, Matthías. 1932. 'Bólstaður við Álftafjörð: Skýrsla um rannsókn 1931'. *Árbók hins íslenzka fornleifafélags*, 1–28.

Þorgils saga ok Hafliða (The Saga of Thorgils and Haflidi). In *Sturlunga saga* 1946 1: 12–50.

Þorgils saga skarða (*The Saga of Thorgils Skardi*). In *Sturlunga saga* 1946 2: 104–226.

Thorgilsson, Ari: see *Íslendingabók*.

Thorkelsson, Thorkel. 1930. 'Alþingi árið 955'. *Skírnir* 104: 49–67.

Þorláks biskups saga hin elzta (*The Older Saga of Bishop Thorlak*). In *Biskupa sögur* 1858, vol. 1: 87–124. Ed. Hið íslenzka bókmentafélag. Copenhagen: S. L. Möller.

Þorláks biskups saga hin ýngri (*The Younger Saga of Bishop Thorlak*). In *Biskupa sögur* 1858, vol. 1: 261–332. Ed. Hið íslenzka bókmentafélag. Copenhagen: S. L. Möller.

Thorláksson, Helgi. 1979a. 'Snorri Sturluson og Oddaverjar'. *Snorri: Átta alda minning*. Ed. Gunnar Karlsson and Helgi Thorláksson, 53–88. Reykjavík: Sögufélag.

———— 1979b. 'Stórbændur gegn goðum: Hugleiðingar um goðavald, konungsvald og sjálfræðishug bænda um miðbik 13. aldar'. *Söguslóðir: Afmælisrit helgað Ólafi Hanssyni sjötugum 18. september 1979*, ed. Bergsteinn Jónsson, Einar Laxness and Heimir Thorleifsson, 227–50. Reykjavík: Sögufélag.

———— 1981. 'Arbeidskvinnens, särlig veverskens, økonomiske stilling på Island i middelalderen'. *Kvinnans ekonomiska ställning under nordisk medeltid*, ed. Hedda Gunneng and Birgit Strand, 50–65. Lindome: Kompendiet.

———— 1982. 'Stéttir, auður og völd á 12. og 13. öld'. *Saga* 20: 63–113.

———— 1987. 'Að vita sann á sögunum: Hvað vitneskju geta Íslendingasögurnar veit um íslenskt þjóðfélag fyrir 1200'. *Ný saga* 1: 87–96.

———— 1988. 'Stéttakúgun eða samfylking bænda? Söguskoðun Björns Þorsteinssonar'. *Saga og kirkja. Afmælisrit Magnúsar Más Lárussonar*, ed. Gunnar Karlsson, Jón Hnefill Aðalsteinsson and Jónas Gíslason, 183–91. Reykjavík: Sögufélag.

———— 1989a. *Gamlar götur og goðavald: Um fornar leiðir og völd Oddaverja í Rangárþingi*. Ritsafn Sagnfrædistofnunar 25. Reykjavík: Sagnfrædistofnun Háskóla Íslands.

———— 1989b. 'Mannfræði og saga. Tvær nýjar bækur um íslenska þjóðveldið'. *Skírnir* 163: 231–48.

———— 1991. *Vaðmál og verðlag. Vaðmál í utanlandsviðskiptum og búskap Íslendinga á 13. og 14. öld*. Reykjavík: Fjölföldun Sigurjóns.

—— 1992a. 'Snorri goði og Snorri Sturluson'. *Skírnir* 166: 295–320.

—— 1992b. 'Social ideals and the concept of profit in thirteenth-century Iceland'. *From Sagas to Society: Comparative Approaches to Early Iceland*, ed. Gísli Pálsson, 231–45. London: Hisarlik Press.

—— 1993. 'Sturlung Age'. *Medieval Scandinavia: An Encyclopedia*, ed. P. Pulsiano and K. Wolf, 615–16. New York: Garland.

—— 1994a. 'Hvað er blóðhefnd?' *Sagnaþing: Helgað Jónasi Kristjánssyni sjötugum 10. apríl 1994*, ed. Gísli Sigurðsson, Guðrún Kvaran and Sigurgeir Steingrímsson, 389–414. Reykjavík: Hið íslenska bókmenntafélag.

—— 1994c. 'Þjóðleið hjá Brekku og Bakka: Um leiðir og völd í Öxnadal við lok Þjóðveldis'. *Samtíðarsögur: The Contemporary Sagas*, vol. I. Níunda Alþjóðlega Fornsagnaþingið, 335–49. Reykjavík: Stofnun Árna Magnússonar.

Thorsteinsson, Björn. 1953. *Íslenzka þjóðveldið*. Annar bókaflokkar Máls og menningar 2. Reykjavík: Heimskringla.

—— 1966. *Ný Íslandssaga: Þjóðveldisöld*. Reykjavík: Heimskringla.

—— 1969. *Enskar heimildir um sögu Íslendinga á 15. og 16. öld*. Reykjavík: Hið íslenzka bökmenntafélag.

—— 1970. *Enska öldin í sögu Íslendinga*. Reykjavík: Mál og menning.

—— 1978. *Íslenzk miðaldasaga*. Reykjavík: Sögufélag.

—— 1985. *Island*. Politikens Danmarks Historie. Aarhus: Politikens Forlag.

—— *Kulturhistoriskt lexikon för nordisk medeltid*: 'Fiskhandel, Island', *KLNM* 4, cols. 370–372; 'Handel: Island', *KLNM* 6, cols. 118–119; 'Tollr', *KLNM* 18, cols. 452–454.

Thorsteinsson, Björn and Sigurður Líndal. 1978. 'Lögfesting konungsvalds'. *Saga Íslands* 3: 17–108.

Tomasson, Richard F. 1980. *Iceland: The First New Society*. Minneapolis: University of Minnesota Press.

Tómasson, Sverrir. 1988. *Formálar íslenskra sagnaritara á miðöldum*. Rannsókn bókmenntahefðar. Reykjavík: Stofnun Árna Magnússonar.

Túlinius, Torfi. 1994. *La 'Matière du nord': Sagas légendaires et fiction dans la littérature islandaise du XIIIe siècle*. Paris: Presses Universitaires de France.

Turner, Victor W. 1971. 'An Anthropological Approach to the Icelandic

Saga'. *The Translation of Culture: Essays to E. E. Evans-Pritchard*, ed. T. O. Beidelman, 349–74. London: Tavistock Publications.

Vápnfirðinga saga (The Saga of the People of Weapon's Fjord). 1950. Ed. Jón Jóhannesson. *Íslenzk fornrit* 11. Reykjavík: Hið íslenzka fornritafélag.

Vasey, Daniel E. 1999. 'Temperature Variation and its Effects upon Livestock and Human Populations in Eighteenth and Nineteenth Century Iceland'. Unpublished paper.

Vatnsdæla saga (The Saga of the People of Vatnsdal). 1939. Ed. Einar Ól. Sveinsson. *Íslenzk fornrit* 8. Reykjavík: Hið íslenzka fornritafélag.

Vésteinsson, Orri. 1996. *The Christianisation of Iceland. Priests, Power and Social Change 1000–1300*. Dissertation. University of London: University College.

——— 1998. 'Patterns of Settlement in Iceland. A Study in Prehistory'. *Saga-Book* 25/1: 1–29.

Vilmundarson, Thórhallur. 1986. 'Um persónunöfn í íslenzkum örnefnum'. *Personnamn i stadnamn*. Norna-rapporter 33: 67–79.

The Vinland Sagas: The Norse Discovery of America, Grænlendinga Saga and Eirik's Saga. 1965. Trans. Magnus Magnusson and Hermann Pálsson. London: Penguin Books.

Wallace, Birgitta Linderoth. 1991. 'L'anse aux Meadows: Gateway to Vinland'. *The Norse of the North Atlantic*, ed. Gerald F. Bigelow. *Acta Archaeologica* vol. 61: 166–97.

Walter, Ernst. 1956. *Studien zur Vápnfirðinga saga. Saga: Untersuchungen zur nordischen Literatur- und Sprachgeschichte* 1. Halle (Saale): Max Niemeyer Verlag.

Wawn, Andrew (ed.). 1994. *Northern Antiquity: The Post-Medieval Reception of Edda and Saga*. London: Hisarlik Press.

Weibull, Lauritz. 1911. *Kritiska undersökningar i Nordens historia omkring år 1000*. Copenhagen: J. L. Lybeckers Forlag.

——— 1913. *Historisk-kritisk metod och nordisk medeltidsforskning*. Lund: C. W. K. Gleerup.

Wickham, C. J. 1995. 'Gossip and Resistance among the Medieval Peasantry'. *Inaugural Lecture*. Birmingham: University of Birmingham.

Wieland, Darryl. 1982. 'Saga, Sacrament, and Struggle: The Concept of the Person in a Modern Icelandic Community'. Ph.D. dissertation, University of Rochester.

Wilson, Stephen. 1988. *Feuding, Conflict and Banditry in Nineteenth Century Corsica*. Cambridge: Cambridge University Press.

Wimmer, Ludvig. 1893–1908. *De danske runemindesmærker*. 6 vols. Copenhagen: Gyldendalske boghandels forlag.

Wormald, Jenny. 1980. 'Bloodfeud, Kindred, and Government in Early Modern Scotland'. *Past and Present* 87: 54–97.

Zóphóníasson, Páll. 1914. 'Naupgriparækt'. *Búnaðarrit* 28: 46–90.

Index

NOTE: References in italics denote illustrations.

INDEX

434

READ MORE IN PENGUIN

In every corner of the world, on every subject under the sun, Penguin represents quality and variety – the very best in publishing today.

For complete information about books available from Penguin – including Puffins, Penguin Classics and Arkana – and how to order them, write to us at the appropriate address below. Please note that for copyright reasons the selection of books varies from country to country.

In the United Kingdom: Please write to *Dept. EP, Penguin Books Ltd, Bath Road, Harmondsworth, West Drayton, Middlesex UB7 ODA*

In the United States: Please write to *Consumer Sales, Penguin Putnam Inc., P.O. Box 12289 Dept. B, Newark, New Jersey 07101-5289*. VISA and MasterCard holders call 1-800-788-6262 to order Penguin titles

In Canada: Please write to *Penguin Books Canada Ltd, 10 Alcorn Avenue, Suite 300, Toronto, Ontario M4V 3B2*

In Australia: Please write to *Penguin Books Australia Ltd, P.O. Box 257, Ringwood, Victoria 3134*

In New Zealand: Please write to *Penguin Books (NZ) Ltd, Private Bag 102902, North Shore Mail Centre, Auckland 10*

In India: Please write to *Penguin Books India Pvt Ltd, 11 Community Centre, Panchsheel Park, New Delhi 110017*

In the Netherlands: Please write to *Penguin Books Netherlands bv, Postbus 3507, NL-1001 AH Amsterdam*

In Germany: Please write to *Penguin Books Deutschland GmbH, Metzlerstrasse 26, 60594 Frankfurt am Main*

In Spain: Please write to *Penguin Books S. A., Bravo Murillo 19, 1° B, 28015 Madrid*

In Italy: Please write to *Penguin Italia s.r.l., Via Benedetto Croce 2, 20094 Corsico, Milano*

In France: Please write to *Penguin France, Le Carré Wilson, 62 rue Benjamin Baillaud, 31500 Toulouse*

In Japan: Please write to *Penguin Books Japan Ltd, Kaneko Building, 2-3-25 Koraku, Bunkyo-Ku, Tokyo 112*

In South Africa: Please write to *Penguin Books South Africa (Pty) Ltd, Private Bag X14, Parkview, 2122 Johannesburg*

READ MORE IN PENGUIN

LITERARY CRITICISM

The Penguin History of Literature

Published in ten volumes, *The Penguin History of Literature* is a superb critical survey of the English and American literature covering fourteen centuries, from the Anglo-Saxons to the present, and written by some of the most distinguished academics in their fields.

New Bearings in English Poetry F. R. Leavis

'*New Bearings in English Poetry* was the first intelligent account of the work of Eliot, Pound and Gerard Manley Hopkins to appear in English and it significantly altered critical awareness . . . Leavis gave to literary criticism a thoroughness and respectability that has never since been equalled' Peter Ackroyd, *Spectator*. 'The most influential literary critic of modern times' *Financial Times*

The Uses of Literacy Richard Hoggart

Mass literacy has opened new worlds to new readers. How far has it also been exploited to debase standards and behaviour? 'A vivid inside view of working-class culture and one of the most influential books of the post-war era' *Observer*

Epistemology of the Closet Eve Kosofsky Sedgwick

Through her brilliant interpretation of the readings of Henry James, Melville, Nietzsche, Proust and Oscar Wilde, Eve Kosofsky Sedgwick shows how questions of sexual definition are at the heart of every form of representation in this century. 'A signal event in the history of late-twentieth-century gay studies' Wayne Koestenbaum

Dangerous Pilgrimages Malcolm Bradbury

'This capacious book tracks Henry James from New England to Rye; Evelyn Waugh to a Hollywood as grotesque as he expected; Gertrude Stein to Spain to be mistaken for a bishop; Oscar Wilde to a rickety stage in Leadsville, Colorado . . . The textbook on the the transatlantic theme' *Guardian*

READ MORE IN PENGUIN

LITERARY CRITICISM

The Practice of Writing   David Lodge

This lively collection examines the work of authors ranging from the two Amises to Nabokov and Pinter; the links between private lives and published works; and the different techniques required in novels, stage plays and screenplays. 'These essays, so easy in manner, so well-built and informative, offer a fine blend of creative writing and criticism' *Sunday Times*

A Lover's Discourse   Roland Barthes

'May be the most detailed, painstaking anatomy of desire we are ever likely to see or need again ... The book is an ecstatic celebration of love and language ... readers interested in either or both ... will enjoy savouring its rich and dark delights' *Washington Post*

The New Pelican Guide to English Literature   Edited by Boris Ford

The indispensable critical guide to English and American literature in nine volumes, erudite yet accessible. From the ages of Chaucer and Shakespeare, via Georgian satirists and Victorian social critics, to the leading writers of the twentieth century, all literary life is here.

The Structure of Complex Words   William Empson

'Twentieth-century England's greatest critic after T. S. Eliot, but whereas Eliot was the high priest, Empson was the *enfant terrible* ... *The Structure of Complex Words* is one of the linguistic masterpieces of the epoch, finding in the feel and tone of our speech whole sedimented social histories' *Guardian*

Vamps and Tramps   Camille Paglia

'Paglia is a genuinely unconventional thinker ... Taken as a whole, the book gives an exceptionally interesting perspective on the last thirty years of intellectual life in America, and is, in its wacky way, a celebration of passion and the pursuit of truth' *Sunday Telegraph*

READ MORE IN PENGUIN

ARCHAEOLOGY

The Penguin Dictionary of Archaeology
Warwick Bray and David Trump

The range of this dictionary is from the earliest prehistory to the civilizations before the rise of classical Greece and Rome. From the Abbevillian handaxe and the god Baal of the Canaanites to the Wisconsin and Würm glaciations of America and Europe, this dictionary concisely describes, in more than 1,600 entries, the sites, cultures, periods, techniques and terms of archaeology.

The Complete Dead Sea Scrolls in English Geza Vermes

The discovery of the Dead Sea Scrolls in the Judaean desert between 1947 and 1956 transformed our understanding of the Hebrew Bible, early Judaism and the origins of Christianity. 'No translation of the Scrolls is either more readable or more authoritative than that of Vermes' *The Times Higher Education Supplement*

Ancient Iraq Georges Roux

Newly revised and now in its third edition, *Ancient Iraq* covers the political, cultural and socio-economic history of Mesopotamia from the days of prehistory to the Christian era and somewhat beyond.

Breaking the Maya Code Michael D. Coe

Over twenty years ago, no one could read the hieroglyphic texts carved on the magnificent Maya temples and palaces; today we can understand almost all of them. The inscriptions reveal a culture obsessed with warfare, dynastic rivalries and ritual blood-letting. 'An entertaining, enlightening and even humorous history of the great searchers after the meaning that lies in the Maya inscriptions' *Observer*

READ MORE IN PENGUIN

RELIGION

The Origin of Satan Elaine Pagels

'Pagels sets out to expose fault lines in the Christian tradition, beginning with the first identification, in the Old Testament, of dissident Jews as personifications of Satan ... Absorbingly, and with balanced insight, she explores this theme of supernatural conflict in its earliest days' *Sunday Times*

A New Handbook of Living Religions
Edited by John R. Hinnells

Comprehensive and informative, this survey of active twentieth-century religions has now been completely revised to include modern developments and recent scholarship. 'Excellent ... This whole book is a joy to read' *The Times Higher Education Supplement*

Sikhism Hew McLeod

A stimulating introduction to Sikh history, doctrine, customs and society. There are about 16 million Sikhs in the world today, 14 million of them living in or near the Punjab. This book explores how their distinctive beliefs emerged from the Hindu background of the times, and examines their ethics, rituals, festivities and ceremonies.

The Historical Figure of Jesus E. P. Sanders

'This book provides a generally convincing picture of the real Jesus, set within the world of Palestinian Judaism, and a practical demonstration of how to distinguish between historical information and theological elaboration in the Gospels' *The Times Literary Supplement*

Islam in the World Malise Ruthven

This informed and informative book places the contemporary Islamic revival in context, providing a fascinating introduction – the first of its kind – to Islamic origins, beliefs, history, geography, politics and society.

READ MORE IN PENGUIN

HISTORY

A History of Twentieth-Century Russia Robert Service

'A remarkable work of scholarship and synthesis . . . [it] demands to be read' *Spectator*. 'A fine book . . . It is a dizzying tale and Service tells it well; he has none of the ideological baggage that has so often bedevilled Western histories of Russia . . . A balanced, dispassionate and painstaking account' *Sunday Times*

A Monarchy Transformed: Britain 1603–1714 Mark Kishlansky

'Kishlansky's century saw one king executed, another exiled, the House of Lords abolished, and the Church of England reconstructed along Presbyterian lines . . . A masterly narrative, shot through with the shrewdness that comes from profound scholarship' *Spectator*

American Frontiers Gregory H. Nobles

'At last someone has written a narrative of America's frontier experience with sensitivity and insight. This is a book which will appeal to both the specialist and the novice' James M. McPherson, Princeton University

The Pleasures of the Past David Cannadine

'This is almost everything you ever wanted to know about the past but were too scared to ask . . . A fascinating book and one to strike up arguments in the pub' *Daily Mail*. 'He is erudite and rigorous, yet always fun. I can imagine no better introduction to historical study than this collection' *Observer*

Prague in Black and Gold Peter Demetz

'A dramatic and compelling history of a city Demetz admits to loving and hating . . . He embraces myth, economics, sociology, linguistics and cultural history . . . His reflections on visiting Prague after almost a half-century are a moving elegy on a world lost through revolutions, velvet or otherwise' *Literary Review*

READ MORE IN PENGUIN

HISTORY

The Vikings Else Roesdahl

Far from being just 'wild, barbaric, axe-wielding pirates', the Vikings created complex social institutions, oversaw the coming of Christianity to Scandinavia and made a major impact on European history through trade, travel and far-flung colonization. This study is a rich and compelling picture of an extraordinary civilization.

A Short History of Byzantium John Julius Norwich

In this abridgement of his celebrated trilogy, John Julius Norwich has created a definitive overview of 'the strange, savage, yet endlessly fascinating world of Byzantium'. 'A real life epic of love and war, accessible to anyone' *Independent on Sunday*

The Eastern Front 1914–1917 Norman Stone

'Without question one of the classics of post-war historical scholarship' Niall Ferguson. 'Fills an enormous gap in our knowledge and understanding of the Great War' *Sunday Telegraph*

The Idea of India Sunil Khilnani

'Many books about India will be published this year; I doubt if any will be wiser and more illuminating about its modern condition than this' *Observer*. 'Sunil Khilnani's meditation on India since Independence is a *tour de force*' *Sunday Telegraph*

The Penguin History of Europe J. M. Roberts

'J. M. Roberts has managed to tell the rich and remarkable tale of European history in fewer than 700 fascinating, well-written pages . . . few would ever be able to match this achievement' *The New York Times Book Review*. 'The best single-volume history of Europe' *The Times Literary Supplement*

READ MORE IN PENGUIN

HISTORY

Hope and Glory: Britain 1900–1990   Peter Clarke

'Splendid ... If you want a text book for the century, this is it'
Independent. 'Clarke has written one of the classic works of modern
history. His erudition is encyclopaedic, yet lightly and wittily borne.
He writes memorably, with an eye for the telling detail, an ear for
aphorism, and an instinct for irony' *Sunday Telegraph*

Instruments of Darkness: Witchcraft in England 1550–1750
James Sharpe

'Learned and enthralling ... Time and again, as I read this scrupu-
lously balanced work of scholarship, I was reminded of contemporary
parallels' Jan Morris, *Independent*

A Social History of England   Asa Briggs

Asa Briggs's magnificent exploration of English society has been
totally revised and brought right up to the present day. 'A treasure
house of scholarly knowledge ... beautifully written, and full of the
author's love of his country, its people and its landscape' *Sunday
Times*

Hatchepsut: The Female Pharaoh   Joyce Tyldesley

Queen – or, as she would prefer to be remembered king – Hatchepsut
was an astonishing woman. Defying tradition, she became the female
embodiment of a male role, dressing in men's clothes and even wearing
a false beard. Joyce Tyldesley's dazzling piece of detection strips away
the myths and restores the female pharaoh to her rightful place.

Fifty Years of Europe: An Album   Jan Morris

'A highly insightful kaleidoscopic encyclopedia of European life ...
Jan Morris writes beautifully ... Like a good vintage wine [*Fifty
Years*] has to be sipped and savoured rather than gulped. Then it will
keep warming your soul for many years to come' *Observer*